CULTURALLY DIVERSE
Library Collections
for Children

Herman L. Totten
Risa W. Brown

NEAL-SCHUMAN PUBLISHERS, INC.

New York   London

Published by Neal-Schuman Publishers, Inc.
100 Varick Street
New York, NY 10013

Library of Congress Cataloging-in-Publication Data

Totten, Herman L.
    Culturally diverse library collections for children / by Herman
L. Totten and Risa W. Brown.
        p.   cm.
    Includes blibliographical references and index.
    ISBN 1-55570-140-X
    1. Minorities—United States—Juvenile literature—Bibliogra-
phy. 2. Children's libraries—United States—Book lists.
I. Brown, Risa W. II. Title
Z1361.E4T68 1994
[E184.A1]   94-25712
016.3058'00973—dc20   CIP

❖ ACKNOWLEDGMENTS ❖

There are many people who have been vital to the completion of this project.

For clerical support, Dexter Evans and Hilary Newton have been extremely helpful.

Credit also goes to the staff of the Dallas Public Library. Their efforts to maintain a culturally diverse collection in a time of budget cuts and staff insecurity are to be commended, and are seldom recognized. Thanks also go to my library colleagues in the Carrollton-Farmers Branch ISD, who responded generously when they received bizarre electronic mail requests for interlibrary loans.

Finally, thanks to my wonderful family. As always, Joe and Thea have provided much needed support.

RISA BROWN

 CONTENTS

✺ INTRODUCTION ✺

There has been a virtual explosion of material described as "multicultural." Lists of these materials are available from many sources. Librarians are being urged to seek out those materials which reflect the multi-ethnic nature of our society; a culturally balanced library collection is considered a must. Yet, librarians have been aware of the lack of materials with characters of different ethnicities for a great many years. Now that we are thinking about the multicultural characteristics of our society, we can only hope that cultural diversity will not merely be a trend, but a development of thought that includes literature by, for, and about all people.

Why is encouragement of this process so important? Tolerance of other ideas and experience is a necessary ingredient to a peaceful world. In our current global society, contact between cultures that are worlds apart geographically is becoming more and more common. Worldwide peace depends on society's ability to understand other humans on this planet. *Hiroshima No Pika,* by Toshi Maruki, offers an insight into the devastation caused by nuclear weapons; it is a profound anti-war statement. The author describes this painful time so that history will not be repeated.

The conflicts in our own nation are becoming more and more evident, as we have seen with the disturbance and turmoil in Los Angeles and the growing fervor of "aryan" groups all over the country. Again, understanding is a primary weapon in the fight for tolerance among the culturally diverse groups who make their homes in communities across the United States.

Literature gives a voice to those of different cultures. Readers can experience a life outside of their own, with values shaped by another cultural heritage. After reading about an Asian child being taught never to look directly at an adult, the reader learns that what some Asian children think is polite may be quite different than what other American children are taught. Cultural conflicts can be vicariously experienced, ultimately teaching the tolerance so badly needed by today's society. In *Where the Broken Heart Still Beats* by Carolyn Meyer, Cynthia Ann Parker returned to Anglo society and yet yearned for her Indian husband and children. Readers can feel her pain, alienation, and lack of understanding she felt from her own relatives.

In addition to our differences, literature emphasizes the things all people have in common, such as love, family, and the search for meaning. The love between parent and child, and the risks a parent will take to protect that child, transcends all cultural barriers, from war-torn Vietnam to El Salvador, from school conflicts in Japan to an American baseball field. Friends can be found in many places, and true friends are a treasure. Those friendships help to bridge the cultural gaps our society faces.

The common thread in many of these stories is the need to find one's place in the larger world. To do that, a person must know about his or her self, and his or her heritage. When that heritage is denied, a valuable part of a person's identity is denied. In *Racing the Sun,* by Paul Pitts, Paul's father had separated himself from his Navajo background, but the relationship between Paul and his dying grandfather makes everyone in the family acknowledge their heritage.

Children's literature is an especially potent medium because children are always faced with the dilemma of "fitting in." Non-Anglo children in the United States feel this dilemma most strongly. There is constant pressure from other children, adults, and the media to be identical to the larger culture. In *My Name is Maria Isabel,* by Alma Flor Ada, a teacher, says that because there are two Marias in the class, she will call Maria Isabel "Mary." Maria Isabel likes her own name because it is hers, so she never answers when the teacher calls her "Mary." Fortunately, the teacher realizes her mistake, and adjusts.

Contemporary children's literature shows alternative approaches and solutions to problems about ethnic background. A character's success can also be a source of pride for a child of the same ethnic background, and an example for children of other cultures. In *Yang the Youngest and His Terrible Ear,* by Lensey Namioka, Yingtao has to prove to his musically talented family that he is more talented at baseball than the violin. His Anglo baseball-playing friend would rather play the violin, but his family thinks that violin playing is for wimps. The two of them team up to satisfy their families by fooling them with violin "syncing," which almost works. The ploy does convince both sets of parents that their boys can have different interests.

Folklore is another way to connect with the heritage of a particular culture. Although folklore is more than "children's stories," there is a respectable body of folklore literature in both picture book and narrative form from countries all over the world. Since the history and social values of a society are expressed in its folklore, the cultural pride embodied in these tales is of great value. They enable children to feel that they belong to the human race.

Another source of cultural pride can be found in biographies. In recent years, historical figures are being treated with fairness, and more of a historical context is provided for a better understanding. Sitting Bull had been previously depicted as a bloodthirsty savage, but in *Sitting Bull and the Battle of the Little Bighorn,* by Sheila Black, he is portrayed as a brave, wise man who fought for his people. Young readers see that some of the same obstacles faced by famous people are similar to the problems children face in their day-to-day lives; problems that can be overcome.

Selection Criteria

A broad selection of new and reprinted materials is being marketed under the multicultural umbrella. Librarians should stick to their selection standards and not alter their selection process simply to accommodate *any* multicultural title. Some criteria that may help evaluate multicultual materials include the following:

1. Is the character a unique individual? Watch out for a character purportedly representing an entire racial or ethnic group.
2. Is the culture of the character accurately and respectfully portrayed?
3. Does the character solve his or her own problem? Avoid titles in which the protagonist's problems are solved by a member of the larger culture.
4. In a biography, is the character overly glamorized? An oversimplification may present an unrealistic portrait of a famous ethnic person.
5. Is the setting authentic and fair to the ethnic group?
6. If historical, are the facts accurate? Watch out for the perpetuation of historical distortions and pertinent omissions.
7. Does the presence of dialect have a legitimate purpose?
8. Watch out for offensive descriptions.
9. Are illustrations accurate?
10. Are females portrayed *realistically?*

About This Book

The annotations in this book will help you become familiar with many of the titles seen in existing multicultural lists so that your decisions can be better informed.

The citations in this book were verified in *Books in Print CD-ROM* using the July 1994 update. In thoses instances where information was not available in *Books in Print,* the primary source was used when possible. In some cases, the primary source did not have data such as LC numbers, and the standard library cataloging sources were used to gather that data.

In the folklore section, individual story titles from collections are included where possible in case a specific tale is being sought. The picture book and fiction sections provide a brief outline of the storyline, characters and conflict. The reference/scholarly works section includes esoteric works that are considered higher levels than many elementary and small public library children's section, but those sources are valuable and may be located through interlibrary loan. Since those materials will be used by you and your professional patrons, grade levels were thought to be unnecessary. In the biography sections, historical and contemporary figures are represented and serve as a quick reference to well-known names. In the non-fiction sections, the background information on significant events in each culture's history in the United States, a representation of that culture in its original setting, and beliefs unique to each culture included in the subject of the books can be valuable in two ways. First, you have information about each book that you select, and second, your awareness of culturally sensitive areas is heightened. In these ways, this book will help you achieve your goal of a culturally balanced library collection.

REFERENCES

1. Based on a list found in Donna E. Norton: Through the eyes of a child, 2nd edition. Columbus, OH: Merrill, 1987; pp. 507-8.

Biography

American Indian warrior chiefs. Jason Hook; Richard Hook, illus. Sterling, 1990. 208 p. (ISBN pbk 1-85314-114-3) Grades 4-6.

Part of the *Heroes and Warriors* series. Previously published volumes are combined in one book. Includes: Tecumseh, visionary chief of the Shawnee; Crazy Horse, sacred warrior of the Sioux; Chief Joseph, guardian of the Nez Perce; Geronimo, last renegade of the Apache. Illustrated with photographs, detailed drawings, and color paintings.

Black Elk: a man with a vision. Carol Greene. Children's Press, 1990. LC 90-39480, 48 p. (ISBN plb 0-516-04213-0; pbk 0-516-442139) Grades K-3.

Part of the *Rookie Biography* series. Black Elk, a medicine man for the Oglala tribe, had visions that showed Native Americans and settlers living in peace. He despaired when time and again his people were killed by soldiers. At the end of his life he still prayed for peace and for his tribe. Simple text format; includes illustrations and photographs.

Charles Eastman: physician, reformer and Native American leader. Peter Anderson. Children's Press, 1992. LC 91-36654, 152 p. (ISBN 0-516-03278-X; pbk 0-516-43278-8) Grades 4 up.

Part of the *People of distinction* seris. Charles Eastman was a Sioux who lived comfortably in two worlds: the Native American world of his youth and the Anglo world of his adulthood. When he was fifteen, his father returned from prison and moved his family to a South Dakota community. He taught his son to accept American ways. Charles, a physician and later a social worker, always worked to bridge the gap between the two cultures.

Chief Joseph and the Nez Perces. Robert A. Scott. Facts on File, 1993. LC 92-15885, 128 p. (ISBN 0-8160-2475-8) Grades 5 up.

Part of the *Makers of America* series. The events of Chief Joseph's life are recreated in vivid detail, starting with the massacre of his tribe by U.S. soldiers. Through their trade network, the Nez Perce had a long tradition of seeking peace by negotiation. Chief Joseph held firm to his belief that the encroaching settlers could be handled that way, until the massacre. Then, deciding that the settlers would not be satisfied until his people were eradicated, he fought until he could fight no more.

Chief Joseph of the Nez Perce Indians: champion of liberty. Mary Virginia Fox. Children's Press, 1992. LC 92-35053, 152 p. (ISBN 0-516-03275-5; pbk 0-516-43275-3) Grades 4 up.

Part of the *People of distinction* series. Joseph received his name after being baptized by missionaries. He was known as Young Joseph to distinguish him from his father. As the settlers' numbers increased, the Native American opinion of them changed. In spite of his personal courage, Chief Joseph reluctantly encouraged the tribe to move to the reservation because he felt survival was essential.

Double life of Pocahontas. Jean Fritz; Ed Young, illus. Cavendish, 1983. LC 90-48g77 128 p. (ISBN plb 1-55905-092-6; pbk 0-14032257-4) Grades 1-10.

Pocahontas lived in two worlds—one was a carefree life as the favorite daughter of her father, an important chief. The other was as the wife of an Englishman living outside of England. Pocahontas' and John Smith's lives became intertwined, as the Indians and British sought a way to live in the same land.

Extraordinary American Indians. Susan Avery; Linda Skinner. Children's Press, 1992. LC 92-11358, 260 p. (ISBN 0-516-00583-9) Grades 4 up.

Brief biographies describe Indians and their accomplishments from the eighteenth century to the present. Some of the notable people covered are: Sacagawea, Chief Joseph, Ishi, Will Rogers, Maria Tallchief, and Wilma Mankiller.

Geronimo. David Jeffery; Tom Redman, illus. Raintree Steck Vaughn, 1390. LC 89-10412, 32 p. (ISBN plb 0-8172-3404-7; pbk 08114-4090-7) Grades 3-6.

Part of the *Raintree American Indian stories* series. Geronimo lived according to Apache values. Seeking revenge on the Mexicans who killed his family, his life was dominated by the conflict between Mexicans and Americans over part of his homeland.

Geronimo and the struggle for Apache freedom. Russell Shorto. Silver Burdette, 1989. LC 88-33687, 144 p. (ISBN plb 0-382-095715; pbk 0-382-09760-2) Grades 5-7.

Part of *Alvin Josephy's biography series of American Indians.* The Apaches were the last nomadic tribe of the Southwest deserts. American civilization threatened their way of life, and the odds were overwhelmingly against them. After each instance where precious Apache lives were lost, Geronimo sought revenge. He fervently fought for freedom for himself and his people.

Hiawatha and the Iroquois league. Megan McClard; George Ypsilantisi Frank Riccio, illus. Silver Burdette, 1989. LC 88-37503, 138 p. (ISBN plb 0-382-09568-5; pbk 0-382-09757-2) Grades 5-7.

Part of *Alvin Josephy's biography series of American Indians*. Hiawatha was a respected medicine man. A tragedy caused him to wander among the tribes of the Northeast. As he contacted different people, he decided that a unifying form of government— a league of Native American nations—would bring peace. Eventually he received support for the idea, and the Iroquois League was formed.

Hiawatha: messenger of peace. Dennis B. Fradin. Macmillan, 1992. LC 90-26312, 48 p. (ISBN 0-689-50519-1) Grades 2-6.

Hiawatha was a respected and prophetic leader. Hiawatha teamed up with his friend, Degandawida, to travel among the warring tribes of the Iroquois. They preached a message of peace and unity. Their work helped to form an Iroquois federation.

Indian chiefs. Russell Freedman. Holiday House, 1987. LC 8646198, 160 p. (ISBN 0-8234-0625-3; pbk 0-8234-0971-6) Grades 4 up.

When Native Americans and settlers began to fight for land, those historic moments of crisis called for great leaders. Biographies of six of those chiefs are included here: Red Cloud of the Oglala Sioux, Satanta of the Kiowas, Quanah Parker of the Comanches, Washakie of the Shoshonis, Joseph of the Nez Perce, and Sitting Bull of the Hukpapa Sioux.

Indian chiefs. Harriet Upton; Jerry Harston, illus. Rourke, 1990. LC 89-34716, 32 p. (ISBN 0-86625-400-5; 0-685-58654-5) Grades 3-8.

Part of the *Wild West in American history* series. Tribal chiefs demonstrated tremendous courage and fortitude in their tragic dealings with settlers, especially the U.S. government. This collection of brief biographies includes: Little Priest, Winnebago; Captain Jack, Modoc; Chief Joseph, Nez Perce; Sitting Bull, Crazy Horse, and Red Cloud, all Sioux; and Geronimo, an Apache.

Ishi: the last of his people. David Petersen. Childrens Press, 1991. LC 90-28887, 32 p. (ISBN 0-516-04179-7; pbk 0-516-44179-5) Grades 2-4.

Part of the *Picture story biography* series. Ishi, who wandered into the small California town of Oroville in 1911, was the sole survivor of the Yana tribe. Although he had lived in fear of the settlers, Ishi was so starved that he decided to give himself up to them. An anthropologist at the University of California in San Francisco gave him a home. Ishi seemed to thrive for a while, but then he caught tuberculosis and died.

Jim Thorpe. William R. Sanford; Carl R. Green. Macmillan, 1992. LC 91-32900, 48 p. (ISBN 0-89686-740-4) Grades 5 up.

Part of the *Sports Immortals* series. Jim Thorpe was a superstar who excelled at football, baseball, and track. He competed in the Olympics, only to have his medals taken away because he was paid to play baseball. Jim pursued professional sports and helped charitable groups, but was reduced to doing odd jobs when his athletic career ended. Includes a trivia quiz.

Jim Thorpe: world's greatest athlete. Gregory Richards. Children's Press, 1984. LC 84-14240, 112 p. (ISBN 0-516-03207-0) Grades 4 up.

Part of the *People of distinction* series. At the 1912 Olympics, Jim Thorpe won the demanding decathlon and was declared the world's greatest athlete. He played professional football and baseball, and always helped out his Native American "family."

King Philip. Robert Cwiklik. Silver Burdette, 1989. LC 89-5952, 144 p. (ISBN 0-382-09573-1; pbk 0-382-09762-9) Grades 5-6.

Part of *Alvin Josephy's biography series of American Indians.* Even though the Indians and the Pilgrims feasted together at the first Thanksgiving, fifteen years later tensions erupted into bloody skirmishes. Metacom, chief of the Wampanoags, also called "King Philip," waged war against the settlers to send them back across the waters.

Maria Martinez: Pueblo potter. Peter Anderson. Children's Press, 1992. LC 92-4807, 32 p. (ISBN 0-516-04184-3; pbk 0-516-44184-1) Grades 2-5.

Part of the *Picture story biography* series. This easy-to-read biography describes Maria Martinez, who developed a new pottery method. She used the ancient designs that her husband found during an excavation at an Anasazi archeological site. Her work became well known to museums and collectors. It continued the tradition of pottery making for her family.

My name is Pocahontas. William Accorsi. Holiday House, 1992. LC 91-24218, 32 p. (ISBN 0-8234-0932-5) Grades K-4.

Pocahontas had a happy childhood as the daughter of the Chief. Then John Smith and the English settlers arrived. Because she wanted to keep the peace, Pochahontas asked her father to spare Smith. She married him and went to England. Pocahontas "narrates" her own story in this colorful picture book.

Native American doctor: the Story of Susan LaFlesche Picotte. Jeri Ferris. Carolrhoda, 1991. LC 90-28503, 80 p. (ISBN plb 0-87614443-1; pbk 0-87614-548-9) Grades 3-6.

Part of the *Trailblazers* series. Susan LaFlesche, an Omaha Indian who grew up in Nebraska, was determined to help her people make a transition from hunting buffalo to living among the settelrs. In 1889, Susan became the first Native American woman to graduate from medical school. On her reservation, she was more than a doctor—she became an advisor and unofficial leader of her people.

Native artists of North America. Reavis Moore. John Muir, 1993. LC 93-16254, 48 p. (ISBN 1-56261-105-4) Grades 4-7.

Part of the *Rainbow Warrior Artist* series. Brief biographies describe the life and work of five Native American artists currently living. Their art reveals both personal exploration and customs of their ancestors. Mariano Valadez is part of the Huichol tribe in Mexico. He creates paintings with yarn dipped in paint. Charlene Teters is a painter of the Spokane tribe. Tammy Rahr is a beader and doll maker of the Cayuga (Iroquois). Robert Mirabel of Taos makes and plays flutes. Jacy Romero of the Chumash is a dancer. Includes photographs, and step-by-step instructions for an activity related to each person's art.

North American Indian tribal chiefs. Karen Liptak. Watts, 1992. LC 91-30261, 64 p. (ISBN 0-531-20101-5; pbk 0-531-15643-5) Grades 3-8.

Part of the *First book* series. The chief of Indian tribes acted as a leader and advisor. Tribe members usually followed the chief's advice out of respect. Brief biographies of well-known tribal chiefs make up this book: Tecumseh, Shawnee; Chief Joseph, Nez Perce; Sitting Bull, Hunkpapa Sioux; and Wilma Mankiller, Cherokee.

Pocahontas. Jan Gleiter; Kathleen Thompson; Deborah L. Chabrian, illus. Raintree Steck-Vaughn, 1984. LC 84-9819, 32 p. (ISBN plb 0-8172-2118-2; plb + cassette 0-8172-2240-5) Grades 2-5.

Part of the *Story Clippers* series. Recounts the "myth" of Pocahontas, and her act of bravery that saved the life of John Smith. The differences between her experiences as a Native American and as an English noblewoman gives her story a bittersweet ending. Illustrated with color paintings.

Sacagawea: American pathfinder. Flora Warren Seymour. Reprint of 1959 ed. Macmillan, 1991. LC 90-23267, 192 p. (ISBN pbk 0-68971482-3) Grades 3-7.

Part of the *Childhood of famous Americans* series. Sacagawea loved adventure, even when she was young. She was excited at each new thing life brought her during her Shoshone childhood. When she was captured, and later returned to her tribe by Lewis and Clark, her love for adventure was affirmed.

Sacagawea: Indian interpreter to Lewis and Clark. Marion Marsh Brown. Children's Press, 1988. LC 87-33810, 119 p. (ISBN 0-51603262-3; pbk 0-516-43262-1) Grades 4 up.

Part of the *People of distinction* series. When Sacagawea was first captured by Hidatsas, she was sad. But she quickly realized that her captors were more prosperous than the Shoshones, so she chose to stay even though she would be a slave. Sacagawea later married a French man, Charbonneau, and soon became pregnant. When other settlers arrived, she was delighted that she and her husband were asked to go along and later to see her tribe again.

Sequoya. Jan Gleiter; Kathleen Thompson; Tom Redman, illus. Raintree Steck-Vaughn, 1988. LC 87-32319, 32 p. (ISBN plb 0-81722678-8; pbk 0-8173-3682-6) Grades 2-5.

Part of the *Raintree stories* series. This biography focuses on Sequoya's struggle to create a written Cherokee alphabet. Working closely with his young daughter, he used pictographs before developing symbols that represented sounds of Cherokee words. Next, Sequoya taught the alphabet to the Cherokee people. Eventually, a newspaper was printed using the Cherokee language.

Sequoya and the Cherokee alphabet. Robert Cwiklik. Silver Burdette, 1989. LC 89-30737, 142 p. (ISBN plb 0-382-09570-7; pbk 0-382-09759-9) Grades 5-7.

Part of *Alvin Josephy's biography series of American Indians.* Sequoya saw that things were changing as early as the 1770s, growing very bad for the Native Americans. The debate was ongoing—get along with the settlers or fight them. His mother encouraged him to attend the mission school. After many years in both cultures, he began devising a method to write or draw the Cherokee language. This was a vital way to preserve and legitimize the culture.

Sequoya: father of the Cherokee alphabet. David Petersen. Children's Press, 1991. LC 91-13313, 32 p. (ISBN 0-516-04180-0; pbk 0-516-44180-9) Grades 2-4.

Part of the *Picture-story biography* series. Sequoya was the first Native American to develop a method of reading and writing his Indian language and oral traditions.

After living among the settlers, Sequoya was fascinated by their ability to communicate on paper. He spent years developing his syllabary, which involves written representations of syllables rather than letters.

Sequoya's gift: a portrait of a Cherokee leader. Janet Klausner. HarperCollins, 1993. LC 92-24939, 128 p. (ISBN 0-06-02123S-7; plb 0-06-021236-5) Grades 4 up.

Sequoya's entire life was influenced by westward pushing settlers. As the result of a mixed marriage, he used his diverse cultural experiences to incorporate a Western method of communication into the Cherokee culture.

Sitting Bull and the battle of the Little Bighorn. Sheila Black. Silver Burdette, 1989. LC 88-27021, 144 p. (ISBN plb 0-382-095723; pbk 0-382-09761-0) Grades 5-7.

Part of the *Alvin Josephy's biography series on American Indians.* Despite his undeserved, fierce reputation, Sitting Bull was a brave, intelligent man who judged situations with insight. He fought for the survival of his people, and tried to preserve their way of life.

Sitting Bull: Tatanka Yotanka. Kathie Billingslea Smith; James Seward, illus. Simon & Schuster, 1987. LC 86-33888, 24 p. (ISBN 0-671-64603-6; plb 0-685-47297-3) Grades K-5.

Part of the *Great Americans* series. Sitting Bull was a Sioux who saw the old ways being replaced. When the new immigrants first came, Native Americans moved to reservations, in return for cattle and farming supplies. Promises were broken, however, and Native Americans were moved from their land forcibly. Different tribes attacked the settlers separately, but Sitting Bull knew they could do nothing unless they joined together. After they defeated Custer, their forces were divided and then defeated.

Story of Geronimo. Zachary Kent. Children's Press, 1989. LC 8837005, 32 p. (ISBN plb 0-516-04743-4; pbk 0-516-44743-2) Grades 3-6.

Part of the *Cornerstones of freedom* series. Geronimo, a proud Apache warior, was obsessed with revenge after his young family was killed by Mexican soldiers. He and his tribe were soon on the run from both the Mexican and U.S. armies. Life became very difficult, and even Geronimo grew tired of the ceaseless struggle and surrendered.

Susette La Flesche: advocate for Native American rights. Marion Marsh Brown. Children's Press, 1992. LC 91-35296, 152 p. (ISBN 0516-03277-1; pbk 0-516-43277-X) Grades 4 up.

Part of the *People of distinction* series. Susette worked diligently to influence public opinion in favor of Native American rights by lecturing and testifying at Congressional hearings. She came from an Omaha reservation. Her sister was the first Native American doctor.

Tecumseh. Russell Shorto. Silver Burdette, 1989. LC 88-32656, 136 p. (ISBN plb 0-382-09569-3; pbk 0-382-09758-0) Grades 5 up.

Part of the *Alvin Josephy's biography series of American Indians.* Tecumseh was a fierce fighter for the honor of his people. He saw that the only way to preserve their way of life was to unite. However, Tecumseh was killed in battle, and the tribes did not stay together without his leadership.

Wilma P. Mankiller: chief of the Cherokee. Charnan Simon. Children's Press, 1991. LC 91-4334, 32 p. (ISBN 0-516-04181-9; pbk 0-516-44181-7) Grades 2-4.

Part of the *Picture-story biography* series. Wilma Mankiller was born on a farm in Oklahoma, but a drought forced her family to move. The government found them a place in San Francisco. After starting her career in sociology, she returned to Oklahoma and became involved in Cherokee tribal affairs, working to fight poverty, discrimination, and despair. She was eventually elected Chief.

Folklore

Animal's ballgame. Lloyd Arneach; Lydia Halverson, illus. Children's Press, 1992. LC 92-9416, 24 p. (ISBN 0-516-05139-3; pbk 0-516-45139-1) Grades ps-3.

Part of the *Adventures in storytelling* series. In this story from the Eastern band of Cherokees, the animals and birds play a ball game to settle an argument. When the animals want neither a little rodent nor a squirrel on their team, two pieces of drum skin are tied to their arms so they can be on the bird team (those later become a bat and a flying squirrel). The game becomes vicious—a condor pulls a strip out of the skunk's back, leaving a white stripe. Similarly, other results of this game are still visible in animals.

Boy who lived with the seals. Rafe Martin; David Shannon, illus. Putnam, 1993. LC 91-46023, 32 p. (ISBN 0-399-22413-0) Grades ps-3.

A Chinook boy wanders away from his parents. Although they fear that he has died, they eventually discover that he is alive and being cared for by seals. His parents try to help him act human again, but he eventually escapes back to the seals.

Buffalo woman. Paul Goble. Macmillan, 1984. LC 83-15704, 32 p. (ISBN 0-02-737720-2; pbk 0-689-71109-3) Grades ps-3.

This story of the kinship between humans and buffaloes was told by tribes who lived in the Great Plains. A young hunter meets a beautiful young woman where the buffalo gather to drink. They fall in love, marry, and have a child. Because his tribe rejects her, the woman takes their child back to her people—the buffalo. With his son's help, the man passes several tests to prove his love for his family, and is allowed to join them.

Clamshell boy: a Makah legend. Terri Cohlene; Charles Reasoner, illus. Rourke, 1990. LC 89-10744, 48 p. (ISBN 0-685-46446-6; plb 0-86593-001-5); Troll, 1990. (ISBN pbk 0-086593-001-5) Grades 3-6.

Part of the *Native American legends* series. Many adults think that children should believe what their elders tell them. This legend depicts some children who did not. They stayed at the river to see if the wild Basket Woman was real. She swooped the children up, planning to make a meal of them. Clamshell Boy arrived, tricked Basket Woman, and returns them to their village. Includes background information on the Makahs.

Coyote steals the blanket: A Ute tale. Janet Stevens. Holiday House, 1993. LC 92-54415, 32 p. (ISBN 0-8234-0996-1; pbk 0-82341129-X) Grades ps-3.

Thinking he was clever enough to handle anything, Coyote takes a blanket that belonges to a spirit that lives in a rock. The rock chases Coyote, crushing anyone who tries to help him. Coyote is saved, but still wants a blanket.

Crow chief: a Plains Indian story. Paul Goble. Orchard, 1992. LC 90-28457, 32 p. (ISBN 0-531-05947-2; plb 0-531-08547-3) Grades ps-2.

In early times, when the buffalo hunt did not go well, everyone in the tribe went hungry. Crows often warned the buffalo that the hunters were coming. Falling Star captured the crow chief and kept him tied up so that he would feel the pangs of hunger and be more cooperative.

Dancing drums: a Cherokee legend. Terri Cohlene; Charles Reasoner, illus. Rourke, 1990. LC 90-8288, 48 p. (ISBN 0-86593-007-4; plb 0-685-46447-4); Troll, 1990. (ISBN pbk 0-8167-2362-1) Grades 3-6.

Part of the *Native American legends* series. Grandmother Sun is insulted when The People do not heed her, so she scorches the earth. When Dancing Drum finds a new way to make music, Grandmother Sun sees The People smiling up at her, and she in turn smiles on them once again. Includes a section on the Cherokees.

Dark way: stories fram the spirit world. Virginia Hamilton; Lambert Davis, illus. Harcourt, 1990. LC 90-36251, 154 p. (ISBN 0-15-222340-1) Grades 3 up.

This collection of scary stories related to strange or supernatural phenomena represents cultures around the world. Two stories with Native American background include: "Manabozo" and "The tiny thing."

Dragonfly's tale. Kristina Rodanus. Houghton Mifflin, 1992. LC 90-28758, 32 p. (ISBN 0-395-57003-4) Grades K-3.

This ancient Zuni tale warns against taking prosperity for granted. The Ashiwi were blessed by the Corn Maidens with bountiful harvests until the elders decided to flaunt their good fortune with a food game. They wasted much of the harvest. When the Corn Maidens sent a famine, two children distracted themselves with toys made from corn shucks. The corn shucks came to life as dragonflies and carried their pleas for help to the Corn Maidens.

Dream wolf. Paul Goble. Macmillan, 1990. LC 89-687, 32 p. (ISBN 0-02-736585-9) Grades 3 up.

Two children lost in the mountains take refuge in a cave. A wolf cares for them and leads them to the safety of their home. The parents are so glad when their children return, they thanked the wolf and always felt a kinship to it. Humankind has lost this sense of kinship with animalkind, but can recapture it by seeking the wolf.

Earthmaker's tales. Gretchen Mayo. Walker, 1989. LC 88-20515, 96 p. (ISBN 0-8027-6839-3; plb 0-8027-6840-7) Grades 5 up.

This collection contains a variety of legends explaining the weather: thunder, lightning, earthquakes, rainbows, snow, ice, volcanoes, hot springs, and fog.

Feathers and tails: animal fables from around the world. David Kherdian; Nonny Hogrogian, illus. Putnam, 1992. LC 91-31270, 96 p. (ISBN 0-399-21876-9) Grades 1 up.

Folk stories everywhere contain stories about the animals of their region. In this collection are animal stories from Native American including: "Coyote and the acorns" (Yurok Indians), "Lemming and the owl" (Eskimo), and "Heron and the hummingbird" (Muskogee Indians).

Fire race: a Karuk coyote tale about how fire came to the people. Jonathan Londan; Lanny Pinola; Sylvia Long, illus. Chronicle, 1993. LC 92-32352, 32 p. (ISBN 0-8118-0241-3) Grades ps up.

Long ago, animals did not have any fire. Coyote decides to get fire from its place at the end of the world, guarded by the Yellow Jacket sisters. Despite the furious pursuit of the sisters, the animals help Coyote bring a smoldering ember to their home.

First strawberries: a Cherokee story. Joseph Bruchac; Anna Vojtech, illus. Dial, 1993. LC 91-31058, 32 p. (ISBN 0-80371331-2; plb 0-8037-1332-0) Grades ps-3.

A Cherokee legend recounts how strawberries came into the world. With the help of the sun, the first man on earth regains the love of the first woman by enticing her with the newly formed fruit she finds delicious.

Figh skin. Jamie Oliviero; Brent Morrisseau, illus. Hyperion, 1993. LC 92-85509, 40 p. (ISBN 1-56282-401-5; plb 1-56282-402-3) Grades ps-2.

This Cree legend tells of a great drought, and a young boy who worries that his grandmother will die from its effects. Desperate, he visits the Great Spirit who gives him fish skin. As a fish, he is able to restore Nature's cycle and bring rain back to the world.

Flute player: an Apache folk tale. Michael Lacapa. Northland, 1990. LC 89-63749, 48 p. (ISBN 0-87358-500-3) Grades 1-3.

It all began at a hoop dance, where a man and a woman became interested in each other. He played a flute and promised to play for her in the canyon. She heard him and sent a leaf down the river to let him know she liked it. He had to go on a hunting trip. The woman became so sad in his absence that she died. When he returned and did not see her, the man disappeared. But his song remained.

Ghost and Lone Warrior: an Arapaho legend. C.J. Taylor. Tundra, 1991. LC 91-65368, 24 p. (ISBN 0-88776-263-8) Grades 1-5.

The nomadic Plains Indians depended on the buffalo to survive. They followed the great herds. Lone Warrior, injured on a hunting party, and tells the others to go on. A blizzard strikes and he faces a spirit who reveals that he will be a great leader.

Her seven brothers. Paul Goble. Macmillan, 1988. LC 86-31776, 32 p. (ISBN 0-02-737960-4) Grades ps-3.

In this Cheyenne legend of the Big Dipper's creation, a girl is destined for great things. When she begins sewing wonderful clothes and moccasins for a nonexistent family, her tribe is puzzled. She leaves and finds her brothers far away. The buffalo are jealous and want her for their sister. Their pursuit drives her and her brothers into the sky.

How Glooskap outwits the ice giants: and other tales of the Maritime Indians. Howard A Norman. Little, Brown, 1989. LC 892379, 60 p. (ISBN 0-316-61181-6) Grades 2-4.

According to some New England tribes, Glooskap is the first person to inhabit the earth. Part god, part hero, he protected and taught the people who came later. Six tales are included in this book: "How Glooskap made human beings;" "How Glooskap outwits the ice giants;" "Why the sea winds have their strength today;" "Glooskap gets two surprises;" "How Magic Friend Fox helped Glooskap against Panther-Witch;" and "How Glooskap sang through the rapids and found a new home."

How rabbit stole the fire: a North American Indian Folk Tale. Joanna Troughton. Bedrick, 1986. LC 85-15629, 32 p. (ISBN 087226-040-2) Grades K-3.

Part of the *Folk Tales of the world* series, based on a Creek tale. Rabbit devises a plan to get fire from the Sky People. He makes a fancy head dress and coats the feathers with resin. Then he offers to teach the Sky People a dance. When Rabbit gets close to the fire, he lights his head dress and runs. In order to escape the Sky People, the animals run until the fire is passed to wood. That is why you get fire when you rub two sticks together.

How Raven brought light to people. Ann Dixon, James Watts, illus. Macmillan, 1992. LC 90-28948, 32 p. (ISBN 0-689-50536-1) Grades K-4.

In this Alaskan Native American tale, Raven takes on a powerful Tlingit chief. The chief has the sun, the moon, and the stars locked away in wooden boxes; the world is in darkness. But Raven magically changes himself into the chief's baby grandson. He asks to play with the wooden boxes and opens them all, enabling the heavenly bodies to escape. When Raven flies through the smoke-hole of the great lodge, he is covered with soot. He remains black to this day.

How the animals got their colors. Marcia Rosen; John Clementson, illus. Harcourt, 1992. LC 91-30113, 48 p. (ISBN 0-15-236783-7) Grades 2-5.

This collection of stories includes myths explaining how a variety of animals got their colors—according to the people who live near them. The Zuni tell about the coyote, and the Ayoreo in South America tell how the sun god gave all the animals their colors.

How the sea began: a Taino myth. George Crespo. Houghton Mifflin, 1993. LC 91-39651, 32 p. (ISBN 0-395-63033-9) Grades K-3.

Yayael, a skilled hunter, catches much of the food his parents eat. When he is caught in a mighty storm, all that is left of him are his bow and arrows. His parents place those into a gourd to honor his memory. One night, the parents take down the gourd and four fat fish flop out. When some mischievous boys drop and break the gourd, water gushes out and creates a sea full of fat fish.

How the seasons came. Joanna Troughton. Bedrick, 1992. LC 9140499, 32 p. (ISBN 0-87226-464-5) Grades K-3.

Part of the *Folk Tales of the world* series, based on an Algonquin legend. Wolf's son was very sick because the weather was always cold. His friend Fisher (similar to an ermine) suggests they go to the land above the sky to bring some warmth back. Together they manage to bring spring, summer, and autumn to the land. But the Thunderers discover Wolf and Fisher, and Fisher is killed. Thanks to his sacrifice, the Earth has seasons, the Thunderers never come to earth, and Fisher is turned into the Big Dipper to remind us of his friendship.

How the stars fell into the sky: a Navajo legend. Jerrie Oughton; Lisa Desimini, illus. Houghton Mifflin, 1992. LC 91-17274, 32 p. (ISBN 0-395-58798-0) Grades K-3.

The First Woman wanted to write laws so the people would know what was expected of them. After considering many ways, she decided to write them in the stars. Patiently positioning stars exactly where she wanted them, she was pleased with her work. But Coyote wanted the job finished and threw the rest of the stars in the sky. This is why the people live in such confusion.

How Two-feather was saved from loneliness: an Abenaki legend. C.J. Taylor. Tundra, 1990. LC 90-70138, 24 p. (ISBN 0-88776-254-9) Grades K-4.

This story is a retelling of the myth "The Origin of Corn;" originating from fire, corn, and communal living. Two-feather is lonely until a strange woman gives him seeds and shows him how to build a fire to make room for crops. He attracts other people who build homes. Although Two-feather marries, he never forgets the Corn Woman.

Iktomi and the berries: a Plains Indian story. Paul Goble. Orchard, 1989. LC 88-23353, 32 p. (ISBN 0-531-05819-0; plb 0-53108419-1; pbk 0-531-07029-8) Grades ps-2.

The Plains Indians tell stories about a trickster, a fool named Iktomi. In this tale, Iktomi is hungry but cannot catch anything to eat. Then he sees some buffalo berries in the water. Iktomi does not realize the berries are a reflection until he nearly drowns. He loses his temper and hits the bushes losing all the berries because they float away. The storytelling tradition of interaction between reader and teller is encouraged throughout the text.

Iktomi and the boulder: a Plains Indian story. Paul Goble. Orchard, 1988. LC 87-35789, 32 p. (ISBN 0-531-05760-7; plb 0-53108360-8; pbk 0-531-07023-9) Grades ps-2.

Iktomi insults a boulder. The boulder traps him underneath and none of the animals can push it off. Finally, he tricks some rats into chipping away at the boulder until he can get up.

Iktomu and the buffalo skull: a Plains Indian story. Paul Goble. Orchard, 1991. LC 90-7716, 32 p. (ISBN 0-531-0599-1; plb. 0-53108511-2) Grades ps-2.

Iktomi is off to charm the young ladies (even though he is a married man). In the process he gets his head stuck in a buffalo skull, finally pleading with his wife to get him out.

Iktomi and the ducks: a Plains Indian story. Paul Goble. Orchard, 1990. LC 89-71025, 32 p. (ISBN 0-531-08483-3; plb 0-531-08483-3; pbk 0-531-07044-1) Grades ps-2.

Iktomi decides that some ducks would make a lovely supper. He coaxes enough ducks for his meal, but as he is cooking Iktomi is distracted by the creaking of some nearby trees. Iktomi gets stuck in the branches and cannot stop a coyote from stealing his supper.

Ishi's tale of Lizard. Leanne Hinton; Susan L. Roth, illus. Farrar, 1992. LC 92-6744, 32 p. (ISBN 0-374-33643-1) Grades 4-7.

Ishi was the last surviving member of the Yahi tribe who secretly lived in the mountains of California. After nearly starving, he moved to San Francisco, sharing Yahi culture. The adventures of Lizard is one of the traditional tales he told the anthropologists he lived with. Includes collage illustrations.

Ka-ha-si and the loon: an Eskimo legend. Terri Cohlene; Charles Reasoner, illus. Rourke, 1990. LC 89-10743, 48 p. (ISBN 0-68546448-2; plb 0-86593-002-3); Troll, 1990. (ISBN pbk 0-8167-2359-1) Grades 4-7.

Part of the *Native American legend* series. At first, Ka-ha-si appears to be a lazy, small boy. But a loon tells Ka-ha-si that he is really strong and his grandfather is depending on him. Ka-ha-si then shows great strength every time his tribe is threatened. Finally it is time for him to join his grandfather at the bottom of a whirlpool. Ka-ha-si is still there, balancing the world on his shoulders. Includes background information on the Eskimos.

Keepers of the earth. Michael Caduto; Joseph Bruchac. Fulcrum, 1988.
LC 88-3620, 209 p. (ISBN 1-55591-027-0; pbk 1-55591-040-8) Grades 1-6.

Native Americans' belief in living in harmony with nature has made them keen observers of the environment. Their perceptions make up a large portion of their folklore. This book is designed to guide children in an interdisciplinary study of nature through Indian legends. Each story is presented with a series of questions and activities for different age groups. Includes experiments, crafts, and outdoor exploration.

Ladder to the sky: how the gift of healing came to the Ojibway nation. Barbara Juster Esbensen; Helen K. Davie, illus. Little, Brown, 1989.
LC 87-22729, 32 p. (ISBN 0-316-24952-1) Grades ps-3.

In the old forgotten time, people were strong and healthy. Everyone lived in harmony and walked with the spirit-messengers. One young man was favored by the spirits, causing jealousy in his tribe. They made the young man so miserable that the spirits took him. The young man's grandmother was so distraught that she tried to follow on the forbidden magic vine. She unleashed suffering and sorrow, but the spirits gave people some ways to heal their suffering.

Legend of Scarface: a Blackfeet Indian tale. Robert San Souci: Daniel San Souci, illus. Doubleday, 1987. LC 77-15170, 40 p. (ISBN pbk 0-385-15874-2) Grades K-3.

Scarface was a young man with an unseemly birthmark on his face. He fell in love with Singing Rains and she with him, but the woman had vowed to Father Sun never to marry. Scarface went to the lodge of Father Sun. Because of an act of bravery he is granted his wish to marry Singing Rains.

Legend of the bluebonnet: an old tale of Texas. Tomie DePaola. Putnam, 1983. LC 82-12391, 32 p. (ISBN 0-399-20937-9; pbk. 0-39920938-7; pbk 0-399-22441-6) Grades ps-3.

This Comanche tale concerns a drought which threatened the tribe's survival. She-who-is-alone has lost all of her family and clings to a doll as a reminder of her loved ones. The shaman says the drought has come because the people are selfish. A sacrifice must be made if the rain is to return. She-who-is-alone sacrifices her doll. The rains come and beautiful blue flowers cover the hills.

Legend of the Indian Paintbrush. Tomie DePaola. Putnam, 1988.
LC 87-20160, 40 p. (ISBN 0-399-21534-4; pbk 0-399-21777-0) Grades ps-2.

Little Gopher is not like other boys. After a Dream-vision, he feels that his destiny is to be an artist, painting pictures of the great events of his tribe. He yearns to paint the sunset, but cannot mix the right colors. One evening the true colors of sunset sprout from the ground. Now every spring the Indian paintbrushes return to the land.

Little Firefly: an Algonquin legend. Terri Cohlene; Charles Reasoner, illus. LC 89-38979, 48 p. (ISBN 0-685-36333-3; plb 086593-005-8); Troll, 1990. (ISBN pbk 0-8167-2363-X) Grades 4-7.

Part of the *Native American legend* series. Little Firefly is frequently the victim of her older sister's vicious teasing and abuse. She has been scarred from years of tending the cookfire. All the young women have been told that if any of them can see the Invisible One, he will marry her. Many try, but only Little Firefly can see him. Includes background information on the Algonquins.

Loon and deer were traveling. Vi Hilbert; Anita Nelson, illus. Children's Press, 1992. LC 92-5450, 24 p. (ISBN 0-516-05140-7; pbk 0-516-45140-5) Grades ps-3.

Part of the *Adventures in storytelling* series. This Skagit tale may be an old one, but its 'stranger danger' message is timely. Loon and Deer are traveling in their canoe. Loon sees two wolves and urges Deer to avoid them. As they get closer, Loon forms an escape plan; Deer does not. She is captured and eaten. Textual backmatter encourages storytelling activities.

Lost children. Paul Goble. Macmillan, 1993. LC 91-44283, 40 p. (ISBN 0-02-736555-7) Grades ps-12.

This Blackfoot legend warns of the dangers of neglecting children. Once there were six orphaned children that no one cared for. They eventually become stars of the Pleiades, beloved by Sun Man and Moon Woman. Sun Man was so angry at their treatment that he caused a drought to punish the People. He relented only when he saw the animals suffering.

Love flute. Paul Goble. Macmillan, 1992. LC 91-19716, 32 p. (ISBN 0-02-736261-2); Reading Adventures, 1993. (ISBN 0-685-648133; cassette 1-882869-80-X) Grades ps up.

Young men often courted women using a flute to express their love. Plains Indians have a legend about the first love flute. A brave warrior was too shy to speak to the beautiful girl he loved. While away from camp, he was given a flute. The man listened to all the songs of the animals and learned them. When he returned, his songs spoke directly to the woman he loved.

Ma'ii and cousin Horned Toad: a traditional Navajo story. Shonto Begay. Scholastic, 1992. LC 91-34888, 32 p. (ISBN 0-590-45391-2) Grades ps-3.

Ma'ii the Coyote is a tricky fellow. He goes from cousin to cousin looking for a hand out. He knows his cousin Horned Toad has a very nice cornfield. When Horned Toad tells Ma'ii he will have to work, Ma'ii eats Horned Toad and keeps the cornfield for himself. From Ma'ii's belly, Horned Toad makes him miserable and teaches Ma'ii a lesson.

Mud pony. Caron Lee Cohen; Shonto Begay, illus. Scholastic, 1988. LC 87-23451, 32 p. (ISBN 0-590-41525-5; pbk 0-590-41526-3; pbk 0590-72838-5) Grades ps-3.

A poor Pawnee boy wants a pony so much that he stops to make one out of mud. When his people leave him behind, Mud Pony comes to life to help him find his people. He eventually becomes a powerful leader, but the day arrives when the pony must return to Mother Earth and the boy must find his own strength.

Muwin and the magic hare. Susan Hand Shetterly; Robert Shetterly, illus. Macmillan, 1993. LC 91-2170, 32 p. (ISBN 0-689-31699-2) Grades 1-5.

Muwin is a bear living during the dream time when people and animals spoke the same language. Although Muwin should be sleeping in his den because winter is near, he sees a snowshoe hare and wants one more meal. He has been tricked by the Great Magic Hare of the woods and goes farther and farther from his den. Happily, the Great Hare makes sure that Muwin gets home safely.

Naked bear: folktales of the Iroquois. John Bierhorst; Dirk Zimmer, illus. Morrow, 1987. LC 86-21836, 144 p. (ISBN 0-68806422-1) Grades 3 up.

These sixteen tales are unique, retaining the style of speech used by old-time story-tellers. There are human characters with their own individuality, as well as animals and monsters.

Native American stories. Joseph Bruchac; John Kahionhes Fadden, illus. Fulcrum, 1991. LC 90-85267, 145 p. (ISBN pbk 1-55591-0947) Grades K-6.

Here are the stories without the activities found in *Keepers of the earth*. The connecting theme that binds these tales and myths is the relationship between humans and nature. A valuable guide to the tribes is included.

Naughty little rabbit and old man coyote: a Tewa story from San Juan Pueblo. Estefanita Martinez; Rick Regan, illus. Children's Press, 1992. LC 92-8992, 24 p. (ISBN 0-516-05141-5; pbk 0-51645141-3) Grades ps-3.

Part of the *Adventures in storytelling* series. In the San Juan Pueblo, a tricky rabbit decides to fool a hungry coyote. The rabbit tells him that there is a piece of cheese in the lake, which is of course a reflection of the moon. Then a frog decides to get into the action, and gives the coyote a haircut. In frustration, he runs away crying.

Prince and the salmon people. Claire Rudolf Murphy; Duane Pasco, illus. Rizzoli, 1993. LC 92-38394, 48 p. (ISBN 0-8478-1662-1) Grades ps-4.

The legend of the salmon people is told beside photos of Tsimshian artifacts and historic portrayals of tribal life. A prince is born in the season that salmon swim up the river. The people perform proper rituals so the fish can swim again. As the boy grows up, his people neglect the ceremonies, and suffer a famine. The boy then goes to the place where salmon are human. They tell him that his people must return to the rituals if they are to have fish.

Quillworker: a Cheyenne legend. Terri Cohlene; Charles Reasoner, illus. Rourke, 1990. LC 89-10742, 48 p. (ISBN 0-86593-004-X; plb 0-685-363-34-1); Troll, 1990. (ISBN pbk 0-8167-2358-3) Grades 4-7.

Part of the *Native American legends* series. A Cheyenne girl named Quillworker begins making seven warrior's outfits she has seen in her dreams. When she is finished, she sets out on a journey to join the seven warriors—her new brothers. The buffalo greatly admired her work and wanted Quillworker to join them. She refused, and the brothers help her flee to the sky to escape. They became the stars of the Big Dipper. Includes background information on the Cheyenne.

Rainbow crow: a Lenape tale. Nancy van Laan; Beatriz Vidal, illus. Knopf, 1989. LC 88-12967, 40 p. (ISBN 0-394-89577-0; plb 0-39499577-5) Grades ps-3.

When the animals first encountered snow, they were not afraid until the smaller animals were covered up. They could not agree on who should ask the sky spirit to stop the snow. Finally, the crow offered to go. The Sky Spirit could not stop the snow, but gave the bird fire to help the animals survive. On the long trip back, the fire singed all the crow's feathers, so now he is black.

Raven: a trickster tale from the Pacific Northwest. Gerald McDermott. Harcourt, 1993. LC 91-14563, 32 p., (ISBN 015-265661-8) Ages 4-8.

Raven uses his magical powers to help humanity. People are living in darkness, and he knows they need light. He travels to the house of the Sky Chief and is able to become his beloved "grandchild." Sky Chief cannot deny anything to his grand-child, even the light box. The child gets the ball of light and changes back into Raven. He flies away and gives light to the People.

Raven's light: a myth from the people of the Northwest coast. Susan H. Shetterly; Robert Shetterly, illus. Macmillan, 1991. LC 8978183, 32 p. (ISBN 0-689-31629-1) Grades 1-5.

After Raven made the earth and its creatures, he realized that it needed light. He went to the Kingdom of Day, changed himself to a piece of cedar frond, and float-ed into the drinking water of the Great Chief's daughter. In that way he made him-self into a "grandson" of the Great Chief, and eventually stole the ball of sunshine.

Rough-face girl. Rafe Martin; David Shannon, illus. LC 91-2921, 32 p. (ISBN 0-399-21859-9) Grades ps-3.

The theme of this Native American Cinderella story is that a kind heart will always be rewarded. Two proud sisters make up their minds to marry an Invisible Being who is said to be rich, powerful, and handsome. Their pride prevents them from being worthy. Their younger sister, though scarred from having to tend the fire, appears beautiful because of her gentle nature. The Invisible Being reveals himself to her.

Sea lion. Ken Kesey; Neil Waldman, illus. Viking, 1991. LC 90-26146, 48 p. (ISBN 0-670-83916-7) Grades ps up.

Eemook was a crippled boy who was raised by an old woman. During a storm, a handsome stranger appears. He is really an evil spirit, luring young maidens out into the storm. Eemook is able to trick the spirit into revealing himself, breaking the spell and saving the tribe from destruction.

Seal oil lamp. Dale DeArmond. Little, Brown, 1988. LC 88-7272, 48 p. (ISBN 0-316-17786-5) Grades K-4.

In this Eskimo tale, a childless couple joyfully anticipate their first child. They are disappointed when they realize that their boy is blind. According to tribal custom, they must leave him to die. He is kept alive by kindly mouse people, who teach him a hunting song that enables him to become a productive member of the tribe.

Spotted Eagle and Black Crow: a Lakota legend. Emery Bernhard; Durga Bernhard, illus. Holiday House, 1993. LC 92-23950, 32 p. (ISBN 0-8234-1007-2) Grades ps-3.

Two brothers loved the same woman. Black Crow left Spotted Eagle to die on the side of a mountain. A pair of eagles helped the warrior live, and eventually return to the tribe. Because Spotted Eagle was true to the natural order of things, he survived a war with the Pawnees, while Black Crow did not.

Star boy. Paul Goble. Macmillan, 1983. LC 82-20599, 32 p. (ISBN 0-02-722660-3; pbk 0-689-71499-8) Grades k up.

This Blackfeet Indian legend is about Star Boy, or Scarface, as he is also known. His father was the Morning Star; his grandparents the Sun and the Moon, but his mother was a mortal. She became unhappy after disobeying the Sun. Back on earth, the boy grew up with a mysterious scar. When he asked the chief's daughter to marry him, she told him to visit Grandfather Sun for his blessing.

Story of Jumping Mouse. John Steptoe. Lothrop, 1984. LC 82-14848, 40 p. (ISBN 0-688-01902-1; plb. 0-688-01903-X; pbk 0-68808740-X) Grades ps-3.

A Native American legend about a mouse who is rewarded for his selflessness by being turned into an eagle.

Story of light. Susan Roth. Morrow, 1990. LC 90-5654, 32 p. (ISBN 0-688-08676-4; plb 0-688-08677-2) Grades ps up.

A Cherokee myth that relates how light came into the world. It was dark and all the animals were bumping into one another. So they decided to get a small part of the sun. First the mole tried to carry it under his tail, but his hair was singed. The buzzard burned all his feathers. The spider then made a jar and carried back the fire successfully.

They dance in the sky: Native American star myths. Jean Guard Monroe; Ray A. Williamson; Edgar Stewart, illus. Houghton Mifflin, 1987. LC 86-27547, 130 p. (ISBN 0-395-39970-X) Grades 6 up.

This collection contains star myths from many tribes. Numerous stories explain the origins of constellations, illustrating with allegory how humans fit into nature's vast realm.

Turquoise Boy: a Navajo legend. Terri Cohlene; Charles Reasoner, illus. Rourke, 1990. LC 89-10795, 48 p. (ISBN 0-685-363-35-X; plb 0-86593-003-1; Troll, 1990. (ISBN pbk 0-8167-2360-5) Grades 48.

Part of the *Native American legends* series. Turquoise Boy sees how hard life is for the Navajo people. He seeks something that will make their lives easier. Turquoise Boy gathers stones, sea shells, and sacred pollen. He then makes gifts for Changing Woman. After a ceremony, the gifts are changed into horses. Includes ackground on the Navajos.

Who will be the sun? Joanna Troughton. Bedrick, 1986. LC 85-15074, 32 p. (ISBN 0-87226-038-0) Grades K-3.

Part of the *Folk Tales of the world* series. All the animals wanted the honor of being the sun, especially Coyote. But it was too hot under him, and everything was dried up or burned. Lynx was a good sun, making Coyote jealous. His jealousy backfired when he was caught in a fire. This taught the people to find a safe trail when fire breaks out.

Woman who fell from the sky. John Bierhorst; Robert Andrew Parker, illus. Morrow, 1993. LC 92-5591, 32 p. (ISBN 0-688-10680-3; plb 0-688-10681) Grades K up.

This simply-told Iroquois story explains how Sky Woman created everything on earth. When she first came to earth there was only water. Gradually land rose where she walked. Then her children were born: one was gentle and one was hard. After that, everything had a little bit of each quality—including humans.

Fiction for Younger Readers
Picture books

Beyond the ridge. Paul Goble. Macmillan, 1989. LC 87-33113, 32 p. (ISBN 0-02-736581-6; pbk 0-689-71731-8) Grades ps-3.

The Plains Indians believed that the spirit did not die with the body. When an elderly woman's spirit is called to a beautiful land "beyond the ridge," she wants to tell her grieving family that everything is good. The land is too beautiful to turn her eyes away.

Big thunder magic. Craig Kee Strete; Craig Brown, illus. Greenwillow, 1990. LC 89-34613, 32 p. (ISBN 0-688-08853-8; plb 0-688-08854-6) Grades ps up.

Thunderspirit was a small and timid ghost. When the Great Chief decides to visit the city and take Nanabee the sheep with him, Thunderspirit is lonely and goes along. The Great Chief does not understand city ways and Nanabee ends up in the zoo. Thunderspirit's magic helps get them home.

Boatride with Lillian Two Blossom. Patricia Polacco. Putnam, 1989. LC 87-2507, 32 p. (ISBN 0-399-21470-4) Grades ps-3.

William and Mabel learn the Native American explanation for wind, rain, sunshine, and moonshine when a mysterious old woman takes them for a magical boatride.

Dancing with the Indians. Angela Shelf Medearis; Samuel Byrd, illus. Holiday House, 1991. LC 90-28666, 32 p. (ISBN plb 0-8234-0893-0; pbk 0-8234-1023-4) Grades ps-3.

This story deals with the relationship between an escaped slave and the Seminole Indians who took him in. The slave's family continues to visit the Native Americans, and his granddaughter describes one of these annual events.

Death of the iron horse. Paul Goble. Macmillan, 1987. LC 85-28011, 32 p. (ISBN 0-02-737830-6; pbk 0-689-71686-9) Grades K-3.

When trains first crossed Native American land, the Cheyennes felt threatened. The Iron Horse seemed impregnable: faster than their horses and too tough for their arrows. Planning to derail the the train, the Cheyennes dismantle the tracks and loot the ensuing wreckage.

Dreamcatcher. Audrey Osofsky; Ed Young, illus. Orchard, 1992. LC 91-20029, 32 p. (ISBN 0-531-05988-X; plb 0-531-08588-0) Grades ps-2.

The Ojibway Indians wove nets to protect their babies from bad dreams. The baby in this picture book is protected from nightmares and other bad things by a warm, loving family. The lullaby lulls him into a sleep of lovely dreams.

Encounter. Jane Yolen; David Shannon, illus. Harcourt, 1992. LC 91-23746, 32 p. (ISBN 0-15-225962-7) Grades K-3.

A young Taino boy is frightened by the arrival of Columbus at his San Salvadoran home. He tries to warn the chief and other adults in the tribe, but they pay no attention because he is a child. As an old man, he recalls why he had good reason to fear the strangers.

Girl who loved wild horses. Paul Goble. Macmillan, 1982. LC 77-20500, 32 p. (ISBN 0-02-736570-0; pbk 0-689-71696-6) Grades K-3.

This Caldecott-winning story tells of a girl who spent more time with horses than her people. She finds herself lost and far away from home after a storm frightens the horses. A leader of the wild horses welcomes her.

Goat in the rug. Charles L. Blood; Martin Link; Nancy Winslow Parker, illus. Macmillan, 1984. LC 80-17315, 40 p. (ISBN 0-02-710920-8; pbk 0-689-71418-1) Grades ps-3.

Geraldine, the goat, loves her Navajo weaver friend Glenmae. Glenmae decides to use Geraldine's hair to make a rug. Geraldine participates at every step of the weaving.

I'm in charge of celebrations. Byrd Baylor; Peter Parnall, illus. Scribner, 1986. LC 85-19633, 32 p. (ISBN 0-684-18579-2) Grades 1-4.

A young girl who lives in the Southwest desert celebrates whenever she sees something that moves her to a happy or wondrous feeling. These phenomena include dust devils, a triple rainbow, and a falling star.

Knots on a counting rope. Bill Martin; John Archambault; Ted Rand, illus. Henry Holt, 1987. LC 87-14832, 32 p. (ISBN 0-8050-0571-4; plb 0-8050-1932-4; pbk 0-8050-2955-9) Grades ps-3.

A Native American boy urges his Grandfather to tell the boy's own story again. They talk about how he almost died at birth, and how he got the name of Boy-Strength-of-Blue-Horses. Each part of the story is a knot in the counting rope, so the boy will always know who he is.

Land of Gray Wolf. Thomas Locker. Dial, 1991. LC 90-3915, 32 p. (ISBN 0-8037-0936-6; ISBN plb 0-8037-0937-4) Grades ps up.

Gray Wolf is the leader of a tribe of Native Americans who live in an unspoiled land. As settlers move in, they clear the land of trees and bushes, and the wildlife leaves. The Native Americans unsuccesfully try to force the settlers out and are subsequently sent to a reservation.

Mama, do you love me? Barbara M. Joosse; Barbara Lavallee, illus. Chronicle, 1991. LC 90-1863, 32 p. (ISBN 0-87701-759-X) Grades ps-1.

Every child can identify with this Inuit family tale. A little girl wants to know that her mother will always love her no matter what she does, even though she may get in trouble. Many aspects of daily Inuit life are woven into the story.

Mystery of Navajo moon. Timothy Green. Northland, 1991. LC 91-52600, 48 p. (ISBN pbk 0-87358-577-1) Grades K-3.

The Navajo moon gives Wilma a diamond star. She soon takes flight on a silver pony. When she reaches for bits of moondust, she falls and lands in her own bed. Did she dream it all? She finds a moonflake lying beside her diamond star.

Nessa's fish. Nancy Luenn; Neil Waldman, illus. Macmillan, 1990. LC 89-15048, 32 p. (ISBN 0-689-31477-9); Reading Adventures, 1993. (ISBN 0-685-64812-5; cassette 1-882869-81-8) Grades K-3.

Nessa and her grandmother go fishing on the Arctic tundra. Their catch is good, but the next morning grandmother is sick. Nessa keeps away a wolf and a bear, protecting grandmother and their catch until help can arrive.

Northern lullaby. Nancy White Carlstrom; Leo and Diane Dillon, illus. Putnam, 1992. LC 90-19719, 32 p. (ISBN 0-399-21806-8) Grades ps-3.

It is bedtime for an Inuit child. First, goodnights must be said to all the inhabitants of the natural world around him—Papa Star, Mama Moon, Grandpa Mountain, Grandma River, Great Uncle Moose and Wolf Uncle Gray, Auntie Willow and Auntie Birch, Cousins Beaver, Deer Mouse, and Red Fox, Sister Owl, and Brother Bear. The Northern Lights then say their own goodnight to the drowsy child.

On Mother's lap. Ann Herbet Scott; Glo Coalson, illus. Houghton Mifflin, 1992. LC 76-39726, 32 p. (ISBN 0-395-58920-7; pbk 0-395-62976-4) Grades ps-K.

Michael, a young Eskimo boy, wants to rock with his mother. When she rocks him with all his playthings, the baby cries. Michael thinks that there is not enough room on mother's lap for him, his stuff, and the baby, but mother finds a way.

One small blue bead. Byrd Baylor; Ronald Himler, illus. Macmillan, 1992. LC 90-28160, 32 p. (ISBN 0-684-19334-5) Grades 2-5.

Set in prehistoric time, only Boy believes in the old man's dream when he sets out to find other people. He promises to do the old man's chores in his absence. When the old man returns, he brings another boy who leaves a blue bead.

Seya's song. Ron Hirschi; Constance Bergum, illus. Sasquatch, 1992. LC 92-5029, 32 p. (ISBN 0-0912365-62-5; pbk 0-0912365-91-9) Grades ps up.

Seya, or Grandmother, is singing to her granddaughter about the traditions of the S'Klallam, a tribe of the Pacific Northwest. The song celebrates nature winding through its cycle. Baby salmon begin their journey; berries ripen; the waves sweep the beach clean; elk call; the salmon return. Includes a pronunciation guide.

Sky dogs. Jane Yolen; Barry Moser, illus. Harcourt, 1990. LC 89-26960, 32 p. (ISBN 0-15-275480-6) Grades ps-2.

This tale is one version of how the Blackfeet Indians first saw horses. They called the strange creatures "sky dogs." The narrator earns a place of honor by learning to get along with them. Illustrated with watercolors.

Storyteller. Joan Weisman; David Bradley, illus. Rizzoli, 1993. LC 93-20460, 32 p. (ISBN 0-8478-1742-3) Grades K-4.

Rama, a nine-year-old Pueblo girl, dislikes her new home in the city. She always had something to do when she lived at the Cochiti Pueblo. Then she becomes friendly with Miss Lottie, a lonely old woman on the third floor. Because Rama is so shy at their first visit, she brings her storyteller doll to encourage the stones to flow. Miss Lottie comes every day after that to share her stories.

Ten little rabbits. Virginia Grossman; Sylvia Long, illus. Chronicle, 1991. LC 90-2011, 32 p. (ISBN 0-87701-552-X) Grades ps-3.

This simple counting book shows rabbits in Native American costume demonstrating various tribal customs. Each rabbit vignette includes a woven pattern and an activity characteristic of a particular tribe. The Afterword contains information on each custom and its background.

Your own best secret place. Byrd Baylor; Peter Parnall, illus. Macmillan, 1991. LC 78-21243, 32 p. (ISBN 0-684-16111-7) Grades 1-3.

The best thing in the world is your own private place. Byrd Baylor shows us hers in the hollow at the foot of a cottonwood tree. She discovers that someone had it before. Other people's private places are shown, but sharing the cottonwood tree is a special gift.

Fiction for Middle Readers

Anpao: an American Indian odyssey. Jamake Highwater; Fritz Scholder, illus. HarperCollins, 1993. LC 77-9264, 256 p. (ISBN plb 0-06-022878-4; pbk 0-06-440437-4; pbk 0-06-131986-4) Grades 7 up.

Many Native American tales converge in this story of Anpao, the brave young man who travels to the sun to ask that his sweetheart be released from her promise to marry the sun and no mortal. His wisdom and experience make him realize that he and his bride must find another home beside this earth.

Bearstone. Will Hobbs. Macmillan, 1989. LC 89-6641, 144 p., (ISBN 0-689-31496-5; pbk 0-380-71249-0) Grades 6-9.

Rancher Walter Landis was young Cloyd's last chance. The boy had lived alone in the mountains, tending his grandmother's goats for years. Now he was expected to fit in at a boarding school. Feeling out of place, he remains troubled. Then Walter, his employer, takes him on a quest for gold in a forgotten mine and the bond between the two is put to the test.

Canyons. Gary Paulsen. Peter Smith, 1992. LC 90-2829, 184 p. (ISBN 0-8446-6590-8); Delacorte, 1990. (ISBN 0-385-30153-7; pbk 0440-21023-2) Grade 4-8.

Brennan Cole becomes obsessed with the skull of an Apache boy he found while camping in an isolated canyon. He then learns that he must return the skull to an ancient sacred place in the mountains.

Courage of Sarah Noble. Alice Dalgliesh; Leonard Weisgard, illus. Macmillan, 1991. Reprint 1959 ed. LC 54-5922, 64 p. (ISBN 0684-18830-9; pbk 0-689-71540-4) Grades 1-5.

When Sarah Noble turns eight, her father takes her with him to the land he just bought from Native Americans to build a new home. She is frightened by stories about Native Americans, but is friendly when she meets a group of children. They become her friends and Sarah stays with them when her father leaves to get the rest of the family.

Dawn rider. Jan Hudson. Putnam, 1990. LC 89-29557, 192 p. (ISBN 0-399-22178-6; pbk 0-590-44987-7) Grades 6 up.

Kit Fox had a vision of her riding a horse, an animal new to her tribe. The Blackfoot captured the beast from the Snake Indians, but no one is able to ride him. Found Arrow, Kit's friend, allows her to visit the horse while he guards it. When their tribe is attacked by Snake Indians, she must convince the men that she can ride for help.

Dogsong. Gary Paulsen. Macmillan, 1985. LC 84-20443, 192 p. (ISBN 0-02-770180-8; pbk 0-14-032235-5) Grades 5-9.

Russell is not sure what is wrong, only that he is restless. Oogruk, an elderly man who follows the old ways, has the only dog team in the village. When Russell takes the dogs out, he realizes that running them is part of him and his heritage. Russell goes on a special journey to find himself and to test his survival strengths.

Haunted igloo. Bonnie Turner. Houghton Mifflin, 1991. LC 9027336, 160 p. (ISBN 0-395-57037-9) Grades 3-6.

Jean-Paul is a young Canadian boy living in the Arctic who must face his fears in that harsh environment. As his family becomes part of the Inuit community, they are able to survive, even though Jean-Paul has a deformed foot. He faces the challenge of staying two hours in an igloo that is believed to be haunted, with the help of his faithful dog, Sasha. That ordeal becomes his greatest strength and fear, as his mother faces having a baby without the hospital's aid.

I am Regina. Sally M. Keehn. Putnam, 1991. LC 90-20098, 192 p. (ISBN 0-399-21797-5) Grades 4-7.

Ten-year-old Regina is kidnapped by Native Americans from her Pennsylvania farm during the French and Indian war. She fears punishment, and even death, if she does not adapt quickly to Native American ways. Regina holds on to the hymn her mother sang to her for comfort and strength. She becomes a beloved part of her Native American family. Recaptured by soldiers ten years later, Regina fears that she will never find her original family. The hymn is the link that will lead her home.

Indian summer. Barbara Girion. Scholastic, 1993. LC 89-10835, 183 p. (ISBN pbk 0-590-42637-0) Grades 4-7.

Joni McCord and Sarah Birdsong are resentful that they have to spend the summer together. Joni's father is going to run the medical clinic for a month on the Iroquois reservation where Sarah's father is chief. The girls try to get along, but Joni thinks like a city girl, and Sarah is quickly angered over her lack of understanding. When they go to the store outside the reservation, Joni cannot believe how badly they are treated—just like Sarah's friends treat Joni. Years of hate cannot be undone by one person, but Joni has to try.

Island of the blue dolphin. Scott O'Dell. Houghton Mifflin, 1960. LC 60-5212, 192 p. (ISBN 0-395-06962-9); Houghton Mifflin, 1990. (ISBN 0-395-53680-4); Dell, 1987. (ISBN pbk 0-440-43988-4; pbk 0440-94000-1) Bantam, 1987. (ISBN Large type 1-55736-002-2) Grades 5 up.

The classic survival story of Karana, who lived alone for many years on an island off the California coast after her tribe left. Based on a true incident. Newbery winner.

Julie of the wolves. Jean Craighead George; John Schoenherr, illus. Harper-Collins, 1974. LC 72-76509, 180 p. (ISBN 0-06021943-2; plb 0-06-021944-0; pbk 0-06-440058-1; pbk 0-06-107034-3); Dell, 1986. (ISBN pbk 0-440-84444-4); Bantam, 1987. (ISBN Large type 1-55736-053-7) Grades 5 up.

Julie was only thirteen, but like many Eskimo girls, a marriage had been arranged for her. She saw no other way of escape but to run away to the Arctic tundra. If wolves had not helped her and made her a part of their pack, she would have starved. Newbery winner.

Little Runner of the longhouse. Betty Baker; Arnold Lobel, illus. Harper-Collins, 1962. LC 62-8040, 64 p. (ISBN plb 0-06-020341-2; pbk 0-06-444122-9) Grades K-3.

An *I can read* book. Little Runner wants to be like the big boys of his village, play tricks on people, and trade for maple sugar.

Morning girl. Michael Dorris. Hyperion, 1992. LC 92-52989, 80 p. (ISBN 1-56282-284-5; plb 1-56282-285-3; pbk 1-56282-661-1) Grades 3-6.

Morning Girl loves to get up early. Her brother, Star Boy, loves to explore and observe the night sky. Their father teases them about not allowing the rest of the house to sleep. This family loves and takes care of one another in their Bahamian island home. The year is 1492. Their harmony with the world is as constant as their warm family life. In stark contrast, when Christopher Columbus arrives and describes them, he only sees their value as a commodity.

Mother's blessing. Penina Keen Spinka. Macmillan, 1992. LC 9131342, 224 p. (ISBN 0-689-31758-1; pbk 0-449-70431-9) Grades 5-9.

A prophecy foretold that Four Cries would be a great leader who would unite the tribes. Her father could not believe that a girl could fulfill the prophecy. She is sent on a path of great travels, searching for a spirit guide to help her find wisdom beyond her years.

Nannabah's friend. Mary Perrine; Leonard Weisgard, illus. Houghton Mifflin, 1989. LC 73-115454, 32 p. (ISBN 0-395-52020-7) Grades K-3.

Nannabah, a young Navajo girl, worries when her grandparents tell her that she must take the sheep to the canyon by herself. She has never been alone before. While in the canyon, she makes two dolls and a little house to keep her company. The next time she goes, another girl joins her.

Next spring an oriole. Gloria Whelan; Pamela Johnson, illus. Random House, 1987. LC 87-4910, 64 p. (ISBN plb 0-394-99125-7; pbk 0-394-89125-2) Grades 2-4.

Part of the *Stepping Stone* series. In the 1830s, Libby and her family travel from their home in Virginia by covered wagon to an unsettled part of Michigan. They make friends with the varied people they meet, including a Native American family that helps them survive their first winter.

Night bird: a story of the Semunole Indians. Kathleen Kudlinski; James Watling, illus. Viking, 1990. LC 92-25935, 64 p. (ISBN 0670-83157-3) Grades 2-5.

Part of the *Once Upon America* series. Night Bird is looking forward to the Green Corn celebration because her grandmother can join them this year. Their celebration is cut short when U.S. soldiers raid them. They try to convince the Seminoles to go to Oklahoma. Some choose to go, and some stay. Night Bird is torn because her parents are going, but her grandmother is staying.

Quanah Parker: warrior for freedom, ambassador for peace. Len Hilts. Harcourt, 1992. LC 87-8488, 192 p. (ISBN pbk 0-15-2644474) Grades 4-7.

Comanches learned the secrets of survival on the bare Texas plains, but everything changed when settlers came in 1836. Quanah Parker, the son of a Comanche chief and a settler, fought fiercely to keep the the other settlers out. When surrender became inevitable, he provided leadership for his people on the reservation.

Racing the sun. Paul Pitts. Avon, 1988. LC 88-91510, 160 p. (ISBN 0-380-75496-7) Grades 5-6.

Brandon was a "regular kid"—until his grandfather moved in. Grandpa was a Navajo who seemed to want to make Brandon follow all the Native American traditions. As Brandon comes to know and love his Grandpa, he begins to discover family bonds, that home is not just a place, but a feeling. Then Grandpa asks Brandon to reteach his father these lessons.

Red Fox and his canoe. Nathaniel Benchley; Arnold Lobel, illus. Harper-Collins, 1964. LC 64-16650, 64 p. (ISBN plb 0-06-020476-1; pbk 0-06-444075-3) Grades K-3.

An I can read book. Red Fox wanted as big a canoe as possible. He and his father made one from the largest tree. When he takes it fishing, a family of bears, two otters, and a raccoon make themselves at home and nearly push him out. A moose decides to join the party, but his weight is too much. The canoe sinks.

Sing down the moon. Scott O'Dell. Houghton Mifflin, 1970. LC 71-98513, 137 p. (ISBN 0-395-10919-1); Dell, 1976. (ISBN 0-44097975-7; pbk 0-440-40673-0); Bantam, 1989. (ISBN Large type 155736-142-8) Grades 5 up.

Bright Morning felt lucky. Her family had many sheep and she loved a fine warrior named Tall Boy. That was before she was kidnapped by Spanish slavers, Tall Boy was wounded in her escape, and the soldiers forced them to leave their homes. Everyone was discouraged by the march to Bosque Redondo. Bright Morning dreamed of going back to their canyon, but Tall Boy was unconvinced until they were forced to flee. Bright Morning had everything hidden in the canyon waiting for their return.

Spider, the cave and the pottery bowl. Eleanor Clymer, Ingrid Fritz, illus. Peter Smith, 1992. LC 73-134815, 80 p. (ISBN 08446-6578-9); Dell, 1989. (ISBN pbk 0-440-40166-6) Grades K-6.

Every summer Kate and her family go to the mesa where her grandmother lives to help with farming and pottery making. This summer is different because there has been no rain and there are fewer crops. Mother worries that they will not have enough food for the winter, so she gets a job. Grandmother is not well and says there is no clay. Then Kate's brother Johnny runs away after breaking the pot that Grandmother says came from the Old Ones.

Squanto: friend of the Pilgrim. Clyde Robert Bulla; Peter Burchard, illus. Scholastic, 1990. LC 54-9145, 112 p. (ISBN 0590-44055-1) Grades 2-4.

Squanto was fascinated by the European men who came to the shore near his home. He accepted their invitation to visit England. Although he learned much about the English way of life, he was too trusting. An unfriendly captain tried to sell him into slavery. He escaped and returned to North America. When the Pilgrims landed, he knew their language and helped them to survive.

Streams to the river, river to the sea: a novel of Sacagawea. Scott O'Dell. Houghton Mifflin, 1986. LC 86-936, 191 p. (ISBN 0-395-40430-4; pbk 0-449-70244-8); Hall, 1989. (ISBN Large print 0-81614811-2) Grades 6 up.

Sacagawea was barely a mother when her husband agreed to go with Lewis and Clark to explore the area leading to the Pacific. With her new baby on her back, she set out on a great adventure. It was a perilous journey. She was a valuable member of the party, while her husband was a complaining nuisance. Sacagawea fell in love with Captain Clark, but knew that the cultural barriers were too great.

Sweetgrass. Jan Hudson. Putnam, 1989. LC 88-25516, 160 p. (ISBN 0-399-21721-5) Grades 5-7.

Fifteen year old Sweetgrass longs to marry her sweetheart, the warrior Eagle-Sun. Even though she is the oldest one of her group who is unmarried, her father is not yet ready to let his favorite daughter go. He says she is not strong enough. Then a harsh winter comes, with little food and a smallpox epidemic. With her father away, Sweetgrass is the only person able to care for her stricken family.

Talking earth. Jean Craighead George. HarperCollins, 1983. LC 82-48850, 160 p. (ISBN 0-06-021975-0; plb 0-06-021976-9; pbk 0-06440212-6) Grades 5 up.

Billie Wind is skeptical of the old Seminole legends, such as those with talking animals. She enters the Florida everglades to better understand her ancestral ways. Billie learns to listen to what animals "say" in order to survive. An otter, a baby panther, and a turtle all contribute to her realization that animals truly know the earth, and can teach people about how to live without destroying the planet.

Thunder rolling in the mountains. Scott O'Dell; Elizabeth Hall. Houghton Mifflin, 1992. LC 91-15961, 144 p. (ISBN 0-395-59966-0; pbk 0-440-40879-2) Grades 5-9.

The story of the last battle between the Nez Perce and the U.S. army is told by Sound of Running Feet, the daughter of Chief Joseph. She bravely perseveres despite many hardships that the tribe endures trying to escape the wrath of the army. She hopes that she can marry her sweetheart and find a peaceful place to live, but there are too many obstacles, too many dead. Her father finally says, "I will fight no more forever."

To walk the sky path. Phyllis Reynolds Naylor. Dell, 1992. 144 p. (ISBN 0-440-40636-6) Grades 4-7.

Billie lives with his family in the Florida everglades in much the same way that Seminoles have lived for generations. He attends the American school because his father and uncles realize that if they are to survive, it will be in mainstream society. Billie's grandfather, Abraham, opposes merging the two cultures. He sees only the loss of the Seminole way, while Billie hopes to improve the situation with the aid of his unique perspective.

Toughboy and Sister. Kirkpatrick Hill. Macmillan, 1990. LC 9031297, 128 p. (ISBN 0-689-50506-X; pbk 0-14-034866-2) Grades 3-7.

John and Annie Laurie—nicknamed Toughboy and Sister—find themselves in a desperate situation. When their father has an accident, the children are stranded at their fishing camp in an isolated part of the Yukon. They must learn to take care of themselves, find food, and escape a marauding bear.

Warrior maiden: a Hopi legend. Ellen Schecter; Laura Kelly, illus. Bantam, 1992. LC 91-41314, 48 p. (ISBN 0-553-08949-8; pbk 0-55337022-7) Grades ps-3.

Part of the *Bank Street ready to read* series. The men of the Hopi pueblo are nervous about working their fields. Apache raiders might attack at any time. Huh-ay-ay's father tells her to be vigilant.
When she sees the warriors approaching she tells everyone in the village to make noise as if they are preparing to do battle. That will give her time to bring the men back from the fields.

Where the broken heart still beats. Carolyn Meyer. Harcourt, 1992. LC 92-257, 197 p. (ISBN 0-15-200639-7; pbk 0-15-295602-6) Grades 4-7.

Part of the *Great Episodes* series. The clash between American and Native American cultures in North America is portrayed in this account of Cynthia Ann Parker's return to her family after many years with the Comanches. During her time with them, she married a Comanche and had several children. The viewpoints here are those of Cynthia and a young cousin who befriended her. Cynthia's longing for her Comanche family becomes stronger because of the hostility she feels from her original family and neighbors. She is never reunited with her Comanche family. When Cynthias's daughter becomes ill and dies, she loses her will to live.

White Hare's horses. Penina Keen Spinka. Macmillan, 1991. LC 90-42777, 160 p. (ISBN 0-689-31654-2; pbk 0-449-70407-6) Grades 5-9.

White Hare, a young Chumash woman, is uncertain about her destiny. She is confused because her visions, instincts, and behavior are different from everyone else's. When Aztecs come to their homeland, the Chumash welcome them. Yet a series of revelations convince White Hare that the Aztecs are not friends. They have come to wage war, capture slaves, and perform human sacrifices. White Hare saves the tribe by setting the Aztecs' horses free.

Reference and Scholarly Works

The American Indian index: a directory of Indian Country, U.S.A.
Gregory W. Frazier; Randolph J. Punley, editor. Arrowstar, 1985. LC 85-20155, 325 p. (ISBN 0-935151-39-7).

A classified list of organizations, serving Native Americans at all levels, is one of the most comprehensive in print. Compiled primarily from official sources, it covers tribes recognized by the Bureau of Indian Affairs, "unrecognized" tribes, Indian interest organizations, government offices (federal and state), education, housing, employment, social service (both reservationbased and urban-based), publications, museums, major pow-wows, and arts and crafts traders. Lack of index makes it necessary to know the agency sought prior to searching.

Atlas of the North American Indian. Carl Waldman. Facts on File, 1985. LC 83-9020, 288 p. (ISBN 0-87196-850-9; pbk 0-81602136-8).

Provides a sound introduction to seven broad topics: "Ancient Indians," "Ancient Civilizations," "Indian Lifeways," "Indians and Explorers," "Indian Wars," "Indian Land cessions," and "Contemporary Indians." Includes over 100 maps, illustrations, a bibliography, and an index.

Dictionary of Indians of North America. Harry Waldmam, ed. Scholarly Press, 1978. 3 Vols., 330 p. (ISBN 0-403-01799-8).

An alphabetical collection of biographies of Native Americans from the time of

Columbus to the present in three volumes. Colorful, poetic, and easy to read.

Encyclopedia of Native American tribes. Carl Waldman; Molly Braun, illus. Facts on File, 1987. LC 86-29066, 308 p. (ISBN 0-8160-1421-3).

Contains concise yet wide-ranging information about the culture and history of more than 150 North American tribes. The author, a former archivist for the NY State Historical Association, compiled the Atlas of the North American Indian (1975). Articles are alphabetically arranged, covering tribal or cultural names, history, housing, areas lived in, migrations, early relations with colonists, wars, and current language families. Includes watercolor illustrations and an index.

First of the Americans: then and now. William H. Hodge. Harcourt, 1981. LC 80-22310, 551 p. (ISBN 0-03-056721-1).

Describes the lives of 13 Native American groups as they were beforethe settlers arrived, and as they developed in the last half of the 20th century. Provides a New World prehistory tracing the development of Native Americans in the Western Hemisphere. The basic approach is a "then and now" description of groups, ranging from the Eskimos to the Navajos. Contains references, black and white photographs, and maps.

Guide to the Indian tribes of the Pacific Northwest. Robert H. Ruby; John A. Brown. University of Oklahoma Press, 1992. LC 8522470, 312 p . (ISBN 0-8061-2479-2) .

This guide describes the various tribes who live in the vast area from the Rockies to the Pacific, and from California to British Columbia. Special events are included. Contains a pronunciation key, with names that the tribes are generally and locally known by. Includes an index.

Handbook of the American frontier: four centuries of Indian-white relationships. Norman Heard. Scarecrow Press, 1987. LC 86-20326, 421 p. V. 1, 1987 (ISBN 0-8108-1931-7); V. 2, 1990 (ISBN 0-81082324-1); V. 3, 1993 (ISBN 0-8108-2767-0).

Reference material on American Indian and non-Indian relationships. Includes topics such as tribes, leaders, frontier settlers, captives, explorers, missionaries, and mountain men. Will contain five volumes when completed—each covering a different area. Volume I covers the Southeastern Woodlands. Volume II covers the Northeast. Volume III covers the Great Plains. Volume IV covers the Southwest and Pacific Coast. Volume V includes a comprehensive index, chronology, and bibliography. Entries listed alphabetically as brief articles.

Handbook of North American Indians: Arctic. Davis Damas, editor. Smithsonian Institute, 1984. LC 77-17162, 862 p. (ISBN 0-87474-185-8).

Includes 59 essays by scholars in the field. Provides an overview of Arctic culture, as well as a historical summary of ethnographic and archeological research. Includes an excellent 77 page bibliography. Lists publications in all the languages in which Arctic researchers have published. Includes photographs and an index.

History of women in America. Carol Hymowitz; Michaele Weissman. Bantam Books, 1984. 400 p. (ISBN 0-553-26914-3).

Details women's contributions to American history. Contains a section called 'The Maverick West," that graphically describes the role and treatment of Native American Indians during the 1800s. Index.

Indian clothing before Cortes: Mesoamerican costumes from the Codices. Patricia Rieff Anawalt. University of Oklahoma, 1990. LC 80-5942, 256 p. (ISBN 0-8061-1650-1; pbk 0-8061-2288-9).

Part of the *Civilization of the American Indian* series. A comprehensive description and analysis of the costumes and clothing of six major groups of Native Americans in Mexico. Includes a broad cultural survey and a discussion of how these clothing styles were reconstructed historically. Contains detailed drawings, figures, color plates, charts, and examples of costumes.

Indian givers: how the Indians of the Americas transformed the world. Jack Weatherford. Crown, 1988. LC 88-3827, 288 p. (ISBN 0-517-56969-8; pbk 0-449-90496-2).

Traces the contributions made by Native Americans to the federal system of government, democratic institutions, modern medicine, agriculture, architecture, and ecology.

Indian wars. Robert M. Utley; Wilcomb E. Washburn. Houghton Mifflin, 1985. LC 85-13474, 362 p. (ISBN pbk 0-685-10831-7).

Part of the *American heritage library* series. Covers the history of over 300 years of warfare between Native Americans and Europeans. Concentrates on the North American continent.

The Indians of Texas: from prehistoric to modern times. W.W. Newcomb, Jr. University of Texas Press, 1961. LC 60-14312, 422 p. (ISBN 0-292-73271-6; pbk 0-292-78425-2).

A comprehensive, scholarly, and authoritative work describing the Native Americans of Texas. Includes a bibliography and an index.

Nations within a nation: historical statistics of American Indians.
Paul Stuart. Greenwood, 1987. LC 86-33618, 261 p. (ISBN 0-313-23813-8).

A well-presented and easy-to-use source for a variety of statistics. Covers such topics as land holdings, population, health care, education, employment, income, and economic development. Each chapter begins with a topic overview and a discussion of the statistical charts presented.

Native American directory: Alaska, Canada, United States. Fred Synder, editor. National Native American Co-operative, 1982. 366 p. (ISBN 0-9610334-0-1).

A comprehensive directory of Native Americans, their events, and organizations. Also includes a guide for acquiring native art forms through galleries, Indian stores, and trading posts. Reserve land information, tribal band names, and data on population, schools, newspapers, and periodicals are also provided.

Native American voluntary organizations. Armand S. La Potin. Greenwood, 1987. LC 86-25764, 193 p. (ISBN 0-313-23633-X).

Part of the *Ethnic Voluntary Organizations* series. An alphabetical listing of voluntary organizations operated by and for Native Americans.

North American Indians, a comprehensive account. Alice Beck Kehoe. Prentice Hall, 1981. LC 80-22335, 564 p. (ISBN pbk 013-623652-9) 2nd ed. Prentice Hall, 1992. 625 p. (ISBN pbk 0-13-624362-29).

A detailed history of Native Americans from Alaska and Canada to Mexico. The book is written from the perspective of the North American native, and deals with those policies or trends that affected them most strongly. Divided by geographic area, each area is in chronological order and includes a detailed bibliography.

Plains Indians of the twentieth century. Peter Iverson, editor. University of Oklahoma Press, 1985. LC 85-40475, 267 p. (ISBN 0-8061-1866-0; pbk 0-8061-1959-4).

An anthology of recent writings on Plains Indians. Attempts to enhance understanding of Native American history as a continuing story. Includes maps, an index, and footnotes to original writings.

Red & white: Indian views of the white man 1492-1982. Annette Rosenstiel. Universe, 1983. LC 82-23901, 192 p. (ISBN 0-87663-657-1).

Indians speak for themselves in excerpts from many documents, letters, books, and speeches. This work shows their determination and presence of mind in the face of genocide. A valuable source for insight into the ordeal. Includes photographs, drawings, a bibliography, and an index.

Reference encyclopedia of the American Indian. Vol. 1. 6th ed. Barry T. Klein, editor. Todd Publications. LC 77-14899, 1,100 p. (ISBN 0-915344-30-0).

Organized by category and arranged alphabetically or alphageographically. A quick reference tool for many aspects of Indian affairs.

Spirit of the New England tribes: Indian history and folklore, 1620-1984. William S. Simmons. University Press of New England, 1986. LC 85-40936, 343 p. (ISBN 0-87451-372-3).

Presents examples of southern New England Indian folklore, from the earliest European contact to the present day. Chapters such as Witches, Ghosts, Giants, and Treasures are presented in chronological order from the 17th century to the present. Includes a bibliography, a general index, and an index of folklore motifs.

Studies in plays and games. Brian Sutton-Smith. Ayer, 1976. 21 vols., (ISBN 0-405-07912-5).

A collection of studies on games, sports, and play activities of tribes and peoples divided into two parts: *Central and South America* and II—*North America*. Includes history, descriptions of games, and some illustrations.

Non-fiction

Abenaki. Colin G. Calloway. Chelsea House, 1989. LC 88-25147, 112 p. (ISBN 1-55546-687-7) Grades 5 up.

Part of the *Indians of North America* series. The Abenaki tribe lived in northern New England, in easily transportable wigwams so that during the warm months they could move around and find enough food to last through the harsh winters. As their lands were taken from them, they seemed to go into hiding. They began a political revival and are buying back their homeland and establishing businesses.

Algonquin. Rita D'Apice; Mary D'Apice; Katherine Ace, illus. Rourke, 1990. LC 90-8648, 32 p. (ISBN 0-86625-388-2) Grades 5-8.

Part of the *Native American people* series. The Algonquins lived along the North Eastern coast. Their daily habits, traditions, and customs are described.

American Indians of the Southwest. Bertha P. Dutton. UNM Press, 1983. LC 80-52274, 317 p. (ISBN pbk 0-8263-0704-3) Grades 5 up.

Describes life in various Native American tribes of the Southwest. The author shows how each tribe adapted to its unique environment and has a unique lifestyle. Includes appendices and an extensive bibliography.

Anasazi. Eleanor Ayer. Walker, 1993. LC 92-14701, 112 p. (ISBN 0-8027-8184-5; plb 0-8027-8185-3) Grades 5 up.

The Anasazi, or ancient ones, are traced from their early appearance to their modern day Pueblo descendants. Using archeological data, their development from basket makers to Pueblo architects is covered.

Anasazi. David Peterson. Children's Press, 1991. LC 91-3036, 48 p. (ISBN 0-516-01121-9; pbk 0-516-41121-7) Grades K-4.

Part of the *New true* series. The Anasazi lived in the Four Corners area of the Southwest. Their descendants joined the Pueblo, the Hopi, and the Zuni Indians. The Anasazi are known for their cliff dwellings which were later abandoned for some unknown reason.

Ancient cliff dwellers of Mesa Verde. Caroline Arnold; Richard Hewett, photographer. Houghton Mifflin, 1992. LC 91-8145, 64 p. (ISBN 0-395-56241-4) Grades 3-6.

The Anasazi were a unique group of people who pre-date the Ute and Navajo Indians in New Mexico and Colorado. Their habits, work, and buildings are studied and analyzed by anthropologists.

Apache. Patricia McKissack. Children's Press, 1984. LC 84-7803, 48 p. (ISBN plb 0-516-41925-0) Grades K-4.

Part of the *New True* series. Describes the history, customs, religion, government, homes, and lifestyle of the Apache Indians. Includes glossary and index.

Apache. Michael E. Melody. Chelsea House, 1989. LC 88-9587, 112 p. (ISBN 1-55546-689-3; pbk 0-7910-0352-3) Grades 5-6.

Part of the *Indians of North America* series. The Apache from Kansas to northern Mexico were nomads in this hard terrain, following game and using portable homes made out of brush. Describes how they were fierce enough to fend off the Spanish colonists, but not the U.S. Army. Apaches are now on reservations in Arizona and New Mexico.

Apache *Indians.* Nicole Claro. Chelsea House, 1992. LC 91-37339, 80 p. (ISBN 0-7910-1656-0) Grades 2-5.

Part of the *Junior library of ATnerican Indians* series. Details this Southwest American tribe's way of life, before and after their troubles with settlers. Discusses famed chiefs, Cochise and Geronimo, as well as the tribe's current legal battles to regain rights and property.

Apaches. Barbara A. McCall; Luciano Lazzarini, illus. Rourke, 1990. LC 89-49498, 32 p. (ISBN 0-86625-384-X; plb 0-685-36387-2) Grades 5-8.

Part of the *Native A7rlerican Peoples* series. The Apaches were fierce survivors in a harsh land, sometimes raiding other tribes. They could move their domiciles quickly, hunting elk, deer, and antelope for food.

Apaches and Navajos. Craig A. Doherty; Katherine M. Doherty. Watts, 1989. LC 89-9079, 64 p. (ISBN 0-531-10743-4; pbk 0-53115602-8) Grades 3-8.

A *First book.* The Apaches and the Navajos were related when they first came to the Southwest, but their bands settled into different areas and separated from the larger group.   Similar tribal customs are discussed in depth.

Arapaho. Loretta Fowler. Chelsea House, 1989. LC 88-22988, 128 p. (ISBN 1-55546-690-7) Grades 5 up.

Part of the *Indians of North America* series. The Arapaho, a nomadic tribe that lived on the Great Plains were pushed out of the Black Hills by Sioux and Cheyenne tribes, and their land in Colorado was taken by miners. In their search for hunting territory, the tribe split, and eventually settled on two reservations set aside for other tribes. Today the Arapaho come together primarily to observe the traditional prayer ceremony.

Archaeology of North America. Dean R. Snow. Chelsea House, 1992. LC 88-18120, 144 p. (ISBN pbk 0-7910-0353-1) Grades 5 up.

Part of the *Indians of North* America series. Archeological data has given scientists much information about the origins and lives of Native Americans. Each region caused them to develop their societies differently. Often their survival required cultivation of corn, beans, and squash. Archaeologists continue to add to society's knowledge, helping to recapture lost civilizations.

Arctic hunter. Diane Hoyt-Goldsmith; Lawrence Migdale, photographer. Holiday House, 1992. LC 92-2563, 32 p., (ISBN 0-8234-0972-4; pbk 0-8234-1124-9) Grades 3-7.

This detailed photoessay follows Reggie, a ten-year-old Inupiat (Eskimo) boy and his family to their summer camp after the winter ice breaks up. He is proud that he can contribute to the hunt. The book emphasizes that the animals will be their food during the winter. Their summer camp is filled with work, play, and warm family times that perpetuate their tribal customs.

Arctic memories. Normee Ekoomiak. Henry Holt, 1990. LC 89-39194, 32 p. (ISBN 0-8050-1254-0; pbk 0-8050-2347-X) Grades 3 up.

Normee Ekoomiak describes the biographical and tribal background on his embroidered pictures of Eskimo life. Text included in English and Inuit.

Boy becomes a man at Wounded Knee. Ted Wood with Wanbli Numpa Afraid of Hawk. Walker, 1992. LC 92-1218, 42 p. (ISBN 0-80278174-8; plb 0-8027-8175-6) Grades 4 up.

The history of the events leading up to the massacre at Wounded Knee is recounted by a Lakota Sioux. An eight-year-old boy goes along the grueling 150 mile ride that retraces their ancestors steps—through snow and rough terrain.

Boy who sailed with Columbus. Michael Foreman; Richard Seaver. Arcade, 1992. LC 91-55518, 80 p. (ISBN 1-55970-178-1) Grades 1-4.

Leif is a Viking orphan who was left at a Spanish monastery. Christopher Columbus recruits him for his voyage to locate a new route to China. When they find land, Leif is fascinated by new sights and sounds. Leif is abandoned and taken in by the Native Americans. He is raised by a wise elder and becomes a medicine man. When he sees the European ships return, he fears what is coming and moves his family west.

Brother Eagle, Sister Sky: a message from Chief Seattle. Chief Seattle; Susan Jeffers, illus. Dial, 1991. LC 90-27713, 32 p. (ISBN 0-8037-0969-2; plb. 0-8037-0963-3) Grades ps up.

Chief Seattle signed the treaty that ended the last Native American War. He rose and addressed the group at the signing: "How can you buy the sky?" His message, to take care of the land as his people did, still speaks volumes.

Buffalo hunt. Russell Freedman. Holiday House, 1988. LC 87-35303, 52 p. (ISBN 0-8234-0702-0) Grades 3-7.

The buffalo was essential to the survival of the people of the Plains. They used it for food, clothing, and shelter. The yearly schedule revolved around the hunt, and their religion honored it. When hunters wiped out the buffalo, they also destroyed the Plains' way of life.

California Indians. C.L. Keyworth. Facts on File, 1990. LC 90-45543, 96 p. (ISBN 0-8160-2386-7) Grades 5-8.

Part of the *First Americans* series. Vivid photographs illustrate the environment and cultures of the Native American tribes of California: Cahuilla, Chumash, Hupa, Miwok, Pomo, and Yurok. The California Indians staged a dramatic protest at Alcatraz in 1969 to fight for their rights.

Catawbas. James H. Merrell. Chelsea House, 1989. LC 88-21821, 112 p. (ISBN 1-55546-694-X) Grades 5 up.

Part of the *Indians of North America* series. The Catawbas made their homeland in the Carolina Piedmont region, living in bark houses protected by large stakes. The tribe grew as war survivors drifted south. Later, they converted to Mormonism. A renewed interest in ancient traditions has led many descendants to a reservation in South Carolina.

Cayuga. Jill Duvall. Children's Press, 1991. LC 91-3038, 48 p. (ISBN 0-516-01123-5; pbk 0-516-41123-3) Grades K-4.

Part of the *New true* series. The Cayuga were part of the Iroquois confederacy, making their home in the Northeastern U.S. After the European arrival, Cayuga societies were scattered. In 1923, when an international "League of Nations" was proposed, a Cayuga chief named Deskaheb traveled to Switzerland to make the point that a league cannot work unless all cultures, large and small, have an equal voice.

Cherokee. Barbara McCall; Luciano Lazzarine, illus. Rourke, 1989. LC 88-3947, 32 p. (ISBN plb 0-86625-376-9; pbk 0-685-58583-2) Grades 5-8.

Part of the *Native American People* series. This history of the Cherokee people briefly describes life before the Europeans, famous Cherokees, and the role the tribes played in the developing United States. Includes the Trail of Tears and the separate bands of Cherokee.

Cherokee. Theda Perdue. Chelsea House, 1989. LC 88-14175, 111 p. (ISBN 1-55546-695-8; pbk 0-7910-0357-4) Grades 5 up.

The Cherokees lived in the southern Appalachians and called themselves the "principal people." Tribal customs dictated that the only cause for war was the killing of a Cherokee and vengeance must be carried out by the victims clan. After the first contact with Europeans, diseases decimated much of the Cherokee nation.
They fought in the French and Indian War and signed a treaty to protect their lands which was violated when they were moved during the "Trail of tears" incident. The surviving Cherokees established a new order for themselves.

Cherokee Indians. Nicole Claro. Chelsea House, l9gl. LC 90-23480, 80 p. (ISBN 0-7910-1652-8) Grades 2-5.

Part of the *Junior library of American Indians* series. Describes how the Cherokees hoped that by adopting the European ways, they could live in harmony. Cherokees were relocated and still fight for rights today.

Cherokee summer. Diane Hoyt-Goldsmith, Lawrence Migdale, photo. Holiday House, 1993. LC 92-54416, 32 p. (ISBN 0-8234-0995-3) Grades 3-7.

Bridget describes her life as a modern Cherokee. Grandmother helps her weave baskets; Grandfather helps to make arrowheads; and father takes them crawdad fishing. There are traditional tribal activities such as the Hog fry and the Stomp dance. Bridget also furnishes information about Cherokee history and language.

Cheyenne. Dennis Fradin. Childrenls Press, 1988. LC 87-33792, 48 p. (ISBN 0-516-01211-8; pbk 0-516-41211-6) Grades K-4.

A New True book. The Cheyenne called themselves "The People." This easy-to-read book gives brief background on their daily lives, their history before and after American settlers, and their lives today.

Cheyenne. Stan Hoig. Chelsea House, 1989. LC 88-17701, 112 p. (ISBN 1-55546-696-6; pbk 0-7910-0358-2) Grades 5 up.

Part of the *Indians of North America* series. The Cheyenne were one of the tribes who lived in the Great Plains, hunting buffalo and fending off hostile tribes. Cheyenne garments were intricate works of art and attracted traders. They fought bitterly against the U.S. army, but the slaughter of the buffalo herds forced them onto reservations. Cheyennes have a reservation in Oklahoma and in Montana.

Cheyenne. Sally Lodge; Luciano Lazzarino, illus. Rourke, 1990. LC 90-8476, 32 p. (ISBN 0-86625-387-4; 0-685-36388-0) Grades 5-8.

Part of the *Native American Peoples* series. Known for painting their faces red, the Cheyenne's lifestyle was transformed from an agricultural to a nomadic culture when they tamed horses. Rituals to prove bravery became more important and war skills were emphasized. The defeat of Custer was a short-lived victory and reservation life was particularly hard on the Cheyenne.

Chickasaw. Duane K. Hale; Arrell M. Gibson. Chelsea House, 1991. LC 90-34775, 112 p. (ISBN 1-55546-697-4; pbk 0-7910-0372-8) Grades 5 up.

Part of the *Indians of North America* series. The Chickasaws settled in the fertile lands of Mississippi, Alabama, and Tennessee after they broke off from a group that became Chocktaw. They revolted against slave-like conditions imposed by the explorer DeSoto. Their alliance with the British resulted in favorable trade agreements, but then the U.S. took over their land and they were forced to relocate to Oklahoma.

Children of clay: a family of Pueblo potters. Rina Swentzell; Bill Steen, photographer. Lerner, 1992. LC 92-8680, 40 p. (ISBN plb 0-8225-2654-9; pbk 0-8225-9627-X) Grades 4-7.

Part of the *We are still here* series. Gathering clay is a vital process for Gia Rose and her family—everyone helps. They pray to the spirit of the clay at every step, especially at the firing. They follow the same tradition as their ancestors did at the Santa Clara Pueblo in New Mexico.

Children's atlas of Native Americans. Rand McNally, 1992. LC 926791, 78 p. (ISBN 0-528-83494-0) Grades K-12.

As native cultures crossed the land bridge and settled in different areas of North and South America, people adjusted their habits to the environment. This atlas furnishes an introduction to the different regions and tribes. Includes maps, photographs, drawings, and descriptions of tribes as background information.

Chinook. Clifford E. Trafzer. Chelsea House, 1990. LC 89-36622, 112 p. (ISBN 1-55546-698-2) Grades 5 up.

Part of the *Indians of North Amerlca* series. The Chinook prospered along the Pacific shore in Oregon and Washington. They thought that flattened foreheads were a sign of beauty. After diseases weakened the tribe, some of them agreed to a reservation, while others refused. They are still fighting for fishing rights on much of their ancient homelands.

Choctaw. Emilie U. Lepthien. Children's Press, 1987. LC 8714583, 48 p. (ISBN 0-516-01240-1; pbk 0-516-41240-X) Grades K-4.

A *New True* book. An easy-to-read book about the Choctaws, who lived in Alabama, Louisiana, and Mississippi and were primarily farmers. There is a brief history of their contact with the Spaniards, the French, and negotiations which resulted in the loss of their land. Some remained in Mississippi, preserving their own culture.

Choctaw. Jesse McKee. Chelsea House, 1989. LC 88-30165, 104 p. (ISBN 1-55546-699-0) Grades 5 up.

Part of the *Indians of North America* series . The Choctaws' early contact with Europeans resulted in many deaths. They were pressured by the American government into trading their rich land for a large tract in Oklahoma. The Choctaws who remained in the South suffered poverty and were sent to a reservation. The two factions come together for festivals.

Chumash. Robert O. Gibson. Chelsea House, 1991. LC 90-34776, 104 p. (ISBN 1-55546-700-8; pbk 0-7910-0376-0) Grades 5 up.

Part of the *Indians of North America* series. The business-oriented Chumash lived on islands along the California coast, operating a thriving trade. Their social system had class divisions, trade unions, and currency. The Spanish destroyed this economic system, using them as slaves, and passing on disease. The remaining Indians moved to the missions, and survived changing governments as laborers. The Chumash have organized, and live on a reservation in California.

Cities in the sand: the ancient civilizations of the Southwest. Scott Warren. Chronicle, 1991. LC 91-38818, 64 p. (ISBN 0-81180012-1) Grades 4-8.

Three main groups of ancient Indians lived in the Southwest: the Anasazi, the Hohokam, and the Mogollon. They had distinctive styles of art, architecture, and patterns of farming and trade. Archaeologists describe what they think life was like for those groups, and speculate on why these Indians abandoned their cities.

Clambake: a Wamponoag tradition. Russell Peters; John Madama, photographer. Lerner, 1992. LC 92-8423, 48 p. (ISBN 0-8225-26514; pbk 0-8225-9621-0) Grades 3-6.

Part of the *We are still here* series. Steven Peters is in the sixth grade, but he is helping his grandfather, Fast Turtle, prepare a traditional appanaug or clambake. Everything must be done according to tradition because Fast Turtle wants Steven to know part of the history of their people.

Coast Salish peoples. Frank W. Porter. Chelsea House, 1989. LC 89-9730, 104 p. (ISBN 1-55546-701-6) Grades 5 up.

Part of the *Indians of North America* series. The Coast Salish peoples are made up of many tribes that settled on the shores of the Puget Sound. Chief Seattle had to give into pressure to turn over their land to non-Indians in return for reservation land. Their reservation was mainly uninhabitable, and they became know as the "landless tribes." They are now fighting back legally.

Comanche. Willard H. Rollings. Chelsea House, 1989. LC 88-33987, 112 p. (ISBN 1-55546-702-4; pbk 0-7910-0359-0) Grades 5 up.

Part of the *Indians of North America* series. Splitting from the Shoshones, the

Comanches formed their own tribe and dominated the southern end of the Great Plains, despite Apache opposition. They were nomads living in tepees and following the buffalo herds. After a protracted struggle with the U.S. army, they were sent to a reservation in Oklahoma.

Comanche Indians. Martin J. Mooney. Chelsea House, 1993. LC 929932, 80 p. (ISBN 0-7910-1653-6) Grades 2-5.

Part of the *Junior library of American Indians* series. The Comanches lived in the desert Southwest, fiercely protecting their hunting lands. Their first threat came from the Spaniards, but after much fighting they came to an agreement. The invading Americans could not be dealt with so effectively. Now they fight for their homeland on the legal front.

Desert is theirs. Byrd Baylor; Peter Parnall, illus. Macmillan, 1975. LC 74-24417, 32 p. (ISBN 0-684-14266-X; pbk 0-689-71105-0) Grades K-5.

The Papago Indians, or the Desert People, have a special closeness to the land. The hawks, the deer, pack rats, the skinny plants, and the fat saguaro cactus share that closeness to the Mother earth. Life in the desert is presented with unique perspective.

Encyclopedia of Native American tribes. Carl Waldman; Molly Braun, illus. Facts on File, 1987. LC 86-29066, 308 p. (ISBN 0-81601421-3) Grades 4-6.

This encyclopedia covers 150 North American tribes, arranged in alphabetical order. Each article has a history of the tribe, its migrations, and it's contact with settlers. Customs and traditions are included: languages, houses, tools, clothing, art, legends and religious beliefs, and ceremonies. Includes illustrations, maps, cross-references, and bibliography.

Eskimo boy: life in an Inupiaq Eskimo village. Russell Kendall. Scholastic, 1992. LC 90-9157, 32 p. (ISBN 0-590-43695-3) Grades 3-6.

This photoessay introduces Norman, a young Inuit, and his family—following them through their lives to show the mixture of modern life and tribal custom in the day-to-day world of the Inuit. Norman goes to school and also ice fishes. Includes information about the Inuit and Alaska.

From Abenaki to Zuni: a dictionary of Native American tribes. Evelyn Wolfson; William Sauts Bock, illus. Walker, 1988. LC 87-27875, 215 p. (ISBN 0-8027-6789-3; plb 0-8027-6790-7) Grades 5 up.

Sixty-eight of the larger tribes are identified and arranged in alphabetical order.

Each article includes information about the land in which they lived and hunted, types of houses they built, the clothing they wore, the foods they ate, their means of travel, and where their descendent live now. Includes illustrations and maps.

Growing up Indian. Evelyn Wolfson; William Sauts Bock, illus. Walker, 1986. LC 86-9053, 96 p. (ISBN 0-8027-6643-9; plb 0-80276644-7) Grades 4 up.

Describes the lives of Native American children from babyhood to their rites of passage by using a question and answer format.

Hidatsa. Mary Jane Schneider. Chelsea House, 1989. LC 88-11702, 112 p. (ISBN 1-55546-707-5) Grades 5 up.

Part of the *Indians of North America* series. The Hidatsa lived in permanent villages along the Missouri River in mud lodges, and were hospitable to European travelers. This village life allowed them to absorb other customs and adapt to reservation life and became more farming oriented. Their reservation was flooded in 1956 when the Garrison Dam was built. They sued successfully.

Hopi. Ann Heinrichs Tomchek. Children's Press, 1987. LC 87-8037, 48 p. (ISBN 0-516-01234-7; pbk 0-516-41234-5) Grades K-4.

A New True book. In this easy-to-read book, Hopi life in Arizona is described. Part of the Pueblo, they built their villages on top of the mesas. They have juggled relations with the Spaniards, the Americans, and other Native Americans so that they can keep their own ways

Houges of bark: tipi, wigwam, and longhouse. Bonnie Shemie. Tundra, 1990. LC 90-70130, 24 p. (ISBN 0-88776-246-8; pbk 088776-306-5) Grades 3-7.

Part of the *Native dwellings* series. The woodland Indians of Canada and the northeastern United States had similar shelters: teepees, wigwams, and longhouses—they use a pole shell covered by tree bark. Teepees were quickly constructed when they Native Americans hunted; wigwams were igloo shaped and more permanent; the longhouses were huge structures.

Houses of hide and earth: tipi and earthlodges. Bonnie Shemie. Tundra, 1991. LC 91-090245-3, 32 p. (ISBN 0-88776-269-7; pbk 088776-307-3) Grades 3-7.

Part of the *Native dwellings* series. The tribes who lived on the plains had to make their homes out of buffalo skins because little wood or other building materials were available. They adapted this type of dwelling into many varieties, based on need and environment.

Houses of snow, skin and bones: native dwellings: the far north. Bonnie Shemie. Tundra, 1989. LC 89-50778, 24 p. (ISBN 0-88776240-9; pbk 0-88776-305-7) Grades 3-7.

Part of the *Native dwellings* series. The Inuit, or Eskimos, have special houses which help them survive the harsh conditions of the far north. Igloos can be quickly constructed as temporary shelters of hard-packed snow, or as more permanent shelters, using rock and whale bone to reinforce them. The shape of the igloo makes it warm inside and wind resistant. Teepee-like tents made out of animals skins are used in the Inuit summer camps.

Huron. Nancy Bonvillain. Chelsea House, 1989. LC 89-930, 112 p. (ISBN 1-55546-708-3) Grades 5 up.

Part of the *Indians of North America* series. The Huron lived in Ontario in huge longhouses behind fortressed palisades. They made intricate embroidered garments and boxes. The French helped expand their trade network, which engendered great jealousy from the Iroquois who eventually waged war on the Hurons. They finally were forced from their homeland, wandering for 200 years until they settled in the Oklahoma territory. Some Huron descendants have formed a reservation in Canada.

Huron carol. Father Jean de Brebeuf; Frances Tyrrell, illus. Dutton, 1990. LC 91-35965, 32 p. (ISBN 0-525-44909-4) Grades ps-4.

Father Jean de Brebeuf, a French missionary who lived among the Huron in the 1600s, composed this Christmas carol in the Huron language. It was later translated into French, and then English.

If you lived with the Sioux Indians. Ann McGovern; Beatrice Darwin, illus. Scholastic, 1992. (ISBN 0-590-45162-6). Grades 3-6.

Describes the daily life of the Sioux Indians—their clothing, food, games, customs, etc.—before and after the coming of the European settlers. Includes a glossary.

Igloo. Charlotte Yue; David Yue. Houghton Mifflin, 1988. LC 88-6154, 128 p. (ISBN 0-395-44613-9; pbk 0-395-62986-1) Grades 3-7.

The igloo is a fascinating shelter used by Eskimos against harsh conditions. The Eskimo's way of life is thoroughly examined and illustrated.

In my mother's house. Ann Nolan Clark. Viking, 1991. 64 p. (ISBN 0-670-83917-5; pbk 0-14-054496-8) Grades 2-4.

Written in verse, this book provides useful information on the Pueblo history, life, and culture from a child's perspective.

In two worlds: a Yup'ik Eskimo family. Aylette Jenness; Alice Rivers. Houghton Mifflin, 1989. LC 88-13887, 84 p. (ISBN 0-39542797-5) Grades 6 up.

A portrait of an Eskimo family dealing with the modern world while maintaining as many of their traditions as possible. Describes how they face their contradictory world together, drawing strength from their heritage with skills learned in the modern society.

Indian festivals. Keith Brandt. Troll, 1985. LC 84-2644, 32 p. (ISBN plb 0-8167-0182-2; pbk 0-8167-0183-0) Grades 3-6.

Brief descriptions offer an overview of various Indian festivals. Samples of their various customs highlight tribes from across North America.

Indian way: learning to communicate with Mother Earth. Gary McLain; Michael Taylor, illus. John Muir, 1990. LC 90-36991, 114 p. (ISBN 0-945465-73-4) Grades 3 up.

Grandpa's stories are used to teach about living in harmony with people and nature. There are thirteen story/lessons, each with a full moon and fond reminiscences. Includes suggested activities to accompany each moon (month) and story.

Indian winter. Russell Freedman. Holiday House, 1992. LC 91-24205, 96 p. (ISBN 0-8234-0930-9) Grades 5 up.

German prince, Maximilian, and Swiss painter, Karl Bodmer, traveled along the wild Missouri river in 1833, recording eye witness accounts of all the Native Americans and trappers they encountered. Daily life, religious ceremonies, and fascinating individuals of the Mandan and the Hidatsa tribes are described and painted in detail as they befriended the European party in a particularly bitter winter. Some of the last years of the Native American way of life was captured.

Indians of the Arctic and Subarctic. Paula Younkin. Facts on File, 1992. LC 90-47675, 96 p. (ISBN 0-8160-2391-3) Grades 5-8.

Part of the *First Americans* series. Offers a detailed look at their rich cultural heritage. Describes how the unique lifestyle of tribes inhabiting the far northern regions is in relation to sharp environmental and historical changes. Illustrated with color photoessays.

Indians of the eastern woodlands. Rae Bains; Mark Hannon, illus. Troll, 1985. LC 84-2664, 32 p. (ISBN plb 0-8167-0118-0; pbk 08167-0119-9) Grades 3-6.

Discusses the natives in the eastern U.S. who met the first waves of European settlers. Their history, customs, religion, government, and homes are generally examined. A few specific tribal details are included on four general groups: the Algonquin, the Iroquois, the Creek confederacy, and the tribes around the Great Lakes.

Indians of the Pacific Northwest. Karen Liptak. Facts on File, 1990. LC 90-45547, 96 p. (ISBN 0-8160-2384-0) Grades 5-8.

Part of the *First Americans* series. Vivid photographs illustrate the environment and cultures of the related tribes of the Pacific Northwest: Bella Coola, Chinook, Coast Salish, Kwakuitt, Nootka, Tlingit, and Tsimshian. Describes how their rituals and daily customs are tied to their coastal homeland.

Indians of the Plains. Elaine Andrews. Facts on File, 1991. LC 90-45545, 96 p. (ISBN 0-8160-2387-5) Grades 5-8.

Part of the *First Americans* series. Vivid photographs illustrate the environment and culture of the nomadic tribes of the Great Plains. They shared similarities due to their co-dependence on the buffalo. Discusses the following tribes: Kiowa, Blackfoot, Plains Cree, Mandan, Hidatsa, Crow, Cheyenne, Sioux, Pawnee, Kansa, and Comanche.

Indians of the Plateau and Great Basin. Victoria Sherrow. Facts on File, 1991. LC 90-47150, 96 p. (ISBN 0-8160-2388-3) Grades 5-8.

Part of the *First Americans* series. These tribes lived in the north-central United States ranging from Colorado to Canada. Harsh living conditions led them to live as nomads in small groups. They did come together for ceremonies centering around hunting or food gathering. Nez Perce is a well-known tribe of the Plateau; Shoshoni is a tribe of the Great Basin. These were some of the last Native Americans to submit to U.S. pressure and live on reservations. Includes color photo inserts of art, costumes, and lands.

Indians of the Southeast. Richard Mancini. Facts on File, 1991. LC 90-46543, 96 p. (ISBN 0-8160-2390-5) Grades 5-8.

Part of the *First Americans* series. Indian tribes in the southeastern United States were able to thrive because of fertile land conditions. Coverage ranges from ancient Hopewell (mound builders) to Seminole, Cherokee, and Creek. These tribes lived in villages, hunted assorted game, and grew a variety of agricultural products. Each tribe had its own customs, but many similarities existed in their daily lives which are described. Includes brief histories after the Europeans arrived, biographies, and efforts to preserve customs.

Indians of the Southwest. Karen Liptak. Facts on File, 1990. LC 90-45546, 96 p. (ISBN 0-8160-2385-9) Grades 5-8.

Part of the *First Americans* series. Vivid photographs illustrate the environment and culture of the tribes in the desert Southwest: Apache, Havasupai, Maricopa, Mohave, Navajo, Pima, Pueblo, Tohono O'odham, Walapai, Yaqui, Yavapai, and Yuma.

Inuit. Bryan Alexander; Cherry Alexander. Raintree Steck Vaughn, 1993. LC 92-9894, 48 p. (ISBN 0-8114-2301-8) Grades 5-6.

Part of the *Threatened cultures* series. The Inuit's unique way of life has been shaped by their harsh Arctic environment. They rely on hunting to survive. As they encounter other cultures and undergo physical changes in their environment, their way of life is threatened. A religion that forbids the abuse of wildlife has been replaced by Western religions that do not teach conservation. Pollution makes the animals unfit to eat. Includes a glossary of English and Inuit words.

Iroquois. Barbara Graymont. Chelsea House, 1988. LC 88-3038, 128 p. (ISBN 1-55546-709-1; pbk 0-7910-0361-2) Grades 5 up.

Part of the *Indians of North America* series. The Iroquois lived in upstate New York, growing food and hunting fish and game. Hiawatha, an Iroquois, began the League of Indian Nations. Many of their numbers died in the French and Indian War and the American Revolutionary war when they sided with the British. The League held on until the early 19th century.

Iroquois. Barbara A. McCall; Luciano Lazzarino, illus. Rourke, 1989. LC 88-18188, 32 p. (ISBN plb 0-86625-378-5; pbk 0-68558582-4) Grades 5-6.

Part of the *Native American People* series. Iroquois were fierce Indians who lived in northern New York, fighting among themselves and other tribes. Deganawidah, an Iroquois, and Hiawatha, a Mohawk, traveled to all the tribes in the region and formed the Indian League of Nations. Discusses the role of women in their lives, their trade habits, their history of war with the settlers, and their current status as master bridge builders.

Iroquois. Craig A. Doherty; Katherine M. Doherty. Watts, 1989. LC 89-33055, 64 p. (ISBN 0-531-10747-7; pbk 0-531-15603-6) Grades 3-8.

Part of the *First book* series. Iroquois Indians, a group of tribes that settled in the northeast United States, formed the League of the Iroquois when confronted with aggressive settlers and other warring tribes. Their confederation is said to have influenced the formation of the U.S. government. Day-to-day life was building longhouses, establishing villages, and hunting and cultivating food. Iroquois reservations can be found today, mainly in New York and Canada.

Iroquois Indians. Victoria Sherrow. Chelsea House, 1993. LC 92-7357, 80 p. (ISBN 0-7910-1655-2) Grades 2-5.

Part of the *Junior library of American Indians* series. The Iroquois were made up of several tribes that became a powerful nation when united by Hiawatha into a confederacy. A folk story is told and customs are described here. The Iroquois are now leaders in the fight for Native American rights.

Ishi, last of his tribe. Theodora Kroeber. Bantam, 1973. LC 64-19401, 224 p. (ISBN pbk 0-553-24898-7) Grades 5-6.

Ishi was part of the small Yahi tribe, the only Native Americans left in the northern California region after gold prospectors came to the area. They barely survived, keeping themselves concealed and holding on to Yahi ways. After disease decimated their numbers, Ishi was the only one left. He gave up living in the Yahi tradition and went to the nearest mining town (San Francisco) where he was taken to the Museum of Anthropology. There, he tells of his way of life, religious code, stories, and songs before he died in 1916 .

Kwakiutl. Stanley Walens. Chelsea House, 1992. LC 90-2310, 112 p. (ISBN 1-55546-711-3) Grades 5 up.

Part of the *Indians of North America* series. The Kwakiutl is a broad name for the groups of Native Americans living along the coast of British Columbia and Vancouver. Their habit of catching and preserving fish in the summer sustained them during the winter, enabling them to have elaborate ceremonials in the cold months. In the late nineteenth century, settlers and missionaries tried to ban the Kwakiutl potlatch ritual, arresting those who tried to continue the practice. Now the ceremony has been revived, and elders are teaching it to younger tribal members.

Kiowa. John R. Wunder. Chelsea House, 1989. LC 88-30159, 112 p. (ISBN 1-55546-710-5) Grades 5 up.

Part of the *Indians of North America* series. As nomads on the Great Plains, the Kiowa controlled the Black Hills in South Dakota. Pressures from other tribes eventually made them move south. Kiowas had written calendars and other artistic works painted on hides. They joined with other tribes in the fight against the U.S. army. After the wars, they were placed on a reservation in Oklahoma. Continuing their painting tradition, Kiowas are still known for their artists.

Lightning inside you: and other Native American riddles. John Bierhorst; Louise Brierley, illus. Morrow, 1992. LC 91-21744, 112 p. (ISBN 0-688-09582-8) Grades 2 up.

Riddles from many Native American tribes are included under categories such as nature, animals, and things that grow.

Literatures of the American Indian. A. LaVonne Brown Ruoff. Chelsea House, 1991. LC 90-44893, 112 p. (ISBN 1-55546-688-5) Grades 5 up.

Part of the *Indians of North America* series. The Native American's literary tradition was mainly oral. The songs, poems, and dramas were taught, memorized, and passed on through the generations. The unique storytelling voice can evoke a special mood which makes it a force for authors recapturing the Indian history and heritage.

Mandans. Emilie U. Lepthien. Children's Press, 1989. LC 8922235, 48 p. (ISBN plb 0-516-01180-4; pbk 0-516-41180-2) Grades K-4.

Part of the *New True* series. The Mandans settled in North Dakota in earth lodges sturdy enough to last for years. They hunted buffalo on foot, using wolf skins as a disguise. Later they used horses. After contact with traders, smallpox spread through the tribe, their numbers were reduced. Three tribes joined together: the Mandans, the Hidatsa, and the Arikaras.

Menomunee. Patricia Ourada. Chelsea House, 1990. LC 89-37073, 112 p. (ISBN 1-55546-715-6) Grades 5 up.

Part of the *Indians of North America* series. The Menominee settled in Wisconsin. The French encouraged them to trap beaver and sell them, but in return they wanted them to fight on their side in the French and Indian War. When settlers came into the region, Chief Oshkosh wisely went straight to the President to petition for reservation land. The lumber industry has kept their tribe going and now they seek to revitalize their ancient customs.

Modoc. Odie B. Faulk; Laura Faulk. Chelsea House, 1988. LC 87-24247, 96 p. (ISBN 1-55546-716-4) Grades 5 up.

Part of the *Indians of North America* series. The Modoc lived at the foot of Mount Shasta in the California-Oregon region. They had a seasonal pattern of cultivating food, using temporary summer shelters, and moving to better quarters in the winter. The Gold Rush in the 1850s brought non-Indians to their region and life changed quickly for them. After they lost the Modoc war of 1872-73, they were taken to a reservation in Oklahoma. Some have been able to move back to Oregon.

Mohawk Indians. Janet Hubbard-Brown. Chelsea House, 1993. LC 9318247, 80 p. (ISBN 0-7910-1667-6; pbk 0-7910-1991-8) Grades 2-5.

Part of the *Junior library of American Indians* series. The Mohawk was one tribe in the Iroquois Confederacy and were called the keepers of the eastern door. Describes their folklore and culture before the coming of the Europeans. Mohawks became dependent on European goods and abandoned their conservationist traditions to keep up with trade demands. Missionaries spread disease and urged further abandonment of tradition. Currently, Mohawks are fighting for their lands and traditions.

Nanticoke. Frank W. Porter. Chelsea House, 1987. LC 86-31775, 96 p. (ISBN 1-55546-686-9) Grades 5 up.

Part of the *Indians of North America* series. The Nanticoke lived along the shore of Chesapeake Bay. Their hunting/gathering way of life became threatened as colonists homesteaded in the Maryland tidewater. Some tribes simply vanished. Today the Nanticoke live in Delaware, finding ways to revitalize their ancient traditions.

Narragansett. William S. Simmons. Chelsea House, 1989. LC 88-28323, 112 p. (ISBN 1-55546-718-0) Grades 5 up.

Part of the *Indians of North America* series. The Narragansetts lived in Rhode Island and gave Roger Williams the land for what is now the city of Providence. They built bark-covered houses and raised food. Their tribe was practically wiped out in a war against the colonists. Tribespeople are gradually gaining back their land.

Native Americans of the West: a sourcebook on the American West.
Carter Smith, editor. Millbrook, 1992. LC 91-31128, 96 p. (ISBN plb 1-56294-131-3) Grades 5-8.

Briefly describes events in the contact between Native Americans and European settlers. The history of their relationship is traced from the first European contact to the massacre at Wounded Knee. Includes illustrations and a timeline covering major events.

Navajo. Susan Stan; Luciano Lazzarino, illus. Rourke, 1989. LC 88-25002, 32 p. (ISBN 0-86625-380-7; 0-685-58580-8) Grades 5-8.

Part of the *Native American People* series. Briefly describes the Navajo history, daily lives, and current situation. They live in the desert Southwest.

Navajo code talkers. Nathan Aaseng. Walker, 1992. LC 92-11408, 114 p. (ISBN 0-8027-8182-9; plb 0-8027-8183-7) Grades 4 up.

During World War II the Navajos developed a code that the Japanese could not break. This book traces the development of code words based on the uniqueness of the Navajo language, the military success of the Navajos, and some of the battles they helped win.

Navajos. Peter Iverson. Chelsea House, 1990. LC 89-36621, 112 p. (ISBN 1-55546-719-9; pbk 0-7910-0390-6) Grades 5 up.

Part of the *Indians of North America* series. The Navajos settled in the desert areas of Arizona, New Mexico, and Utah. Their way of life involved raising sheep and livestock, growing food, weaving, silversmithing, and building round homes called hogans. The U.S. army forced them to relocate to New Mexico, later returning them to their homeland to live on a reservation. They bitterly opposed the livestock reduction forced on them, but served in large numbers during World War II. The tribe is currently growing and organizing.

Nez Perce. Kathi Howes; Luciano Lazzarino, illus. Rourke, 1990. LC 88-24997, 32 p. (ISBN 0-86625-379-3; 0-685-36389-9) Grades 5-8.

Part of the *Native American People* series. The Nez Perce lived in small villages in the Northeast. Describes their lifestyle, government, religion, success with horse breeding, relations with traders, and crafts. Nez Perce were especially interested in the ability of settlers to send written messages and wanted to learn that. The discovery of gold, coupled with the miners violation of the treaty signed between the Nez Perce and the government, increased tensions until war broke out.

Nez Perce. Alice Osinski. Children's Press, 1988. LC 88-11822, 48 p. (ISBN plb 0-516-01154-5; pbk 0-516-41154-3) Grades K-4.

A New True book. Nez Perce Indians lived in the Northwest, primarily Idaho. Their main food was salmon, and they hunted and gathered plants. They conducted an annual harvest at which several tribes enjoyed festivals. The Nez Perce were also excellent horse breeders and trainers. This was one reason they did well against U.S. soldiers. They still have reservations in Idaho and Washington.

North American Indian medicine people. Karen Liptak. Watts, 1990. LC 90-12337, 64 p. (ISBN 0-531-10868-6; pbk 0-531-15640-0) Grades 5-8.

Part of the *First book* series. This work provides an overview of the medicine person, his or her social status, and the variety of methods used to identify and train the person in the medicine society ways. Types of herbal cures are described as well as the role of traditional native medicine today.

North American Indian survival skills. Karen Liptak. Watts, 1990. LC 90-12354, 64 p. (ISBN 0-531-10870-8; pbk 0-531-15642-7) Grades 5-8.

Part of the *First book* series. Describes how Native Americans found food and water, made easily-built shelters, and generally lived off of the land. Includes a list of edible herbs used for medicines.

Ojibwa. Helen Hornbeck Tanner. Chelsea House, 1992. LC 90-2455, 120 p. (ISBN 1-55546-721-0; pbk 0-7910-0392-2) Grades 5 up.

Part of the *Indians of North America* series . The Ojibwa settled in the Great Lakes area, living off the great natural resources of the land. They successfully repelled an Iroquois invasion, traded with French fur traders, and negotiated with other Indian tribes for hunting agreements. After years of being dispersed on various reservations, they are now coming together to rekindle traditions such as the rice gathering ceremony and fishing rights.

Ojibwe. Susan Stan; Luciano Lazzarino, illus. Rourke, 1989. LC 88-24998, 32 p. (ISBN 0-86625-381-5; 0-685-58581-6) Grades 5-6.

Part of the *Native American People* series. The Ojibwe, also known as Chippewa, were a large tribe living in the Great Lakes area. Their villages consisted of groups of wigwams, and they cultivated food, such as wild rice, for their food source. Their gentle nature allowed abuses as European settlers came in and took control of their land. Currently, many are learning the traditional ways.

Oneida. Jill Duvall. Children's Press, 1991. LC 91-8893, 48 p. (ISBN 0-516-01125-1; pbk 0-516-41125-X) Grades K-4.

Part of the *New True* series. The Oneida was a strong part of the Iroquois confederacy in the northeastern U.S. They were known as fishermen, using fish as a trade commodity. Relations with incoming Europeans were devastating, so many moved to Wisconsin. Strong leaders kept them from scattering. They reorganized, using laws passed to help them, so that today there are viable Oneida communities in Wisconsin and New York. Traditional arts and crafts are still alive, and land is being bought back for the tribe.

Osage. Terry P. Wilson. Chelsea House, 1988. LC 87-34105, 111 p. (ISBN 1-55546-722-9) Grades 5 up.

Part of the *Indians of North Arrerica* series. The Osages lived in the fertile Mississippi valley. They became business partners with French fur traders in the 18th century. In the 19th century, they had to fight to stay in control of their lives. Oil was discovered on their property, that enabled them to have more freedom and mobility in mainstream society.

Paiute. Pamela A. Bunte; Robert J. Franklin. Chelsea House, 1990. LC 89-37072, 112 p. (ISBN 1-55546-723-7) Grades 5 up.

Part of the *Indians of North America* series. The Paiutes lived in Utah and parts of Nevada and Arizona. They were primarily farmers. Gold prospectors traveling through their land were the first settlers they saw. In a few years, they were working as laborers for the farmers who had taken their lands. A reservation was formed for them and they have been able to achieve some self-sufficiency.

Pawnee. Dennis B. Fradin. Children's Press, 1988. LC 88-11820, 48 p. (ISBN 0-516-01155-3; pbk 0-516-41155-1) Grades K-4.

Part of the *New True* series. The Pawnee settled in Nebraska and built villages of domed earth lodges. They held buffalo hunts twice a year when the entire tribe went along in their teepees. They were often in wars with the Cheyenne and the Sioux, usually using surprise attacks to steal horses. When the settlers came, they either bought Pawnee land or gave their enemies guns. The Pawnee finally settled on a reservation in Oklahoma.

Penobscot. Jill Duvall. Children's Press, 1993. LC 93-796, 48 p. (ISBN 0-516-01194-4; pbk 0-516-41194-2) Grades K-4.

Part of the *New True* series. The Penobscots lived in Maine, using permanent winter villages, travelling to summer camps to gather food, and hunting in the fall to survive the frozen winters. Incoming French, and later English colonists, changed their lives. The Penobscots continue to fight for laws giving them the right to their ancestral lands.

People of the breaking day. Marcia Sewall. Macmillan, 1990. LC 89-18194, 48 p. (ISBN 0-689031407-8) Grades 1 up.

A young member of the Wampanoags tells the story of his tribe. He describes how his group works, prays, plays, provides for the family, and survives the winter.

People of the sacred arrow: the Southern Cheyenne today. Stan Hoig. Dutton, 1992. LC 91-44428, 144 p. (ISBN 0-525-65088-1) Grades 6 up.

The Southern Cheyenne have lived in Oklahoma for several generations, not even having a reservation. Their pride and strength has endured in spite of pressure to conform to traditional U.S. society. This is the story of the modern Southern Cheyenne: a people influenced by the traditions and beliefs of their culture in conflict with the society that surrounds them.

People shall continue. Simon Ortiz. Children's Book Press, 1988. LC 88-18929, 24 p. (ISBN 0-89239-041-7) Grades 2-7.

Using the voice of a poetic storyteller, the history of the Native American people is traced from creation to current times. The message is simple: people must work together in harmony with nature in order for humanity to continue. Learn from the Native American, says the poet, and learn about life.

Peoples of the Arctic. Keven Osborn. Chelsea House, 1990. LC 90-1362, 112 p. (ISBN 0-685-18912-0) Grades 5 up.

Part of the *Peoples of North America* series. The people of the Arctic are different from other Native American peoples. They have been isolated until fairly recently by their environment, and their language is unlike any other. This book focuses on their culture: hunting, religion, history, and other traditions.

Pima-Maricopa. Henry F. Dobyns. Chelsea House, 1989. LC 88-30289, 112 p. (ISBN 1-55546-724-5) Grades 5 up.

Part of the *Indians of North America* series. The Pimas and the Maricopas were peaceful farming tribes living along the Gila River in Arizona. They formed a league to defend themselves against the Apache. When prospectors came through, they saved many of them with food, water, and protection from hostile Native Americans. They are still fighting to preserve their water rights along the Gila.

Plains Indians of North America. Robin May. Rourke, 1987. LC 87-4293, 48 p. (ISBN 0-86625-258-4; 0-685-67607-2) Grades 4-8.

Part of the *Original Peoples* series. The Plains Indians were nomads when the use of horses made their tribes flourish. The destruction of the buffalo herds made them vulnerable to the settlers and the armies who protected them. Today's tribes are fighting for an identity which will enable them to survive *and* preserve their culture.

Potawatomi. James Clifton. Chelsea House, 1987. LC 87-5170, 99 p. (ISBN 1-55546-725-3) Grades 5 up.

Part of the *Indians of North America* series. The Potawatomi lived in the Great Lakes region, and became an agriculture-based tribe. The Iroquois pushed them west, where they were caught up in the French and Indian War, and then the American Revolution. The Potawatomi were dependent on European goods, so they always tried to negotiate. They were scattered, but are currently working to revitalize tribal customs.

Powhatan tribes. Christian F. Feest. Chelsea House, 1990. LC 89-9975, 112 p. (ISBN 1-55546-726-1) Grades 5-7.

Part of the *Indians of North America* series. Powhatan was chief of several tribes who lived in Virginia, and were the first to encounter British explorers. The tribes suffered from contact with the Europeans. In addition to hostilities resulting in bloodshed and the capture of Indians for slaves, diseases took their toll. Virginia is now the site of the Powhatan reservation.

Powwow. George Ancona. Harcourt, 1993. LC 92-15912, 48 p. (ISBN 0-15-263268-9; pbk 0-15-263269-7) Grades 4-7.

Powwows are Native American celebrations in which several tribes gather to honor their traditions. This photoessay shows dancers performing, and explains the history of the dances and the costumes.

Pueblo. Charlotte Yue; David Yue. Houghton Mifflin, 1986. LC 85-27087, 117 p. (ISBN 0-395-38350-1; 0-395-54961-2) Grades 4-7.

Beautiful sculptured villages were built by the Pueblos long before explorers came to this continent. This book shows how those structures were built, the significance of some of the features, and other everyday items and their use.

Pueblo. Mary D'Apice; Katherine Ace, illus. Rourke, 1990. LC 89-77841, 32 p. (ISBN 0-86625-385-8; 0-685-36390-2) Grades 5-8.

Part of the *Native American People* series. This tribe was named for their unique sculpture-like villages that appear throughout the southwestern desert. Their history is a harsh one, first living under Spanish rule, and then American. They tried to revolt under Chief Pope's leadership, but failed. Their traditional daily lives are described.

Pueblo boy: growing up in two worlds. Marcia Keegan. Dutton, 1991. LC 90-45187, 48 p. (ISBN 0-525-65060-1) Grades 2-6.

Timmy Roybal lives at the San Ildefonso Pueblo. He plays the same way many other ten-year-old boys do, but is also learning the traditions of his people. He describes their crafts and parts of the ceremonial dances.

Pueblo storyteller. Diane Hoyt-Goldsmith; Lawrence Migdale, photographer. Holiday House, 1991. LC 90-46405, 32 p. (ISBN 08234-0864-7; pbk 0-8234-1080-3) Grades 3-7.

April describes Pueblo traditions and daily lifestyle. She shows her grandmother baking bread and making the Pueblo storyteller clay figure. Her grandfather makes a Cochiti drum. April learns the Buffalo dance and saves all the stories she hears so she can pass them on.

Quapaws. W. David Baird. Chelsea House, 1989. LC 89-25943, 112 p. (ISBN 1-55546-728-8) Grades 5 up.

Part of the *Indians of North America* series. The Quapaws controlled the region where the Arkansas River enters the Mississippi and were sought by many allies. They were forced to leave their homeland for relocation in Oklahoma. After many years of poverty, the Quapaws were able to lease their land, first to ranchers, and then to miners. The Quapaws are rediscovering their rituals and traditions.

River ran wild. Lynne Cherry. Gulliver/Harcourt, 1992. LC 91-12892, 32 p. (ISBN 0-15-200542-0) Grades K-4.

The Nashua river in Massachusetts once supported many Indians. As Europeans settled along its shore, towns grew and the Industrial Revolution progressed. The river was polluted to the point that it became ecologically dead. In the spirit of those early Indians who relied on the Nashua for survival, a girl named Marion organized a clean up. The river lives again.

Sacred harvest: Ojibway wild rice gathering. Gordon Regguinti; Dale Kakkak, photographer. Lerner, 1992. LC 92-1167, 48 p. (ISBN plb 0-8225-2650-6; pbk 0-8225-9620-2) Grades 3-7.

Part of the *We are still here* series. Eleven-year-old Glen Jackson learns traditional ways to harvest the wild rice around the Great Lakes and rivers of northern Minnesota.

Semunole. Barbara Brooks; Luciano Lazzarino, illus. Rourke, 1989. LC 88-6920, 32 p. (ISBN 0-86625-377-7; 0-685-58584-0) Grades 5-8.

Part of the *Native American people* series. This series uses an oversized format and numerous color drawings to describe the Seminole culture, as well as their current situation. Includes a time line.

Seminole. Merwyn S. Garbarino. Chelsea House, 1989. LC 88-5103, 112 p. (ISBN 1-55546-729-6) Grades 5 up.

Part of the *Indians of North America* series. The Seminole tribe was really a combination of Indian tribes from the Southeast who fled to Florida, that was settled by the Spanish. When the U.S. annexed Florida, a war between the Seminoles and the U.S. government broke out. Most Seminoles were forcibly relocated. Some remained and survived to form their own communities. Includes a short biography of the Seminole leader, Osceola.

Seminole. Martin Lee. Watts, 1991. LC 89-8900, 64 p. (ISBN pbk 0-531-15604-4) Grades 4-6.

Part of the *First book* series. The Seminole were made up of several tribes that escaped American rule to settle in Florida while under Spanish rule. When the U.S. annexed Florida, the Seminoles were forced to move to Oklahoma on the "Trail of tears." They had adapted their ways to the Florida marshlands, and their chief Osceola bitterly fought U.S. control. One Seminole reservation is now in Florida and the other is in Oklahoma.

Shoshoni. Alden R. Carter. Watts, 1989. LC 89-31102, 64 p. (ISBN 0-531-10753-1; pbk 0-531-15605-2) Grades 3 up.

Part of the *First book* series. Life for the Shoshones was hard. They were foragers who lived in the Great Basin in small family groups, finding food where they could. Settlers made life especially hard in the Great Basin because of scarce resources. Tribespeople still live on or near the Basin.

Shoshoni. Dennis B. Fradin. Children's Press, 1988. LC 88-11821, 48 p. (ISBN plb 0-516-01156-1; pbk 0-516-41156-X) Grades K-2.

A New True book. Shoshonis lived a nomadic life in the Northern states. Their day-to-day life and customs are described. Famous Shoshones include Sacagawea and Chief Washakie. Shoshones today live on reservations in Idaho and Wyoming.

Sioux. Barbara Brooks; Luciano Lazzarino, illus. Rourke, 1989. LC 88-25001, 32 p. (ISBN 0-86625-382-3; 0-685-5858-9) Grades 5-8.

Part of the *Native American People* series. The Sioux were a restless people that roamed the Great Plains, though nomadic, families stored food in special wigwams and would retrieve it when they needed it. Some of the most famous battles between Native Americans and the U.S. Army involved the Sioux.

Sioux. Elaine Landau. Watts, 1989. LC 89-5654, 64 p. (ISBN 0531-10754-X; pbk 0-531-15606-0) Grades 4-7.

Part of the *First book* series . This tribe's painted teepees could be easily taken down for quick travel. Their religion was tied into the hunt, and young men had to prove themselves in ceremonies such as the painful Sun Dance. Sioux suffered from the U.S. advancement because of dwindling land and vanishing buffalo. Several fierce Sioux chiefs tried to fight away the threat, including Red Cloud, Sitting Bull, and Crazy Horse.

Trail of Tears. R. Conrad Stein. Children's Press, 1993. LC 9233422, 32 p. (ISBN plb 0-516-06666-8; pbk 0-516-46666-6). Grades 3-6.

Describes the Federal Government's seizure of Cherokee land in Georgia and the forced migration of the Cherokee Nation along the "Trail of Tears" to Oklahoma.

Tainos: the people who welcomed Columbus. Francine Jacobs.Putnam, 1992. LC 91-3215, 112 p. (ISBN 0-399-22116-6) Grades 5-9.

October 12, 1492 marked a change for the gentle Taino Indians in the Bahamas. On that day, European men in huge ships landed on their shores. The Spaniards' lust for gold would dominate the rest of the natives' existence. Little by little, the Taino population would die out due to starvation, suicide in fear of Spanish capture, or direct Spanish violence.

Tarahumara. John G. Kennedy. Chelsea House, 1990. LC 89-71237, 112 p. (ISBN 1-55546-730-X) Grades 5 up.

Part of the *Indians of North America* series. The Tarahumara live in their ancestral home in a series of forbidden canyons in northern Mexico. They live on small farming compounds, or ranchos, consisting of a main house and grain storage facility, raising nearly everything they need. Tarahumara had brief contact with Spanish priests and miners, but they still live essentially as they have for centuries.

Teton Sioux: people of the plains. Evelyn Wolfson. Millbrook, 1992. LC 92-4633, 64 p. (ISBN 1-56294-077-5) Grades 4-6.

Part of the *Native Americans* series. A detailed account of everyday life includes food, traditions, games, yearly calendars, and other customs. There is also a tribal history and a view of contemporary life for reservation inhabitants. Includes a glossary of Sioux words and a detailed bibliography.

Thirteen moons on turtle's back: a Native American year of moons. Joseph Bruchac; Jonathan London; Thomas Locker, illus. Putnam, 1992. LC , 32 p. (ISBN 0-399-22141-7) Grades ps-8.

Each scale on the turtlels shell is thought to represent a month in many native American cultures. In this collection of poems, based on legend, each month is celebrated with observations of its unique nature until each season is honored.

Totem pole. Diane Hoyt-Goldsmith; Lawrence Migdale, photographer. Holiday House, 1990. LC 89-26720, 32 p. (ISBN 0-8234-0809-4; pbk 0-8234-1135-4) Grades 3-7.

In this photoessay, David is a Tsimshian Indian and his father carves totem poles in the way taught by his father and grandfather. David's father is working on a totem pole for the Klallam tribe and David helps. David and his father perform the Carver's dance during a pole-raising ceremony.

Totem pole Indians of the Northwest. Don E. Beyer. Watts, 1989. LC 89-31170, 64 p. (ISBN 0-531-10750-7; pbk 0-531-15607-9) Grades 4-7.

Part of the *First books* series. The Native Americans who carved totem poles inhabited the land of the Pacific Northwest. Their sea-based food source and fascinating crafts (totem poles, baskets, and masks) are discussed at length. Other day-to-day routines are described.

Trees stand shining: poetry of the North American Indians. Hettie Jones; Robert Andrew Parker, illus. Dial, 1993. LC 79-142452, 32 p. (ISBN 0-8037-9083-X; plb 0-8037-9084-8) Grades 4-7.

These poems were gathered from a variety of Indian tribes. The scarcity of language allows the imagination of the reader to recreate images, and experience the animals, weather, wind, rainbows, and feelings captured in each poem.

Turkeys, pilgrims and Indian corn: the story of the m anksgiving symbols. Edna Barth; Ursula Arndt, illus. Houghton Mifflin, 1979. LC 75-4703, 96 p. (ISBN 0-395-28846-0; pbk 0-89919-039-1) Grades 3-6.

Although the primary focus of the book concerns the Pilgrim origins of Thanksgiving traditions, there is a discussion of the roles Indians played and how their food and assistance enabled the settlers to survive.

Urban Indians. Donald L. Fixico. Chelsea House, 1991. LC 9049754, 104 p. (ISBN 1-55546-732-6) Grades 5 up.

Part of the *Indians of North America* series. Many Native American tribes organized city-based societies before the European settlers built their towns. In order to trade or find work, Native Americans often moved to U.S. cities. Some have prospered, but many have been victimized by poverty and discrimination. Describes Native Americans in urban areas who are coping and supporting others like them in order to thrive.

Village of blue stone. Stephen Trimble; Jennifer Dewey, illus; Deborah Reade, illus. Macmillan, 1990. LC 88-34194, 64 p. (ISBN 0-02-789501-7) Grades 3-7.

Recreates the everyday life and customs of the cliff dwellers, or the Anasazi. The story of two clans is followed through a year of preparing for annual celebrations, crop planting and harvesting, the birth of a baby, a wedding, and a funeral. In the end, a new Sun Watcher (or holy man) is chosen to carry the traditions forward. Includes details of the archeological expedition.

Voices from America's past. Raintree Steck-Vaughn, 1990. LC 90-44955, 128 p. (ISBN 0-8114-2770-6) Grades 5-9.

Different eras in American history are described by the people who lived them. Historical documents such as letters, speeches, diaries, and reminiscences set the tone for the eyewitness accounts of what happened. Native Americans are represented by Chief Red Cloud's speech to a New York City audience.

Wampanoag. Laurie Weinstein-Farson. Chelsea House, 1988. LC 88-2828, 96 p. (ISBN 1-55546-733-4; pbk 0-7910-0368-X) Grades 5 up.

Part of the *Indians of North America* series. The Wamponoag fished, hunted, and foraged in Massachusetts. They built wigwams of woven mats. Their tribes and others fought the English led by Metacomet, known as King Philip. They lived on reservations during the 18th and 19th centuries, laboring on farms, whaling boats, and running businesses.

Wounded Knee: the death of a dream. Laurie O'Neill. Millbrook, 1993. LC 92-12998, 64 p. (ISBN plb 1-56294-253-0; pbk 1-56294748-6) Grades 4-6.

Part of the *Spotlight on American history* series. Examines the events leading up to the battle of Wounded Knee. The massacre at Wounded Knee, South Dakota broke the last bit of resistance Native Americans could muster to face the U.S. troops. Big Foot, the last of their warrior-chiefs, was killed along with other warriors, women, and children.

Yakima. Helen H. Schuster. Chelsea House, 1990. LC 89-23903, 112 p. (ISBN 1-55546-735-0) Grades 5 up.

Part of the *Indians of North America* series. The Yakima were descendants of the first migration to the continent and settled in Washington State. In their seasonal routine, they hunted and gathered food in the warm months, staying in their villages in cold months. Their first contact with Americans was the Lewis and Clark expedition. Settlers rushed in and took over land even when the treaty promised areas to Native Americans. They still fight to control the fish, water, and timber resources on their reservation.

Yankton Sioux. Herbert T. Hoover. Chelsea House, 1988. LC 87-18221, 112 p. (ISBN 1-55546-736-9; pbk 0-7910-0369-8) Grades 5 up.

Part of the *Indians of North America* series. The Yankton Sioux lived in Minnesota and had a thriving trade business with settlers. When the U.S. proposed putting them on a reservation, their warriors could have joined the Sioux and other tribes who planned to fight. The Yankton Sioux hoped to keep their business going and peacefully went to the reservation.

Yuma. Robert L. Bee. Chelsea House, 1989. LC 88-39463, 112 p. (ISBN 1-55546-737-7) Grades 5 up.

Part of the *Indians of North America* series. The Yuma fought Apaches and others to control the Colorado River basin in Arizona. In the fertile floodplain, they farmed and hunted, building domes with attached ramadas for their livestock. They successfully repelled Spanish settlers, but could not turn away the U.S. army protecting gold prospectors. On their reservation in Arizona, they fight to keep their traditions alive and for economic opportunity.

✻ ASIAN AMERICANS ✻

Biography

Chingis Khan. Demi. Henry Holt, 1991. LC 90-28807, 64 p.
(ISBN 0-8050-1708-9) Grades 3-5.

The story of Genghis Khan, the Mongol leader who unified an empire, is told in a
legend-like style. Beautiful illustrations add to the myth.

Connie Chung: broadcast journalist. Mary Malone. Enslow, 1992.
LC 91-25396, 128 p. (ISBN 0-89490-332-2) Grades 6 up.

Part of the *Contemporary Women* series. Connie is a well-known television newscast-
er whose success is a result of persistence and hard work. Her parents escaped political persecution in China. She went to work for a TV station as a copy clerk and
was given a chance to be a reporter. Her dedication to reporting led to her break
during Watergate. Sparsely illustrated with photographs.

El Chino. Allen Say. Houghton Mifflin, 1990. LC 90-35026, 32 p.
(ISBN 0-395-52023-1) Grades 2-8.

Billy's father always told his children they could be anything they wanted in America, but he never expected Billy to be a bullfighter. Billy could not find a sport right
for him until he went to Spain. He loved the bullfights but was told that only
Spaniards could be bullfighters. By finding his own style, he was able to win over
the Spanish people and become what he dreamed of being. This picture book is
appropriate for a read-aloud.

Famous Asian Americans. Janet Nomura Morey; Wendy Dunn. Dutton,
1992. LC 91-17255, 192 p. (ISBN 0-525-65080-6) Grades 5 up.

Short articles describe the life and accomplishments of these Asian Americans:
Jose Aruego, author-illustrator; Michael Chang, tennis champion; Connie
Chung, broadcast journalist; Myung-Whun Chung, music director; Wendy Lee
Gramm, Chairman, Commodity Futures Trading Commission; Daniel K.

Inouye, U.S. Senator; Maxine Hong Kingston, writer and educator; Nainy Ngor, physician and actor; Dustin Nguyen, actor; Ellison S. Onizuka, astronaut; I.M. Pei, architect; Samuel C.C. Ting, physicist; and An Wang, inventor (Wang laboratories).

Genghis Khan. Judy Humphrey. Chelsea House, 1987. LC 87-5194, 112 p. (ISBN 0-87754-527-8) Grades 5 up.

Part of the *World leaders past and present* series. By using carefully planned strategies and strong-arm tactics, Genghis Khan established the largest empire in the world. He built it region by region, allowing trade to continue. His leadership provided unity for a huge land, but his violence and viciousness were unending. Illustrated with drawings and photographs.

Hirohito. Karen Severns. Chelsea House, 1988. LC 87-26828, 112 p. (ISBN 1-55546-837-3) Grade 5 up.

Part of the *World leaders past and present* series. Hirohito went from being the nominal ruler of a traditional, emperor-led government to being the leader of a government that had to cooperate with conquering Allied forces after World War II. He showed his flexibility when he helped build up the Japanese economy in the uncertain post-war economic climate. Illustrated with photographs.

Ho Chi Minh. Dana Ohlmeyer Lloyd. Chelsea House, 1987. LC 86-13707, 112 p. (ISBN 0-87754-571-5) Grades 5 up.

Part of the *World leaders past and present* series. Ho Chi Minh wanted to free his Vietnam from foreign rule, and he believed that a Communist system adapted to Vietnam was the best course. He fought and won independence from France, then sought to overthrow South Vietnam's government. He inspired tenacious fighting against the U.S.-backed South Vietnamese. After his death, peace talks led to the U.S. troop withdrawal, and the two countries united as a Socialist Republic. Illustrated with photographs.

The invisible thread: an autobiography. Yoshiko Uchida. Simon & Schuster, 1991. LC 91-12398, 136 p. (ISBN 0-671-74164-0) Grades 5 up.

Part of the *In my own words* series. Yoshiko Uchida relates her nightmarish experiences when thousands of Japanese-Americans were interned during World War II. She tried very hard to appear American in everything she did and said as a child. But as an adult, she discovered many positive things about her Japanese heritage, and that is the driving force behind her stories. Illustrated with photographs.

Kublai Khan. Kim Dramer. Chelsea House, 1990. LC 89-48915, 112 p. (ISBN 1-55546-812-8) Grades 5 up.

Part of the *World leaders past and present* series. Kublai Khan followed in the footsteps of his grandfather, Genghis Khan. He maintained the same bloody, ruthless tradition as he and his brothers struggled to keep the mighty empire together. Once there was a cautious peace, Kublai encouraged arts, sciences, and business ventures. Illustrated with drawing and photographs.

Last princess: the story of Princess Ka'iulani of Hawaii. Fay Stanley; Diane Stanley, illus. Macmillan, 1991. LC 89-71445, 40 p. (ISBN 0-02-786785-4) Grades 1-4.

In a picture book format, the life of Hawaii's last heir to the royal throne is simplistically told. She lived an aristocratic life, but Ka'iulani would never be queen. The monarchy was overthrown by American soldiers representing large companies. Then a native revolt to take the country back was squelched. Ka'iulani died in despair over the loss of her nation.

Lost garden. Laurence Yep. Simon & Schuster, 1991. LC 90-40647, 128 p. (ISBN 0-685-58838-6; s.p. 0-685-47021-0; pbk 0-685-58839-4; pbk 0-685-47022-9; plb 0-671-74159-4) Grades 5-7.

Part of the *In my own words* series. Feeling that he was an outsider, Laurence Yep spent a lifetime of writing, searching for an identity. He was not Chinese and was not American, yet both cultures helped to mold his identity. He grew up in San Francisco trying to avoid Chinatown. His writing came to embody the plight of immigrants who seek to understand themselves and their identities. Illustrated with photographs.

Mao Zedong. Hedda Garza. Chelsea House, 1988. LC 87-18331, 112 p. (ISBN 0-87754-564-2) Grades 5 up.

Part of the *World leaders past and present* series. The Chinese leader, Mao Zedong, was committed to instituting Communism in a country long-ruled by emperors. The Communists and Chiang Kai-shek briefly joined forces against foreign exploitation and China's own dissident warlords. Once power was restored to the central government, the two great leaders split and Mao Zedong organized the Long March, a 6000-mile march which consolidated popular support for the Communists. While many of his plans did not work, he made strides in modernizing China. Illustrated with photographs.

Michael Chang: tennis champion. Pamela Dell. Children's Press, 1992. LC 92-6384, 32 p. (ISBN 0-516-04185-1; pbk 0-516-44185-X) Grades 2-5.

Part of the *Picture story biography* series. Michael was the youngest man to win pro tennis' French Open. He became a professional tennis player at sixteen, which meant leaving school and finishing on his own. Michael does not live as "normal" young people do because he works relentlessly at his sport. Illustrated with photographs and text in an easy to read format.

Nien Cheng: courage in China. Leila Merrell Foster. Children's Press, 1992. LC 92-9333, 152 p. (ISBN 0-516-03279-8; pbk 0-516-43279-6) Grades 4 up.

Part of the *People of distinction* series. Nien Cheng was imprisoned during the Cultural Revolution in China. Her eyewitness accounts were the only reports of the political situation beside the official propaganda. She endured inhumane treatment because she suspected of having foreign ties. After her release, Nien was determined to have the truth told. Includes Nien's portrait.

Seija Ozawa, symphony conductor. Charnan Simon. Children's Press, 1992. LC 91-36741, 32 p. (ISBN 0-516-44182-7) Grades 2-5.

An easy to read book that is part of the *Picture story biography* series. Seija Ozawa's parents loved Western symphonic music. When it became clear that he was a talented musician, they sent him to Europe to study. Contending with cautious public opinion in both the West and the East, he became a world-respected conductor, and opened doors for Asians in the field of classical music. Illustrated with photographs.

Sun Yet-sen. Jeffrey Barlow. Chelsea House, 1987. LC 86-31732, 112 p. (ISBN 0-87754-441-7) Grades 5 up.

Part of the *World leaders past and present* series. Sun Yet-sen knew that the old dynasty system was no longer effective. As he became part of the growing revolutionary forces, he could see the destructiveness of the many factions trying to gain power. Sun Yat-sen worked to unify his nation, wanting both capitalist and socialist forces to operate in China's best interests. Illustrated with photographs.

West coast Chinese boy. Sing Lim. Tundra, 1991. LC 79-67110, 64 p. (ISBN 0-88776-270-0) Grades 5 up.

Sing Lim grew up in 1920s Canada when there was a great deal of anti-Chinese feeling. Sing reacted with humor to lighten his experiences. This biography is told with anecdotes and is illustrated with cartoon-like drawings and a section of color plates. His childhood was filled with wondrous and funny things, such as shaving babies' heads, Chinese opera, and a bear paw feast.

Young painter: the life and paintings of Wang Yani—China's extraordinary young artist. Zheng Zhensun; Alice Low. Scholastic, 1991.
LC 90-29319, 80 p. (ISBN 0-590-44906-0) Grades 4 up.

Beautiful color illustrations show a young Chinese girl's special art. She began painting when she was only two. When her father saw signs of her great talent, he created a world in which she could freely paint. They spent a lot of time studying nature, from which she drew inspiration. Wang is the youngest artist to have a one-person show at the Smithsonian Institute.

Folklore

Anno's Aesop: a book of fables by Aesop and Mr. Fox. Mitsumasa Anno. Orchard, 1989. LC 88-60087, 64 p. (ISBN 0-531-05774-7; plb 0-531-08374-8) Grades ps-2.

Little Freddy Fox discovers a book in the forest and begs his father to read to him. But the stories from Father Fox are slightly different from Aesop's although both are illustrated by the same Japanese illustrator.

Artist and the architect. Demi. Henry Holt, 1991. LC 90-40936, 32 p. (ISBN 0-8050-1580-9; plb 0-8050-1685-6) Grades ps-2.

Being jealous of another's talent will only lead to trouble. So it is with a Chinese artist who plots to get rid of the palace architect. He convinces the Emperor to burn the architect and send him to heaven. The architect devises a secret hiding place and escapes the flames. He returns, telling the Emperor that he has come back because they need the artist in heaven now. Apparently, the threat of burning changes the artist's mind, and he becomes much more accepting of other's talents.

Badger and the magic fan. Tony Johnston; Tomie dePaola, illus. Putnam, 1990. LC 89-4027, 32 p. (ISBN 0-399-21945-5) Grades ps-3.

A badger tricks some young Japanese goblins out of their magic fan, which makes any nose grow long and then short again. He makes a certain princess have a long nose. No matter who tries to shorten it, only the badger can do it. Of course he earns a fortune, but he gets the nose job in the end.

Bamboo hats and a rice cake. Ann Tompert; Demi, illus. Crown, 1993. LC 92-26849, 32 p. (ISBN 0-517-59272-X; plb 0-517-59273-8) Grades ps-3.

In Japan, the proper celebration of the New Year is a serious matter. When an old, poor couple have no rice cakes to eat on the New Year, the wife tells her husband to sell her wedding kimono. He cannot sell it but trades for a variety of things. At the end of the day, he still has no rice cakes but he does have hats which he leaves with the statues of Jizo, the protector of children. Jizo repays his homage with huge rice cakes which last through the New Year celebration and beyond.

Brocaded slipper and other Vietnamese tales. Lynette Dyer Vuong; Vo-Dinh Mai, illus. HarperCollins, 1992. LC 84-40746, 96 p. (ISBN plb 0-397-32508-8); LC 81-19139, 128 p. (ISBN pbk 0-06-440440-4) Grades 2-7.

Here are many familiar fairy story characters from their Vietnamese versions. Tam is mistreated by a cruel stepmother and discovered by a prince in the *Brocaded slipper*. Other tales include *Little finger of the watermelon patch, The fairy grotto,* and *Master frog and the lampstand princess.*

China's bravest girl: the legend of Hua Mu Lan. Charlie Chin; Tomie Arai, illus. Children's Book Press, 1993. LC 93-15255, 32 p. (ISBN 0-89239-120-0) Grades K up.

The story of Hua Mu Lan is told in verse as if sung by a court minstrel, or pipa player. The Emperor demands a male from every household to serve in the military, but Hua Mu Lan's father is elderly. She goes in her father's place, dressed as a boy, and distinguishes herself. Her final courageous act is revealing that she is a woman to her comrade in arms.

Chinese mirror. Mirra Ginsburg; Margot Zemach, illus. Harcourt, 1988. LC 86-22940, 26 p. (ISBN 0-15-200420-3; pbk 0-15-217508-3) Grades ps-3.

"There was a time long, long ago when no one in our village had ever seen a mirror." So begins a tale in which each character sees a different stranger in the mirror and thinks something really unusual is going on.

Dark way: stories from the spirit world. Virginia Hamilton; Lambert Davis, illus. Harcourt, 1990. LC 90-36251, 154 p. (ISBN 0-15-222340-1) Grades 3 up.

This collection of scary tales is tied to strange and supernatural phenomena and represents cultures from around the world. Stories that have an Asian background include: *The one-inch boy; Everlasting life;* and *Tanuki's magic teakettle.*

Dragon's pearl. Julie Lawson; Paul Morin, illus. Houghton Mifflin, 1993. LC 92-2574, 32 p. (ISBN 0-395-63623-X) Grades K-3.

Xiao Sheng loves to sing. When a drought dries everything up, he has little to sing about. Then he finds a magic pearl that fills the rice jar and the money box. When robbers come, Xiao Sheng swallows it. He is transformed into a dragon and creates so many clouds that the drought is ended. Illustrations are lush paintings.

Dragon's robe. Deborah Nourse Lattimore. HarperCollins, 1990. LC 89-34512, 32 p. (ISBN 0-06-023719-8; plb 0-06-023723-6; pbk 0-06-443321-8) Grades 1-5.

A young girl named Kwan Yin was orphaned, poor, and had only her loom to earn her way. She came upon a man who was ill and could not tend to the dragon shrines of China. The old man hired emissaries to tend to the shrines for him, but they stole the offerings for themselves. Kwan Yin offers her gift, a robe woven from the loom, to the dragon and is greatly rewarded.

Emperor and the kite. Jane Yolen; Ed Young, illus. Putnam, 1988. LC 87-18600, 32 p. (ISBN 0-399-21499-2; pbk 0-399-22512-0) Grades ps up.

The youngest daughter of the Emperor was so little that no one thought much of her. When evil men overthrew the government and imprisoned her father, the little girl sent food up to him in a basket attached to her kite. She built a very large kite with a strong cord, and her father climbed down from his tower prison. He reclaimed his throne, always keeping his little daughter by his side.

Empty pot. Demi. Holt, 1990. LC 89-39062, 32 p. (ISBN 0-8050-1217-6) Grades ps-2.

The Emperor wants to name a successor. He tells all the children in his kingdom that whoever grows the best flower from his seeds will be the next emperor. Ping has a dilemma—his plant did not grow in spite of his loving care. Since he did his best, he decides to take his empty pot to the Emperor. He finds out that the Emperor cooked all the seeds he gave out, so none of the plants could grow. Ping was the only one brave enough to be honest.

Enchanted tapestry. Robert San Souci; Laszlo Gal, illus. Dial, 1987. LC 85-29283, 32 p. (ISBN 0-8037-0304-X; plb 0-8037-0306-6; pbk 0-8037-0862-9) Grades ps-3.

A woman who is a skilled weaver begins an especially beautiful tapestry and becomes so involved in it that she neglects everything. Two of her sons become upset, but one encourages her to follow her heart. Once finished, the tapestry is stolen by fairies, and only one son has the character to retrieve it and save his mother.

Feathers and tails: animal fables from around the world.
David Kherdian; Nonny Hogrogian, illus. Putnam, 1992. LC 91-31270, 95 p.
(ISBN 0-399-21876-9) Grades 1-4.

Folk stories everywhere contain tales about the animals of their region. Includes the
Chinese story, *Monkey*. Some animals are friends to each other, others are enemies,
but they all teach us something.

Future of Yen-tzu. Winifred Morris; Frisco Henstra, illus. Macmillan, 1992.
LC 90-26989, 32 p. (ISBN 0-689-31501-5) Grades ps-3.

In this traditional Chinese tale, a farmer's son named Yen-tzu wants more than a
simple farming life. He sets out to find a better life. A bizarre turn of events convinces the Emperor that Yen-tzu is a not only wise but brave. The Emperor now
expects even greater things from him based on his past "performance." Yen-tzu
quickly collects his reward and leaves.

Greatest of all: a Japanese folktale. Eric A. Kimmel; Giora Carmi, illus.
Holiday House, 1991. LC 90-23658, 32 p. (ISBN 0-8234-0885-X) Grades ps-3.

There was a family of mice who lived with the Emperor. Father Mouse is proud of
living in a palace. When his daughter wants to marry a humble field mouse, Father
Mouse sets out to find the best possible candidate to marry his daughter. He, too,
chooses the field mouse after a lengthy search.

Hawaiian legends of tricksters and riddlers. Vivian Thompson; Patricia
Wozniak, illus. University of Hawaii Press, 1990. LC 90-44432, 112 p. (ISBN pbk
0-8248-1302-2) Grades 4-8.

Hawaiian myths of earth, sea, and sky. Vivian Thompson; Marilyn Kahale-
wai, illus. Reprint of 1966 ed. University of Hawaii Press, 1988. LC 88-1325, 88 p.
(ISBN pbk 0-8248-1171-2) Grades 3-8.

Each book includes a glossary and bibliography. Early legends of survival through
trickery against superior gods are supplanted by tales of riddlers who seek to
improve their social status. Hawaiian myths seek to explain creation, the seasons,
and natural wonders of the islands.

How the animals got their colors. Marcia Rosen; John Clementson, illus.
Harcourt, 1992. LC 91-30113, 48 p. (ISBN 0-15-236783-7) Grades 2-5.

This collection of stories are myths explaining how a variety of animals got their
colors—according to the people who live near them. The Chinese story in this
collection tells about the tiger.

How the ox star fell from heaven. Lily Toy Hong. Whitman, 1991.
LC 90-38978, 32 p. (ISBN 0-8075-3428-5) Grades K-3.

Oxen used to live with the Emperor of all the Heavens and had many luxuries. But down on earth, people worked terribly hard. They were always tired and never had enough to eat. The Emperor took pity on the peasants and sent the Ox Star to deliver a message. But the Ox got mixed up and delivered the wrong message. He was banished from heaven and from then on helped the peasants.

Jade stone: a Chinese Folktale. Caryn Yacowitz; Jui-Hong Chen, illus. Holiday House, 1992. LC 91-17934, 32 p. (ISBN 0-8234-0919-8) Grades ps-3.

Artists must be true to their art, even when the Emperor commands otherwise. Chan Lo realizes this when the Emperor asks him to carve a fearsome dragon from a jade stone. Chan Lo hears something in the stone which compels him to carve three carp. The Emperor is furious but the fish speak to him as nothing has before.

Journey of Meng. Doreen Rappaport; Yang Ming-Yi, illus. Dial, 1991.
LC 90-19257, 32 p. (ISBN 0-8037-0895-5; plb 0-8037-0896-3) Grades ps-3.

The emperor is a cruel dictator in this Chinese tale about the building of the Great Wall. Many men are captured and forced to work as slaves, including Meng's scholar-husband Wan. As winter approaches, she worries about his working in the cold. After a terrible journey to be by his side, she learns that he died. She faces the Emperor responsible for her husband's death and defies him in a startling way.

Judge Rabbit and the tree spirit: a folktale from Cambodia. Lina Mao Wall; Cathy Spagnoli; Nancy Hom, illus. Children's Book Press, 1991.
LC 90-26240, 32 p. (ISBN 0-89239-071-9) Grades K-5.

When a husband is drafted into the king's army, a tree spirit takes the form of the husband and lives with the wife. When the man returns, a judge must decide who is the real husband. Judge Rabbit tricks the tree spirit into a bottle and he never bothers the couple again.

Korean Cinderella. Shirley Climo; Ruth Heller, illus. HarperCollins, 1993.
LC 93-23268, 48 p. (ISBN 0-06-020432-X; plb 0-06-020433-8) Grades K-3.

This version of Cinderella takes place in ancient Korea. Pear Blossom is the mistreated stepchild. The stepmother becomes so demanding that Pear Blossom gets helps from some magical animals. With their help, a magistrate catches sight of her and wants to marry her.

Korean folk and fairy tales. Suzanne Crowder Han; Won-taek Chong, illus. Hollyn, 1992. LC 90-85304, 256 p. (ISBN 0-930878-03-5) Grades 5 up.

This is a collection for both enjoyment and the serious study of folktales. It provides a unique view of Korean culture and values. The stories are grouped into these categories: animals; ghosts, goblins, and demons; supernatural spouses; reward and punishment; cleverness and stupidity; and potpourri. Information about Korean history and religion is included.

Legend of the Milky Way. Jeanne M. Lee. Henry Holt, 1982. LC 81-6906, 32 p. (ISBN 0-8050-0271-0; pbk 0-8050-1361-X) Grades ps-2.

In Chinese legends, the Milky Way is called the Silver River. Two of the brightest stars are Vega and Altair. One of the stars was once a princess who fell in love with a mortal and married him. When the Queen Mother found out, she turned them into stars and separated them on each side of the Silver River. On the seventh day of the seventh month, they are allowed to visit each other.

Liang and the magic paintbrush. Demi. Henry Holt, 1980. LC 80-11351, 32 p. (ISBN 0-8050-0220-0; pbk 0-8050-0801-2) Grades ps-2.

In this Chinese folktale, Liang is given the gift of a magic paintbrush. The pictures he paints come to life. A greedy emperor orders him to paint pictures of fierce animals and winds of destruction. Liang paints so much wind that it destroys the royal family. Then Liang disappears. Some think he wanders the earth helping the poor.

Lon Po Po: a Red Riding Hood story from China. Ed Young. Putnam, 1989. LC 88-15222, 32 p. (ISBN 0-399-21619-7) Grades K-4.

Long ago in China a woman lived with her three daughters. One day she had to visit their grandmother and left the girls by themselves. A wolf knew the sisters were alone and came to them at night claiming to be their grandmother. The animal tricked them into letting him in. Shang, who was the oldest, realized they were in danger and tricked the wolf.

Magic boat. Demi. Henry Holt, 1989. LC 90-4425, 32 p. (ISBN 0-8050-1141-2) Grades ps-2.

When good and honest Chang rescues an old man, he receives a magic boat. It saves Chang, his mother, and some animal friends. They also save a wicked man named Ying, who tricks Chang out of his magic boat and uses it to win a fortune in the Emperor's court. With perseverance and the help of his friends, Chang wins back the boat.

Magic spring: a Korean folktale. Nami Rhee. Putnam, 1993. LC 92-7728, 32 p. (ISBN 0-399-22420-3) Grades ps-3.

An old couple longs for a child. They never complain about the injustices in their lives or the hateful remarks of their neighbor. One day, the man discovers the fountain of youth. He shows it to his wife who sips and also becomes young again. When the neighbor hears of it, he drinks so much that he becomes a baby—the child the couple always wanted.

Make-believe tales: a folk tale from Burma. Joanna Troughton. Bedrick, 1991. LC 90-48962, 32 p. (ISBN 0-87226-451-3) Grades K-3.

Part of the *Folktales of the world* series. A cat, a mouse, a parrot, and a monkey bet a rich traveler that he will not believe their stories. They tell him outlandish tales, which he accepts with a nod. Then he tells a story, claiming they are his slaves. If the animals do not believe his story, they lose the bet. If they accept his story, they are his slaves. They must consult the Princess Learned-in-law who gives them a fair settlement.

Mighty Mountain and the three strong women. Irene Hedlund; Judith Elkin. Volcano, 1990. LC 89-28052, 32 p. (ISBN 0-912078-86-3) Grades 2-5.

Mighty Mountain earned fame in his small village and journeys to the city for the grand wrestling match. He meets Kuniko, who decides to help him become the strongest wrestler. She takes him home to train with Grandma and Kuniko's mother. These very strong women prepare him for the match, which he easily wins.

Moles and the mireuk: a Korean folktale. Holly Kwon; Woodleigh Hubbard, illus. Houghton Mifflin, 1993. LC 92-437, 32 p. (ISBN 0-395-64347-3) Grades K-3.

A large stone statue called a mireuk stands beside a temple and a family of moles. The mole parents seek the most powerful husband for their dear daughter. They ask the king, the sun, the clouds, and the wind. Finally they ask the mireuk, who says that a mole hole could topple him. So the mole parents choose a nice mole boy for their son-in-law.

Momotaro the peach boy. Linda Shute. Lothrop, 1986. LC 85-9997, 32 p. (ISBN 0-688-05863-9; plb 0-688-05864-7) Grades ps-3.

A kindly old couple wish fervently for a child. They get their wish when a huge peach appears with a baby inside. According to ancient Japanese belief, a peach will bring happiness. The child grows into a hero who gains the help of animal friends to defeat a demon.

Mouse's marriage. Junko Morimoto. Puffin, 1988. LC 85-31458, 32 p. (ISBN pbk 0-14-050678-0) Grades ps-1.

A mother and father mouse want the mightiest husband for their daughter. They ask the sun, the clouds, the wind, and a wall to marry her. Then they see mice inhabiting the mighty wall and find their son-in-law at last—a mouse.

Nine-in-one Grr! Grr! Blia Xiong; Cathy Spagnoli; Nancy Hom, illus. Childrens Book Press, 1989. LC 89-9891, 32 p. (ISBN 0-89239-048-4; pbk 0-89239-110-3) Grades ps-5.

Based on a Hmong (Laotian) folktale. Tiger is so lonely that she travels to the great god Shao to find out how many cubs she will have. The god tells her she will have nine cubs a year for as long as she can remember his words. Tiger worries that she will forget, so she makes up a song, "Nine-in-one, grr! grr!" When Bird hears this, he worries about tigers eating all the animals. So he tricks Tiger into thinking her song was "One-in-nine grr! grr!" Illustrations are embroidered story cloths.

Painter and the wild swans. Claude Clement; Frederic Clement, illus. Dial, 1986. LC 86-2154, 32 p. (ISBN 0-8037-0268-X; pbk 0-8037-0840-8) Grades K-4.

Teiji is a Japanese painter who feels that his work is empty after he sees a beautiful flock of wild swans. He feels that he cannot paint until he sees them again. He goes to their Siberian nesting grounds and is overcome by the cold. Before dying, he is able to capture part of their beauty and becomes a swan himself.

Princess and the beggar: a Korean folktale. Anne Sibley O'Brien. Scholastic, 1993. LC 92-11988, 32 p. (ISBN 0-590-46092-7) Grades K-4.

The youngest daughter of the royal family is frequently moved to tears, especially by injustices done to a village beggar named Pabo Ondal. In exasperation, her father jokingly suggests that she marry him. Later when the father seriously urges her to marry, she rejects his choice saying that he named Pabo first. She is banished for her impudence, and Pabo reluctantly accepts her as his wife. She teaches him the "courtly" arts, and their family is eventually accepted by the king. They find true happiness in their own home.

Rainbow people. Laurence Yep; David Wiesner, illus. HarperCollins, 1989. LC 88-21203, 208 p. (ISBN 0-06-026760-7; plb 0-06-026761-5; pbk 0-06-440441-2) Grades 3-6.

These stories reflect the rich culture that Chinese-Americans brought with them to this country to keep their traditions alive. There are twenty tales grouped by these themes: tricksters, fools, virtues and vices, and love.

Samurai's daughter. Robert D. San Souci; Stephen T. Johnson, illus. Dial, 1992. LC 91-15585, 32 p. (ISBN 0-8037-1135-2; plb 0-8037-1136-0) Grades ps-3.

Tokoyo is a noble woman, but spends a lot of time with the local female divers who gather abalone and oysters. When her father is exiled to a distant island, Tokoyo resolves to make the perilous journey. Her bravery helps her find safe passage. Once there, her commitment to help the less fortunate leads her to fight the curse of the land. She breaks the curse and prosperity is restored.

Seven Chinese brothers. Margaret Mahy; Jean and Mou-sien Tseng, illus. Scholastic, 1990. LC 88-33668, 32 p. (ISBN 0-590-42055-0; pbk 0-590-42057-7) Grades ps-3.

When Ch'in Shih Huang was Emperor, seven identical brothers with amazing powers are the only ones who can best the tyrant. They escape execution by switching with one another, so that the one with the power best suited to the sentence could face it—until the youngest brother bursts into tears and washes everybody away.

Shell woman and the king. Laurence Yep; Yang Ming-Yi, illus. Dial, 1993. LC 92-9583, 32 p. (ISBN 0-8037-1394-0; plb 0-8037-1395-9) Grades K-3.

Uncle Wu fell in love with a woman he met at the seashore. When he proposed marriage, the woman called Shell confessed that she could turn into a shell. When an evil king found out about this, he imprisoned Uncle Wu and commanded Shell to perform three wonders. To save her husband's life, Shell does the tasks, but tricks the king in the process allowing Uncle Wu and herself to escape.

Shining princess and other Japanese legends. Eric Quayle; Michael Foreman, illus. Arcade, 1989. LC 89-84076, 112 p. (ISBN 1-55970-039-4) Grades K-5.

These Japanese tales have familiar moral lessons with their own distinctive flavor. Included is *Shining princess; White hare and the crocodiles; My lord bag o' rice; Tongue-cut sparrow; Adventures of a fisher lad; Old man who made dead tree bloom; Momotaro-peach warrior; Matsuyama mirror; Wooden bowl;* and *Ogre of Rashomon.*

Sim Chung and the river dragon: a folktale from Korea. Ellen Schecter; June Otani, illus. Bantam, 1993. LC 92-7652, 48 p. (ISBN 0-553-09117-4; pbk 0-553-37109-6) Grades ps-3.

Part of the *Bank Street ready-to-read* series. Sim Chung is devoted to her blind father. When a priest tells him that for 300 bags of rice his sight will be restored, Sim Chung is determined to get the rice. A rich man offers 300 bags of rice to any maiden willing to live with a dragon, and Sim Chung goes to the beast. The dragon is moved by her homesickness and allows her to return to her father and the rich man who becomes her husband.

Sir Whong and the golden pig. Oki Han; Stephanie Haboush Plunkett. Dial, 1993. LC 91-43389, 32 p. (ISBN 0-8037-1344-4; plb 0-8037-1345-2) Grades ps-3.

In this Korean folktale, Sir Whong is known for his kindness and generosity. He is surprised by a stranger's request for a loan of 1,000 nyung. The stranger says he has a poor, sick mother who needs expensive medicine. He offers their family's prized possession for security: a pig made of gold. Whong makes the loan, and then learns that the "golden" pig is a fake. Whong cleverly tricks the stranger into paying back the money.

Song of stars. Tom Birdseye; Ju-Hong Chen, illus. Holiday House, 1990. LC 89-20066, 32 p. (ISBN 0-8234-0790-X) Grades 4-8.

On the seventh night of the seventh month, the Chinese celebrate love in the Festival of the Milky Way. The myth involves the annual joining of the stars Vega and Altair, a princess and a herdsman who love each very much. They are banished to opposite sides of the Milky Way, meeting only once a year.

South and north, east and west: the Oxfam book of children's stories. Michael Rosen, editor. Candlewick, 1992. LC 91-58749, 96 p. (ISBN 1-56402-117-3; pbk 1-56402-396-6) Grades ps up.

Oxfam is a British organization whose fund raising operations send aid to poverty ridden areas of the world. Some of the stories in this collection were first heard by Oxfam staff working in the countries represented. Asian stories include: *The daughter* (Vietnam); *Strongest person in the world* (Korea); *Dog, cat and monkey* (Indonesia); *Sunkaissa, the golden-haired princess* (Nepal); *Ears, eyes, legs and arms* (China); and *Good morning* (Bangladesh).

Stonecutter. Patricia Newton. Putnam, 1990. LC 89-32920, 32 p. (ISBN 0-399-22187-5) Grades ps-3.

A stonecutter was contented and proud of his work until he delivered stone to the luxurious home of a rich man. Then he wanted more: the riches of the merchant, the luxury of the king, the power of the sun, the shade of the clouds, the majesty of the mountain, and, finally, the power of the stone cutter.

Stonecutter: a Japanese folktale. Gerald McDermott. Puffin, 1978. LC 74-26823, 32 p. (ISBN pbk 0-14-050289-0) Grades 1-3.

A stonecutter chips away at a mountain and is content, until he sees a prince and his procession go by. He wants the power of a prince, and the spirit of the mountain grants his wish. The man sees that the sun is more powerful, but while he is the sun, he burns everything up. He sees that the cloud is more powerful, but then he washes everything away. Only the mountain remains. He wants to be a mountain until a stonecutter begins chipping away at him.

Story of Yuriwaka. Erik and Masako Haugaard; Birgitta Saflund, illus. Roberts Rinehart, 1991. LC 91-65681, 42 p. (ISBN 1-879373-02-5) Grades 3-6.

When European travelers landed in Japan in the sixteenth century, they told the story of Odysseus. The story was so popular that it was transformed into a Japanese tale. Yuriwaka is the strongest man in Japan. The Emperor sends him to control the pirates plundering Kyushu. After defeating them, his companions become jealous and power hungry; leaving him on a deserted island. Yurikawa manages to return and proves who he is with his skill as an archer.

Tales from Gold Mountain. Paul Yee; Simon Ng, illus. Macmillan, 1990. LC 89-12643, 64 p. (ISBN 0-02-793621-X) Grades ps up.

This collection of stories is based on the experience of Chinese men and women who came to America to find a better life. The Chinese in these folktales face adversity on the frontier with their traditions. In spite of everything, they find their own place, often with an unexpected solution.

Tales from the bamboo grove. Yoko Kawashima Watkins; Jean and Mou-sien Tseng, illus. Macmillan, 1992. LC 91-38218, 64 p. (ISBN 0-02-792525-0) Grades 4-11.

These folktales were told to young Yoko when her Japanese family lived in Northern Korea. Her parents, homesick for their homeland, told the stories to hold on to their customs. They also teach lessons that were important to Yoko's parents. They include *Dragon princess, Tatsuko; Fox wife; Why is seawater salty; Yoyoi and the spirit tree; Monkey and crab;* and *The grandmother who became an island.*

Three strong women: a tall tale from Japan. Claus Stamm; Jean and Mou-sien Tseng, illus. Viking, 1990. LC 92-25331, 32 p. (ISBN 0-670-83323-1); Puffin, 1993. (ISBN pbk 0-14-054530-1) Grades 2-5.

Forever Mountain is on his way to the wrestling match in the capital when he decides to play a trick on a cute girl he meets. He tickles her, but she traps his hand and takes him home with her. Her mother and grandmother are so strong that he stays with them to train for the wrestling match he goes on to win.

Tiger and the Brahmin. Brian Gleeson; Kurt Vargo, illus. Rabbit Ears, 1992. LC 91-45715, 40 p. (ISBN 0-88708-233-5; book + cassette 0-88708-232-7) Grades K up.

Part of the *We all have tales* series. A Brahmin well-known for his kindness is moved by a caged tiger's piteous cries. When the Brahmin lets him out, the tiger prepares to eat him as he had planned even though he promised not to. The elephant, the pipal tree, and the water buffalo see no hope for the Brahmin. But the jackal tricks the tiger back into the cage just in time.

Tongues of jade. Laurence Yep; David Wiesner, illus. HarperCollins, 1991. LC 91-2119, 208 p. (ISBN 0-06-022470-3; plb 0-06-022471-1) Grades 3-7.

Chinese immigrants used stories to keep memories of their homeland alive. This collection is taken from stories about relationships, mysticism, magic, and ghosts. In ancient times, jade was thought to preserve a body. Tongues of jade are a storytellers gift to preserve Chinese culture through the oral tradition.

Two of everything. Lily Toy Hong. Whitman, 1993. LC 92-29880, 32 p. (ISBN 0-8075-8157-7) Grades K-3.

A Chinese couple, Mr. and Mrs. Haktak, are very poor. They get excited when Mr. Haktak finds a strange pot. Quite by accident, they discover that the pot will duplicate anything they put into it. They make a lot of money so they can buy food. In the midst of celebrating, Mrs. Haktak falls in the pot. Then there are two of her. Naturally, a dilemma ensues.

Tye May and the magic brush. Molly Garrett Bang. Morrow, 1992. LC 80-16488, 56 p. (ISBN pbk 0-688-11504-7) Grades 1 up.

Part of the *Greenwillow read-alone* series. Tye May is an orphan who lives on the street. She wants to paint but cannot buy a brush. One night she is visited by an old woman who gives her a magic brush. Everything Tye May paints comes to life. When the Emperor hears this, he commands her to paint. She paints an ocean, a boat, and a wind that carries him away.

Weaving of a dream: a Chinese folktale. Marilee Heyer. Viking, 1986. LC 85-20187, 32 p. (ISBN 0-670-80555-6); Puffin, 1989. (ISBN pbk 0-14-050528-8) Grades K-6.

Based on an ancient Chinese legend. A widow who has the gift of weaving beautiful brocades sees a painting of a palace. She yearns so much to live there that she decides to recreate it in one of her weavings. A fairy steals her brocade, and her sons must get it back.

Why ducks sleep on one leg. Sherry Garland; Jean and Mou-sien Tseng, illus. Scholastic, 1993. LC 92-9709, 32 p. (ISBN 0-590-45697-0) Grades ps 3.

This Vietnamese tale explains a curious duck habit. There were once three ducks who each only had one leg. They had trouble doing everything: swimming, hunting for food, even getting out of the way. They asked the village guardian spirit to plead their case to the Jade Emperor, but the spirit impatiently tells them that something created cannot be undone. He is getting rid of some solid gold legs from incense burners, which the ducks take. So the ducks tuck their precious gold legs under them when they sleep, and all other ducks copied them.

Why rat comes first: a story of the Chinese zodiac. Clara Yen; Hideo C. Yoshida, illus. Children's Book Press, 1991. LC 90-26536, 32 p. (ISBN 0-89239-072-7) Grades 3-4.

Here is a Chinese folktale that explains why Rat begins the 12 year Chinese calendar cycle. Includes the Zodiac cycle, characteristics of persons born in various years, and relations among the signs.

Yeh-shen: a Cinderella story from China. Ai-Ling Louis; Ed Young, illus. Putnam, 1990. LC 80-11745, 32 p. (ISBN 0-399-20900-X; pbk 0-399-21594-8) Grades ps-2.

Long ago in Southern China, there was a beautiful girl named Yeh-Shen. She lived with her stepmother, who treated her very badly. When she found that the girl had a secret pet fish, the stepmother killed it so that the girl would have nothing. The spirit of the fish magically transforms Yeh-Shen into a well-dressed woman so that she can attend a festival. Her stepsister recognizes her, and when Yeh-Shen flees, she loses one golden slipper. A prince finds it and becomes obsessed with the woman who wore such a tiny slipper.

Fiction for Young Readers
Picture books

Amoko and Efua Bear. Sonia Appiah; Carol Easmon, illus. Macmillan, 1989. LC 88-8343, 32 p. (ISBN 0-02-705591-4) Grades ps-1.

Everywhere Amoko goes, her favorite bear Efua goes, too. When Amoko gets a new drum, she is so excited that she loses Efua. Everyone is happy when they are reunited even though Efua is quite worn for her adventure.

Anna in charge. Yoriko Tsutsui; Akiko Hayashi, illus. Viking, 1989.
LC 89-987964, 32 p. (ISBN 0-670-81672-8; pbk 0-14-050733-7) Grades ps-1.

When Anna's mother runs an errand, younger sister Katy is asleep. Mother asks
Anna to watch over her. Soon after her mother leaves, Katy wakes up, and Anna
brings her outside to play. Suddenly, Anna looks around and does not see Katy anywhere. She looks everywhere and finally finds her at the park.

Anna's special present. Yoriko Tsutsui; Akiko Hayashi, illus. Viking, 1988.
LC 89-10844, 32 p. (ISBN 0-670-81671-X; pbk 0-14-054219-1) Grades ps-3.

Anna frequently gets upset when Katy borrows her favorite doll, Emily. When Katy
gets sick and has to go to the hospital, Anna worries. Her mother and Katy stay
away all night, but finally Anna can go to see Katy in the hospital. Anna decides to
give Katy something that is sure to make her happy—Emily.

Before the picnic. Yoriko Tsutsui; Akiko Hayashi, illus. Putnam, 1987.
LC 86-30382, 24 p. (ISBN 0-399-21458-5) Grades ps-2.

Sashi is excited about going on a picnic and wants to help. What she thinks is helping is not helping at all, but Mother is very understanding.

Bicycle man. Allen Say. Houghton Mifflin, 1982. LC 82-2980, 48 p.
(ISBN 0-685-05704-6; pbk 0-395-50652-2) Grades ps-3.

The festivities on Sports Day in a small Japanese mountain village are energetic and
exciting. Regular school activities are put aside, parents come to visit, and mishaps
occur. Then a hush falls over the school yard when the residents notice two American
servicemen watching. The large black man asks to borrow the principal's bicycle, and
then performs amazing tricks. The visit becomes a pleasant surprise for everyone.

Big Al. Andre Clements; Yoshi, illus. Picture Book Studio, 1991. LC 88-15129, 28
p. (ISBN pbk 0-88708-075-8); Scholastic, 1991. (ISBN pbk 0-590-44455-7); 2nd
edition. Picture Book Studio, 1991. (ISBN 0-88708-154-1) Grades ps-2.

Big Al is a large, scary-looking fish with huge teeth. He has no friends, but wants at least
one. He does everything he can to look friendly but cannot convince anyone. When all
the little fish are scooped up in a net, Big Al tears through the net, freeing them but tan-
gling himself. The fisherman takes one look at him and throws him back.

Boy of the three-year nap. Dianne Snyder; Allen Say, illus. Houghton Mifflin, 1988. LC 87-30674, 32 p. (ISBN 0-395-44090-4; pbk 0-395-66957-X)
Grades ps-3.

Taro is a lazy boy—all he does is eat and sleep. Any time his mother tries to get him to work, he refuses. He decides to marry a wealthy girl and tricks her father into making the arrangements. The girl realizes what has happened. She agrees to the marriage only if the father gives Taro a job. Everything ends well.

Bravo, Tanya. Patricia Lee Gauch; Satomi Ichikawa, illus. Putnam, 1992. LC 91-16005, 40 p. (ISBN 0-399-22145-X) Grades ps-3.

In this sequel to **Dance, Tanya,** the dancing protaganist joins a dance class, but despite her love of dance, she has trouble following the piano music and the counting of her ballet teacher. When Tanya dances the way she does in the park to the sound of the wind, she does much better in her class.

Butterfly hunt. Yoshi. Picture Book Studio, 1991. LC 90-7361, 32 p. (ISBN pbk 0-88708-137-1; mini book 0-88708-270-X) Grades K up.

A boy admires a butterfly so much that he decides to catch it and keep it forever. It is not easy to catch. It is always just out of reach, fluttering away from him. He finally catches it—then realizes that life in a jar is different than one in the wild. He learns that he will keep the memory of it long after he has released the butterfly.

Chin Yu Min and the ginger cat. Jennifer Armstrong; Mary GrandPre, illus. Crown, 1993. LC 92-8658, 32 p. (ISBN 0-517-58656-8; plb 0-517-58657-6) Grades ps-4.

Chin Yu Min is the proud and haughty wife of a rich man left to fend for herself when he dies. She is on the verge of starvation when a cat helps her catch fish. She asks the cat to stay, and together they increase her fortune by selling the fish they catch. Unfortunately, her haughty ways almost cause her to lose the cat's friendship. When she realizes her error, she invites everyone to her house celebrate her newfound sincerity.

Chinese Mother Goose Rhymes. Robert Wyndham; Ed Young, illus. Putnam, 1989. LC 68-28479, 48 p. (ISBN pbk 0-399-21718-5) Grades ps-1.

Many of these traditional Chinese children's poems will be familiar because variations appear in many cultures. These poems are used as lullabies, games, songs, counting lessons, and guessing games—for fun and teaching.

Cleversticks. Bernard Ashley; Derek Brazell, illus. Crown, 1992. LC 91-34669, 32 p. (ISBN 0-571-58878-1; plb 0-517-58879-X) Grades ps-2.

Ling Sung does not like school because he does everything wrong there. The other kids are good at something—tying shoes, printing their names, buttoning coats. Ling Sung finds something he can do that no one else can do. He can use chopsticks, and everyone wants to learn how.

Coco can't wait. Taro Gomi. Puffin, 1985. LC 83-17295, 32 p. (ISBN pbk 0-14-050522-9) Grades ps 1.

This is a travel story. Coco wants to see her grandmother, and grandmother wants to see Coco. Each is so anxious to see the other that they keep missing each other on the way.

Crow boy. Taro Yashima. Viking, 1955. LC 55-13626, 38 p. (ISBN 0-670-24931-9; pbk 0-14-050172-X) Grades K-3.

A quiet, somewhat backward boy is ridiculed during most of his school life until a special teacher recognizes that the boy may know more than the other children realize. He is able to imitate crows perfectly because he hears them all along the long walk from his mountain home. Once his talents are recognized, he is accepted.

Dance, Tanya. Patricia Lee Gauch; Satomi Ichikawa, illus. Putnam, 1989. LC 88-9935, 32 p. (ISBN 0-399-21521-2; mini book + doll 0-399-22795-4) Grades ps 3.

Little Tanya loved to dance. Not only did she practice with her older sister, Elise, she danced on her own. Tanya was too little to take ballet lessons, so she had to be content to watch her sister's class. Elise had a dance recital and everyone came to watch. Later Tanya surprised everyone with a recital of her own.

Dancer. Fred Burstein; Joan Auclair, illus. Macmillan, 1993. LC 91-41429, 40 p. (ISBN 0-02-715625-7) Grades ps-3.

A young girl and her father walk through their neighborhood to her dance class. Along the way, they identify everyday things in English, Spanish, and Japanese with phonetic spellings to try out pronunciations.

Dawn. Molly Bang. Morrow, 1983. LC 83-886, 32 p. (ISBN 0-688-02400-9; plb 0-688-02404-1; pbk 0-688-10989-6) Grades ps up.

Dawn's father tells the story of her mother, a mysterious woman who weaves sails as strong as steel, but makes her husband promise never to watch her when she weaves.

Dawn. Uri Shulevitz. Farrar, 1974. LC 74-9761, 32 p. (ISBN 0-374-31707-0; 0-374-41689-3; pbk 0-317-59335-8) Grades ps up.

Muted illustrations show a grandfather and his grandson enjoying nature on a camping trip. As the animals awaken, the two row out on the lake to appreciate the flow of colors that form the dawn.

Dragon kite of the autumn moon. Valerie Reddix; Jean and Mou-sien Tseng, illus. Lothrop, 1992. LC 91-1506, 32 p. (ISBN 0-688-11030-4; plb 0-688-11031-2) Grades ps-3.

Grandfather always celebrates Kite Day with Tad-Tin by making a special kite, sending it up in the air, and releasing it to carry away all their troubles. But this year Grandfather is sick. Tad-Tin worries about Grandfather and the Kite Day tradition, so Tad-Tin flies his treasured dragon kite and magic happens that very night.

Dragon parade: a Chinese New Year story. Steven A. Chin; Mou-Sien Tseng, illus. Raintree Steck Vaughn, 1992. LC 92-18079, 32 p. (ISBN plb 0-8114-7215-9) Grades 2-5.

Part of the *Stories of America* series. Norman-Ah Sing hopes to find riches in America when he leaves China. But, when he arrives in San Francisco in the 1850s, it looks like his poor village in China. He sets up his grocery store and celebrates the new year, glad to find a new life in America. He shares his special customs by cooking a meal for everyone in town.

Dwarf giant. Anita Lobel. Holiday House, 1991. LC 90-39214, 32 p. (ISBN 0-8234-0852-3) Grades ps-3.

The peaceful life of a Japanese prince and princess is shattered by a rude dwarf. During his visit, the prince is thrilled that something exciting is going on, but the wild dancing that ensues tears up their beautiful home. The princess tries to get them to stop, but they will not. She enlists the aid of their farmer neighbors, and together they send the dwarf away.

Emma's dragon hunt. Catherine Stock. Lothrop, Lee and Shepard, 1984. LC 83-25109, 32 p. (ISBN 0-688-02696-6; plb 0-688-02698-2) Grades K up.

Emma is excited about her grandfather from China coming to live with her. At first his dragon stories frighten her. Each day as they go out to look for dragons, Emma learns that they are not to be feared. Then her grandfather gives her her own dragon—a beautiful dragon kite.

Emperor and the nightingale. Meila So. Macmillan, 1992. LC 91-40693, 32 p. (ISBN 0-02-786045-0) Grades ps-2.

This retelling of the story by Hans Christian Andersen is a simpler version of the classic. The Emperor takes in a nightingale after a foreign traveler praises its song. He is enchanted by the beautiful singing and gives her a lovely gold cage. Then someone makes a mechanical bird for the Emperor. He grows to like the mechanical bird better and the real bird flies away. Eventually, the mechanical bird wears out, and the Emperor falls into poor health. The nightingale returns, and its song eases the Emperor's pain.

Families are different. Nina Pellegrini. Holiday House, 1991. LC 90-22876, 32 p. (ISBN 0-8234-0887-6) Grades ps-3.

When an adopted Korean girl is angry that she does not look like her mother and father, her mother explains that there are many different kinds of families. They have one thing in common: love. She looks around and sees all kinds of families that love each other.

Funny little woman. Arlene Mosel; Blair Lent, illus. Dutton, 1972. LC 75-179046, 40 p. (ISBN 0-525-30265-4; pbk 0-525-45036-X) Grades ps-4.

A funny little woman chases a rolling rice dumpling, and finds herself in a strange place inhabited by an oni (which is like a troll). He takes her to his house to cook for him and his friends. The oni gives her a magic paddle that turned one grain of rice into a pot full. She proceeds to escape (not easily) with the magic paddle, and becomes rich from making rice dumplings.

Girl who loved caterpillars. Jean Merrill; Floyd Cooper, illus. Putnam, 1992. LC 91-29054, 32 p. (ISBN 0-399-21871-8) Grades ps up.

Izumi is determined to do what she wants to do—she studies caterpillars with little regard for the conventional habits of well-bred girls. Despite pressures, Izumi continues to collect them with the help of some scruffy-looking boys. She attracts the attentions of a nobleman, who sends her presents and notes. But she is still only interested in caterpillars.

Girl who loved the wind. Jane Yolen; Ed Young, illus. HarperCollins, 1982. LC 71-171012, 32 p. (ISBN 0-690-33100-2; plb 0-690-33101-0; pbk 0-06-443088-X) Grades ps-3.

Princess Danina was very protected. She never knew any sadness. Then the wind spoke to her not only of sadness but joy, and the variety that is found in the world. Princess Danina began to feel trapped rather than protected, until the wind could take her away.

Grain of rice. Helena Clare Pittman. Hastings, 1986. LC 84-4670, 40 p. (ISBN 0-8038-2728-8; plb 0-8038-9289-6; pbk 0-553-15986-0) Grades K-4.

Pong Lo is a peasant who proposes marriage to the Emperor's daughter. The Princess is impressed by the courageous man and urges her father to give him a job.

Pong Lo performs all his tasks well and with good humor. When the princess becomes ill and Pong Lo saves her, he asks for a grain of rice, each to be doubled for a hundred days. By the end of that time, there is so much rice that he is a rich man, rich enough to marry the Emperor's daughter.

Grandfather's journey. Allan Say. Houghton Mifflin, 1993. LC 93-18836, 32 p. (ISBN 0-395-57035-2) Grades K-4.

Grandfather traveled from Japan to America, and loved its sprawling land. He returned to Japan to marry his sweetheart and brought her back to America. Eventually he returned to Japan, but always longed for America. Now that the grandson has traveled back and forth between the two countries, he understands his grandfather's homesickness and dilemma.

Hoang breaks the lucky teapot. Rosemary Breckler; Adrian Frankel, illus. Houghton Mifflin, 1992. LC 90-24265, 32 p. (ISBN 0-395-57031-X) Grades K-3.

Hoang feels terrible when he broke the gia truyen, the teapot his grandmother gave him the night they left Vietnam. It is part of their tradition of providing a place for good fortune to dwell and keeping away the evil spirits. Hoang worries about the evil spirits locating them in their new American home. So he finds a way to make good fortune want to live in another teapot.

How my parents learned to eat. Ina R. Friedman; Allen Say, illus. Houghton Mifflin, 1987. LC 84-18553, 32 p. (ISBN 0-395-35379-3; pbk 0-395-44235-4) Grades K-3.

While an American sailor dates a Japanese girl, each one is worried about learning to eat with the others utensils. So, in secret, the sailor learns how to eat with chopsticks, and the Japanese girl learns how to eat with a fork and knife. Then they surprise each other.

I hate English. Ellen Levine; Steve Bjorkman, illus. Scholastic, 1989. LC 88-38265, 32 p. (ISBN 0-590-42305-3) Grades K-2.

Mei Mei hates English. It is so hard and so different from Chinese. Mei Mei dreams of everyone else speaking Chinese so she can have fun with them. Then one day she meets a new teacher. By the time Mei Mei learns to speak English, she has made a new friend.

Kenji and the magic geese. Ryerson Johnson; Jean and Mou-sien Tseng, illus. Simon & Schuster, 1992. LC 91-3644, 32 p. (ISBN 0-671-75974-4) Grades ps-3.

Kenji loves the painting of the five geese that has always hung in his parents' house. After a flood, his parents need to sell it to survive the winter. When the art collector comes, one of the geese mysteriously disappears and he refuses to buy the painting. After the goose reappears, the art collector complains about some strange marks. When two baby geese appear, Kenji's family charges people to see their unique seven-goose painting.

Letter to the king. Leong Va. HarperCollins, 1991. LC 91-9469, 32 p. (ISBN 0-06-020079-0; plb 0-06-020070-7) Grades K-3.

In a society that values only sons, a daughter is able to change the mind of a king and save her father. When he is wrongly sent to prison, Ti Ying decides to deliver a letter to the king pleading for her father's life. No one has ever done that before, and the king is so moved that the father is set free.

Lost lake. Allen Say. Houghton Mifflin, 1989. LC 89-11026, 32 p. (ISBN 0-395-50933-5; pbk 0-395-63036-3) Grades K-3.

A young boy and his father are having a difficult time getting to know one another. They never talk much. One day, Dad surprises the boy by taking him on a camping trip. He takes him to a site that Dad and his father used, but lots of people are already camping there. So Dad and the boy backpack until they find their own secret camping place.

Lotus seed. Sherry Garland; Tatsuro Kuichi, illus. Harcourt, 1993. LC 92-2913, 32 p. (ISBN 0-15-249465-0) Grades 4-7.

Grandmother has seen much change in Vietnam. After the fall of the Emperor, she sneaked into his garden and saved a lotus seed to remember him. She keeps it safe through all the changes in her life—marriage, children, war, and destruction—and takes it to America. Then one of her grandchildren takes the seed and plants it in the pond. She is distraught—until the plant flowers. She gathers the seeds, gives one to each grandchild, and keeps one for herself.

Magical hands. Marjorie Baker; Yoshi, illus. Picture Book Studio, 1991. LC 89-31373, 32 p. (ISBN pbk 0-88708-103-7) Grades ps up.

Four friends always meet for lunch, and one day three teasingly wish for their chores to be done as a birthday surprise. William listens, and as each birthday comes around, he gets up early and makes each birthday wish come true. When his birthday comes, he is surprised to find that his chores have been "magically" done.

Min-Yo and the moon dragon. Elizabeth Hillman; John Wallner, illus. Harcourt, 1992. LC 89-36462, 32 p. (ISBN 0-15-254230-2) Grades ps-3.

All over China, people worry when the moon gets bigger and bigger. It looks as if the moon is coming to the earth. They decide to ask the moon dragon if they are in any danger. The staircase to the moon dragon is very fragile, so Min Yo is elected to go because she is the lightest one in China. What she finds will change the night sky forever.

Moon dragon. Moira Miller; Ian Deuchar, illus. Dial, 1989. LC 88-3902, 32 p. (ISBN 0-8037-0566-2) Grades ps-3.

Ling Po is the most boastful young man in all of China. He claims that he can do things bigger and better than everyone else. So when he insists that he can build a kite that will take him to the moon, word traveled through the countryside, and eventually to the Emperor. He wants to see this great event. Now Ling Po will have to prove his bold claim.

Moon lady. Amy Tan; Gretchen Schields, illus. Macmillan, 1992. LC 91-22321, 32 p. (ISBN 0-02-788830-4) Grades 1 up.

One rainy afternoon, Nai-Nai entertains her granddaughters with a tale of her childhood in China. As a child, Nai-Nai misbehaved a lot, but she tries to be good when she hears that she might be granted a secret wish by the Moon Lady. In a fit of anger, she wishes to be away from her family. Once separated from her loved ones, she realizes her mistake.

"More, more, more," said the baby. Vera B. Williams. Greenwillow, 1990. LC 89-2023, 32 p. (ISBN 0-688-09173-3; plb 0-688-09174-1) Grades ps up.

Three sets of babies and grownups play games that show how much they love one another. One set is an Asian family, depicted at bedtime.

Mountains of Tibet. Mordicai Gerstein. HarperCollins, 1987. LC 85-45684, 32 p. (ISBN 0-06-022144-5; plb 0-06-022149-6; pbk 0-06-443211-4) Grades 2 up.

There once was a boy who loved to fly his kite and dreamed of seeing the world. He grows up, becomes busy with work and family, and never sees the world. Then he dies and is offered unlimited choices to live as anything he wishes. With each choice, he is closer and closer to what he used to be—only this time he chooses to be a girl who loves to fly kites.

My friends. Taro Gomi. Chronicle, 1990. LC 89-23940, 40 p. (ISBN 0-87701-688-7) Grades ps-1.

First published in Japan, this book describes how a little girl learned her basic skills from animals: "I learned to climb from my friend the monkey;" "I learned to smell the flowers from my friend the butterfly;" "I learned to kick from my friend the gorilla." Good for creative dramatics.

Nightingale. Michael Bedard; Regolo Ricci, illus. Houghton Mifflin, 1992. LC 91-4195, 32 p. (ISBN 0-395-60735-3) Grades K-4.

This retelling of Hans Christian Andersen's tale features lush illustrations and folk-tale-oriented text. The Emperor loves a nightingale's song so much that he cages the bird until a mechanical nightingale wins his affection. He does not care that the nightingale escaped the gold cage until the mechanical bird breaks and the Emperor becomes ill. Then the nightingale returns out of love for the Emperor, and sings so beautifully that he is saved from dying.

Nora's duck. Satomi Ichikawa. Putnam, 1991. LC 90-20160, 40 p. (ISBN 0-399-21805-X) Grades ps-3.

Nora goes for a walk and finds an injured baby duck. She takes it to Doctor John, a kind "people" doctor. Nora discovers that he has taken in many animals who need help. She has confidence that Doctor John can help her duck, too.

Nora's roses. Satomi Ichikawa. Putnam, 1993. LC 91-46145, 32 p. (ISBN 0-399-21968-4) Grades ps up.

Nora is sick in bed. Her nose is red and she is bored. Outside her window, a rose bush is full of flowers. One by one, they are picked and taken to the exciting places where she would like to go. Then Nora has a special dream in which the flowers take her to some of the places they have gone.

One, two, three. Yoshi. Picture Book Studio, 1991. LC 90-23918, 28 p. (ISBN 0-88708-159-2) Grades K up.

One impetuous inchworm falls off his tree branch and sets into motion a cumulative story that excites the entire meadow. This is also a counting story involving two famished fish, three tired turtles, four grumpy grasshoppers, and so on.

Our home is the sea. Riki Levinson; Dennis Luzak, illus. Dutton, 1988. LC 87-36419, 32 p. (ISBN 0-525-44406-8; pbk 0-14-054552-2) Grades K-3.

For a Chinese boy whose school year has just ended, the streets of Hong Kong seem especially busy with people and vehicles. He runs all the way to his family's house boat, so that he can spend summer at his father's and grandfather's profession: fishing.

Over the deep blue sea. Daisaku Ikeda; Brian Wildsmith, illus. Knopf, 1993. LC 92-22557, 32 p. (ISBN 0-679-84184-9; plb 0-679-94184-3) Grades ps-3.

Akiko and her brother move to an island and make friends with Pablo. He shows them how to paddle a canoe on the water and how the sea turtles hatch. They explore the wreck of a war ship. Pablo's grandmother talks about the war, making Pablo angry and resentful toward Akiko and her brother. The children must learn that the war between the adults is over, and they can be friends.

Paper boats. Rabindranath Tagore; Grayce Bochak, illus. Boyd Mill, 1992. LC 91-72987, 32 p. (ISBN 1-878093-12-6) Grades ps-3.

A young boy launches some boats he made, decorated with flowers, from his garden. As they drift down the river, he imagines the distance they will travel and hopes that by reaching out he will make new friends. Tagore is a Nobel prize winner.

Paper crane. Molly Bang. Greenwillow, 1985. LC 84-13546, 32 p. (ISBN 0-688-04108-6; plb 0-688-04109-4; pbk 0-688-07333-6) Grades K up.

Because of an act of kindness to a mysterious old man, a restaurant owner is given an origami paper crane, which magically comes alive and brings him good fortune.

Princess and the moon. Daisaku Ikeda; Brian Wildsmith, illus.; Geraldine McCaughrean, trans. Knopf, 1992. LC 92-148, 32 p. (ISBN 0-679-83620-9; plb 0-679-93620-3) Grades ps-3.

When the moon sends Moon Rabbit to fetch Sophie, the girl is worried. Is it because she is bad-tempered or naughty at school? Moon Rabbit is able to show Sophie that she can be polite and happy if she feels better about herself. In the world of the moon, everyone is a prince or princess. In the sunlight, their crowns do not show. Sophie goes home with a new understanding of people and herself.

Red thread. Ed Young. Putnam, 1993. LC 91-45442, 32 p. (ISBN 0-399-21969-2) Grades ps-3.

Wei Gu is the orphan of well-born parents but a marriage was never been arranged for him in the Chinese tradition. He hopes to convince a matchmaker to find him a good wife. An old man from the spirit world insists that Wei Gu is fated to marry someone who is only three now, and poor. Wei Gu is angry and pays a servant to kill the child. Many years later he finally marries a woman who bears an unusual scar. They realize that the thread of fate, the red thread of the old man, has always bound them.

River dream. Allen Say. Houghton Mifflin, 1988. LC 88-14740, 32 p. (ISBN 0-395-48294-1; pbk 0-395-65749-0) Grades K-3.

While Mark is sick in bed, his uncle sends him a get-well present: the fly box they used on their last fishing trip. The memories of that event cause him to fantasize of a fishing trip where he and his uncle catch some very large trout.

Roses sing on new snow: a delicious tale. Paul Yee; Harvey Chan, illus. Macmillan, 1992. LC 91-755, 32 p. (ISBN 0-02-793622-8) Grades ps-3.

Maylin cooks in her father's restaurant. Her cooking is the most famous in Chinatown, but her father never gives her the credit, saying his two sons do all the cooking. The governor of South China decides to visit and asks all the restaurants to send their best dish. Maylin sends hers and her father gets into a lot of trouble trying to conceal the cook. Finally Maylin gets the credit she deserves.

Screen of frogs: an old tale. Sheila Hamanaka. Orchard, 1993. LC 92-24172, 32 p. (ISBN 0-531-05464-0; plb 0-531-08614-3) Grades ps-2.

A spoiled child grows to be a spoiled man, and lives on his inheritance without doing any real work. Finally, he runs out of money and land to sell. He decides to sell his big house and the lake beside it. While taking a nap, a frog appears in a dream and begs him not to sell because someone else would ruin it. The man is shaken. He keeps the land, sells his fancy things, and works at farming. Miraculously, frogs appear on a blank screen in his home and keep him company all his days.

Silent Lotus. Jeanne M. Lee. Farrar, 1991. LC 90-55141, 32 p. (ISBN 0-374-36911-9) Grades K-3.

Lotus is a beautiful, but sad child because she was born deaf and could not learn to speak. She longs to play with other children, but they rebuff her. So she plays with the birds in her own private world. When her parents take her to the palace to see the temple dancers, Lotus at last finds a place for herself and a way to communicate with others.

Snow country prince. Daisaku Ikeda; Brian Wildsmith, illus.; Geraldine McCaughrean, trans. Knopf, 1991. LC 90-24908, 32 p. (ISBN 0-679-81965-7; plb 0-679-91965-1) Grades ps-3.

Mariko and her brother Kazuo dread winter because their Papa leaves them to find work. They fill their time by feeding the swans who winter near their village. One night the Snow Country Prince appears, praises them, and urges them to never give up. These words bolster them when their mother must leave to nurse their father when he becomes injured.

Story about Ping. Marjorie Flack; Kurt Wiese, illus. Viking, 1933. LC 33-29356, 32 p. (ISBN 0-670-67223-8); Puffin, 1977. (ISBN 0-14-050241-6); Puffin, 1989. (ISBN 0-14-095038-9; pbk + cassette 0-14-095117-2) Grades ps-1.

Every day Ping and his family leave their boat on the Yangtze river to eat along the shore. And every day they return to the boat. Ping hates to be the last one in line because that duck always got a spanking on the back. One day when he was late, he hid and the boat left. Many adventures happen to Ping before he is reunited with his family, but he still gets a spanking on the back.

Terrible Eek. Patricia Compton; Sheila Hamanaka. Simon & Schuster, 1991. LC 91-6421, 40 p. (ISBN 0-671-73737-6; pbk 0-671-87169-2) Grades ps-6.

A small family sits around their cozy fire one stormy night, and the son asks his father if he is afraid. His father replied yes, he was afraid of thieves, wolves, and leaks. A thief and a wolf overhear this and wonders what a leak is. They each startle the other. Through a series of misadventures, each is glad to escape the terrible leak with an Eek of their own.

Through moon and stars and night skies. Ann Turner; James Graham Hale, illus. HarperCollins, 1990. LC 87-35044, 32 p. (ISBN 0-06-026189-7; plb 0-06-026190-0; pbk 0-06-443308-0) Grades ps-3.

A boy from a far-off nation was adopted in this country and tells how he felt during the process. He received pictures, then traveled a long way, and he was afraid of everything, in spite of his wonderful new parents. The boy gradually got used to all the new things. He felt safe enough to sleep in his new bed because he had some-one to watch over him.

Tikki Tikki Tembo. Arlene Mosel; Blair Lent, illus. Henry Holt, 1968. LC 68-11839, 32 p. (ISBN 0-8050-0662-1; pbk 0-8050-1166-8; big book 0-8050-2345-3) Grades ps-2.

Because Tikki Tikki Tembo (there's more to his name than that) has such a long name, his brother Chang has a difficult time getting help when Tikki Tikki Tembo falls in the well. That is how the Chinese came to give all their children short names.

Tree of cranes. Allen Say. Houghton Mifflin, 1991. LC 91-14107, 32 p. (ISBN 0-395-52024-X) Grades K-3.

The spirit of Christmas carries across cultural lines as a young Japanese boy learns about Christmas from his American-born mother. She decorates a pine tree with paper cranes and candles, and then makes a special request of him. In return he gets a Samurai kite, and knows that his family loves him.

Tucking Mommy in. Morag Loh; Donna Rawlins, illus. Orchard, 1988. LC 87-16740, 40 p. (ISBN 0-531-05740-2; plb 0-531-08340-3; pbk 0-531-07025-5) Grades ps-2.

Mommy is so tired that she is going to bed as soon as she tucks her two girls in. She falls asleep as the girls are telling their goodnight story. The girls take Mommy to her room, help her prepare for bed, and tuck her in. The girls are ready for bed when Daddy gets home, and he is proud of them for taking good care of Mommy.

Umbrella. Taro Yashima. Viking, 1958. LC 58-14714, 32 p. (ISBN 0-670-73858-1; pbk 0-14-050240-8) Grades ps-1.

Momo is so excited about her new umbrella and rain boots that she wants to use them in the sunshine and wind. She must wait until it rains. When she is finally able to use her lovely umbrella and boots, she walks down the street like a grownup holding her umbrella rather than Mommy or Daddy's hand.

What comes in spring? Barbara Savadge Horton; Ed Young, illus. Knopf, 1992. LC 89-39695, 40 p. (ISBN 0-679-80268-1; plb 0-679-90268-6) Grades ps-1.

As a mother tells her daughter about the seasons, the family's history is told. In the spring, Mama first saw Daddy. In the summer, they enjoyed the outdoors. Mama and Daddy were married in another summer. With autumn, Mama remembers how her daughter began to grow inside her. When the daughter is born, Mama and Daddy were happy—and they still are.

Who's hiding here? Yoshi. Picture Book Studios, 1991. LC 86-25455, 36 p. (ISBN 0-88708-041-3; pbk 0-88708-277-7) Grades ps up.

This beautiful book features cut-outs which hint at the animal on the next page and demonstrates how animals protect themselves with their natural camouflage. They are able to blend in with their surroundings just as those animals hiding on the page underneath. The format and rhyming text create a game-like feeling.

Will you come back for me? Ann Tompert; Robin Kramer, illus. Whitman, 1988. LC 87-37258, 32 p. (ISBN 0-8075-9112-2; pbk 0-8075-9113-0) Grades ps-K.

Four-year-old Suki worries when her mother talks about taking her to a daycare center. She is especially worried when they visit one. Then Suki's mother gives her a special heart to remind her that mother is always thinking of her and will return.

Fiction for Older Readers

Angel child, dragon child. Michele Maria Surat; Vo-Dinh Mai, illus. Raintree Steck Vaughn, 1983. LC 83-8606, 32 p. (ISBN 0-940742-12-8); Scholastic, 1989. (ISBN pbk 0-590-42271-5) Grades 3-6.

Ut misses her mother who stayed behind in Vietnam so that all of her children could come to America. Ut is afraid to go to school and hates being teased by Raymond. When they get into trouble for fighting, the principal makes Raymond write while Ut tells her story. Once everyone learns that Ut's mother was left in Vietnam, they have a Vietnamese fair to raise the money to help reunite the family.

Best bad thing. Yoshiko Uchida. Macmillan, 1983. LC 83-2833, 132 p. (ISBN 0-689-50290-7; pbk 0-689-71745-8) Grades 4-7.

Sequel to **A jar of dreams.** Rinko cannot believe that her mother wants her to stay with a friend of the family, Mrs. Hata, to help on their farm. Rinko thinks that her stay will be fun, but then bad things begin to happen. One of the Hata boys has an accident and a welfare worker comes to take them away from the farm. Rinko has to think of something to help.

Boat to nowhere. Maureen Crane Wartski; Dick Teicher, illus. NAL/Dutton, 1989. LC 79-28139, 160 p. (ISBN pbk 0-451-162854-4) Grades 4-6.

Mai, Loc, and their grandfather lead a quiet life in their small Vietnamese village. Then, Kien shows up—he is rude and disrespectful, but calm when everyone else panics. When Communists overrun the village, Kien leads Mai, Loc, and grandfather to escape in a fishing boat. Storms blow them off course, sharks swim around their boat, and pirates threaten them. They wonder if they are destined to die at sea.

Born in the year of courage. Emily Crofford. Carolrhoda, 1991. LC 91-10883, 184 p. (ISBN 0-87614-679-5) Grades 4-6.

Manjiro is a bright, curious fifteen-year-old. When he goes fishing with some friends, they become stranded on a barren island. In the mid 1800s, Japan allowed no contact with the outside world. When an American whaler picks up the fishermen, their lives are changed completely. Manjiro and the captain become friends, and he takes the boy to America. Manjiro dreams of returning to Japan one day and creating trade between the countries. Based on a true story.

Boy and the samurai. Erik Christian Haugaard. Houghton Mifflin, 1991. LC 90-47535, 256 p. (ISBN 0-395-56398-4) Grades 5-9.

Saru is an orphan and on his own very early in his life in a large, feudal Japanese town. Despite his adventures, Saru is glad to find a home with a priest where he has companionship and education. A samurai comes to them for help, telling of his wife being held hostage. Saru and the priest help the samurai free his wife, and they all escape over the mountains.

China year. Emily Cheney Neville. HarperCollins, 1991. LC 90-39899, 256 p. (ISBN 0-06-024383-X; plb 0-06-024384-8) Grades 5-9.

Henrietta spends one year living in China. When she returns to New York, nothing is the same because her outlook on life has changed. Her extraordinary friendship with Minyuan impacts her life. He showed her what life is really like in China behind the shrines and historical places, and why the students led the revolution in Tienanmen square.

Dragon cauldron. Laurence Yep. HarperCollins, 1991. LC 90-39584, 320 p. (ISBN 0-06-026753-4; plb 0-06-026754-2) Grades 7 up.

Sequel to **Dragon of the lost sea** and **Dragon steel**. After Shimmer, Thorn, and Cizet capture the magic cauldron, they need help in using it to restore the dragon's lost sea. In their search for help, the party encounters terrible evil which must be battled and vanquished if the world is to survive. Although the recommended grade is higher, elementary readers who began the series will want to finish.

Dragon of the lost sea. Laurence Yep. HarperCollins, 1988. LC 81-48644, 224 p. (ISBN 0-06-026746-1; pbk 0-06-440227-4) Grades 6 up.

First in a series of fantasy novels based on a Chinese folktale. Shimmer, a dragon, has wandered among humans (in disguise, of course) for many years, but she never lets herself get attached to one until she meets Thorn. He insists on helping her find the witch who stole the Dragon's sea. Together they become a team and overcome the witch.

Dragon steel. Laurence Yep. HarperCollins, 1985. LC 84-48338, 288 p. (ISBN plb 0-06-026751-8; pbk 0-06-440486-2) Grades 6 up.

Sequel to **The Dragon of the lost sea**. Shimmer and Thorn capture the witch (Cizet) who stole the dragon's sea. In order to restore the sea, they need more magic from the High King, who enslaved the other dragons. Underwater, the party must find ways to free the dragons, steal a magic cauldron, and deal with another pesky human.

Dragon war. Laurence Yep. HarperCollins, 1992. LC 91-28921, 320 p. (ISBN 0-06-020302-1; plb 0-06-020303-X; pbk 0-06-440525-7) Grades 6 up.

The conclusion to the saga which began in **Dragon of the Lost Sea**. The dragon princess Shimmer and her companions find themselves drawn into war as the only way to defeat the Boneless King, rescue Thorn, and restore the dragon's underwater home.

Dragonwings. Laurence Yep. HarperCollins, 1975. LC 74-2625, 256 p. (ISBN 0-06-026738-0; pbk 0-06-440085-9); Bantam, 1990. (ISBN large type 1-55736-168-1) Grades 6 up.

In 1908, Moon Shadow, only eight years old, travels across the great ocean to join a father he has never met. He soon comes to love his father and shares his dream of building a machine that could fly. Based on a true historical incident.

Echoes of the white giraffe. Sook Nyul Choi. Houghton Mifflin, 1993. LC 92-17476, 144 p. (ISBN 0-395-64721-5) Grades 5 up.

Sequel to **Year of impossible goodbyes.** Sookan is a refugee far from her home, unsure of her father and brother's safety and trying to find some stability in a new school. Her friendship with a young man helps her face the changes that war has brought, but her feelings bring confusion and rebellion from the strict Korean society. Finally, she finds the determination to make her life as meaningful as possible.

Farewell to Manzanar. Jeanne Wakatsuki Houston. Bantam, 1983. LC 75-11267, 160 p. (ISBN pbk 0-553-27258-6) Grade 7 up.

Based on the true story of a Japanese-American family's internment during World War II. It is written by a woman who, as a child, was interned at Manzanar with her family. Despite its high-grade recommendation, the child's perspective of these troubling times has value for students studying this period.

Fu-Dog. Rumer Godden; Valerie Littlewood, illus. Viking, 1990. LC 89-50858, 64 p. (ISBN 0-670-82300-7) Grades ps-2.

Li-la gets a lovely birthday present from her great uncle—a Fu-dog. He tells Li-la about China and Chinese customs, and convinces her to go to Chinatown to visit her great uncle. She and her brother travel into London and find great uncle's restaurant (with help from Fu-Dog). When Fu-Dog is lost in a New Year celebration, Li-la is sad until great uncle gives her a live dog to take Fu-Dog's place.

Goodbye, Vietnam. Gloria Whelan. Knopf, 1992. LC 91-3660, 112 p. (ISBN 0-679-82263-1; plb 0-679-92263-6); Random House, 1993. (ISBN pbk 0-679-82376-x) Grades 3-7.

Mai and her family are only hours ahead of the police who plan to put them in prison because her grandmother practices the healing arts. Their journey is a dangerous one—overland to the coast, and then on a boat with mechanical difficulties. But they make friends and celebrate Tet—the New Year. Once in Hong Kong, they anxiously wait for word about when they can go to America.

Great grandfather's house. Rumer Godden; Valerie Littlewood, illus. Green-willow, 1993. LC 91-48030, 80 p. (ISBN 0-688-11319-2) Grades 1 up.

Seven-year-old Keiko is a spoiled city girl who does not want to go to her grandparents house. Her cousin Yoji loves everything at the house in the country. Keiko feels out of place, causing careless accidents and feeling like she never does anything right. But with some patient coaxing, Keiko learns to do things cautiously, even saving Yoji's life when he has an accident in the snow.

Hello, my name is Scrambled eggs. Jamie Gilson; John Wallner, illus. Lothrop, 1985. LC 84-10075, 160 p. (ISBN 0-688-04095-0); Pocket, 1991. (ISBN pbk 0-671-74104-7) Grades 4-6.

When Harvey's family decides to take in Vietnamese refugees, everyone is nervous about their ability to make the immigrants feel at home. Harvey likes Tuan immediately and makes it his job to Americanize Tuan. But things are happening too fast for Tuan, and Harvey learns how much American is too much.

Homesick: my own story. Jean Fritz; Margot Tomes, illus. Putnam, 1982. LC 82-7646, 160 p. (ISBN 0-399-20933-6); Dell,1984. (ISBN pbk 0-440-43683-4; large type 1-55736-070-7) Grades 3-7.

Ten-year-old Jean looked at her father's globe and knew that her home in America was far from where she was living—China. Even though Jean is homesick, she has many adventures and relates them with humor, energy, and her own unique perspective.

House of sixty fathers. Meindert Dejong; Maurice Sendak, illus. Harper-Collins, 1956. LC 56-8148, 192 p. (ISBN plb 0-06-021481-3; pbk 0-06-440200-2) Grades 5-8.

Tien Pao and his family narrowly escape advancing Japanese troops in World War II China, only to become separated. With only his pig, Tien Pao must make his way across a war-torn land to find his family. With courage and persistence, Tien Pao evades soldiers, joins the Chinese resistance, and fights loneliness in a barrack filled with U.S. airmen.

If it hadn't been for Yoon Jun. Marie Lee. Houghton Mifflin, 1993. LC 92-9557, 144 p. (ISBN 0-395-62941-1) Grades 3-7.

Alice was adopted when she was a baby, so she does not remember anything about Korea or her birth family. She has always wanted to fit in with her American family—she is popular in school and is a cheerleader. When Yoon Jun and his mother move from Korea, she is uncomfortable with comparisons and her father's suggestions that she learn something about that country. Alice is forced to learn about Korea when she and Yoon Jun are paired up for International Day.

In the eye of war. Margaret and Raymond Chang. Macmillan, 1990. LC 89-38027, 208 p. (ISBN 0-689-50503-5) Grades 4-7.

Ten-year-old Shao-shao and his family hope to live peacefully despite the war that rages around them. Their home, Shanghai, is occupied by the Japanese: his father works with the Chinese underground even though one of the neighbors works with the Japanese. The conflict that most worries Shao-shao is the one he has with his father. When Father has to leave because of his underground connection, Shao-shao worries that he might never see him again.

Jar of dreams. Yoshiko Uchida. Macmillan, 1981. LC 81-3480, 144 p. (ISBN 0-689-50210-9); Reprint, LC 92-18803, 144 p. (ISBN pbk 0-689-71672-9) Grades 5-7.

Being Japanese in California during the Depression is hard. Even though Rinko's family has dreams, they are not sure if any of them can come true. When Aunt Waka arrives from Japan, her liveliness cheer and strengthen them. By loving and supporting each other, Rinko's family find ways to overcome adversity and realize all of their dreams.

Journey home. Yoshiko Uchida; Charles Robinson, illus. Macmillan, 1978. LC 78-8792, 144 p. (ISBN 0-689-50126-9); Reprint. LC 91-40149, 144 p. (ISBN pbk 0-689-71641-9) Grades 4-6.

Sequel to **Journey to Topaz.** Yuki's father is paroled out of the Utah internment camp but nothing is back to the way it was. Even when they return to their hometown in California, the Japanese-Americans cannot find jobs or housing. The family is able to find ways to survive with the help of their friends until everyone is together and hopeful for the future.

Journey to Topaz. Yoshiko Uchida; Donald Carrick, illus. Creative Arts, 1985. LC 84-70422, 160 p. (ISBN 0-916870-85-5) Grades 4-12.

Yuki and her family become suspects after Pearl Harbor is attacked by the Japanese. Their comfortable life comes apart when they are told that they must live in an internment camp. They packed their belongings, sold what they could, and found a new home for Yuki's dog, Pepper. They endure the prison camp, make friends, and start school when they are moved to a camp in Utah. Because their family is together, they are able to face everything with courage and dignity.

Little brother. Allan Baillie. Viking, 1992. LC 91-28797, 144 p.
(ISBN 0-670-84381-4; pbk 0-14-036862-0) Grades 3-7.

Vithy and his older brother Mang try to escape the Khmer Rouge soldiers who take them into the forest presumably to kill them, but the brothers get separated. Vithy hears a shot, so he struggles on alone, hoping that Mang escaped and will meet him at the Thailand border. Vithy finds a home in a refugee camp assisting a doctor. He cannot find his brother anywhere and must finally accept his death, Vithy leaves for Australia with the doctor.

Little weaver of Thai-Yen village. Tran-Khanh-Tuyet; Nany Hom, illus.; Christopher Jenkins, trans. Children's Book Press, 1987. LC 86-17186, 24 p.
(ISBN 0-89239-030-1) Grades 2-9.

Part of the *Fifth World Tales* series. Hien lives a simple life on a Vietnamese farm with her mother and grandmother. She loves to weave and sing. But war changes that—her mother and grandmother are killed, and she is badly injured. Hein is taken to America and after her operation, a family took care of her. Even though the family is kind, she always misses her family and country as she learns American customs.

Mieko and the fifth treasure. Eleanor Coerr; Cecil H. Uyehara, illus. Putnam, 1993. LC 92-14660, 64 p. (ISBN 0-399-22434-3) Grades 2-5.

Mieko's art teacher says she has the fifth treasure—beauty in the heart. But, Mieko fears she has lost it because of her anger and bitterness after the atomic bomb was dropped. Her new friend Yoshi helps Mieko to heal and to achieve a beauty in her heart again.

Moon bridge. Marcia Savin. Scholastic, 1992. LC 92-2601, 231 p.
(ISBN 0-590-45873-6) Grades 5 up.

Ruthie and Shirl have been friends for a long time. However, Ruthie is surprised by the malicious way that Shirl treats Mitzi, a Japanese-American girl. Ruthie finds herself siding with Mitzi and they form a friendship despite the prejudice that flares because of World War II and the bombing of Pearl Harbor. When Mitzi and her family are taken to internment camps, Ruthie fears that she will never see Mitzi again.

My name is San Ho. Jayne Pettit. Scholastic, 1992. LC 91-9230, 192 p.
(ISBN 0-590-44172-8) Grades 6 up.

San Ho tries to live a normal life in his small Vietnamese village. Yet he has never known peace. When his father was killed, his mother leaves him with relatives in

Saigon to go to school. He finds that his mother has left the country and married an American serviceman. His story of escape and adjustment to life in America without war is a new perspective to the story of freedom.

Of nightingales that weep. Katherine Paterson; Haru Wells, illus. Harper-Collins, 1974. LC 74-8294, 170 p. (ISBN 0-690-00485-0; pbk 0-06-440282-7) Grades 5 up.

Wars between clans in feudal Japan affect every aspect of Takiko's life. When her samuri father is killed, she and her mother find a new home in the country. As Takiko grows, she is offered a place in the Japanese court. While serving the young emperor, Takiko falls in love with a warrior in the opposing clan.

Onion tears. Diana Kidd; Lucy Montgomery, illus. Orchard, 1991. LC 90-43011, 72 p. (ISBN 0-531-05870-0; plb 0-531-08470-1); Morrow, 1993. LC 92-46601, 80 p. (ISBN pbk 0-688-11862-3) Grades 4-6.

Nam Huong does not speak, smile or talk. She misses her parents and wonders if they are alive in Vietnam. Her life with her "Auntie" in the restaurant is so different from the farm where she grew up. Nam Huong befriends her teacher who lives nearby and has become sick. When she worries that she will lose her only friend, it is then in a flood of tears that she is able to tell about the horrors of her escape and how she lost her grandfather in the sea.

Pearl Harbor is burning: a story of World War II. Kathleen V. Kudlinski; Ronald Himler, illus. Viking, 1991. LC 93-15135, 64 p. (ISBN 0-670-83475-0; pbk 0-14-034509-4) Grades 4-6.

Part of the *Once Upon America* series. Frank has just moved to Hawaii and makes friends with Kenji, the only boy in school who does not make fun of him. Early one morning when they are playing in the backyard, the two boys witness the Japanese attack on Pearl Harbor.

Star-fisher. Laurence Yep. Morrow, 1991. LC 90-23785, 150 p. (ISBN 0-688-09365-5; pbk 0-14-036003-4) Grades 4-6.

Joan Lee and her family leave their home in Ohio and move to a small West Virginia town. Papa is sure that they will find prosperity in a town with no Chinese laundry. The odds are overwhelming, but they battle the isolation, the lack of acceptance, and communication problems to find a place for themselves.

Vatsana's lucky new year. Sara Gogol. Lerner, 1992. LC 92-11243, 156 p. (ISBN 0-8225-0734-X) Grades 5-6.

Vatsana is always impatient when her mother insists she learn about her Laotian culture. She feels more American than Laotian. Then her aunt and cousin arrive from Laos, and Vatsana must reevaluate her background. She faces prejudice from a bully at school and her own resentment from pressures at home.

Yang the youngest and his terrible ear. Lensey Namioka; Kees de Kiefte, illus. Little, Brown, 1992. LC 91-30345, 112 p. (ISBN 0-316-59701-5; pbk 0-440-40917-9) Grades 3-7.

Yingtao is the youngest child of a musically talented family, but he is tone deaf. When he plays with his three siblings he ruins their sound. But their father wants them all to play in a recital. Because Yingtao's friend Matthew plays so much better than Yingtao, the boys wonder whether the Yang family can understand why Yingtao does not want to play, and why Matthew does want to play.

Year of impossible goodbyes. Sook Nyul Choi. Houghton Mifflin, 1991. LC 91-10502, 176 p. (ISBN 0-395-57419-6; pbk 0-440-40759-1) Grades 5-6.

A suspenseful account of a young girl's experiences in North Korea during the Japanese and later the Russian occupation at the end of World War II. Their family must rely on each other for survival even as they risk their lives to find freedom in the South.

Year of the panda. Miriam Schlein; Kam Mak, illus. HarperCollins, 1990. LC 89-71307, 96 p. (ISBN plb 0-690-04866-1) Grades 3-7.

Lu Yi knows that the government is doing a lot to save pandas. When Lu Yi and his father find a dead panda and her grieving baby, they feel they must take it in or the baby will die. Lu Yi is given a reward, but he is sad because he has to give up the baby. He is allowed to go to the science center and help them with the pandas.

Reference and Scholarly Works

Asian America: Chinese and Japanese in the United States since 1850. Roger Daniels. University of Washington Press, 1988. LC 88-5643, 384 p., (ISBN 0-295-96669-6).

An account of Chinese and Japanese Americans that concentrates on individual contributions to their adopted country, rather than the exclusions that were imposed upon them. Includes and index and illustrations.

Asian American: a study guide and source guide. Lynn P. Dunn. R&E Publishers, 1975. LC 74-31620, 111 p. (ISBN 0-88247-304-2).

Part of a four volume series on American minorities titled *Ethnic Studies.* Each volume covers three themes: identity, conflict, and integration/nationalism. This volume serves as a guide for students (includes high school level) studying Asian Americans. In each thematic section, the development of the "study outline" is historical and chronological. The "notes and sources" column parallels the "study outline." Includes a "glossary and who's who" features.

Asian American experiences in the United States. Joann Faung Jean Lee. McFarland, 1991. LC 90-53804, 228 p., (ISBN 0-89950-585-6).

Depicts the experiences of Chinese-Americans in oral history interviews. Lee begins with important distinctions in traditions, rituals and values that define each Asian group, even though society perceives Asians as a singular racial group. She includes judicial rulings and Acts of Congress which affected the immigration, citizenship, marriage, and employment opportunities of Asians. Interviews are short, yet insightful, but are not grouped according to ethnic-national origin.

Asian and Pacific American perspectives in bilingual education: comparative research. Mae Chu Chang. Columbia University, Teachers College Press, 1982. LC 82-10764. (ISBN pbk 0-8077-2723-7).

A collection of papers dealing with bilingual education concerning Asian and Pacific Americans. Areas covered include the structure of Asian languages, English language idiosyncrasies, and practical issues such as testing and assessment.

Becoming Americans: Asian sojourners, immigrants, and refugees in the Western United States. Tricia Knoll. Coast to Coast Books, 1982. LC 82-4539, 356 p. (ISBN 0-9602664-3-7; ISBN pbk 0-9602664-4-5).

Knoll provides brief accounts of the people from seven different countries, including Cambodia. Each chapter describes a brief recent history of the country, their culture, explains why people left, and introduces some of the individuals who came to the U.S. Includes a brief chronology, several appendices, an index, and maps.

Cambodia: traditional music #1. Chinary Ung, compiler and annotator. Folkways Records, 1978. One phonodisc. (ISBN 0-937703-36-X).

A survey of Cambodian music that includes vocal and instrumental selections, with examples from village folk celebrations and recreational music, as well as the classical Cambodian dance repertoire. Notes accompanying the selections explain the context of each piece and describe the instruments used, however none of the songs are translated. Provides some black and white photographs of the instruments described.

Cambodian system of writing and beginning reader with drills and glossary. Franklin E. Huffman. Yale University Press, 1970. LC 78-104614, 365 p. (ISBN 0-300-01199-7, reprint ISBN 0-300-01314-0).

Designed to be used in conjunction with the author's *Modern Spoken Cambodian*, it prepares students to read and write Cambodian. The book consists of three parts: Part One is a formal analysis of the relationship between the phonology of modern Cambodian and the symbols used to represent them; Part Two provides the student with a systematic, step-by-step approach to reading and writing Cambodian syllables; and Part Three consists of fifty reading selections graded in difficulty, ranging from short simple narratives to essays on various aspects of Cambodian culture. A glossary includes approximately 2,000 vocabulary items introduced in the reader and examples used throughout the other sections of the book.

Chinese in San Francisco: a pictorial history. Laverne Mau Dicker. Dover Publications, 1979. LC 79-50669, (ISBN 0-486-23868-7).

Documents Chinese-American history in San Francisco from 1847 to 1979 in a series of short articles listing historical dates of significance. Contains 168 black and white photographs from public and private collections. Includes a bibliography.

Chinese of America. Jack Chen. Harper, 1981. LC 80-7749, 288 p., (ISBN 0-06-250-139-9).

Covers the Chinese-American experience from the arrival of the first Chinese 1785, to the issues and achievements of the present.

Contemporary American immigrants: patterns of Filipino, Korean, and Chinese American settlement in the United States. Luciano Mangiafico. Greenwood, 1988. LC 87-17752, 229 p. (ISBN 0275-92726-1).

The author devotes four chapters on the statistics from the United States Bureau of Census on Chinese immigrants to the U.S. in contemporary period. The data covers information of history, social and demographic characteristics, current emigration trends and problems, and prospects for the future about Chinese immigration.

Dictionary of Asian American history. Hyung-Chan Kim, editor. Greenwood, 1986. LC 85-30188, 642 p. (ISBN 0313-23760-3).

This reference work contains short essays about the Chinese and several other Asian American groups. It includes an extensive dictionary that lists people and events in alphabetical order, and a chronology of Asian American history and 1980 Census data.

Folklore communication among Filipinos in California. Herminia Quimpo Meñez. Ayer, 1980. 257 p. (ISBN 0-405-13320-0).

This study examines folklore communication—specifically among the Delano Filipino community in Kern County, CA and among the community in Monterey County, CA—to show how certain social situations affect folklore performance and the dynamics of the communication of folklore. Includes an index, a bibliography, and five appendices.

Handbook of Korea. 9th ed. Korean Overseas Information Service, Irvington Publishers. 824 p. (ISBN 0-8290-2631-2).

A publication of the South Korean Government that provides information on almost every aspect of Korean life and culture. Includes a bibliography, index, color plates, and a map.

Hawaii handbook. 3rd ed. J.D. Bisigname. Moon, 1991. (ISBN pbk 0-918373-48-4).

A traveler's resource guide to Hawaii that provides an introduction to the geography, history, and society of the islands.

Hawaii's people. 4th ed. Andrew W. Lind. University of Hawaii Press, 1980. LC 80-10764.

An account of the poly-racial population in Hawaii covering who the people are, how they live, and their culture.

Hearts of sorrow. James F. Freeman. Stanford University Press, 1989. LC 89-32115, 446 p. (ISBN 0-8047-1585-8; pbk 0-8047-1890-3).

Interviews of a wide range of Vietnamese-American refugees provide a glimpse into the lives of Vietnamese-Americans, revealing their hopes and fears, and their successes and failures. An extensive bibliography is provided, and many of these other studies and works are referred to in the introductions that precede each section to provide a background for the personal narratives.

History of Cambodia. 2nd ed. David P. Chandler. Westview Press, 1992. LC 83-1391 287 p. (ISBN 0-8133-0926-3).

This book chronicles Cambodian history from its beginning to the twentieth century by using 19th and 20th century Khmer archives and documents. It is the first scholarly history of Cambodia to appear in English. Includes Illustrations, a bibliographic essay, and an index.

Intermediate Cambodian reader. Franklin E. Huffman; In Proum, ed. Yale University Press, 1982. 499 p.(ISBN 0-300-01552-6).

This sequel to *Cambodian System of Writing and Beginning Reader With Drills and Glossary,* serves as an intermediate reader to develop a student's ability to the point of reading unedited Cambodian with the aid of a dictionary.

Justice delayed: the record of the Japanese American internment cases. Peter Irons, ed. Wesleyan Univ. Press, 1989. LC 88-20880. 448 p. (ISBN 0-8195-5168-6; pbk 0-8195-6175-4).

A comprehensive record of the events of the Pearl Harbor attack and its consequences to the Japanese Americans in the U.S. Covers the court cases of three young men who had the courage to challenge the military curfew and exclusion orders preceding the mass internment of the Japanese Americans.

Kenkyusha's new English-Japanese dictionary. Yoshio Koine, editor. Kenkyusha, State Mutual Book and Periodical Service, 1980. 2477 p. (ISBN 0-8288-1013-3); 1990 edition, 2119 p. (ISBN 0-317-59316-1).

This work is patterned after the Webster and Oxford dictionaries, and is considered one of the most widely used standard dictionaries. After the English entry and pronunciation guide, Japanese characters follow to indicate the subject matter and definition. Includes a list of widely used phrases entitled Foreign Phrases and Quotations, mainly in Latin, French, and German. There is also a companion Japanese-English edition.

Korea annual 1992: a comprehensive handbook on Korea. Yonhap News Agency, Western Publications Service, 1992. 812 p. (ISBN 89-7433-005-9).

An annual publication committed to keeping abreast of current trends in Korea. It is divided into 11 sections: Chronology, Highlights in Korean current events, Government, Economy, Social Affairs, Education and Culture, Korean Ginseng, General Information, Law and Documents, Directories, Who's Who.

Korea: tradition and transformation, a history of the Korean people. Andrew C. Nahm. Hollym International Corporation, 1988. LC 86-81681, 583 p. (ISBN 0-930878-56-6).

This work covers North and South Korea in one comprehensive volume describing the land, climate, people, and major historical developments in political, economic, cultural, and social aspects. Includes a chronology, appendices, bibliography, maps, charts, and an index.

Korean dance, theater and cinema. Korean National Commission for UNESCO, editors. Pace International Research, 1983. LC 83-97102, 205 p. (ISBN 0-89209-017-0).

Part of the Korean Art, Folklore, Language, and Thought series of Korean culture dedicated to promoting an understanding of Korea's past and present. The individual articles contain tables, photos, and bibliographies.

Korean immigrants. Won Moo Hurh; Kwang Chung Kim. Fairleigh Dickenson University, 1984. LC 82-48466, 280 p. (ISBN 0-8386-3145-2).

This work shows general patterns of the cultural and socio-economic adaptation of Korean immigrants as compared to other immigrants. Includes an extensive appendix of survey information and a selected bibliography on Korean-American research studies.

Koreans in America. Bong-youn Choy. Nelson Hall, 1979. LC 79-9791, 376 p. (ISBN 0-88229-352-4).

Divided in three sections, this book describes the socioeconomic, cultural, and political activities of Koreans in America from 1882 to 1976, in addition to giving an account of Korea's domestic and external conditions during this same period. Includes a bibliography and an index.

Korea's cultural roots. 3rd ed. Jon Carter Covell. Hollym International, 1986. LC 83-81319, 132 p. (ISBN 0-930878-32-9).

Explains some of the complex mutations, Eastern myths, religions, architecture of the Shaman, Buddhist, and neo-Confucian roots, and symbolism of Korea. Includes an index and illustrations of religious ceremonies, symbols, and art, however, It does not include the effect of Christianity on Korean history.

Literature for children about Asians and Asian Americans: analysis and annotated bibliography with additional readings for adults. Esther C. Jenkins; Mary C. Austin. Greenwood, 1987. LC 87-23627, 320 p. (ISBN 0-313-25970-4).

Although the main focus of this book is children's literature, a section is devoted to additional reading for adults on Japanese and Japanese Americans as well as other Asians. Literature for children is divided into two categories: folk literature and contemporary literature. The informative summary of the history and trends of each category is provided, in addition to individual annotations.

Modern spoken Cambodian. Reprint. Franklin E. Huffman. Cornell University, 1987. 451 p. (ISBN 0-300-01316-7).

A guide to the basic structures of standard spoken Cambodian that includes pronunciation drills, useful words and phrases in 28 different situations, and a Cambodian-English/English-Cambodian glossary (both transliterated). Includes an index. Recommended to come before *Cambodian Writing System and Beginning Reader*.

Path of the ocean: traditional poetry of Polynesia. Marjorie Sinclair, ed. University of Hawaii Press, 1982. LC 82-8611, 239 p. (ISBN 0-8248-0804-5).

An anthology of Polynesian poetry arranged geographically from Hawaii to new Zealand.

Quiet Odyssey: a pioneer Korean woman in America. Mary Paik Lee. University of Washington Press, 1990. LC 89-28077, 264 p. (pbk 0-295-96969-5).

This autobiography chronicles the experiences of Ms. Lee from the age of five to the age of eighty-six. Includes maps, photographs, a bibliographic essay, and three appendices.

South Pacific handbook. 5th ed. David Stanley. Moon, 1993. 778 p. (ISBN 0-918373-99-9).

A comprehensive guide to the history, politics, economics, cultures, and customs of the Pacific Islands.

Southeast Asia on a shoestring. 6th edition. Tony Wheeler. Lonely Planet Pub., 1989. 688 p., (ISBN 0-86442-056-0).

A travel guide that provides useful up-to-date information about Southeast Asia covering history, general travel information, and what to expect when traveling. Only a few pages are devoted to Cambodia because traveling there is difficult for Westerners.

Strangers from a different shore. Ronald Takaki. Viking, 1990. LC 89-2816, 584 p. (ISBN 0-14-013885-4).

A collection of essays about the hardships and history of Asian immigrants. The section on Korean Americans provides personal accounts of their fight to be identified by their own ethnic identity and to be free of the grasp Japan had on their homeland. Includes a section of notes and an extensive index.

Strangers to these shores: race and ethnic relations in the United States. 4th Edition. Vincent N. Parrillo. Macmillan, 1993. LC93-12047, 613 p. (ISBN 0-02-391752-0).

Provides a conceptual and theoretical overview of immigration from all points in the world, and is divided into 5 major parts, providing treatment to each separate ethnic group. Each chapter consists of firsthand immigrant accounts and text summary highlights, as well as extensive map, photo, and line art illustrations. Includes key terms, review questions, an annotated bibliography at the end of each chapter, and an appendix.

Swimming to Cambodia. Spaulding Gray, producer. Distributed by Lorimar Home Video. 1987. 85 min.

A 'concert film' of Spaulding Gray's off-Broadway monologue detailing his thoughts and experiences in Southeast Asia during the filming of "The Killing Fields".

Non-fiction

A to Zen: a book of Japanese culture. Ruth Wells; Yoshi, illus. Picture book studio, 1992. LC 91-14183, 28 p. (ISBN pbk 0-88708-175-4) Grades K up.

An alphabet book that introduces young readers to ancient and modern Japan. Traditions, history, and everyday life stories are woven into each portrait.

Animals: selected poems. Michio Mado; Mitsumasa Anno, illus.; Empress Michiko of Japan, trans. Macmillan, 1992. LC 92-10356, 48 p. (ISBN 0-689-50574-4) Grades ps up.

This book is well-known Japanese poet Mado's first English publication. Each poem captures a truth about its animal subject with simplicity, giving this volume ageless appeal. Anno has created delicate cut-paper illustrations.

Asian crafts. Judith Hoffman Corwin. Watts, 1992. LC 91-13500, 48 p. (ISBN 0-531-11013-3) Grades 1-4.

Collection of art activities and recipes from the entire Asian continent—China,

India, Japan, and Russia. Step-by-step instructions are given and materials are common. Ideas come from ancient and modern Asia and activities include painting, paper cutting, making toys and games, and cooking snacks.

Between two cultures: the Vietnamese in America. Alan Henkin; Liem Thanh Nguyen. R&E Publishers, 1981. LC 80-69333, 125 p. (ISBN 0-8548-039-7) Grades 3-6.

A comprehensive history and study of Vietnam. The book gives an overview of the religion and culture. It also describes the challenges that the Vietnamese must face when they arrive in the U.S.

Cambodia. Claudia Canesso. Chelsea House, 1989. LC 88-30435, 96 p. (ISBN 1-55546-798-9) Grades 6 up.

Part of the Places and Peoples of the World series. Describes the history of Cambodia and a study of the current situation in that country, providing a broad overview of Cambodians and their country. Contains information about the geography, history, government, economy, people and culture of Cambodia, a quick facts section, a glossary, and an index.

Chi-Hoon: a Korean girl. Patricia McMahon; Michael O'Brien, photographer. Boyd Mills, 1993. LC 92-81331, 48 p. (ISBN 1-56397-026-0) Grades 4-7.

Covers one week in the life of an eight-year-old girl who lives in Seoul, Korea. Her family and school are the focus, but aspects of Korean culture are also explained. Includes color photographs of an engaging family to illustrate the girl's attempts to be a good daughter and student.

Child in prison camp. Shizuye Takashima. Tundra, 1991. LC 74-1265, 100 p. (ISBN 0-88776-241-7) Grades 4 up.

A young Japanese-Canadian girl describes her life after she and her family are forced to live in a Canadian internment camp during World War II. She relates the hardships, the fears, and the humiliation of camp life in the form of a journal.

Children of China. Matti A. Pitkanen, illus.; Reijo Harkonen. Carolrhoda, 1990. LC 89-35063, 40 p. (ISBN plb 0-87614-394-X) Grades 3-6.

Part of the World's Children series. Life in China is portrayed through the eyes of children with text and color photography. Includes children in rural Tibet. Includes a facts and a pronunciation guide.

China homecoming. Jean Fritz; Michael Fritz, photographer. Putnam, 1985.
LC 84-24775, 144 p. (ISBN 0-399-21182-9) Grades 5 up.

Sequel to Homesick: my own story. As an American child growing up in China, Jean
was homesick for America. Yet once back in America, she was homesick for China.
China has gone through much cultural upheaval since she left, and Jean is anxious
about returning. Through her anticipation and later her travels, she savors all things
Chinese and shares that with her readers with her unique, lively perspective.

China's long march: 6,000 miles of danger. Jean Fritz; Yang Zhr Cheng,
illus. Putnam, 1988. LC 87-31171, 128 p. (ISBN 0-399-21512-3) Grades 7 up.

Despite its YA recommendation, this period of Chinese history is a unique subject
for a juvenile book. Jean Fritz uses her distinctive style to describe the Communist
army of Mao Zedong marching 6,000 miles to defeat Chiang Kai-shek and the
Nationalist Army. Provides descriptions of why people felt so strongly about the
cause that they endured such terrible conditions.

Chinese. Jodine Mayberry. Watts, 1990. LC 90-12273, 64 p.
(ISBN 0-531-10977-1) Grades 5-8.

Part of the Recent American Immigrants series. Many Chinese immigrated to this
country to search for gold during the California Gold Rush of 1849. Once in California, many began working for the railroads. Chinese-Americans have faced discrimination and laws which discouraged their coming into this country. In spite of
these odds, Chinese-Americans have distinguished themselves. Brief biographies
and food recipes are included.

Chinese-American experience. Dana Ying-Hui Wu; Jeffrey Dao-Sheng Tung.
Millbrook, 1993. LC 92-15649, 64 p. (ISBN plb 1-56294-271-9) Grades 4-6.

Part of the Coming to America series. Provides history of why the Chinese left
China, the hardships of coming to a new country, and the bias they endured.

Chinese-Americans. William Daley. Chelsea House, 1988. LC 86-322732,
112 p. (ISBN 0-87754-867-6; pbk 0-7910-0260-8) Grades 4-7.

Part of the Peoples of North America series. Describes the Chinese struggle to find
a place in American society.

Chinese American heritage. David M. Brownstone. Facts on File, 1988.
LC 88-10970, 144 p. (ISBN 0-8160-1627-5). Grades 6 up.

Part of America's Ethnic Heritage Series. Describes the history of China before introducing the Chinese Americans, including a chapter on the Chinese in Hawaii. Includes illustrations, an index, and a bibliography.

Chinese New Year. Tricia Brown; Fran Ortiz, photographer. Henry Holt, 1987. LC 87-8532, 48 p. (ISBN 0-8050-0497-1) Grades ps-2.

A photographic portrayal of the Chinese New Year and the customs associated with the celebration.

Chinese women of America: a pictorial history. Judy Yung. University of Washington Press, 1986. LC 85-40974, 128 p. (ISBN 0-295-96357-3). Grades 6 up.

A history of Chinese women in America between 1834 and 1985. Over 130 photographs document this time period of pioneers, focusing on the struggle and development of contemporary Chinese women. Includes tables and maps of the female population, education, labor force, and major occupations.

City kids in China. Peggy Thomson; Paul S. Conklin, photographer. Harper-Collins, 1991. LC 90-1993, 128 p. (ISBN 0-06-021654-9) Grades 3-7.

Describes the lives of children in the city of Changsha, China. Includes their day-to-day lives, the special treat of the sights, sounds, and smells of the market place, and their hopes for the future. Their parents' feelings about the "one child per family" law is briefly explored.

Count your way through Korea. Jim Haskins; Dennis Hockerman, illus. Carolrhoda, 1989. LC 88-25897, 24 p. (ISBN 0-87614-348-6; pbk 0-87614-516-0) Grades 1-4.

Part of the Count Your way series. Each number from one through ten is used to present concepts about Korean customs and culture.

Dan Thuy's new life in America. Karen O'Connor. Lerner, 1992. LC 91-28915, 40 p. (ISBN 0-8225-2555-0) Grades 4-8.

Part of the In my shoes series. Dan Thuy and her family spent three years in a refugee camp waiting to come to America. This book looks at their lives after three months of American life. Dan Thuy and her family are finally beginning to adjust. Trying to maintain their traditions and adopt the American way of life cause some conflicts, but determination for a better life helps them.

English-Korean picture dictionary. Francis M. Koh; Denise S. Vignes, illus. EastWest 1987. LC 87-83309, 4p p. (ISBN pbk 0-9606090-3-2) Grades ps up.

This book is designed to help people who have adopted Korean children and need to teach them how to speak English. It can be used by anyone trying to learn either language. The introduction compares the two languages to help the English speaking user. In each picture, the English word, the phonetic pronunciation for the Korean word, and the Korean word are shown. Includes a list of nouns, verbs, adjectives, and a section of phrases for everyday situations.

Ethnic celebrations around the world. Nancy Everix. Good Apple, 1991. 154 p. (ISBN 0-86653-607-8) Grades 3-8.

Contains games, puzzles, maps, coloring pages, and craft instructions for projects connected with holidays of different countries. Each holiday, arranged by country, is discussed with an accompanying bibliography. The Asian country is represented by Taiwan.

Filipinos in America. Frank H. Winter. Lerner, 1988. LC 88-613, 80 p. (ISBN 0-8225-0237-2; pbk 0-8225-1035-9) Grades 5-6.

Part of the In America series. Describes the Filipino immigration to the United States and their adjustment to American life.

Forever family: a book about adoption. Roslyn Banish; Jennifer Jordan-Wong. HarperCollins, 1992. LC 90-28725, 48 p. (ISBN 0-06-021673-5; plb 0-06-021674-3; pbk 0-06-446116-5) Grades K-3.

Eight-year-old Jennifer Jordan-Wong has a new bi-racial family who adopted her. She has a Chinese-American father and a new set of relatives who help her learn new things. Before Jennifer was adopted she lived in foster homes, and she often thinks of those families. Although her biological parents are not shown, Jennifer wonders why they could not keep her. Usually she is too busy growing up to think about it.

Hawaiian word book. Robin Burningham, illustrator. Bess Press, 1982. 104 p. (ISBN 0-935848-12-6) Grades 2-5.

Designed to teach over 200 basic Hawaiian words and to introduce the Hawaiian language and culture. Illustrated words deal with various aspects of Hawaiian culture, nature, lifestyle, food, and clothing.

Hiroshima no pika. Toshi Maruki. Lothrop, 1982. LC 82-15365, 48 p. (ISBN 0-688-01297-3) Grade 7 up.

Mii's family's account of their experiences when the atomic bomb was dropped at Hiroshima is described in a picture book format. Although death and destruction surround them, the family manages to stay together even after Mii's mother carries her father across two rivers. At the end, Mii and her family rebuild but always carry the memories, hoping it will not happen again. Scenes of death, the burned-out city, people struggling to survive are haunting, thus the higher grade level recommendation.

Hoang Anh: a Vietnamese-American boy. Diane Hoyt-Goldsmith; Lawrence Migdale, photographer. Holiday House, 1992. LC 91-28880, 32 p. (ISBN 0-8234-0948-1) Grades 3-7.

Hoang Anh lives in San Rafael, California. His family escaped from Vietnam because they feared Communist takeover of their country because his father fought in the war. Hoang Anh describes how his life is a combination of American and Vietnamese customs.

How my family lives in America. Susan Kuklin. Macmillan, 1992. LC 91-22949, 40 p. (ISBN 0-02-751239-8) Grades ps-2.

Children of three families and three different cultures relate stories of how they adjust to American traditions and still maintain the unique aspects of their original culture. The Asian family represented is from China. Includes a recipe for cold sesame noodles.

In the eyes of the cat: Japanese poetry for all seasons. Demi; Tze-si Huang, trans. Holt, 1992. LC 91-27728, 80 p. (ISBN 0-8050-1955-3; pbk 0-8050-3383-1) Grades ps-3.

A collection of nature poetry organized by seasons. Each poem captures a moment in the life of an animal. The author of every poem is identified with birth and death dates. Distinctive illustrations.

Japanese-Americans. Harry Kitano. Chelsea House, 1987. LC 86-28365, 112 p. (ISBN 0-87754-856-0; pbk 0-7910-0269-1) Grades 4-7.

Part of the Peoples of North America series. This book documents the struggles of Japanese emigrants and their desire to maintain their cultural heritage. Successful individuals of Japanese heritage are detailed.

Japanese in America. Noel L. Leathers. Lerner, 1991. LC 67-15684, 72 p. (ISBN plb 0-8225-0241-0; pbk 0-8225-1042-1; pbk 0-8225-1014-6) Grades 2-5.

Part of the In America series. Describes the history of the Japanese in America with pictures and charts. Includes an index.

Japanese Texans. Thomas K. Walls. University of Texas Institute of Texan Cultures, 1987. LC 87-50131, 256 p. (ISBN 0-86701-021-5; pbk 0-86701-022-3) Grades 4-6.

Describes the history of the Japanese in Texas from 1885 to the present. Many interesting stories of individuals. Includes photographs and a chronology. Indexed.

Journey: Japanese-Americans, racism and renewal. Sheila Hamanaka. Orchard, 1990. LC 89-22877, 40 p. (ISBN 0-531-05849-2; plb 0-531-08449-3) Grades 5 up.

Sheila Hamanaka painted a five-panel mural depicting her family in the United States from 1941-1945. It is a bleak picture of Japanese-Americans struggling for survival and being imprisoned in internment camps. There is hope in the last panel for freedom and reparation.

Kanu of Kathmandu: a journey in Nepal. Barbara Margolis. Macmillan, 1992. LC 92-12482, 40 p. (ISBN 0-02-762282-7) Grades 1-4.

Eight-year-old Kanu is proud to act as tour guide and show off the Nepalese city where he lives. He describes every day situations, special details of the city such as the architecture, and the natural beauty of Mt. Everest.

Korean-Americans. Brian Lehrer. Chelsea House, 1988. LC 87-18219, 112 p. (ISBN 0-87754-888-9) Grades 5 up.

Part of the Peoples of North America series. Provides an overview of Korean history, culture, the conditions which encouraged emigration away from Korea, and the Korean's life in the United States.

Korean holidays and festivals. Frances M. Koh; Liz B. Dodson, illus. East-West Press, 1990. LC 90-84031, 32 p. (ISBN 0-9606090-5-9) Grades 2-5.

A chronological history of traditional Korean holidays and festivals. Provides background about the Korean culture and customs, as well as the way these holidays are still celebrated with activities, games, food, and dress.

Koreans. Jodine Mayberry. Watts, 1991. LC 90-12987, 64 p. (ISBN 0-531-11106-7) Grades 5-10.

Part of the Recent American Immigrants series. Describes the life of Koreans after their immigration to the United States and the hardships they faced. Includes biographies of successful Korean-Americans, how conditions changed after World War II and the Korean war, and Korean celebrations.

Land of yesterday, land of tomorrow: discovering Chinese Central Asia. Paul, David, and Peter Conklin, photographers; Brent Ashabranner. Dutton, 1992. LC 91-25145, 96 p. (ISBN 0-525-65086-5) Grades 5 up.

The Xinjiang Province is a barren and harsh region, located in the middle of the Asian continent, that was closed to outsiders by the Communist government. Recently it was opened for a brief time and the Conklin family traveled there. This book chronicles their visit.

Lee Ann: the story of a Vietnamese-American girl. Tricia Brown; Ted Thai, photographer. Putnam, 1991. LC 90-25708, 48 p. (ISBN 0-399-21842-4) Grades 5 up.

Third grader Lee Ann describes her life with a Vietnamese family living in America. She relates her family's escape from war-torn Vietnam and how her parents think about relatives left behind.

Lion dancer: Ernie Wan's Chinese New Year. Kate Waters; Madeline Slovenz-Low; Martha Cooper, photographer. Scholastic, 1990. LC 89-6423, 32 p. (ISBN 0-590-43046-7; pbk 0-590-43047-5) Grades ps-3.

Eddie Wan and his family prepare for their Chinese New Year celebration. This year Eddie will perform his first Lion Dance on the streets of New York. Finally the waiting is over, and Eddie is inside his colorful costume, keeping in step with all the other dancers inside his costume. Illustrated with color photos.

Look what we've brought you from Vietnam. Phyllis Shalant. Simon & Schuster, 1988. LC 87-20276, 48 p. (ISBN plb 0-671-63919-6; pbk 0-671-65978-2) Grades 2-6.

A how-to book with instruction for things to make and do to celebrate Vietnamese holidays. Includes recipes, a puppet show, a storytelling activity, and games.

Making Chinese papercuts. Robert and Corinne Borja. Whitman, 1980. LC 79-18358, 40 p. (ISBN plb 0-8075-4948-7) Grades 3-8.

The history of this Chinese folk art is based on creating art in an inexpensive but very expressive way. Papercuts are frequently used as party and holiday decorations. Includes instructions, patterns, and usage suggestions.

Matsuri! Festival!: Japanese American celebrations and activities. Nancy K. Araki; Jane N. Horii. Reprint from 1979. Heian International, 1985. 140 p. (ISBN 0-89346-019-2). Grades ps-2.

Describes five Japanese traditions and corresponding activities—dancing, cooking, etc.

My Hiroshima. Junko Morimoto. Viking, 1990. LC 89-51483, 32 p.
(ISBN pbk 0-670-83181-6); Puffin, 1992. (ISBN pbk 0-14-054524-7) Grades 2-5.

A young girl describes her life in Hiroshima before and after the bomb was
dropped. She relates the hardships the city faced and its eventual return to peace
and beauty.

Pianist's debut: preparing for the concert stage. Barbara Beirne. Carolrhoda, 1990. LC 90-2238, 56 p. (ISBN plb 0-87614-432-6) Grades 2-5.

Part of the In the Spotlight series. Eleven-year-old and American born Leah Yoon is
a gifted piano student. The Asian-American girl describes her early experiences
with learning music and how seemingly easy it was to earn prestigious awards. She
also relates her hard work, diligent practice at Julliard Music School, and the hope
to have a career on the concert stage.

Public defender: lawyer for the people. Joan Hewett; Richard Hewett, photographer. Dutton, 1991. LC 90-26389, 48 p. (ISBN 0-525-67340-7) Grades 4-8.

Janice Fukai is a public defender in Los Angeles County for people who cannot
afford to hire a lawyer. This book follows her through a typical workday and gives
background information about her job

Red dragonfly on my shoulder: haiku. Sylvia Cassedy; Kunihiro Suetake;
Molly Bang, illus. HarperCollins, 1992. LC 91-18443, 32 p. (ISBN 0-06-022624-
2; plb 0-06-022625-0) Grades K-5.

Presents thirteen haikus. Each one is translated from Japanese, describes an animal,
and is illustrated with unusual collages.

Sadako and the thousand paper cranes. Eleanor Coerr; Ronald Himler,
illus. Putnam, 1977. LC 76-9872, 64 p. (ISBN 0-399-20520-0); Dell, 1979.
(ISBN pbk 0-440-47465-5) Grades 2-5.

Based on letters written between Sadako Sasaki and her classmates. Sadako was a
lively, energetic girl who wanted to run on the girls track team. When dizzy spells
finally forced her to slow down, doctors discovered that Sadako had contracted
leukemia as a result of radiation from the atomic bomb that was dropped on
Hiroshima.

Sachiko means happiness. Kimiko Sakai; Tomie Arai, illus. Children's, 1990.
LC 90-2248, 32 p. (ISBN 0-89239-065-4) Grades K-5.

The touching story of young Sachiko and her grandmother who thinks she is five years old. Describes how Sachiko comes to terms with her grandmother's memory-debilitating illness and finds happiness.

South Pacific islanders. Patricia H. Vilsoni. Rourke, 1987. LC 87-4332, 48 p. (ISBN 0-685-67606-4; plb 0-86625-259-2) Grades 4-6.

Part of the Original Peoples series. Describes the origins, history, and culture of the people inhabiting the South Pacific islands, especially Tonga, Samoa, and Fiji. Examines the impact of Western influence and the problems they face. Includes maps, a glossary, a bibliography, and an index.

Southeast Asians. William McGuire. Watts, 1991. LC 90-12996, 64 p. (ISBN 0-531-11108-3) Grades 5-10.

Describes the hardships and eventual flight by refugees from Vietnam, Cambodia, and Laos because of war. Relates how these people attempt to preserve their culture as they find a place in American society.

Story of the Saigon airlift. Zachary Kent. Children's, 1991. LC 91-15847, 32 p. (ISBN plb 0-516-04760-4; pbk 0-516-44760-2) Grades 3-6.

Part of the Cornerstones of Freedom series. Describes the North Vietnamese surprise attack on Saigon, in 1975, that was the final hold-out of the Republic of South Vietnam. American soldiers and South Vietnamese had to evacuate—a helicopter rescue was ordered and thousands of people were airlifted out of Saigon.

Vietnamese in America. Paul Rutledge. Lerner, 1987. LC 87-4030, 64 p. (ISBN plb 0-8225-0235-6; pbk 0-8225-1033-2) Grades 5 up.

Part of the In America series. Provides background on the war which made many Vietnamese leave their country. There are stories about Vietnamese children, how they escaped, and how they adjusted to life in the United States.

We adopted you, Benjamin Koo. Linda Walvoord Girard; Linda Shute, illus. Whitman, 1989. LC 88-23653, 32 p. (ISBN 0-8075-8694-3; pbk 0-8075-8695-1) Grades 2-6.

Benjamin was born in Korea and his American parents adopted him when he was still a baby. He tells his story and describes his life.

We came from Vietnam. Muriel Stanek; William Frank McMahon, illus. Whitman, 1985. LC 84-29927, 48 p. (ISBN plb 0-8075-8699-4) Grades 1-6.

The Nguyen family escaped Vietnam in 1982, survived the boat journey and life in a refugee camp, and made it safely to settle in Chicago. They are adjusting to life there, learning English and sending their children to public school. The Nguyen's new life in America is a blend of two cultures.

Where the river runs: a portrait of a refugee family. Nancy Price Graff; Richard Howard, photograher. Little, Brown, 1993. LC 92-24184, 71 p. (ISBN 0-316-32287-3) Grades 4-8.

Relates the story of a Cambodian family who was forced to flee their native country and their adjustment to life in the United States with the help of Cambodian traditions.

❈ HISPANIC AMERICANS ❈

Biography

Antonia Novello, U.S. surgeon general. Joan C. Hawxhurst. Millbrook, 1993. LC 9219564, 32 p. (ISBN plb 1-56294299-9) Grades 2-4.

Part of the *Hispanic heritage* series. Antonia Novello came from a poor Puerto Rican family. When she developed health problems as a child, Antonia decided she wanted to be a doctor. It was not easy to obtain the required education, but she became a pediatrician. As surgeon general, she focuses on children's health issues and life style choices.

Benito Juarez. Jan Gleiter, Francis Balistreri, illus. Raintree Steck-Vaughn, 1990. LC 38017, 32 p. (ISBN plb 0-8172-3381-4) Grades 3-6.

Part of the *Raintree Hispanic stonries* series. This short, picture book biogtaphy of Mexico's beloved president is written in English and Spanish. Benito Juarez was born to poor peasant farmers. He became a lawyer and challenged the Roman Catholic church's power. He also survived wars and political upheavals before becoming president. Unfortunately he died in office before his reforms could take effect.

Benito Juarez. Dennis Wepman. Chelsea House, 1987. LC 86-6802, 112 p. (ISBN 087754-537-5) Grades 5 up.

Part of the *World leaders past and present* series. This longer biography focuses on his motivation and achievements. Benito Juarez was determined to fight the laws, the church, and the caste system which Mexican society used to oppress Indian peasants. He became a lawyer, moved into politics, and eventually organized a revolution. Juarez was elected president before and after the French attempted to control Mexico. He was the symbol of freedom and democracy.

Benito Juarez, president of Mexico. Frank De Varona. Millbrook, 1993. LC 92-19349, 32 p. (ISBN plb 1-56294279-4; pbk 1-56294807-5) Grades 2-4.

Part of the *Hispanic heritage* series. Benito Juarez's dream was a Mexico governed by native inhabitants. Spain and its European allies had ruled there from the time when the Aztecs were conquered. Juarez was a Zapotec Indian who became a governor, and later president, despite strong European opposition. Easy to read format; includes illustrations.

Bernardo de Galvez. Frank de Varona; Tom Redman, illus. Raintree/Steck-Vaughn, 1990. LC 89-38079, 32 p. (ISBN 0-8172-3379-2) Grades 3-6.

Part of the *Raintree Hispanic stories* series. Bernardo de Galvez was a Spaniard who played an important role in America's fight for independence against the British. After serving as a soldier in the Spanish army, he was appointed governor of Louisiana as a reward for his bravery. He allowed American forces to use land near New Orleans as a base. When war was declared he raised an army to drive the British out of the Mississippi Valley and around the Gulf of Mexico region. Picture book format; includes text in Spanish and English.

Carlos Finlay. Christine Sumption, Kathleen Thompson; Les Didier, illus. Raintree/Steck-Vaughn, 1990. LC 89-38770, 32 p. (ISBN plb 0-8172-33784) Grades 3-6

Part of the *Raintree Hispanic stories series*. Carlos Finlay was a Cuban citizen born of European parents. After studying medicine abroad, he returned to Cuba and began studying yellow fever. Although he formulated the original theory that malaria was spread by mosquitoes, Walter Reed received the credit. Picture book format; includes text in Spanish and English.

Carolina Herrera: international fashion designer. Janet Riehecky. Children's Press, 1991. LC 90-28886, 32 p. (ISBN 0-516-04178-9; ISBN pbk 0-516-44178-7) Grades 2-4.

Part of the *Picture-story biography* series. Venezuelan born fashion designer Carolina Herrera is known for designing simple yet elegant clothes. Simple text format; includes photographs.

Cesar Chavez. Consuelo Rodriguez. Chelsea House, 1991. LC 90-4217, 112 p. (ISBN plb 0-7910-1232-8) Grades 5 up.

Part of the *Hispanics of achicvement* series. This longer biography focuses on his motivation and achievements. Cesar Chavez's youth in Arizona was difficult. The Great Depression forced his family to become migrant workers. Very little was done to improve the situation of migrant workers until Chavez and his colleagues became community organizers. Gaining widespread support from Mexican American laborers, they organized the National Farm Workers Association. Chavez's persistence and organizational skills helped migrant workers bargain for better wages, safer working conditions, and greater dignity. Includes photographs.

Cesar Chavez and La Causa. Naurice Roberts. Children's Press, 1986. LC 85-27980, 32 p. (ISBN 0-516-03484-7; pbk 0-51643484-5) Grades 2-4.

Part of the *Picture-story biographies* series. Chavez came from a poor migrant family and only finished school through the eighth grade. He felt passionately that there had to be a better way of life for migrant families. Chavez founded the National Farm Workers Association—an organization committed to securing better benefits from the growers. Simple text format; includes photographs.

Cesar Chavez: labor leader. Maria Cedeno. Millbrook, 1993. LC 92-22620, 32 p. (ISBN plb 1-56294280-8; pbk 1-56294-808-3) Grades 2-4.

Part of the *Hispanic heritage* series. Cesar Chavez had many upheavals in his childhood because of the Depression and his family farm's crop failure. His life's work reflected his commitment to improving the plight of migrant workers.Does not include his death. Easy to ready format; includes photographs.

Chico Mendes: fight for the forest. Susan DeStefano; Larry Raymond, illus. Twenty-first century, 1992. LC 91-19734, 76 p. (ISBN 0-8050-2887-0) Grades 4-8.

Part of the *Earth keepers* series. Chico Mendes was a rubber tapper in the Amazon rain forest, just as his father had been. Their methods preserved the trees so that the ecosystem continued to provide them with a living. But cattle ranchers, farmers, and industrialists began destroying the rain forests for personal gain. After a newspaper reporter taught him to read and write, Mendes began organizing other rubber tappers to read and form labor unions. His courageous fight ultimately cost him his life. Includes illustrations.

Daniel Ortega. James Stockwell. Chelsea House, 1991. LC 90-19464, 112 p. (ISBN 1-55546-846-2) Grades 5-6.

Part of the *World leaders past and present* series. Daniel Ortega studied law as a way to promote social change. He was forced to go underground after organizing students to protest the Somoza government. Ortega and other Sandonistas fought Somoza and finally won. Ortega was elected president, but rebels made the victory hard to maintain. Ortega held on until the rebels stopped fighting. He then asked them to help rebuild the country. Indudes background on Central American history and photographs.

David Farragut. Abbott Chrisman; Francis Balistreri, illus. Raintree Steck-Vaughn, 1988. LC 8837398, 32 p. (ISBN plb 0-8172-2904-3) Grades 3-6.

Part of the *Raintree Hispanic stories* senes. David Farragut's father was a Spanish sailor who fought in the Revolutionary war. Farragut also become a sailor, and was a hero in the Civil War. He distinguished himself in the Union Navy as the first U.S. Admiral. Picture book format; includes text in English and Spanish.

Diego. Jonah WInter; Jeanette Winter, illus.; Amy Prince, translator. Knopf, 1991. LC 90-25923, 40 p. (ISBN 0-679-81987-8; plb. 0-679-91987-2; pbk 0-679-85617-X. Grades K-4.

This Spanish/English picture book shows how the childhood of Diego Rivera helped shape his art. Due to an illness, Rivera was taken to the mountains, where he saw beautiful things from nature. When he retumed, Rivera began to draw everywhere, especially on walls. Although he traveled all over the world, Rivera continued to paint the Mexico he loved on walls.

Diego Rivera. James D. Cockaoft. Chelsea House, 1991. LC 91-6277,112 p. (ISBN plb 0-7910-1252-2) Grades 5 up.

Part of the *Hispanics of achievement* series. This longer biography recounts the life of Rivera, and the political history and events which shaped his views. It traces the development of an art that produced many moving and authentic murals. Includes photographs.

Diego Rivera. Jan Gleiter, Kathleen Thompson; Yoshi Miyake, illus. Raintree/SteckVaughn, 1988. LC 88-39314, 32 p. (ISBN 0-8172-2908-6; pbk 0-8114-6764 3) Grades 2-5.

Part of the *Raintree Hispanic stories* series. This short biography relates that at an early age Rivera showed great artistic talent and energy. His political beliefs are traced, from his anger over Mexican tyranny to his support of the Communist party. Rivera painted murals on walls so that everyone could have access to his art. Picture book format; includes text in Spanish and English.

Diego Rivera: artist of the people. Anne Neimark. HarperCollins, 1992. LC 91-25209, 128 p. (ISBN 0-06-021783-9; plb 0-06-0217847) Grades 3-6.

Rivera's determination to convey his artistic and social message caused his work to be censored. Hist determination and ability to portray the common people was inspiring.

Diego Rivera: Mexican muralist. Jim Hargrove. Children's Press, 1990. LC 89-25453, 128 p. (ISBN plb 0-516-03268-2; pbk 0-516-43268-0) Grades 4 up.

Part of the *People of distinction* seriss. The flamboyancy of Diego Rivera is captured with humor and directness. He loved to tell a tall tale, but every attempt is made to separate fact from fiction. Art was the primary focus of his life; all of his relationships suffered because of that focus. Includes illustrations.

Emiliano Zapata. John David Ragan. Chelsea House, 1989. LC 88-27326, 112 p. (ISBN 1-55546-823-3) Grades 5 up.

Part of the *World leaders past and present* series. Zapata was a modest village farmer who could read, write, and speak with clarity. At the age of 30 he was was elected president of his region. Outraged because the government was controlled by hacienda owners who ignored the people's desperate needs, Zapata organized an armed force to rebel. Although many other regional leaders joined him, Zapata was betrayed and killed in an ambush.

Emesto "Che" Guevara. Douglas Kellner. Chelsea House, 1989. LC 87-32579, 112 p. (ISBN 1-55546-835-7) Grades 5 up.

Part of the *World leaders past and present* series. "Che" Guevara had the ability to inspire people to action and he became a driving force in Cuba's revolution. In his youth, Che's determination helped him overcome asthma, become a doctor, and dedicate his life to helping the oppressed. Rut change did not come quickly enough, so Che learned guerrilla tactics. He was killed while fighting in Bolivia.

Evelyn Cisneros: prima ballerina. Charnan Simon. Children's Press, 1990. LC 9040104, 32 p. (ISBN 0-516-04276-9; pbk 0-516-44276-7) Grades 2-4.

Part of the Picture story *biography* series. Evelyn Cisneros is prima ballerina of the San Francisco Ballet. Her mother thought that dance classes would help her overcome shyness. Cisneros overcame personal setbacks to develop a unique style of dancing. Simple text format; includes photographs.

Everett Alvarez, Jr.: a hero for our times. Susan Maloney Clinton. Children's Press, 1990. LC 90-38375, 32 p. (ISBN 0-516-04277-7; pbk 0-516-44277-5) Grades 2-4.

A Picture *story biography.* Everett Alvarez was the first American prisoner-of-war captured in Vietnam. He showed courage during his ordeal, never giving up. When he was released he went on to a productive life in civil service. Simple text format; includes photographs.

Famous Mexican-Americans. Janet Morey and Wendy Dunn. Dutton, 1989. LC 8 7218,176 p. (ISBN 0-525 65012-1) Grades 5 up.

Some of the most famous and accomplished contemporary Mexican-Americans are presented here: Cesar Chavez; Henry Cisneros; Archbishop Patrick Flores; Dolores Huerta, labor leader; Nancy Lopez, golfer; Vilma Martinez, attorney; Luis Nogales, business executive; Edward James Olmos, actor; Katherine Davalos Ortega, U.S. treasurer; Blandina Cardenas Ramirez, member, U.S. Commission on Civil Rights;

Edward Roybal, Congressman; Dan Sosa, Jr., state Supreme Court justice; Luis Valdez, film director; and William Velasquez, Former President of Southwest Voter Registration Education project.

Father Miguel Hildalgo: a cry for fredom D. E. Perlin; Tim McClure, illus. Hendrick Long, 1991. LC 90-27375, 32 p. (ISBN 0-937460-67-2) Grades K-4.

A simple biography of the Mexican priest who urged the Indian peasants to become independent of the Spanish govemment. He taught them skills to enable them to become self-sufficient. After Spanish troops attacked the peasants and captured Father Hidalgo, a revolution to establish a more democratic government began.

Ferdinand and Isabella. Paul Stevens. Chelsea House, 1988. LC 87-20822,112 p. (ISBN plb 0-87754-523-5) Grades 5 up.

Part of the *World leaders past and present* series. Ferdinand and Isabella shared a dream of a unified Spain. They married in secret and spent the rest of their lives in a struggle to rule. Ferdinand and Isabella fought wars and established policies to strengthen the nation. In an effort to rid their country of alleged religious heretics, they sponsored the Spanish Inquisition. Isabella also financed the explorations of Christopher Columbus.

Fidel Castro. John Vail. Chelsea House, 1986. LC 86-6853, 112 p., (ISBN 87754-566-9) Grades 5-6.

Part of the World *leaders past and present* series. Fidel Castro contributed heavily to changing the course of history in the Westem hemisphere when he helped end one of Latin America's oldest dictatorships and begin one of his own. Includes background on Cuba's history, Castro's motivation, and photographs.

Fidel Castro of Cuba. Judith BenUey. Simon & Schuster, 1991. LC 90-26057,128 p. (ISBN 0-671-70198-3; pbk 0-671-70199-1) Grades 4-7.

An *In-Focus* biography. The illegitimate son of a wealthy landowner, Fidel Castro had a fine education and knew important people. He felt that Cuba was too unstable and wanted change. Castro inspired an organization to revolt under conditions that seemed impossible. When Castro gained power, he seized property and assets causing landowners and many business people to leave.

Francisco Franco. Hedda Garza. Chelsea House, 1987. LC 86-29963, 112 p. (ISBN 87754-5243) Grades 5 up.

Part of the World *leaders past and present* series. Francisco Franco ruled Spain after Hitler and Mussolini helped him overthrow the Republican govemment. Under his fascist rule, the country was modemized, but this was achieved only by using tyrannical methods—censorship, imprisoning anyone who opposed him, and the execution of thousands of dissenters.

Frida Kahlo. Robyn Montana Tumer. Little, Brown, 1993. LC 91-29556, 32 p. (ISBN 316-85651-7) Grades 4-7.

Part of the *Portraits of women artists* series. This picture book biography features full-color reproductions of Kahlo's work, photographs of the artist, and an easy text. Her energy and love of life are evident throughout the story, including a difficult marriage to Diego Rivera. Her paintings reveal humor and disappointment in a unique style. Their significance is explained in the context of her life experiences.

Gloria Estefan. Rebecca Stefoff. Chelsea House, 1991. LC 90-26286,104 p. (ISBN 07910-1244-1) Grades 5 up.

Part of the *Hispanics of achievement* series. Superstar Gloria Estefan has struggled most of her life. Her parents brought her from Cuba to seek financial security. After her bumpy rise to stardom, a terrible accident left her with a broken back. Once again Estefan fought back and regained the ability to perform. Includes photographs and drawings.

Henry Cisneros: Alcalde Mexicano Americano. Naurice Roberts. Children's Press, 1987. LC 85-29057, 32 p. (ISBN 0-516-03485-5; pbk 0-516-53485-8) Grades 2-5.

A Picture story biography. Henry Cisneros achieved success as a political figure by becoming mayor of San Antonio. He believes in striving for excellence and being true to his Mexican-American heritage. Does not include latest achievements.

Hemando de Soto. Abbott Chrisman; Rick Whipple, illus. Raintree/Steck-Vaughn, 1988. LC 88-38955, 32 p. (ISBN plb 0-8172-2903-5; pbk 0-8114-6753-8) Grades 3-6.

Part of the *Raintree Hispanic stories* series. Because De Soto was the youngest son, he could not inherit anything from his father. Realizing that his fortune lay somewhere else, De Soto's yearning for adventure led him to the New World. De Soto was with Pizarro when he conquered the Incas. He took up further exploration by charting the Southeastem U.S., including the Mississippi River. Picture book format; includes text in Spanish and English.

Hernando de Soto. Robert Carson. Children's Press, 1991. LC 91-12665, 128 p. (ISBN 0-516-03065-5) Grades 3 up.

Part of the *World's great explorers* series. Hemando de Soto traveled with expeditions that discovered the Inca Indians in Peru and explored the territory that later became the Southeastem United States. The first European to reach the Mississippi, De Soto was overcome by malaria, and buried near the river. Color format; includes maps, paintings, and information in fact boxes.

Jose Canseco. James. R. Rothaus. Child's World, 1991. LC 91-16385, 32 p. (ISBN 89565-73-X) Grades 3-5.

Part of the *Sports Superstars series.* Born in Cuba, Jose Canseco came here as a young boy and began playing baseball at the age of 12. His desire to be the best and please his father enabled him to be drafted by the Oakland A's and hit over forty home runs and steal over forty bases during the 1988 season. Describes his career with the Oakland A's, but does not include his trade to the Texas Rangers. Action color photographs.

Jose Canseco: baseball's forty-forty man. Nathan Aaseng. Lerner,1989. LC 892279, 56 p. (ISBN plb 0-8225-0493-6; pbk 0-8225-9586-9) Grades 4-9.

Part of the *Achievers* series. Jose Canseco was born in Cuba. His parents left when Castro came to power. Even though Jose and his twin brother were both picked by professional baseball teams, he is better known. Although at first Canseco's performance was disappointing, persistent hard work and belief in himself helped him come back.

Jose Marti. Jan Gleiter; Kathleen Thompson; Les Didier, illus. Raintree Steck-Vaughn, 1988. LC 88-39174, 32 p. (ISBN plb 0-8172-2906-X); (ISBN pbk 0-81146761-9) Grades 3-6.

Part of the *Raintree Hispanic stories* series. Jose Marti was a poet, lawyer, journalist and revolutionary who worked for the freedom of Cuba. As a youth, one of his poems landed him in prison, and later in exile to Spain. Marti returned to Cuba again and again, finally leading a revolution in which he was killed. His words inspired others to continue the flght. Picture book format; indudes text in English and Spanish.

Juan Peron. John DeChancie. Chelsea House, 1987. LC 86-31749, 112 p. (ISBN 087754-548-0) Grades 5 up.

Part of the *Worid leaders past and present series.* Juan Peron, President of Argentina from 1946 to 1955, was the nation's first popularly chosen leader. Peron tried to win the military's complete support, and put down several revolts by officers trying to gain control. His charismatic personality attracted the people, but he was unable to unify the country behind his economic programs.

Juan Seguin: a hero of the Texas Revolution. Rita Kerr. Sunbelt Media, 1985. 64 p. (ISBN 0-89015-502-X) Grades 5-8.

Juan Seguin grew up on a hacienda near San Antonio as part of a well-respected family involved in their community. As a young man he did not like Santa Anna, the general who became president of Mexico. He supported the Americans and fought beside them to help Texas become independent. Reads like a work of fiction.

Junipero Serra. Jan Gleiter; Kathleen Thompson; Charles Shaw, illus. Raintree Steck-Vaughn, 1988. LC 88-39173, 32 p. (ISBN plb 0-8172-29094); (ISBN pbk 0-8114 676 1) Grades 3-6.

Part of the *Raintree Hispanic stories* series. Serra was a bright student and devout Catholic. He traveled into Califomia where he founded several missions, and ran them efficiently. His leadership inspired many to settle in California. Picture book format; indudes text in English and Spanish.

Luis Munoz Marin. Abbott Chrisman; Dennis Matz, illus. Raintree Steck-Vaughn, 1988. LC 88-38062, 32 p. (ISBN plb 0-8172-2907-8) Grades 3-6.

Part of the *Raintree Hispanic stories* series. Marin advocated reforms in Puerto Rico at a time when living conditions kept growing worse. He campaigned tirelessly to become the Puerto Rican representative in Congress, and was able to obtain some help for the country. Marin became govemor and worked for economic improvement. Although he later resigned because of illness, his vision remains. Picture book format; includes text in English and Spanish.

Luis W. Alvarez. Corinn Codye; Bob Masheris, illus. Raintree Steck-Vaughn, 1990. LC 89-38768, 32 p. (ISBN plb 0-8172-3376-8; pbk 0-8114-6750-3) Grades 2-6.

Part of the *Raintree Hispanic stories* series. Alvarez contributed to the development of the atomic bomb and a radar system used in fighter planes. Alvarez received the Nobel prize in physics for isolating parts of the atom. He and his son formulated the theory that dinosaur extinction was due to a tremendous meteor explosion. Picture book format; includes text in Spanish and English.

Martin Sheen: actor and activist. Jim Hargrove. Children's Press, 1991. LC 91-7793, 152 p. (ISBN 0-516-032747; ISBN pbk 0-516-432745) Grades 4 up.

Part of the *People of distinction* series. Ramon Estevez, whose stage name is Martin

Sheen, realized that applying for acting jobs under his real name meant he would only be considered for Hispanic roles. Now Sheen uses his recognition to advance causes that he feels will save and improve people's lives, such as banning nuclear weapons and improving environmental safety.

Oscar Arias: peacemaker and leader among nations. Kelli Peduzzi Ronnie Cummins. Gareth Stevens, 1991. LC 90-39917, 64 p. (ISBN 0-8368-0102-4) Grades 5-6

Part of the *People who have helped the world* series. Oscar Arias won the Nobel Peace Prize in 1987 for bringing the leaders of Central American nations together with his peace plan. He was elected president of his homeland, Costa Rica, in 1986. Background information is organized into fact boxes and sidebars; includes photographs and drawings.

Pablo Casals: cellist of conscience. Jim Hargrove. Children's Press, 1991. LC 9021047, 128 p. (ISBN 0-516-03272-0;) Grades 4-6.

Part of the *People of distinction* sefies. Casals grew up in a musical family and knew several instruments before he ever saw a cello. When he finally heard one, he knew he had to play it. His parents made sure that he received excellent instruction, and Casals began performing very early to supplement the small family coffers. His fame grew, but his nation, Spain, was overcome by fascism. Casals refused to perform there until the govemment was removed. He also would not play in any country that started a war or condoned it. Includes a portrait of him.

Pedro Menendez de Aviles. Kathleen Thompson; Charles Shaw, illus. Raintree Steck-Vaughn, 1990. LC 89-38081, 32 p. (ISBN plb 0-8172-3383-0) Grades 3-6.

Part of the *Raintree Hispanic stories* series. De Aviles started his rough life as an adventurer very young. After he eamed a reputation as a cruel sea captain, the Spanish king sent him to America. De Aviles helped drive the French out of Florida and claim it for Spain. Picture book fommat; includes text in Spanish and English.

Pele: the king of soccer. Caroline Amold. Watts, 1992. LC 91-33557, 64 p. (ISBN 0531-20077-9) Grades 3-6.

Part of the *First book* series. Pele's father, who played soccer for a minor league soccer team, recognized athletic potential early in his young son. He was a major league player in Brazil, but achieved more world renown when he played for the Cosmos. Pele helped professional soccer become popular in the United States. Easy text format; includes photographs.

Picture book of Simon Bolivar. David Adler; Robert Casilla, illus. Holiday House, 1992. LC 91-19419, 32 p. (ISBN 0-8234-0927-9) Grades ps-3.

An easy read aloud book about the man known as El Lebertador, (The Liberator). Bolivars eccentric past and the influences on him are examined to show how he decided that South America needed its independence from Spain. Includes paintings.

Pride of Puerto Rico: the life of Roberto Clemente. Paul Robert Walker. Harcourt, 1991. LC 90-45521, 132 p. (ISBN pbk 0-15-200562-5) Grades 4-6.

Roberto Clemente played great baseball in the barrios of Puerto Rico and the major leagues of the U.S. Clemente had 3,000 hits before he was killed trying to bring aid to earthquake victims in Nicaragua.

Queen Isabella the first. Corinn Codye; Rick Whipple, illus. Raintree Steck-Vaughn, 1990. LC 89-38080, 32 p. (ISBN plb 0-8172-3380-6; pbk 0-8114-6758-9) Grades 3-6.

Part of the *Raintree Hispanic stories* series. Isabella had a dream of a unified Spain. Ferdinand commanded the army, and Isabella traveled to gain support from the people. Isabella and Ferdinand also wanted a strong church and local militia. They decreed laws encouraging business, and decided to help Columbus in order to bring in more riches. Picture book format; includes text in Spanish and English.

Roberto Clemente. Tom Gilbert. Chelsea House, 1991. LC 90-44690, 112 p. (ISBN 0-7910-1240-9) Grades 5 up.

Part of the *Hispanics of achievement series.* Growing up in a poor laborer's home in Puerto Rico, Roberto Clemente was a respecfful youngster who leamed the value of hard work earty. He fell in love with baseball and spent every moment possible playing. In high school he signed with a professional team in San Juan and went on to a brilliant career in the United States. Clemente was the first Hispanic admitted to the Hall of Fame. He was killed in a plane crash while attempting to take supplies to earthquake victims in Nicaragua.

Simon Bolivar. Jan Gleiter; Kathleen Thompson; Tom Redman, illus. Raintree Steck-Vaughn, 1988. LC 88-38060, 32 p. (ISBN plb 0-8172-2902-7; pbk 0-684-28500-6) Grades 3-5.

Part of the *Raintree Hispanic* stories series. Simon Bolivar was of Spanish descent and lived in Venezuela. After trips to France, he became inspired by the example of Napoleon Bonaparte, and longed to free his country from Spanish dictators. After many military heroics he achieved a short-lived victory. Bolivar was forced to flee civil war but succeeded in introducing the concept of liberation. Picture book format; includes text in Spanish and English.

Simon Bolivar: Latin Amencan liberator. Frank de Varona. Millbrook, 1993. LC 9219459, 32 p. (ISBN 1-56294278-6; pbk 1-56294812-1) Grades 2-5.

Part of the *Hispanic heritage* series. Inspired by his teacher and ideals of democracy, Simon Bolivar dedicated his life to leading Venezuela to self-rule to end centuries of Spanish domination. As a Venezuelan native, he was unable to hold a position with the Spanish government. While traveling in Europe, Bolivar decided that a revolution, such as the ones which occurred in America and France, was the best solution. Easy to read format; includes drawings.

Simon Bolivar: South American liberator. Carol Greene. Children's Press. 1989. LC 89-34663, 116 p. (ISBN 0-516-03267-4) Grades 4 up.

Part of the *People of distinction* series. Fired with the revolutionary spirit that he saw in France, Simon Bolivar was determined to free his country from Spanish tyranny. His revolution swept across the South American continent. Bolivar wrote a constitution for some of the nations he helped to liberate, and fought unsuccessfully for a united South America. Includes his protrait.

Sor Juana Ines De La Cruz. Kathleen Thompson; Rick Karpinski, illus. Raintree Steck-Vaughn, 1990. LC 89-38767, 32 p. (ISBN plb 0-8172-3377-6; pbk 0-8114-6752-X) Grades 2-6.

Part of the *Raintree Hispanic stories* series. Juana loved leaming. Even from early childhood she pursued education with a passion. A series of misfortunes left her in Mexico City, where the Viceroy's wife asked her to be an attendant. At the court Juana was asked to demonstrate her intellectual abilities. She became a nun and spent most of her life reading, writing, and studying. Juana's poetry was well-known, but she became a political pawn in an archbishop's rise to power. Picture book format; includes text in Spanish and English.

Summer life. Gary Soto. University Press of New England, 1990. LC 89-40614, 127 p. (ISBN 0-87451-523-8); Dell, 1991. (ISBN 0-440-21024-0) Grades 4 up.

Gary Soto presents his autobiography in short poetic vignettes that recreate his childhood experiences, and the sights, sounds, and smells that relate to each memory. A rich view of Hispanic family life in 1950s Califomia.

Vilma Martinez Corinn Codye; Susi Kilgore, illus. Raintree Steck-Vaughn, 1990. LC 89-38766, 32 p. (ISBN 0-8172-3382-2; ISBN pbk 0-8114-6762-7) Grades 3-6.

Part of the *Raintree Hispanic stories* series. Vilma Martinez became a lawyer at a time when Hispanic men were limited to menial jobs and women were expected to stay home and have children. Determined to improve life for Hispanics, she fought and won many civil rights cases, in private practice and as head of the Mexican-American Legal Defense and Education Fund. Picture book format; includes text in Spanish and English.

Folklore

All of you was singing. Richard Lewis; Ed Young, illus. Macmillan, 1991. LC 89-18263, 32 p. (ISBN 0-689-31596-1; pbk 0-689-71853-5) Grades K-3.

A poetical version of an Aztec myth explaining creation and the beginnings of music. The poem captures the Aztec idea of being alive in each part of nature.

Atariba and Niguayona. Harriet Rohmer; Jesus Guerrero Rea; Consuelo Castillo, illus. Children's Book Press, 1988. LC 76-17495, 24 p., (ISBN 0-89239-026-3) Grades 2-6.

Part of the *Tales of the Americas* series. Based on a Taino Indian legend. Niguayona sees that his dear friend Atariba is dying. A macaw tells him of a cure from the fruit of the ciamoni tree. Niguayona is determined to find this fruit. He searches diligently, and is finally aided by the *anona* lights. He listens to nature around him and saves his friend. In English and Spanish.

Blacksmith and the devils. Maria Cristina Brusca and Tona Wilson. Henry Holt, 1992. LC 92-176, 40 p. (ISBN 0-8050-1954-5) Grades 1-4.

An Argentinian folktale about a blacksmith who is granted three wishes and picks foolish ones. Then he makes a deal with the devil for twenty years of life and a bag of gold. When time is up, his foolish wishes keep him out of the devil's clutches, but also exclude him from heaven. So the spirit of the blacksmith wanders on the pampas.

Borreguita and the coyote. Vema Aardema; Petra Mathers, illus. Knopf, 1991. LC 9039419, 40 p. (IS8N 0-679-80921-X; plb 0-679-909214) Grades ps-3.

In this Mexican folk tale a little lamb tricks a coyote to again and again keep him from eating her until he finally leaves her alone.

Boy who could do anything: and other Mexican folk tales. Anita Brenner; Jean Charlot, illus. Shoestring, 1992. LC 92-3903, 128 p. (ISBN 0-208-02353-4) Grades 3-6.

Anita Brenner and Jean Charlot were two activists who were instrumental in the artistic rebirth of Mexico after the revolution. They collected a series of tales from a storyteller named Luz in a small Indian village. This work includes legends of Tepozton, a boy who could do anything. There are three kinds: stories of everyday life; stories from long ago; and stories of magic.

Brother Anansi and the cattle ranch. James De Sauza; Stephen Von Mason, illus. Children's Book Press, 1989. LC 88-37091, 32 p. (ISBN 0-89239-0441; book and cassette 0-89239-063-8) Grades ps-7.

Part of the *Tales of the Americas* series. The Anansi character from African folklore has found its way to Nicaragua with a modem twist. After Brother Tiger wins the lottery Anansi talks him into going into the ranching business. They buy a herd of cattle, and after a few years Anansi finds a way to trick Brother Tiger out of all his cows. In English and Spanish.

Chancay and the secret of fire: a Peruvian folk tale. Donald Charles. Putnam, 1992. LC 91-16629, 32 p. (ISBN 0-399-22129-8) Grades ps-3.

Chancay performs an act of kindness by releasing a beautiful fish that he caught. In return the fish offers Chancay a favor. All he wants is a way to ease the suffering of his people. The fish says he needs fire. Chancay must pass difficult tests to prove himself. He finally captures the sun's mirror, that enables him to start a fire any time he needs one.

Coyote rings the wrong bell: a Mexican folktale. Francisco Mora. Children's Press, 1991. LC 91-13163, 24 p. (ISBN 0-516-05136-9; pbk 0-51645136-7) Grades ps-3.

Part of the *Adventures in storytelling* series. The text is printed after the illustrations to let readers try their own storytelling. This tale involves a hungry coyote who captures a rabbit. The rabbit is able to escape by telling the coyote that a nearby bell will summon young school bunnies, but it only attracts hornets.

Dark Way: stories from the spirit world. Virginia Hamilton; Lambert Davis, illus. Harcourt, 1990. LC 90-36251, 154 p. (ISBN 0-15-222340-1) Grades 3 up.

A collection of scary tales is related to strange or supernatural phenomena. They represent cultures around the world. A story with a Hispanic background is *The pretender*.

Dwarf-wizard of Uxmal. Susan Hand Shetterly; Robert SheKerly, illus. Macmillan, 1990. LC 89-32864, 32 p. (ISBN 0-689-31445-8) Grades K-3.

Based on a Yucatan Mayan legend. Tol was hatched from an egg because an old woman prayed over it and a snake kept it warm. When Tol was bom, he was very small and afraid of normal sized people. The old woman said he was destined to be a nuler and should challenge the governor. By carrying out a series of challenges, Tol fulflls the prophecy with the aid of the old woman and some animal friends.

Flame of Peace: a tale of the Aztecs. Deborah N. Lattimore. HarperCollins, 1987. LC 86-26934, 48 p. (ISBN plb 0-06-23709-0; pbk 0-06-443272-6) Grades K-3.

Two Flint knew when his father did not return from a diplomatic mission to a neighbonng tribe that war was about to break out. He decides to search for Lord Monning Star, the god of peace. First he had to battle nine evil demons with only his wits. Lord Moming Star was impressed with his valiant stnuggle and rewarded him with a new Fire of Peace.

How the animals got their colors. Marcia Rosen; John Clementson, illus. Harcourt, 1992. LC 91-30113, 48 p. (ISBN 0-15-236783-7) Grades 2-5.

This collection of myths explain how a variety of animals got their colors according to the people who live near them. The Ayoreo in South America recount how the sun god gave all the animals their colors.

How the birds changed their feathers. Joanna Troughton. Bedrick, 1986. LC 861251, 32 p. (ISBN 0-87226-080-1) Grades K-3.

Part of the *Folk tales of the world* series. In this South American folk tale, all the birds were white. A cruel young boy found some brightly colored rocks, and when he strung them around his neck became a rainbow snake that preyed on everyone. The cormorant was the only animal brave enough to bite the snake, and asked for the skin as his reward. It was too big for him to carry, but all the birds helped. Wherever a bird touched the skin, it turned into that color.

How we came to the fifth world. Harriet Rohmer; Mary Anchondes, Graciela Carrillo, illus. Children's Book Press, 1988. LC76-7240, 24 p. (ISBN 0-89239-0247) Grades 2-6

Part of the *Tales of the Americas* series. Based on an Aztec legend. When each world becomes corrupt, the gods find the last good couple and save them, while destroying everyone else. Each world was ruled and ultimately destroyed by a god representing one of the four elements—Water, Air, Fire, and Earth. We are in the fifth world, and are doomed unless we can rid our hearts of evil. In English and Spanish.

Invisible hunters: los cazadores invisibles. Harriet Rohmer, Octavio Chow; Morris Vidaure; Joe Sam, illus. Children's Book Press, 1987. LC 86-32658,32 p. (ISBN 089239-031-X; pbk 0-892390109-X; book and cassette 0-89239-036-0) Grades 2-6.

In this Nicaraguan folk tale, three hunters discover a magic that makes them invisible and capable of good hunting. However, when accepting the magic, they agree that they will never sell the meat or kill animals with guns. Then traders arrive and manipulate the hunters into doing the very things they said they would not do. As a result, the hunters become permanently invisible.

Legend of El Dorado: a Latin American tale. Nancy Van Laan, adapter; Beatriz Vidal. Knopf, 1991. LC 89-7998, 40 p. (ISBN 0-679-80136; plb 0-679-90136-1)Grades ps-4.

El Dorado, a gold treasure, lured many Spaniards to search, even to kill, to obtain riches. Here is one version: A king once lived in a palace by a lake. A serpent who lived there lured his beloved wife and child into the water with him. After the serpent promised they would be reunited, the king had a ceremony every year. He was covered with gold dust, offered treasures, and then himself to the serpent. Finally the king joined his family. The new king repeats the ceremony so that the serpent will keep the kingdom safe.

Legend of Food Mountain. Harriet Rohmer; Graciela Carrillo, illus. Children's Book Press, 1982. LC81-7163424, 32 p. (ISBN 0-89239-022-0) Grades K-8.

Based on an Aztec legend. The gods do not know what the newly formed humans eat. A little ant shows the god Quetzalcoatl the inside of Food Mountain. They open it with lightning, letting the humans eat and leaving the mountain unguarded. The rain dwarfs steal all the food, and that's why Humans still ask the rains to return and help the crops to grow.

Legend of the two moons. Francisco X. Mora. Highsmith, 1993. LC 92-31552, 32 p. (ISBN 0-91784615-X)Grades ps-K.

Based on a Mexican folktale. Chucho, Felipe's dog, and a little green parrot notice two moons shining in the night sky. Parrot decides that he must have one of them. He loosens one, but the moon is so heavy that both of them fall into the lake. Just as the friends despair, they notice that the fallen moon is now shining in the lake.

Magic dogs of the volcanoes. Manlio Argueta; Elly Simmons, illus.; Sbcey Ross, trans. Children's Book Press, 1990. LC 90-2254, 32 p. (ISBN 0-89239-0646) Grades K-5.

Based on a Salvadorian legend. Magic dogs protected the villagers from harm. Don

Tonio and his brothers owned the land and did not like the dogs helping the peasants, so they sent soldiers to find them. The soldiers destroyed their food, and the dogs were in danger. They called on the volcanoes for help. The volcanoes melted the soldiers, and Don Tonio never bothered the people again. In English and Spanish.

Moon rope: a Peruvian folktale. Lois Ehlert. Harcourt, 1992. LC 91-36438, 32 p., (ISBN 0-15-255343-6) Grades ps-3.

Fox wants to go to the moon and convinces Mole to go with him. They braid grass into a very long rope, and convince the birds to carry the end of it to the point of the crescent. The trip was a disaster for Mole, and now he hides in shame in a deep tunnel. But Fox? On a clear night during the full moon, he looks down at earth. The collage illustrations are based on ancient Peruvian designs. In Spanish and English.

Moon was tired of walking on air: origin myths of South American Indians. Natalia Belting; Will Hillenbrand, illus. Houghton Mifflin, 1992. LC 91-20946, 48 p. (ISBN 0-395-53806-8) Grades 4-7.

This collection contains creation myths from the tribes of South America. As they settled in different parts of the continent, the tribes wondered how the earth began. Included is *Daughter of tain; why rainbow is bent; When Orekeke wrestled tornado; Fox and the parakeet woman; World above, worlds below; How birds got new beaks;* and *Men got teeth.* Preview before recommending.

Mother Scorpion country. Harriet Rohmer; Dorminster Wilson. Children's Book Press, 1987. LC 86-32649, 32 p. (ISBN 0-89239-032-8; book and cassette 0-89239-037-9) Grades 2-7.

Part of the *Stories from Central America* series. This Nicaraguan tale features a young couple who love each other very much. When Kati, the young wife, dies, her husband Naklili follows her to the land of the spirits. He cannot share paradise with her as a living being, so he returns to the land of the living until he can join her in death. In Spanish and English.

The mythology of Mexico and Central America. John Bierhorst. Morrow, 1990. LC 90-5879, 256 p. (ISBN 0-688-06721-2; pbk 0-688-11280 3) Grades 7 up.

This is a valuable study of a people through their prehistory. Indian stories have been preserved by a variety of means—written and oral. The tales of different cultures are compared and similarities are apparent. Origins are traced and specific tales are presented. Useful for storytelling.

Papagayo: the mischief maker. Gerald McDermott. Harcourt, 1992.
LC 91-40364, 40 p. (ISBN 0-15-259465-5; pbk 0-15-2594647) Grades ps-3.

Papagayo the parrot is a noisy trouble maker in the Amazon jungle. He squawks to tease the other animals, especially the day-sleeping animals with night habits. Those are the ones who observe the moon-dog eating the moon and worry about how to stop him. Papagayo helps them chase the moon-dog away before it eats all of the moon.

Pancho's pinata. Stefan Czernecki; Timothy Rhodes. Hypefion, 1992.
LC 92-7325, 32 p. (ISBN 1-56282-277-2; plb 1-56282-278-0) Grades K-4.

When Pancho was still a little boy, he led the Christmas posada in his Mexican village. He dressed as an angel and sang so sweetly that a star came down to hear him. Pancho helped the star escape when it became caught on a cactus. It then showered the boy with stardust. When Pancho was an old man he wanted to share some of his happiness. He made a pinata that looked like a star. When broken, it showered happiness on the children.

Rain player. David Wisiniewski. Houghton Mifflin. 1991. LC 90-44101, 32 p.
(ISBN 0395-55112-9) Grades K-4.

An ancient Mayan village is doomed to a terrible drought until Pik challenges the rain god to a game of pok-a-tok. He gets help from the jaguar, the quetzal, (a brightly feathered bird), and the cenote, (a great natural well of water); because all of them depend on the rain for survival. Illustrations are intricate paper cut-outs.

Rooster who went to his uncle's wedding: a Latin American folktale.
Alma Flor Ada; Kathleen Kuchera, illus. Putnam, 1992. LC 92-14087, 32 p.
(ISBN 0-399-22412-2) Grades ps-3

Rooster was in such a hurry to get ready for his uncle's wedding that he forgot breakfast. On his way, he became very hungry and saw a single kernel of corn in a mud puddle that was irresistible. But he got his beak was dirty and no one would help him clean if off until the sun offered his help.

Sleeping bread. Stefan Czernecki; Timothy Rhodes. Hyperion, 1993. LC 91-75422, 40 p. (ISBN 1-56282-183-0; plb 1-56282-207-1; pbk 1-56282-5194) Grades K-4.

Beto's bread delighted everyone in his small Guatemalan village, but he always saved a little for a beggar named Zafiro. As the village prepared for a festival, they wanted Zafiro to leave because he embarrassed them. When he left, Beto's bread no longer rose. After many attempts to make it rise, Beto brought Zafiro back. Together they figured out how to make the bread rise once again.

Song of the chirimia: a Guatemalan folktale. Jane Anne Volkmer. Carolrhoda, 1992. LC 90-2069, 40 p. (ISBN 0-87614423-7; pbk 0-87614592-6) Grades ps-3.

Once a Mayan king had a daughter whom he loved very much because she had a sparkle in her eyes. One day she became quite unhappy. The king's advisors suggested marriage as a cure. All the eligible bachelors brought her gifts, but the king said 'whoever makes my daughter laugh shall marry her.' A simple young man who learned to play a bird-like flute song won her heart. In English and Spanish.

South and north, east and west: the Oxfam book of children's stories. Michael Rosen, editor. Candlewick, 1992. LC 91-58749, 96 p. (ISBN 1-56402-117-3) Grades ps-3.

Oxfam is a British organization whose fund raising operations send aid and education to poverty ridden areas of the world. Some of the stories in this collection were first heard by Oxfam staff working in the countries represented. South American stories include: *Beginning of history* (Brazilian Indian); *Pedro and his dog* (Bolivia); and *Little green frog* (Dominican Republic).

Thunder king: a Peruvian folktale. Amanda Loveseed. Bedrick, 1991. LC 90-14416, 32 p. (ISBN 0-87226 450-5) Grades K-3.

Part of the *Folk tales of the world* series. Twin brothers Illanti and Tantay take special care of each other. When Tantay is captured by the Thunder King, Illanti is determined to rescue him from the King's icy castle. He receives help from a llama and a condor, and the twins are able to get home for supper.

Tiger and the rabbit: a Puerto Rican folktale. Francisco X. Mora. Children's Press, 1991. LC 91-3500, 32 p. (ISBN 0-516-05137-7; pbk 0-51645137-5) Grades ps-3.

Part of the *Adventures in storytelling* series. The text is printed after the illustrations to let readers try their own storytelling. This tale involves a trickster rabbit. He outsmarts Senor Tiger, first to save his own life, but then just for fun. Finally Rabbit rides Senor Tiger with a saddle .

Twenty-five Mixtec cats. Matthew Gollob; Leovigildo Martinez, illus. Tambourine, 1993. LC 92-13585, 32 p., (ISBN 0-688-11639-6; plb 0-688-11640-X) Grades 1-4.

A story based on Oaxaca tradition. A healer brings home twenty-five kittens after shopping in a neighboring town. Until he brought them there were no cats in his village. The townspeople feared the cats until they helped to save the butcher and the healer from an evil spell.

Uncle Nacho's hat. Harriet Rohmer; Veg Reisberg, illus. Children's Book Press, 1989. LC 88-37090, 32 p., (ISBN 0-89239-043-3) Ages 3-8.

Based on a Nicaraguan folktale. Uncle Nacho is unhappy with his worn out hat. When his niece Ambrosia gives him a new one he worries about what to do with his old hat. No matter how hard he tries to get rid of it, the hat keeps coming back to him. Then Ambrosia suggests that he is thinking about it too much—he should think of his new one. So Uncle Nacho goes out to show it off. In Spanish and English.

Why there is no arguirg in heaven: a Mayan myth. Deborah Nourse Lattimore. Harper, 1989. LC 87-35045,32 p., (ISBN 0-06-023717-1; plb 0-06 023718-X) Grades 1-5.

An argument between Lizard House and the Moon Goddess over who was the greatest god prompted Hunab Ku, the first Creator God, to prove his greatness by creating the earth. Hunab Ku then challenged them to create a being to worship him. Lizard House and Moon Goddess tried to do this, but could not. Maize God watched everything, and then created a strong race of people who work hard and sing beautiful songs. Maize God now sits beside Hunab Ku.

Woman who outshone the sun: the legend of Lucia Zenteno. Alejandro Cruz Martinez; Femando Olivera, illus.; Rosalma Zubizarreta, trans. Children's Book Press, 1991. LC 91-16646, 32 p., (ISBN 0-89239-1014) Grades K-3.

This Zapotec legend tells about a beautiful, magical woman named Lucia Zenteno. Some welcomed Lucia to their village, but others were frightened by the things she was able to do. Unhappy about the villagers' suspicions, she leaves. The river goes too because it loves her. The people suffer—only then do they apologize. She convinces them to be kind.

Fiction for Younger Readers
Picture books

Abuela. Arthur Dorros; Elisa Kleven, illus. Dutton, 1991. LC 90-21459, 40 p. (ISBN 0-525-44750-4) Grades ps-2.

When Rosalba is on an outing with her abuela (her grandmother), she imagines that the two of them can fly. They see all of New York City and visit all their Puerto Rican friends and relatives. At last they enjoy the adventure they usually have: a beautiful day in the park.

Abuela's weave. Omar S. Castaneda; Enrique O. Sanchez, illus. Lee and Low, 1993. LC 92-71927, 32 p. (ISBN 1-880000-00-8) Grades K-3.

Esperanza loves to help her grandmother with her weaving. Grandmother worries that her traditional Guatemalan hand weaving cannot compete with machine made items, especially when people are so put off by the birthmark on her face that they will not buy. After preparing many woven pieces, Esperanza and her grandmother travel to the market, but are not seen together. Esperanza sets up the booth and sells all the merchandise.

Abuelita's paradise. Carmen Santiago Nodar; Diane Paterson, illus. Whitman, 1992. LC 91-42330, 32 p. (ISBN 0-8075-0129-8); Reading Adventures, 1993. (ISBN 0-685-66422-8; bk + cassette 1-882869-79-6) Grades K-3.

Marita loved to sit with her grandmother in her rocking chair and listen to stories of her childhood in Puerto Rico. Grandmother's stories were very real for Marita. Grandmother has died but Marita still sits in the rocking chair. When she sits with her mother, they remember the stories and grandmother's special love.

Adventures of Connie and Diego. Maria Garcia; Malaquias Montoya, illus.; Alma Flor Ada, trans. Children's Book Press, 1987. LC 86-17132, 32 p. (ISBN 0-89239-028-X; bk + cassette 0-89239-033-6; cassette 0-89239-051-4) Grades 2-9.

Part of the *Fifth world tales* series. In this original story told as a Mexican folk tale, Connie and Diego are twins who are born with many colors across their bodies. Everyone laughs at them, so they begin wandering, looking for a place just for them. Their travels make them realize that they are humans, and belong with humans. They return, content in their new found self-acceptance. In English and Spanish.

Amazon boy. Ted Lewin. Macmillan, 1993. LC 92-15798, 32 p. (ISBN 0-02-757383-4) Grades K-3.

Paulo's father has always promised to take him into the great city near the mouth of the Amazon for his birthday. He is very excited as the boat steams down the river. At the market they see amazing varieties of fish. Paulo notices that his father is sad because there used to be much larger fish in the river. He fears that some day the fish will be gone. The next time Paulo fishes, he catches a big fish—and lets it go.

Amelia's road. Linda Jacobs Altman; Enrique O. Sanchez, illus. Lee and Low, 1993. LC 92-59982, 32 p. (ISBN 1-880000-04-0) Grades K-3.

Amelia is tired of all the moving around that her migrant family has to do. Her parents remember her birth date by the crops they were picking when she was born.

Amelia's last teacher did not even bother to learn her name. Fortunately her new teacher does. With her encouragement, Amelia draws a picture of her dearest dream, a home. She finds a path through the field and pretends she is going to that home. Amelia stores her precious dreams in a metal box and buries it under a tree on her path, calling that her permanent home.

And Sunday makes seven. Robert Baden; Michelle Edwards, illus. Whitman, 1990. LC 89-37823, 40 p. (ISBN 0-8075-0356-8) Grades ps-3.

Carlos was poor but kind. His cousin Ricardo was rich but selfish. Carlos worked all day and found himself in the forest at nightfall. He came to a house of witches and listened to their song. Carlos could not help himself—the perfect rhyme came into his head and he added it to their song. The witches were delighted and rewarded him. Ricardo was so jealous that he demanded the same chance.

Armando asked, "Why?" Jay Hulbert; Sid Kantor; Pat Hoggan, illus. Raintree Steck-Vaughn, 1990. LC 90-8021, 24 p. (ISBN 0-8172-3576-0; set of 3 pbks 0-685-58548-4) Ages 3-8.

A Ready, set, read book. Everyone in Armando's family is too busy to answer his questions. Mami has an idea. They take a trip to the library. The librarian helps him find books that will answer his questions.

Bicycle for Rosaura. Daniel Barbot; Morella Fuenmayor, illus. Kane/Miller, 1991. LC 90-47215, 24 p. (ISBN 0-916291-34-0) Grades ps-3.

Rosaura wants a bicycle for her birthday—but she is a hen. Senora Amelia is surprised but decides to look around for a hen-sized bicycle. She nearly gives up when a peddler comes around with all sorts of strange things. He says all he needs are some measurements to make a bicycle for Rosaura. What a nice birthday surprise—except the peddlar forgot the brakes!

Birthday basket for Tia. Pat Mora; Cecily Lang, illus. Macmillan, 1992. LC 91-15753, 32 p. (ISBN 0-02-767400-2); Reading Adventures, 1993. (ISBN 0-685-64816-8; cassette 1-882869-78-8) Grades ps-1.

Cecilia wants to give her great aunt Tia a special present because they love each other very much. She collects things that remind her of their special times: their favorite book, a cup for the mint tea her aunt makes, and the red ball they throw back and forth. She puts these things in a basket and gives it to her at a surprise party. The cat who is their constant companion also surprises Tia and Cecilia.

Chair for my mother. Vera B. Williams. Greenwillow, 1982. LC 81-7010. 32 p.
(ISBN 0-688-00914-X; plb. 0-688-00915-8; pbk 0-688-08400-1; big book 0-688-
12612-X; Spanish 0-688-13200-6) Grades K-3.

All the coins that Rosa's family saves go into a big jar. Finally it is full. They have
been saving for a big comfortable chair. The family has no sofa or easy chair
because all their things were burned in a fire. They were able to put their lives back
together with their relatives', friends' and neighbors' help. Now they can get a big
chair for themselves.

Dancer. Fred Burstein; Joan Auclair, illus. Macmillan, 1993. LC 91-41429, 40 p.
(ISBN 0-02-715625-7) Grades ps-3.

A young Japanese-American girl and her father walk through their neighborhood to
her dance class. Along the way, they identify everyday things in Spanish, English,
and Japanese. Includes phonetic spellings to try pronounciations.

Desert mermaid. Alberto Blanco; Patricia Revah, illus.; Barbara Paschke, trans.
Children's Book Press, 1992. LC 92-1105, 32 p. (ISBN 0-89239-106-5) Grades K-5.

A mermaid lives in a Sonora, Mexico desert oasis. She does not know that she is the
last oasis mermaid. She goes on a quest to learn ancestral songs in order to save herself. Once she has learned the music, the words, and the accompaniment, she follows
her heart to the sea, where she finds hundreds like her. This original story is old in a
folk tale style and illustrated by tapestry photographs. In English and Spanish.

Esteban and the ghost. Sibyl Hancock; Dirk Zimmer, illus. Dial, 1983.
LC 82-22125, 32 p. (ISBN 0-8037-2443-8; plb 0-8037-2411-X;
pbk 0-8037-0230-2) Grades ps-3.

Once there was a castle in Toledo, Spain that was haunted. A merry tinker named
Esteban decides to spend All Hallows Eve there to see for himself. He meets the
ghost and agrees to help him get to heaven by finding his money.

Family pictures. Carmen Lomas Garcia. Children's Book Press, 1990.
LC 89-27845, 32 p. (ISBN 0-89239-050-6; pbk 0-89239-108-1) Grades 1-7.

In Spanish and English, Carmen Lomas describes the background of her paintings.
Her childhood in Kingsville, Texas inspired these portraits of Mexican-American
life.

Fiesta! Beatriz McConnie Zapater; Jose Ortega, illus. Simon & Schuster, 1993. 32
p. (ISBN pbk 0-671-79842-1) Grades 2-5.

Chucho and his family are very excited. They are going to a fiesta in America that is like the ones they celebrated in their former home in Columbia. The family spends the week making costumes. Papi surprises them with a brightly painted cow mask. He is on a team that will climb the greased pole to win the prize money at the top. He can almost reach it. Chucho helps by climbing on Papi's shoulders. If they win the prize money they may be able to visit Columbia.

Friends from the other side = Amigos del otro lado. Gloria Anzaldua; Consuelo Mendez, illus. Children's Book Press, 1993. LC 92-34384, 32 p. (ISBN 0-89239-113-8) Grades 2-7.

Prietita has seen Joaquin when he delivered some firewood to her house, but their friendship begins when she chases away some bullies who harass him. She walks him home to his makeshift shelter. Joaquin and his mother have come to the U.S. illegally and are trying desperately to make a new life. When the Border Patrol comes, Prietita seeks help for Joaquin and his mother.

Gilberto and the wind. Marie Hall Ets. Viking, 1963. LC 63-8527, 32 p. (ISBN plb 670-34025-1; pbk 0-14-050276-9) Grades ps-1.

Gilberto plays with the wind. Sometimes the wind is mischievous and takes away Gilberto's balloon and kite. Sometimes it is kind and sails his boat. Sometimes the wind is scary. And sometimes Gilberto wonders if it will come back to play.

Gold coin. Alma Flor Ada; Neil Waldman, illus. Bernice Randall, translator. Macmillan, 1991. LC 90-32806, 32 p. (ISBN 0-689-31633-X; pbk 0-689-71793-8) Grades K-3.

In Central America, Juan has been a thief for many years, traveling by night and rarely contacting other people. As he passes an old woman's hut, he sees that she has a gold coin. He is obsessed by the coin and follows her when she leaves her hut at night. He travels quite a distance, trading his labor for guides to find the old woman. Juan learns what a generous woman she is, and finally cannot bring himself to keep the coin when she gives it to him.

How many days to America: a Thanksgiving story. Eve Bunting; Beth Peck, illus. Houghton Mifflin, 1988. LC 88-2590, 32 p. (ISBN 0-89919-521-0; pbk 0-395-54777-6) Grades ps-3.

In the Caribbean, a family has to flee for their lives. They experience many hardships on the boat. They do not see land for many days and their food and water run low. The family is glad to be alive when they reach America, and the feast that is prepared for them is a true Thanksgiving celebration.

I want to go home. Alice McLerran; Jill Kastner, illus. Morrow, 1992.
LC 91-9599, 32 p. (ISBN 0-688-10144-5; plb 0-688-10145-3) Grades ps-3.

Marta is not happy about moving into her new house. Then they get a cat named
Sammy, and he does not like the new house either. Marta becomes worried about
Sammy because he hides from everyone and will not eat. Finally they become
friends, which makes the new house feel more like home.

Little painter of Sabana Grande. Patricia Maloney Markun; Robert Casilla,
illus. Macmillan, 1993. LC 91-35230, 32 p. (ISBN 0-02-762205-3) Grades ps-2.

Fernando has worked hard to make his own paints and get his brushes, but after all
that work, he still has no paper. He wants to paint very badly and is miserable.
Finally Fernando's parents agree to let him paint on their adobe house. He creates
beautiful pictures on the walls. When the neighbors see his art, they want him to
paint the sides of their houses, too. Soon their Panamaian village is transformed
into a beautiful art gallery.

Lorenzo the naughty parrot. Tony Johnston; Leo Politi, illus. Harcourt, 1992.
LC 91-8006, 32 p. (ISBN 0-15-249350-6) Grades K-3.

Lorenzo is a bright green parrot who loves his family in Mexico. He squawks to let
them know when company arrives, whether it is a birthday party or San Nicolas.
Lorenzo is very curious about family activities. This leads to his falling in the oil
when Papa changes it in the car and scratching the bricks that Papa makes for
Mama's new floor. Yet Lorenzo saves the day when Papa loses his wedding ring and
no one can find it.

Maya and the town that loved a tree. Kiki Suarez; Kathryn Shaw. Rizzoli,
1992. 32 p. (ISBN 0-8478-1563-3); Universe, 1993. (ISBN 0-87663-796-9) Grades
ps-3.

There once was a little Mexican town that grew into a city. The pollution was so
bad that all the trees died. It happened so gradually that the people forgot what
they were missing. Then one day Maya arrived with a healthy tree and made the
people promise to take care of it. They built a park in the middle of the city. When
the tree became too big, children took its fruit and planted trees all over town.

Music, music for everyone. Vera B. Williams. Greenwillow, 1984. LC 83-
14196, 32 p. (ISBN 0-688-02603-6; plb 0-688-02604-4; pbk 0-688-07811-7)
Grades K-3.

Sequel to **Something Special for Me**. Rosa returns after her family buys the big
chair and her accordion, but the big jar where they save all their coins remains

empty. Grandma is sick and all the money is used to take care of her. Rosa gets an idea for making money when her friends play their instruments. She forms a band and they arrange some new songs. They are thrilled when they get their first playing job.

Nine days to Christmas. Marie Hall Ets; Aurora Labastida. Viking, 1959. LC 59-16438, 48 p. (ISBN 0-670-51350-4; pbk 0-14-054442-9) Grades ps-3.

This classic story of a Mexican family's Christmas celebration of posadas is told from little Ceci's viewpoint. She can hardly wait for their Christmas party and keeps getting into trouble for trying to help. Ceci finally goes with her mother to pick out a pinata, but frets over the fact that her beautiful pinata will be broken at the posadas.

On a hot, hot day. Nicki Weiss. Putnam, 1992. LC 91-13234, 32 p. (ISBN 0-399-22119-0) Grades ps-1.

Mama and Angel share many special moments in all the seasons in their New York City neighborhood. They splash in the water on a hot day; they snuggle and read in the cold winter; and at the end of each day, Mama tucks Angel into bed.

On the pampas. Maria Cristina Brusca. Henry Holt, 1991. LC 90-40938, 40 p. (ISBN 0-8050-1548-5; pbk 0-8050-2919-2) Grades ps-2.

Maria reminisces about the summers she spent on her grandparents ranch in Argentina. She and her cousin Susanita spent their days riding horses and taking care of them. Their adventures included working the cattle, riding to the general store, and finding ostrich eggs. They celebrated grandmother's birthday, and most evenings they told stories. At the end of that summer Maria anxiously anticipated the next one. End pages show a map of South America and word definitions.

Pedro and the Padre: a tale from Jalisco, Mexico. Verna Aardema; Frisco Henstra, illus. Dial, 1991. LC 87-24476, 32 p. (ISBN 0-8037-0522-0; plb 0-8037-0523-9) Grades ps-3.

Pedro's father sends him to look for work, thinking that Pedro might get over his laziness if he worked for a stranger. The Padre is glad to get someone to help him until Pedro begins telling tall tales to cover up his laziness. His lies get him into many adventures, until some men want to throw him into the river. Pedro then promises never to tell another lie.

Something special for me. Vera B. Williams. Greenwillow, 1983. LC 82-11884, 32 p. (ISBN 0-688-01806-8; plb 0-688-01807-6; pbk 0-688-06526-0) Grades K-3.

Sequel to **Chair for my mother.** All the coins that Rosa's family save go into a big jar to buy her a special birthday present. When Rosa and her mother go downtown to shop for her it, she cannot decide what to get. Nothing is right until she sees a man playing an accordion and making everyone around him happy. Rosa wants to play one to make people happy.

Tamarindo puppy. Charlotte Pomerantz; Byron Barton, illus. Greenwillow, 1993. LC 79-16584, 32 p. (ISBN 0-688-11902-6; plb 0-688-11903-4; pbk 0-688-11514-4) Grades ps up.

These poems, in Spanish and English, reflect the way some people speak—a little Spanish to say one thing, a little English to say another. All the poems describe special times that loving families share: a mother-daughter good-bye, a trip to the bakery, a puppy sleeping on the bed, even four brothers and what they are doing now.

This home we have made = esta casa que hemos hecho. Anna Hammond and Joseph Mantunis; Olga Karman Mendell, trans. Crown, 1993. LC 92-28954, 24 p. (ISBN 0-517-59339-4) Grades ps-3.

A homeless child finds herself unable to sleep under the stairway with her mother and brother. She comes out and discovers a magical parade with brightly colored animals and musicians playing. She joins the parade and is rewarded with a home of her own where she and her family can lead a normal life. This story is the result of a mural painted by homeless children in the South Bronx. For them too the dream came true. In Spanish and English.

Three stalks of corn. Leo Politi. Macmillan, 1993. LC 75-35009, 32 p. (ISBN 0-684-19538-0; pbk 0-689-71782-2) Grades K-3.

Angelica and her grandmother live in Pico Rivera, California. Their family has roots in Mexico. Grandmother grows corn in her yard and tells Angelica stories about its significance for their people. Angelica's school principal asks Grandmother to teach the children how to cook tacos and enchiladas.

Tonight is carnaval. Arthur Dorros. Dutton, 1991. LC 90-32391, 32 p. (ISBN 0-525-44641-9) Grades K-3.

A Peruvian family anticipates a celebration. A young boy eagerly prepares for the festivities. As he does his chores, he practices the flute in order to play in a band with his father. The story is illustrated with photographs of hand-made wall hangings called arpilleras. This patchwork type of art tells stories of events from every-day - life. They occasionally have pockets to hold a written version in the quilt. A folk art treatment of life in the Andes mountains.

Treasure nap. Juanita Havill; Elivia Savadier, illus. Houghton Mifflin, 1992. LC 91-28700, 32 p. (ISBN 0-395-57817-5) Grades K-3.

One hot afternoon when it is too hot to sleep Alicia asks for a story. So Mama talks about her great-great grandmother Rita, and how she traveled into the Mexican mountains to her grandparents' house. Rita learned about birds and how to play the pito, a flute. When she left Grandfather gave her a flute, a bird cage, and a serape, which she kept. When Alicia wakes from her nap she wants to see these things stored away in the family chest, and play the pito.

Vejigante masquerader. Lulu Delacre. Scholastic, 1993. LC 92-15480, 40 p. (ISBN 0-590-45776-4) Grades K-3.

Ramon has worked hard to get a costume for Carnival. His family is poor and his mother does not have time to help, so Ramon sews a costume himself and saves money for a mask. He hopes to be accepted by the older boys by participating in pranks that are part of the celebration. In the process his costume is ripped. His mother comes up with a solution. A lively and colorful Puerto Rican story in Spanish and English.

Visit to Mexico. Mary Packard; Benrei Huang, illus. Western Publishing, 1992. LC 91-72928, 24 p. (ISBN 0-307-12665-X) Grades ps-3.

Juanito and his sister Lupita have the same birthday, but this year is different. Lupita will be fifteen and she celebrates her quince anos. Everyone is so busy preparing for Lupita's party that Juanito worries that no one will remember his. What he thought were preparations for Lupita's celebration are actually for his surprise party.

Wall. Eve Bunting; Ronald Himler, illus. Houghton Mifflin, 1990. LC 89-17429, 32 p. (ISBN 0-395-51588-2; pbk 0-395-62977-2) Grades ps-3.

The wall is the Vietnam Veterans Memorial in Washington, D.C. A boy and his father have come to find the name of the boy's grandfather, one of those killed in the war. People come to look, learn, or remember. Although the boy is proud that his grandfather is honored this way, he knows his family would much rather have Grandfather with them.

With my brother/Con mi hermano. Eileen Roe; Robert Casilla, illus. Macmillan, 1991. LC 90-33983, 32 p. (ISBN 0-02-777373-6) Grades ps-3.

When a young boy's brother is too busy to play, he remembers the things they did together, and dreams of the time when they can do them again. Text in Spanish and English.

Fiction for Older Readers

... and now Miguel. Joseph Krumgold; Jean Charlot, illus. HarperCollins, 1987. LC 53-8415, 245 p. (ISBN 0-690-09118-4; plb 0-690-04696-0; pbk 0-06-440143-X) Grades 5 up.

Miguel Chavez is twelve and anxious to prove that he is old enough to tend sheep at the family ranch in Taos, New Mexico. He tries very hard but something always goes wrong. When Miguel thinks he will never succeed, he finds a way to be a vital part of the family. Newbery winner.

Baseball in April: and other stories. Gary Soto. Harcourt, 1990. LC 89-36460, 111 p. (ISBN 0-15-205720-X; pbk 0-15-205721-8) Grades 3-7.

Each story in this collection is an everyday experience of a Mexican-American young person growing up in California and how his or her dream and desire become real.

Centerfield Ballhawk. Matt Christopher; Ellen Beier, illus. Little, Brown, 1992. LC 91-28989, 64 p. (ISBN 0-316-14079-1; pbk 0-316-14272-7) Grades 2-4.

An easy-to-read chapter book about Jose Mendez, a boy who loves baseball. He hopes to win his father's affection by playing well. First he breaks a neighbor's window and is not allowed to practice. Then his best bat breaks. When his sister hits better than he does, Jose feels miserable. In the end, Jose learns to appreciate his own abilities.

Class president. Johanna Hurwitz; Sheila Hamanaka, illus. Morrow, 1990. LC 89-28600, 96 p. (ISBN 0-688-09114-8; pbk 0-590-44064-0) Grades 2-7.

Julio Sanchez enjoys the fresh ideas of Mr. Flores, the school's newest fifth grade teacher, especially his idea of holding a class election. Julio would love to run for president, but does not think he could win. He enthusiastically backs his best friend, unconsiously showing leadership potential. When nominations are made, a surprise is in store for Julio, but not everyone else.

Crossing. Gary Paulsen. Orchard, 1987. LC 87-7738, 128 p.
(ISBN 0-531-05709-7; plb 0-531-08309-8; pbk 0-440-20582-4) Grades 6-8.

Manny Bustos is an orphan trying to survive on the streets of Juarez. He dreams of finding a better life across the river in North America before the slavers can sell him. Then he meets the strange sergeant who drinks to forget all the killing he has seen. Manny wonders if he can get through the fog in the sergeant's brain to obtain help to cross the river.

Fear the condor. David Nelson Blair. Dutton, 1992. LC 91-46921, 160 p.
(ISBN 0-525-67381-4) Grades 7 up.

Bartolina fears everything. Her life is controlled by the patron's family on the hacienda where she and her family live in Bolivia. Hacienda authorities are all-powerful, forcing the people to farm on unproductive land. Then war with Paraquay comes, and Bartolina's father is sent to fight. Because her grandparents must work harder to compensate for the loss of young men, they die. Each one plants ideas of social change in the minds of the people. Despite the secondary grade recommendation, this gives insight into Latin American life.

Forty-third war. Louise Moeri. Houghton Mifflin, 1989. LC 89-31178, 208 p.
(ISBN 0-395-50215-2; pbk 0-395-66955-3) Grades 5-9.

One minute Uno Ramirez is a normal twelve-year-old villager, the next one he is pressed into military service. This story recounts his eight days as a soldier with revolutionaries. He spends time training, learning to shoot and going on patrol. Uno wonders if he has the personal strength to be a soldier, especially as the big battle approaches. He learns that even boys can be heroic.

Ghost catcher. Dennis Haseley; Lloyd Bloom, illus. HarperCollins, 1991. LC 91-4426, 40 p. (ISBN plb 0-06-022247-6) Grades 1-5.

The Ghost Catcher can get close to ghosts without turning into one himself. He makes the families of the ghosts very happy by bringing back the loved ones before it is too late. But he gets too curious and decides to go to the place where ghosts go. When he thinks he is trapped, his friends from the village find a way to help him return safely.

Going home. Nicholasa Mohr. Dial, 1986. LC 85-20621, 176 p. (ISBN 0-8037-0269-8; plb 0-8037-0338-4; pbk 0-553-15699-3) Grades 5-8.

When Felita turns twelve, everything seems to change. Her parents treat her much differently than her brothers and she finds that she likes Vinny, a boy she tutors in English. The biggest surprise of all is that she will spend two months in Puerto Rico. There she spends time with her relatives and makes new friends, but some girls resent her because she is an American. Felita battles homesickness but eventually finds her own identity.

Grab hands and run. Frances Temple. Orchard, 1993. LC 92-34063, 176 p. (ISBN 0-531-05480-2; plb 0-531-08630-5) Grades 5 up.

Danger is all around Felipe's family in their Salvadoran home. He narrowly escapes being captured to serve in the military, and then his father disappears. Father had told them if anything happened to him, they should go north to Canada. So they take what they can and leave. After a harrowing and exhausting journey, they are granted asylum, and an opportunity to start over again.

Guero. Elizabeth Borton de Trevino; Leslie W. Bowman, illus. Farrar, 1989. LC 88-46133, 112 p. (ISBN 0-374-31995-2; pbk 0-374-42028-9) Grades 3 up.

El Guero— the Blond one—is the son of a respected Mexican judge. When the revolutionary Diaz takes control of Mexico, El Guero's father is exiled to a province far removed from civilization in Mexico City. Their life changes from affluence to pioneer isolation. They make friends with sailors, Indians and missionaries, while building a home and establishing law for the area. When desperados take over their little settlement and imprison his father, El Guero must travel many days to the next town for help.

Hill of fire. Thomas Lewis; Joan Sandin, illus. HarperCollins, 1971. LC 70-121802, 64 p. (ISBN plb 0-06-023804-6; pbk 0-06-444040-0; pbk + cassette 0-694-00175-9) Grades K-3.

An *I can read history book*. Pablo's father complained that nothing ever happened. He worked in his field and then came home. One day, the farmer's plow opened up a big hole in the earth, with smoke coming out, followed by hot lava. It grew into a mountain, destroyed most of the village, and forced the people to flee. After they rebuilt, Pablo's father no longer sought excitement.

Journey of the sparrows. Fran Leeper Buss. Dutton, 1991. LC 91-11110, 160 p. (ISBN 0-525-67362-8; pbk 0-440-40785-0) Grades 4-9.

Maria does not expect an easy life in America, but she knows she will die if she stays in El Salvador. Maria, her pregnant sister Julia, and little brother Oscar are smuggled to Chicago in crates. They lead a hand to mouth existence, constantly worrying about getting caught by immigration agents. Single-handedly Maria keeps the family going. When her mother writes begging them to come for their baby sister, Maria fears she is not capable of handling more responsibility.

Laura loves horses. Joan Hewett; Richard Hewett, photo. Houghton Mifflin, 1990. LC 89-34987, 48 p. (ISBN 0-89919-844-9) Grades 2-5.

Laura Santana lives on a ranch and is around horses constantly. She rides, takes care of the horses, and plays with them. Now that Laura is eight, she has begun to compete in horse shows. Yet she still enjoys riding in the wild Southern California countryside.

Local news. Gary Soto. Harcourt, 1993. LC 92-37905, 148 p. (ISBN 0-15-248117-6) Grades 5 up.

These short stories offer vivid potrayals of life in a California Hispanic neighborhood. The stories feature young characters in strong conflicts—often with themselves.

Most beautiful place in the world. Ann Cameron; Thomas Allen, illus. Knopf, 1988. LC 88-532, 64 p. (ISBN 0-394-89463-4; plb 0-394-99463-9) Grades ps-3.

This is Juan's story. He tells of his village in Guatemala, his early life, and how he came to live with grandmother after his parents left him. His grandmother has a successful business selling a type of rice pudding. After Juan shows interest in the business, Grandmother lets him help her. He takes pride in doing his job well, but he also wants to go to school. Juan has pride as a student too, and the teachers want to promote him early.

My Aunt Otilia's spirits. Richard Garcia; Robin Cherin and Roger Reyes, illus.; Jesus Guerrero Rea, trans. Children's Book Press, 1987. LC 86-17129, 24 p. (ISBN 0-89239-029-8) Grades 2-9.

Part of the *Fifth world tales* series. Aunt Otilia lives in Puerto Rico. The narrator remembers her as tall and skinny. Strange things happen in the night near Aunt Otilia. Her bed shakes and she says, "That's just my spirits." One night the narrator only pretends to sleep. He sees Aunt Otilia's bones leave her body. He is so startled that he gathers the disjointed parts of her body but cannot put them back together before dawn.

My name is Maria Isabel. Alma Flor Ada; K. Dyble Thompson, illus. Macmillan, 1993. LC 91-44910, 64 p. (ISBN 0-689-31517-1) Grades 2-5.

When Maria Isabel starts in a new school, her teacher calls her Mary because there are two other Marias. Maria Isabel never knows when the teacher is talking to her, and she misses her chance to have a part in the winter pageant. Maria is too shy to tell her teacher about the problem with her name, but she writes her feelings in an essay. Her teacher then understands, calls her by her full name, and lets her lead a song in the play.

Pacific crossing. Gary Soto. Harcourt, 1992. LC 91-46909, 134 p. (ISBN 0-15-259187-7; pbk 0-15-259188-5) Grades 4-7.

Lincoln Mendoza and his barrio brother Tony Contreras go to Japan for the summer and learn first hand what the people are like. They become part of two families—help with chores, eat Japanese food, and learn Japanese history and traditions. Lincoln feels lucky to continue his martial arts studies and gains strength and understanding about himself.

Pedro's journal: a journey with Christopher Columbus. Pam Conrad; Peter Koeppen, illus. Boyds Mills, 1991. LC 90-85723, 96 p. (ISBN 1-878093-17-7; pbk 0-590-46206-7) Grades 3-7.

Christopher Columbus's discovery of America is presented through the eyes of a young cabin boy, Pedro de Salcedo. In his diary, Pedro comments on aspects of the voyage: the crew's attitudes, their fears of the unknown, and their resentment after failing to find treasure. Pedro especially criticizes their taking Indian women as slaves and is disheartened about the trip home.

Santiago's silver mine. Eleanor Clymer; Ingrid Fetz, illus. Dell, 1989. LC 72-86930, 80 p. (ISBN 0-440-40157-7) Grades K-6.

Santiago's family is desperate for money. The crops are bad and Santiago's father must go to Mexico City to find work. Santiago thinks that all their problems would be solved if they found some money. They might find treasure in the old silver mine that was abandoned by the mining company. Santiago and his friend do find treasure, but not the kind they expect.

Skirt. Gary Soto. Delacorte, 1992. LC 91-26145, 74 p. (ISBN 0-385-30665-2; pbk 0-440-40924-1) Grades 4-7.

Miata loses everything. When she loses her mother's Mexican folklorico skirt, which she borrowed for her school dance group, she does not want to admit to her parents that she lost something so important. Miata and her friend Ana go to great lengths to get the skirt back, and she finds new pride in her accomplishments at the folklorico dance.

Soccer Sam. Jean Marzollo; Blanche Sims, illus. Random House, 1987. LC 86-47533, 48 p. (ISBN plb 0-394-98406-4; pbk 0-394-88406-X) Grades 1-3.

Part of the *Step into reading* series. When Sam's cousin Marco arrives from Mexico, the boys are uncomfortable with each other because Marco does not know much English. Sam is embarrassed because Marco does dumb things, such as kicking the basketball instead of dribbling it on the floor. Then Marco shows how he plays soccer, and teaches the game to Sam and his friends. This enables the second graders to challenge the third graders to a soccer play-off.

Sunrise song. Minnie Gilbert. Sunbelt Media, 1984. 96 p. (ISBN 0-89015-468-6) Grades 4-6.

The traditional celebration of a daughter's fifteenth birthday, also known as quinceanera, is a much anticipated event in a Mexican family. Rosita wishes for it on her fourteenth birthday. As the last year of her childhood unfolds, a great deal happens to force her into facing adulthood: friendships change, her family suffers loss, and violence occurs. Yet the celebration is still a joyous event.

Reference and Scholarly Works

A bicultural heritage: themes for the exploration of Mexican and Mexican-American culture in books for children and adolescents.
Isabel Schon. Scarecrow, 1978. LC 78-4332, 164 p. (ISBN 0-8108-1128-6).

Designed to promote understanding, appreciation, and respect for Mexican-American culture. The author emphasizes literature that promotes a bicultural heritage. Contents are arranged according to grade levels, and include titles dealing with customs, lifestyles, heroes, folklore, and history of Mexican-Americans. Expected outcomes, discussions, evaluations, and follow-up activities are also arranged by grade levels. A pre- and post-attitude survey and three appendices, that contain additional readings and references, are also included. Of the 265 titles, a majority are fiction; however, biographical, historical, and artistic works are listed.

Books in Spanish for children and young adults: an annotated guide/libros infantiles y juveniles espanol: una guia anotada. Isabel Schon, compiler. Scarecrow, 1978. LC 78-10299, 165 p. (ISBN 0-8108-1176-6); Scarecrow, 1983. LC 83-3315, 172 p. (ISBN 0-8108-1620-2); Scarecrow, 1985. LC 85-2196, 220 p. (ISBN 0-8108-1807-8); Scarecrow, 1987. LC 87-9785, 313 p. (ISBN 0-8108-2004-8); Scarecrow, 1989. LC 89-10526, 180 p. (ISBN 0-8108-2238-5); Scarecrow, 1993. LC 92-33302, 305 p. (ISBN 0-8108-2622-4)

Highlighted in this bibliography are works in Spanish by Hispanic authors from Latin American countries and Spain. This book is particularly useful in selecting Spanish language materials for children. Entries are organized by broad subject categories, (fiction, history, etc.,) within each country.

Chicano organization directory. Cesar Caballero, compiler. Neal-Schuman, 1985. LC 83-8333, 221 p. (ISBN 0-918212-65-0).

A directory of active organizations that responded to a questionnaire. Includes the following: non-profit agencies that provide services primarily to Mexican-Americans, Chicano Studies programs in colleges and universities, in addition to social, business, educational, and professional organizations. Listings provide names, addresses, type of organization, purposes and goals, officers, and publications (if any).

Chicano scholars and writers: a bio-bibliographical directory. Julio A. Martinez, editor. Scarecrow, 1979. LC 78-32076, 589 p. (ISBN 0-8108-1205-3).

Documents information on 500 scholars and writers including Chicanos and Anglo-Americans who have had an interest in Chicano themes. Entries contain personal data, educational, attainments, professional and/or community affiliations, honors, and publications. Includes a subject index.

El Diccionario del Espanol/chicano. Roberto A. Galvan; Richard V. Teschner. NTC Publishing Group, 1991. 152 p. (ISBN 0-8325-9634-5).

This is a revised edition of *El Diccionario del Espanol de Tejas,* 1975. It was expanded to a total of 8,000 entries, and the scope was broadened to include lexicons from other Southwestern states.

Dictionary of Mexican American history. Matt S. Meier; Feliciana Rivera, editors. Greenwood, 1981. LC 80-24750, 472 p. (ISBN 0-313-21203-1).

Although written from a historical perspective, this work contains entries that relate to Chicano culture and literature. It contains short articles, cross-references, and suggested readings, and a complete text of the Treaty of Guadalupe/Hidalgo, (which officially ended the war between the U.S. and Mexico in 1848). Includes a short glossary of Chicano terms, historical maps, and statistical tables.

A dictionary of Mexican American proverbs. Mark Glazer, compiler. Greenwood, 1987. LC 87-23721, 376 p. (ISBN 0-313-25385-4).

Arranged alphabetically in Spanish, this dictionary includes phrases and their variants along with the English translation. Key words are underlined. Gives the source of each proverb and tells how many times it was included in the collection survey. Includes index.

Extraordinary Hispanic Americans. Susan Sinnott. Children's Press, 1991. LC 91-13909, 260 p. (ISBN plb 0-516-00582-0) Grades 4-8.

Brief articles describe the lives of Hispanics from Spain, Mexico, Cuba, Puerto Rico and Central and South America who influenced the history of the United States. Includes the Age of exploration; early Hispanic America; America from sea to sea; the twentieth century; and looking toward the twenty-first century.

Guide to the history of Texas. Light Townsend Cummins, Alvin R. Bailey, Jr., editors. Greenwood, 1988. LC 87-15021, 320 p. (ISBN 0-313-24563-0).

Divided into two parts, this guide contains historical essays and records of the major archival repositories of Texas. Due to space limitations, it does not include comprehensive information. Intended to be used by research students and beginners.

Hispanic Americans information directory 1994-95. 3rd ed. Charles B. Montney, editor. Gale Research, 1994. 515 p. (ISBN 0-8103-7810-X).

Provides information on agencies, programs, publications, and services for Hispanic Americans. Has contact data and descriptive information for more than 4,700 entries. Includes approximately 250 nonprofit organizations. Hispanic library and museum collections are identified, as well as approximately fifty awards, honors, and prizes bestowed upon those who serve the Hispanic community. The entries also include colleges and universities that offer Hispanic study programs, government agencies and their programs, and university related and non-profit organization research centers. Contains information on the top 500 Hispanic owned businesses, bilingual and migrant worker education, Hispanic radio and television stations, publishers, and videos. Each entry is indexed by name and key word.

Hispanic heritage: a guide to juvenile books about Hispanic people and cultures. Isabel Schon. Scarecrow, 1988. LC 88-18094, 158 p. (ISBN 0-8108-2133-8); Scarecrow, 1980. LC 80-10935, 178 p. (ISBN 0-8108-1290-8)

Designed to instill understanding and appreciation for the people, history, art, and the political, social, and economic problems of Hispanic-heritage people. The emphasis is on books published in the United States from 1960 to the early 1970's that relate to ten Spanish-speaking countries—Argentina, Chile, Colombia, Cuba, Mexico, Panama, Peru, Puerto Rico, Spain, and Venezuela. Includes people of Hispanic heritage in the United States. A short analysis summarizes specific ideas explored, provides critical reviews, and indicates recommended titles. Contains author, subject and title indexes. A useful tool for librarians who want to develop or reevaluate their collections, for teachers, and for students in both high schools and universities who want to explore this culture.

Hispanic resource directory 1992-1994: a comprehensive guide to over 6,000 national, state and local organizations, agencies, programs and media concerned with Hispanic Americans. Alan Edward Schorr. Denali Press, 1992. 384 p. (ISBN 0-938737-26-0).

Designed to provide easy access to data on organizations and agencies that serve

Hispanics, the Hispanic community, and organizations whose membership is primarily Hispanic. Contents, are arranged by state and city, and include contact information for 951 local, regional, and national groups, and a coded list of services. When available, the entries contain the name of the key contact person, staff size and number of members, chapters or affiliates. Many listings also contain annual budgets, ongoing publications, and a brief overview of the organization's purpose. This guide omits groups and agencies which focus on service to Hispanic refugees and immigrants. Nine appendices and three indexes supplement the directory with approximately 1,300 additional organizations.

Hispanics and the humanities in the Southwest: a directory of resources. F. Arturo Rosales, David William Foster, ed. Center for Latin American Studies, Arizona State University, 1983. LC 83-20993, 256 p. (ISBN 0-87918-055-2).

Acquaints people with the potential of humanities projects in California, Arizona, Texas, and New Mexico. Includes essays on the history of Hispanics in these areas which are useful in classrooms and media outlets that focus on the Hispanic community. Contains annotated listings of scholars, media outlets, libraries, and museums. Also lists groups that are willing to cooperate in Hispanic-oriented projects.

Latino materials: a multimedia guide for children and young adults. Daniel Flores Duran, compiler. Neal-Schuman, 1979. LC 78-18470, 264 p. (ISBN 0-87436-262-8).

Part of the *Selection Guide* series. Dr. Duran's work is an annotated bibliography of books and 16mm films suitable for Chicano and Puerto Rican children and young adults. Includes materials useful to librarians and educators serving Chicano youth.

Latinos in the United States: a historical bibliography. Albert Camarillo, editor. ABC-Clio, 1986. 332 p. (ISBN 0-87436-458-2).

Contains journal literature on all of the Hispanic-origin populations in the United States. Emphasis is on materials published in *America: History and Life* between 1973 and 1985. Contents are arranged according to national origin, except Chapter I, which deals with general materials, (bibliographies, historiography, archives, and collections), and Chapter II, which concentrates on Latinos in the borderlands prior to 1848. The 1,382 citations are primarily drawn from the humanities and social sciences. Includes contemporary and historical studies. This interdisciplinary work is useful for college and university students, scholars, reference librarians, and readers who are interested in research.

Mexican American biographies: a historical dictionary 1836-1987.
Matt S. Meier. Greenwood, 1988. LC 87-12025, 300 p. (ISBN 0-313-24521-5).

Alphabetically lists and reproduces biographical sketches of prominent Mexican Americans from 1836 to 1987. Individuals are also indexed by professional activity and state.

Non-Fiction

Antonio's rain forest. Anna Lewington; Edward Parker, photo. Carolrhoda, 1993. LC 91-46972, 48 p. (ISBN plb 0-87614-749-X) Grades 2-5.

Antonio and his family's story coincides with the history of the rubber industry. Includes an account of the tappers union's efforts to break the hold of the land owners and to obtain government assistance for schools and medical care.

Arroz con leche: popular songs and rhymes from Latin America.
Lulu Delacre. Scholastic, 1989. LC 88-751962, 32 p. (ISBN pbk 0-590-41887-4; pbk 0-590-41886-6; pbk + cassette 0-590-60035-4) Grades ps-4.

Latin American culture is rich in songs and rhymes. This is a collection of songs with music and instructions for games. Illustrated with colorful drawings.

Aztecs. Frances F. Berdan. Chelsea, 1989. LC 88-10077, 112 p. (ISBN 1-55546-692-3; pbk 0-7910-0354-X) Grades 5-up.

Part of the *Indians of North America* series. The Aztecs built and maintained their empire in Mexico from 1325 to 1521, when the Spaniards conquered them. Their strengths lay in alliances with their neighbors, trading networks, and their warriors. Despite Spain's rule for three hundred years, Aztec influence continues in modern Mexico.

Aztecs. Jacqueline Dineen. Macmillan, 1992. LC 91-36169, 64 p. (ISBN 0-02-730652-6) Grades 6 up.

Part of the *Worlds of the past* series. Using archeological and primary sources, data about this fascinating ancient civilization is presented in a series of short articles. The text is reinforced by photographs of gylphs, artifacts and recreations, diagrams, and maps. The history of the Aztecs is portrayed along with daily life, religious beliefs, and the final confrontation with the Spaniards.

Aztecs. Peter Hicks. Thomson, 1993. LC 92-44377, 32 p. (ISBN 1-56847-058-4) Grades 4-6.

Part of the *Looking into the past* series. Information is presented in captions to color photographs of artifacts, archeological sites, glyphs, and art work. The visual presentation of Aztec life and culture will appeal to low ability readers.

Aztecs. Pamela Odijk. Silver Burdette, 1990. LC 89-24197, 48 p. (ISBN 0-382-09887-0) Grades 5-8.

Part of the *Ancient world* series. With vivid photographs and detailed illustrations, aspects of the daily lives of the Aztecs are discussed. Family life, clothing, religion, art, and architecture comprise some of the history that is shown. A timeline, glossary, and list of important names are helpful special features.

Aztecs. Ruth Thomson. Watts, 1992. LC 92-14747, 32 p. (ISBN 0-531-14245-0) Grades 3-6.

Part of the *Craft topics* series. Aztec customs and traditions are described in short articles with an abundance of drawings and photographs of artifacts. Along side many Aztec items are craft instructions for making similar ones from readily available materials. Contains Instructions for a headdress, a mosaic painting, a helmet, and jewelry.

Aztecs. Tim Wood. Viking, 1992. LC 91-68542, 48 p. (ISBN 0-670-84492-6) Grades 3-7.

Part of the *See through history* series. This well-illustrated history of Aztec life reveals a brilliant, but cruel, people who built magnificent buildings to make human sacrifices to their gods. Short articles with subheadings facilitate easy to understand reading. See-through cutaways show the amazing architecture.

Children of the world: Bolivia. Yoshiyuki Ikuhara. Gareth Stevens, 1988. LC 87-42616, 64 p. (ISBN plb 1-55532-321-9) Grades 5-6.

Porfirio and his family live on the shore of Lake Titicaca, South America's largest lake. Their life style is simple, and many of their habits are reminiscent of their Incan ancestors. Background on Bolivia includes ethnic groups, history, geography, and a description of La Paz, the capital. Includes a glossary and list of suggested activities.

Children of the world: Mexico. Yoshiyuki Ikuhara. Gareth Stevens, 1987. LC 86-42800, 64 p. (ISBN 1-55532-186-0; plb 1-55532-161-5) Grades 5-6.

Maria Elena and her family live in Guadalajara. Through photographs and written descriptions, her day-to-day routines come to life. Her school, food, play, home life, and religious ceremonies are shown. History and facts about Mexico are presented in short articles. Includes a glossary, ideas for research, and other activities.

Count your way through Mexico. Jim Haskins; Helen Byers, illus. Carolrhoda, 1989. LC 88-25899, 24 p. (ISBN plb 0-87614-349-4; pbk 0-87614-517-9) Grades 1-4.

In this counting book, Spanish numbers are phonetically presented. Each number introduces an aspect of Mexican history and culture, including crafts, celebrations, food, wildlife, and historical events.

Cuba. Ronnie Cummins; Mercedes Lopez, photo. Gareth Stevens, 1991. LC 89-43170, 64 p. (ISBN 0-8368-0219-5) Grades 5-6.

Part of the *Children of the world* series. Alain and his family live in Havana. He goes on a tour of historic buildings. His grandmother was part of the rebel force that put Castro into power. Alain's story focuses on his day-to-day life: school, family, friends, and outings. In the "For your information" section, there is an article with facts on history, culture, and government. Includes suggested activities.

Cuba is my home. Gini Holland; Mercedes Lopez, photo; adapted from a book by Ronnie Cummins. Gareth Stevens, 1992. LC 92-17725, 48 p. (ISBN 0-8368-0848-7) Grades 1-4.

Part of *My Home Country* series. This is an easy-to-read version of **Children of the world—Cuba**. Alain's daily life in Havana is described as he goes to school and plays in his neighborhood. Includes fact section and color map.

Cuban Americans. Renee Gernand. Chelsea House, 1989. LC 87-30954, 112 p. (ISBN 0-87754-869-2) Grades 5 up.

Part of the *Peoples of North America* series. Portrays Cuba's history, and the political and economic situation which caused many of its people to leave. They have settled mostly in Florida, but try to maintain their special culture.

Cubans. Barbara Grenquist. Watts, 1991. LC 90-12984, 64 p. (ISBN 0-531-11107-5) Grades 5-10.

Part of the *Recent American immigrants* series. Includes geographical and historical information about Cuba. This small island country has been dominated by foreign nations. When Castro attained power, he set up a Communist rule which caused many people of the business and educated middle class to leave. Settling mostly in Miami, the immigrants of the first two decades quickly integrated into United States economic life.

Ethnic celebrations around the world. Nancy Everix. Good Apple, 1991. 160 p. (ISBN 0-86653-607-8, GA 1326) Grades 3-6.

This book contains games, puzzles, maps, coloring pages, and craft instructions for projects that teachers can suggest in connection with holidays of different nations. Each holiday is discussed with an accompanying bibliography. Arranged by country. Hispanic countries include Brazil, Mexico, and Spain.

Fiesta! June Behrens; Scott Taylor, photographer. Children's Press, 1978. LC 78-8468, 32 p. (ISBN plb 0-516-08815-7; pbk 0-516-48815-5; Spanish 0-516-38815-0; Spanish pbk 0-516-58815-X) Grades K-4.

Part of the *Festivals and holidays* series. Cinco de Mayo means big parties. Mariachis play, everyone wears bright Mexican costumes, and dancers don ruffled skirts. Cinco de Mayo falls on May 5. On this date ragged Mexican troops drove out a well-outfitted French army.

Fiesta!: Mexico's great celebrations. Elizabeth Silverthorne. Millbrook, 1992. LC 91-37178, 64 p. (ISBN 1-56294-055-4; pbk 1-56294-836-9) Grades 3-6.

People in Mexico frequently celebrate special occasions with a fiesta. Some are tied to Mexican history and are patriotic in nature. Others are religious. Different regions have special events. Mexico's cultural make-up of Indians, Spaniards, and a mixture of the two is a part of its unique celebrations. There are instructions for crafts and recipes associated with fiestas.

Getting elected: the diary of a campaign. Joan Hewett; Richard Hewett, photographer. Dutton, 1989. LC 88-11109, 48 p. (ISBN 0-525-67259-1) Grades 4-7.

This photo essay documents the political campaign of Gloria Molina for a Los Angeles city council seat. The routine of recruiting volunteers and raising funds, securing media coverage and rushing to appointments shows the hard work involved in running for office. The last few days are unbelievably tiring, and election day is an anxious wait. Finally the results are in and Molina wins.

Grandchildren of the Incas. Matti A. Pitkanen, illus.; Ritva Lehtinen. Carolrhoda, 1992. LC 90-35507, 40 p. (ISBN plb 0-87614-397-4; pbk 0-87614-566-7) Grades 3-7.

Part of the *World's children* series. The Incas once thrived in South America, rich in culture and wealth. Their descendants now live in poverty, trying to preserve their heritage. Their daily lives are shown with vivid color photos of their children. Includes facts about Incas, the modern Quechuan Indians, and a pronunciation guide.

Hector lives in the United States now: the story of a Mexican-American child. Joan Hewett; Richard Hewett, photographer. HarperCollins, 1990. LC 89-36572, 48 p. (ISBN 0-397-32295-X; plb 0-397-32278-X) Grades 2-5.

Hector's day-to-day life is documented in this photo essay as his family approaches two special events—Hector's first communion and their application for amnesty.

Hello, Amigos. Tricia Brown; Fran Ortiz, photographer. Henry Holt, 1992. LC 86-9882, 48 p. (ISBN 0-8050-0090-9; pbk 0-8050-1891-3) Grades ps-2.

Today is Frankie Valdez's birthday. Special things happen at school. When he gets home, he and his family will celebrate with his favorite foods, sing songs with a mariachi, and break his birthday piñata.

How my family lives in America. Susan Kuklin. Macmillan, 1992. LC 91-22949, 40 p. (ISBN 0-02-751239) Grades ps-3.

Children from three families and three cultures, African, Puerto Rican, and Chinese, tell stories of their families' adjustment to American traditions, while maintaining unique aspects of their original cultures. Eric's father was born in Puerto Rico and his family speaks English and Spanish. Includes a recipe for habichuelas.

I speak English for my Mom. Muriel Stanek; Judith Freeman, illus. Whitman, 1989. LC 88-20546, 32 p. (ISBN plb 0-8075-3659-8) Grades 2-5.

Lupe feels grown-up when she helps her mother by translating English into Spanish. When Mrs. Gomez realizes that she needs to speak English by herself to improve their family's situation, Lupe helps her with English classes.

Incas. Sarita Kendall. Macmillan, 1992. LC 91-513, 64 p. (ISBN 0-02-750160-4) Grades 6 up.

Part of the *Worlds of the past* series. Relying on archeological data and eyewitness accounts from conquering Spaniards, Inca culture and history is described. The Incas flourished in what is now Peru, building cities, roads, and fortresses, until they were defeated by the Spanish army. Includes short, eye-catching articles, a time line, and a glossary.

Inspirations: stories about women artists. Leslie Sills. Whitman, 1989. LC 88-80, 56 p. (ISBN 0-8075-3649-0) Grades 4 up.

Four artists are studied and their life experiences are illuminated by their artistry. Frida Kahlo, the Mexican painter, is one of the artists presented. She had tremendous struggles but her artistic vision helped her to survive.

Kids explore America's Hispanic heritage. Westridge Young Writers Workshop. John Muir Publications, 1992. LC 91-42232, 112 p. (ISBN 1-56261-034-1) Grades 3 up.

Completely student written, this collection of essays explores aspects of Hispanic culture. There is history, festivals, dance, cooking and recipes, crafts, a phrase guide, short biographies of artists and unknown Hispanics (mostly family members). The students convey their pride in themselves as a people and a community.

Latin American and Caribbean crafts. Judith Hoffman Corwin. Watts, 1992. LC 91-13466, 48 p. (ISBN 0-531-11014-1) Grades 1-4.

Art activities and recipes are collected in this book. Drawing from ancient and recent folk patterns, readily available materials are used. There are instructions for wearable art, murals, paintings, sculptures, and tasty snacks.

Maya. Lawanna Hooper Trout. Chelsea House, 1991. LC 90-2309, 128 p. (ISBN 1-55546-714-8; pbk 0-7910-0387-6) Grades 5 up.

Part of the *Indians of North America* series. The Mayans lived along the Yucatan Peninsula in a complex society of nobles, warriors, and peasants. They were mathematicians and astronomers, and used a hieroglyphic language. They built complex cities based on a trade economy. When these declined, they became vulnerable to the conquering Spaniards.

Maya. Patricia McKissack. Children's Press, 1985. LC 85-9927, 45 p. (ISBN 0-516-01270-3; pbk 0-516-41270-1) Grades 2-3.

Part of the *New true book* series. The Mayan society strictly observed their caste system. Babies who had their heads flattened, their faces scarred, and their eyes crossed had the signs of beauty and prestige. Mayan arts included sculpture, murals, and musical instruments. Their calendar was an advanced one. Some Mayan traditions remain among the people of Central America.

Mexican Americans. Julie Catalano. Chelsea House, 1988. LC 87-893, 112 p. (ISBN 0-87754-857-9; pbk 0-7910-0272-1) Grades 5 up.

Part of the *Peoples of North America* series. Mexican history and government policies caused conditions that have encouraged numerous Mexicans to come to the United States. Includes individuals of Mexican heritage who have become famous.

Mexicans in America. Jane Pinchot. Lerner, 1989. LC 72-3587, 104 p. (ISBN plb 0-8225-0222-4; pbk 0-8225-1016-2) Grades 5 up.

Part of the *In America* series, this book furnishes background on the Mexican people and outside influences that sought to control their country. It also attempts to explain clashes between different cultures. Highlights famous Mexican-Americans and their contributions.

Migrant family. Larry D. Brimmer. Lerner, 1992. LC 91-27019, 40 p. (ISBN 0-8225-2554-2) Grades 5-6.

Part of the *In My Shoes* series. This photo essay portrays the daily life of twelve year old Juan Medina and his family who are migrant workers in California. Their life is hard, full of despair and setbacks. The system they live under does them more harm than good, so Juan's family relies only on each other. They urge Juan to get an education despite incredible odds.

Montezuma's missing treasure. Anita Larsen; Pamela Johnson, illus. Macmillan, 1992. LC 91-19259, 48 p. (ISBN 0-89686-615-7) Grades 5-6.

Part of the *History's mysteries* series. A true life mystery has long existed about Aztec treasure. Hernan Cortes was so convinced that there were huge stores of gold that he conquered an entire race. Yet after much killing, when the Aztec capitol fell, no gold was found. Possible solutions to the whereabouts of the missing gold are presented.

Puerto Ricans. Jerome J. Aliotta. Chelsea House, 1991. LC 90-31972, 112 p. (ISBN 0-87754-897-8) Grades 5-6.

Part of the *Peoples of North America* series. Puerto Ricans have spent many generations trying to better themselves on the United States mainland. Puerto Rican history contains much hardship as a result of dealing with foreign societies. Many Puerto Ricans have emigrated because of the resulting poverty. Includes brief biographies of famous Puerto Rican Americans.

Puerto Ricans in America. Ronald J. Larsen. Lerner, 1989. LC 89-2840, 80 p. (ISBN 0-8225-0238-0; pbk 0-8225-1036-7) Grades 2-5.

Part of the *In America* series. The history of Puerto Rico includes Columbus' control of the island and United States suppression of its efforts for independence. Even though Puerto Rico is part of the United States, it does not have the full privileges of a state. To escape the poverty of their country, many Puerto Ricans come to large American cities.

Spanish pioneers of the southwest. Joan Anderson; George Ancona, photo. Dutton, 1989. LC 88-16121, 64 p. (ISBN 0-525-67264-8) Grades 3-6.

Spanish pioneers settled in parts of the Southwest before the Pilgrims landed at Plymouth. This photo essay shows the day-to-day life of the Spanish settlers. The desert environment is harsh, and there is opposition from Indians. Comfort from a Catholic priest occurs only when he can travel to people's homes. Photographed at El Rancho de las Golondrinas, near Santa Fe, New Mexico.

Spirit child: a story of the Nativity. John Bierhorst, trans.; Barbara Cooney, illus. Morrow, 1990. LC 84-720, 32 p. (ISBN pbk 0-688-09926-2) Grades ps up.

The Christmas story became part of Aztec folklore as a result of missionary activity, and was absorbed into the culture. This is a translation of the Aztec version, with beautiful Indian characters illustrating the story.

Tortillitas para Mama: and other nursery rhymes. Margot C. Griego; Barbara Cooney, illus. Henry Holt, 1981. LC 81-4823, 32 p. (ISBN 0-8050-0285-5) Grades ps-2.

These nursery rhymes were collected from many parts of Latin America. Stories are presented in English and Spanish, with fingerplays and creative dramatics instructions.

Ubel Velez: lawyer. Jennifer Bryant; Pamela Brown, photo. Twenty-first Century, 1991. LC 90-25322, 40 p. (ISBN 0-941477-52-5) Grades 2-4.

Part of the *Working Moms* series. Ubel is a lawyer specializing in immigration law. She helps people become naturalized citizens by guiding them through the legal process. She also helps to manage a household for Manuel, her husband, and two teenage daughters.

Uncertain journey: stories of illegal aliens in El Norte. Margaret Poynter. Macmillan, 1992. LC 91-8857, 176 p. (ISBN 0-689-31623-2) Grades 5 up.

Millions of illegal aliens risk everything to come to the United States because they are desperate to find a better life for themselves and their families. Twelve people tell of their uncertain job and housing prospects, and their efforts to avoid deportation.

Voices from America's past. Raintree Steck-Vaughn, 1990. LC 90-44955, 128 p. (ISBN 0-8114-2770-6) Grades 5-9.

Different eras in U.S. history are described by people who lived through them. Historical documents such as letters, speeches, diaries, and reminiscences set the tone for these eyewitness accounts. Hispanics are represented by Cesar Chavez, leader of the farm workers.

AFRICAN AMERICANS

Biography

Against all opposition: black explorers in America. Jim Haskins. Walker, 1992. LC 91-30203, 128 p. (ISBN 0-8027-8137-3; plb 0-8027-8138-1) Grades 6 up.

Brief biographies of African-American adventurers are presented: Estevanico, who searched for the Seven cities of Cibola; Jean Baptiste Point du Sable, founder of Chicago; York, who accompanied Lewis and Clark; James Beckwourth, the mountain man; Matthew Henson, who accompanied Perry to the North Pole; Guion Bluford, first Black in space; and Ronald McNair, astronaut who died in the Challenger explosion.

Amos Fortune: free man. Elizabeth Yates; Nora S. Unwin, illus. Dutton, 1967. (ISBN 0-525-25570-2) Puffin, 1989. 192 p. (ISBN pbk 0-14-034158-7) Grades 3-7.

Resembling a work of fiction, Amos Fortune's story is traced from his life as a prince of his tribe in Africa, through the hardships of his trip to America and his life as a slave. Amos learned English and the trade of tanner. Then, when he was seventy, he found a wife he loved and decided to go to the wilderness and make the kind of home he always wanted. Illustrated with drawings, this Newbery winner has been reprinted in paperback.

Arctic explorer: the story of Matthew Henson. Jeri Ferris. Carolrhoda, 1989. LC 88-34449, 80 p. (ISBN plb 0-87614-370-2; pbk 0-87614-507-1) Grades 3-6.

Matthew Henson and Robert Peary met while surveying for the Panama Canal, and later decided to team up again for a different goal: reaching the Arctic circle. They did so together, but once back in the United States, Peary got all the glory and credit while none was given to Henson. Illustrated with photographs from their expeditions, this book is at a fairly easy reading level.

Barbara Jordan: Congresswoman. Linda Carlson Johnson. Blackbirch, 1993. LC 90-40026, 64 p. (ISBN 1-56711-031-2; pbk 1-56711-050-9) Grades 3-7.

Part of the *Library of Famous Women* series. Barbara Jordan was born and raised in Houston. Barbara thrived as a debate student and a leader in her youth. She went to law school, and later became a state legislator and a member of the U.S. Congress. Illustrated with photographs, this biography focuses on Barbara's accomplishments.

Barbara Jordan. Corinne Naden; Rose Blue. Chelsea House, 1992. LC 91-24410, 112 p. (ISBN 0-7910-1131-3; pbk 0-7910-1156-9) Grades 5 up.

Part of the *Black Americans of Achievement* series. Another treatment of the inspirational Congresswoman's life, covering her family, upbringing, and political rise to power. Also delves into her career after she left Washington. Illustrated with photographs, Barbara's life-long motivations are explained with quotes from her and her family, friends, and colleagues.

Barry Sanders. James Rothaus. Child's World, 1991. LC 91-17850, 32 p. (ISBN 0-89565-737-6; s.p. 0-685-55134-2) Grades 3-5.

Part of the *Sports Superstars* series. Barry Sanders is an exciting running back who plays for the Detroit Lions. For all his flashy moves on the playing field, he is a serious and quiet person off the field. He won the Heisman trophy in 1988. High interest-very easy reading level, color action photographs included.

Benjamin Banneker. Kevin Conley. Chelsea House, 1989. LC 89-34598, 112 p. (ISBN 1-55546-573-0) Grades 5 up.

Part of the *Black Americans of Achievement* series. Benjamin Banneker was a free African-American, living a quiet life, running his family farm, doing astronomical research, and writing his findings, which included an almanac—the first to be published in the U.S. Uses historical sources and Banneker's writings where possible. Illustrated with artistic representations and photographs of landmarks.

Benjamin Davis, Jr. Catherine Reef. Twenty-first Century, 1992. LC 91-43504, 80 p. (ISBN plb 0-8050-2137-X) Grades 4-6.

Part of the *African American Soldiers* series. Benjamin Davis was a West Point cadet who wanted to be a pilot. In 1935, the military was strictly segregated and Davis had to settle for non-combat assignments. World War II changed everything. A black air squad was formed and Davis excelled in its operations. Fighting segregation throughout his career, he flew in World War II, Korea, and Vietnam. Illustrated with photographs.

Best book of Black biographies. Carole Marsh. Gallopade, 1989. 57 p. (ISBN plb 1-55609-330-6; pbk 1-55609-329-2; computer disk 1-55609-331-4) Grades 3-12.

Part of the *Our Black Heritage* series. This collection of facts, trivia, and activities is done in a folksy style that is easy to read. Although there is not enough information to write a report, curiosity is stimulated, and could encourage every reader to write his or her own biography.

Bicycle rider. Mary Scioscia; Ed Young, illus. HarperCollins, 1983. LC 82-47702, 48 p. (ISBN 0-06-025222-7; plb 0-02-025223-5); HarperCollins, 1993. (ISBN pbk 0-06-443295-5) Grades 2-6.

Marshall Taylor was a world-class bicycle racer from 1896-1910. In a picture book format, Marshall's beginnings are portrayed as an adolescent who loved to ride his bicycle fast. An owner of a bicycle store offers Marshall a job because the boy's speed and tricks could draw in customers. As a fluke, Mr. Hay enters Marshall in the annual Indianapolis bicycle race.

Bill Cosby: America's most famous father. Jim Haskins. Walker, 1988. LC 87-33951, 128 p. (ISBN 0-8027-6785-0; plb 0-8027-6786-9) Grades 7-9.

This biography focuses on Bill Cosby's personality, how his life experiences effect him, and what makes him try so hard. A portrait of the unique person that Bill Cosby is. Illustrated with photographs.

Bill Cosby: family funny man. Larry Kettelkamp. Messner, 1987. LC 86-23809, 128 p. (ISBN 0-671-62382-6; pbk 0-671-64029-1) Grades 3 up.

Bill Cosby's success is characterized by the projects he undertakes. Focusing on Cosby's accomplishments, detailed background is given on his curtailed sports career, his stand-up comedy routines, his acting roles on TV and movies, as well as his educational work on "Sesame Street," "Electric Company," and other programs which contributed to his doctorate. Of course, the development of his most popular program, "The Cosby Show," is included. Illustrated with photographs.

Black heroes and heroines, book three: Paul Laurence Dunbar. Ida R. Bellegarde. Bell Enterprises, 1983. LC 79-51798, 61 p. (ISBN 0-918340-11-X) Grades 5 up.

This biography focuses on Dunbar's youth and development as a writer, emphasizing his serious nature and his perseverance to be a published author. Sparsely illustrated with drawings.

Black people who made the old West. William L. Katz. Africa World Press, 1992. LC 92-26779, 181 p. (ISBN 0-86543-363-1; pbk 0-86543-364-X) Grades 5-6.

African American pioneers struggled for their place in the West along with people from many other nationalities, yet their stories are not always known. Some courageous settlers are featured: explorers, fur traders, early settlers, gold prospectors, cow hands, law men, and soldiers. Photographs included.

Black pioneers of science and invention. Louis Haber. Harcourt, 1970. LC 77-109090, 181 p. (ISBN 0-15-208565-3; pbk 0-15-208566-1) Grades 5 up.

Despite its age, this collective biography is a good source of information about African American scientists and inventors, both well-known and lesser known. Inventors include: Benjamin Banneker, Norbert Rillieux, Jan E. Matzeliger, Elijah McCoy, Granville Woods, Lewis Howard Latimer, and Garrett Morgan. Scientists include: George Washington Carver, Percy Lavon Julian, Lloyd A. Hall, Ernest Everett Just, Daniel Hale Williams, Louis Tompkins Wright, and Charles Richard Drew. Each fairly brief articles gives family background and life events, significance of each person's work, and the recognition they received. Illustrated by portraits, photographs and detailed drawings.

Black scientists. Lisa Yount. Facts on File, 1991. LC 90-19159, 112 p. (ISBN 0-8160-2549-5) Grades 5-12.

The scientists in this collection faced a common dilemma: excelling in a science during an era that denied African Americans many educational opportunities. Featured in this book: Daniel Hale Williams, surgeon; George Washington Carver, agriculturalist; Ernest Everett Just, microbiologist; Percy Lavon Julian, organic chemist; Charles Richard Drew, surgeon; Jane Cooke Wright, cancer researcher; Beltraim O. Fraser-Reid, organic chemist; and John P. Moon, computer engineer. Includes chronologies and bibliographies for each scientist.

Bo Jackson. John Rolfe. Lerner, 1991. LC 90-55742, 124 p. (ISBN pbk 0-316-75457-9); Little, Brown, 1991. (ISBN plb 0-8225-3109-7) Grades 3-6.

Bo Jackson was the first athlete in the modern era to play professional football and baseball at the same time. The format and writing style of this book is similar to the popular magazine, *Sports Illustrated for kids*. It focuses on Bo's accomplishments and includes color and black and white photographs as well as a glossary of sports terms. Published before the hip injury that ended his football career.

Bo Jackson: pro sports superstar. Thomas Raber. Lerner, 1991. LC 90-34897, 64 p. (ISBN plb 0-8225-0487-1; pbk 0-8225-9585-0) Grades 4-9.

Part of the *Achievers* series. Bo Jackson played professional baseball and football because he loved both sports, but also because he is anxious to fully develop his special gifts and talents. His accomplishments are described, including a chart of career statistics, but his personal motivation is used to explain how he achieved success. Published prior to football career-ending hip injury.

Carter G. Woodson: the father of Black history. Patricia and Fredrick McKissack; Ned Ostendorf, illus. Enslow, 1991. LC 91-8813, 32 p. (ISBN 0-89490-309-8) Grades 1-4.

Part of the *Great African Americans* series. Carter Woodson wanted to show that African Americans had contributed many things to the progress of humanity. He founded the Negro History Week which became Black History Month and created the Association for the Study of Negro Life and History. In an easy to read format, the African American educator's life is illustrated with drawings and photographs.

Charles Richard Drew, M. D. Rinna E. Wolfe. Watts, 1991. LC 90-13106, 64 p. (ISBN 0-531-20021-3) Grades 3-6.

Charles Drew discovered that plasma could be separated from blood. The first life-saving transfusions from stored blood began because of this research. He went to medical school in Canada because of discrimination in this country, where he met and studied with John Beattie, a British doctor doing blood research. When World War II broke out, Beattie contacted Charles for his plasma research and many lives were saved. Well illustrated with photographs, the book also includes a glossary, bibliography and index.

Clarence Thomas, Supreme Court justice. Warren Halliburton. Enslow, 1993. LC 92-30951, 104 p. (ISBN 0-89490-414-0) Grades 6 up.

Part of the *People to know* series. Clarence Thomas was raised in a poor home in the South, but his grandfather was determined that he get a good education. He attended Yale Law school, and later became chair of the Equal Employment Opportunity Committee. He was nominated to the U.S. Supreme Court in 1991, and despite the controversy that arose because of accusations of sexual harassment, Thomas became the second African-American justice to serve on the court. Well illustrated with photos, Thomas's works are quoted to explain his motivations. Includes a chronology and a bibliography.

Colin Powell. Catherine Reef. Twenty-first Century, 1992. LC 91-45129, 80 p. (ISBN 0-8050-2136-1) Grades 4-7.

Part of the *African-American Soldiers* series. Seeing that an education and persistence created opportunities, Colin Powell carved a place for himself in the military. He promoted equal opportunities for African Americans, emphasized hard work, and respected those who showed it. Illustrated with photographs, this book focuses on his contributions to the military.

Colin Powell: a man of war and peace. Carl Senna. Walker, 1992. LC 92-16099, 150 p. (ISBN 0-8027-8180-2; plb 0-8027-8181-0) Grades 5 up.

Colin Powell is well-known for his dignified leadership throughout the Persian Gulf war. He has had his share of struggles and disappointments, but his ability to overcome adversities and become a person of strength and courage is shown here. This book uses interviews with family members and other research to make this a personal biography.

Colin Powell: four-star general. Elaine Landau. Watts, 1991. LC 91-12860, 64 p. (ISBN 0-531-20143-0) Grades 5-8.

Part of the *First Book* series. This short biography details Powell's early experiences, his military time in Vietnam, his successful political career, and his compassionate and effective leadership during the Persian Gulf war. Excellent photographs.

Colin Powell: straight to the top. Rose Blue and Corinne J. Naden. Millbrook, 1991. LC 91-19121, 48 p. (ISBN 1-56294-052-X) Grades 2-4.

Part of the *Gateway biography* series. Powell's rise through the ranks of the military and politics resulted from his dedication and steady hard work to achieve goals and do his best at all available opportunities. Colin's contribution to the civil rights movement is emphasized and illustrated with photographs.

Coretta Scott King. Diane Patrick. Watts, 1991. LC 91-17032, 144 p. (ISBN plb 0-531-13005-3) Grades 9-12.

An *Impact* biography. For too long, Coretta Scott King was only known as Martin Luther King, Jr.'s wife. She, too, has been an agent of change in her own right by providing support to the Civil Rights movement and carrying on with her husband's work after his death. She has pushed for legislation creating a national holiday in his honor and established the Center for Nonviolent Social Change. Includes an insert of photographs and a bibliography.

Daniel "Chappie" James. Neil Super. Twenty-first Century, 1992. LC 91-43503, 80 p. (ISBN 0-8050-2138-8) Grades 4-7.

Part of the *African-American Soldiers* series. "Chappie" James was an energetic, enthusiastic man who excelled because of his unwavering faith in excellence and hard work. He was a fighter pilot in World War II, Korea and Viet Nam in a time when segregation plagued the military. His perseverance was rewarded—he was the first African-American to become a four-star general. Illustrated with photographs.

David Robinson. James R. Rothaus. Child's World, 1991. LC 91-24880, 32 p. (ISBN 0-89565-784-8; s.p. 0-685-55140-7) Grades 3-5.

This high interest-easy reading level biography focuses on the career of basketball player and former naval cadet David Robinson. After completing his college career at the Naval academy, the 7-foot Robinson fulfilled his service obligation before turning pro with the San Antonio Spurs. Color action photographs included.

David Robinson: backboard admiral. Dawn M. Miller. Lerner, 1991. LC 90-44936, 64 p. (ISBN plb 0-8225-0494-4; pbk 0-9225-9600-8) Grades 4-9.

Part of the *Achievers* series. This is another treatment of Robinson's delayed voyage from the naval academy to the National Basketball Association. Now a premier center in the league, Robinson's feelings and motivations are used to explain his service in the Navy before turning pro. Illustrated throughout with black and white photographs and a chart of career statistics is included.

Denmark Vesey. Lillie Johnson Edwards. Chelsea House, 1990. LC 89-22336. 110 p. (ISBN 1-55546-614-1; pbk 0-7910-0250-0) Grade 5 up.

Part of the *Black Americans of Achievement* series. Using his winnings from the state lottery, Denmark was able to buy his freedom, educate himself, and run his own carpentry business. He found out about the slave uprising in St. Domingue and planned his own revolt to free slaves in the United States. He recruited a huge army of slaves but the conspiracy was betrayed. Illustrated with photographs and drawings.

Desmond Tutu: bishop of peace. Carol Greene. Children's, 1986. LC 86-9582, 32 p. (ISBN 0-516-03634-3; pbk 0-516-43634-1) Grades 2-5.

A *Picture story* biography. Desmond Tutu won the Nobel Peace Prize in 1984 for his contributions to the fight for equal rights in South Africa. He was a teacher before he became an Anglican priest. After being appointed Bishop of South Africa, he worked from this position to dismantle apartheid. Short and fairly easy to read, this biography is well illustrated with photographs.

Duke Ellington. James Lincoln Collier. Macmillan, 1991. LC 90-26303, 144 p. (ISBN 0-02-722985-8); Macmillan, 1994. (ISBN pbk 0-02-042675-5) Grades 5-9.

Duke Ellington, who was self-taught as a pianist and a composer, put together a band composed of some of the greatest jazz musicians of the time. He won renown as one of America's most important composers of the 20th century. For advanced readers and musical enthusiasts because of its musical background. The book is not illustrated.

Dwight Gooden: strikeout king. Nathan Aasang. Lerner, 1988. LC 87-4072, 56 p. (ISBN plb 0-8225-0478-2; pbk 0-8225-9549-4) Grades 4-9.

Part of the *Achievers* series. Dwight Gooden was an incredibly gifted baseball player who succumbed to the pressures of the game and living up to everyone's expectations. After overcoming a problem with drugs, Gooden is struggling to make up lost ground both with his reputation and with his game. Gooden's problems are unemotionally described, his accomplishments are detailed. Illustrated with photographs and includes a chart of career statistics.

Eddie Murphy. Teresa Koenig. Lerner, 1985. LC 84-29696, 48 p. (ISBN plb 0-8225-1602-0) Grades 4-9.

Part of the *Entertainment World* series. Eddie Murphy clowned around at home and school and dreamed of having a career making people laugh. His rise to fame was a quick jump from being a cast member on Saturday Night Live to becoming a famous movie star. A fairly easy to read format is well illustrated with photographs.

Eleven African American doctors. Robert C. Hayden. Twenty-first century, 1992. LC 91-44195, 208 p. (ISBN 0-8050-2135-3) Grades 5-8.

Part of the *Achievers: African Americans in Science and Technology* series. Each detailed article describes the work of these physicians and how their contributions helped raise health standards. Physicians and researchers include: Solomon Carter Fuller, William Hinton, Louis Wright, William Montague Cobb, Arthur Logan, Daniel Collins. Jane Wright, Eugene Adams, Angella Ferguson, Charles Drew, and Daniel Hale Williams. Illustrated with photographs.

Florence Griffith Joyner: dazzling Olympian. Nathan Aaseng. Lerner, 1989. LC 89-2278, 56 p. (ISBN plb 0-8225-0495-2; pbk 0-8225-9587-7) Grades 3-6.

Part of the *Achievers* series. "Flo Jo" is a record breaking runner with an exuberant style. She trained with dedication to win Olympic gold medals at the 1988 games in Seoul. Her accomplishments are described with a sparse, sports writing style. Includes a chart of career statistics, photographs, and illustrated action shots.

Frank Robinson. Norman L. Macht. Chelsea House, 1991. LC 90-38510, 64 p. (ISBN plb 0-7910-1187-9) Grades 3 up.

Part of the *Baseball Legends* series. After a legendary playing career, Frank Robinson became the first African American to be hired as a manager of a major league baseball team. Focusing on Frank's professional accomplishments, this book is illustrated with photographs.

Frederick Douglass fights for freedom. Margaret Davidson. Scholastic, 1989. LC 75-124185, 80 p. (ISBN pbk 0-590-42218-9) Grades 2-5.

An easy-to-read book, this biography devotes space to Frederick Douglass's childhood as a slave. Once he escaped slavery, he was recruited by Abolitionists to be a spokesman for the cause.

Frederick Douglass: leader against slavery. Patricia and Fredrick McKissack; Ned Ostendorf, illus. Enslow, 1991. LC 91-3084, 32 p. (ISBN 0-89490-306-3) Grades 1-4.

Part of the *Great African-Americans* series. This very easy-to-read biography traces Douglass' life from his childhood as a slave, his early adulthood as a freedman struggling to help other slaves, and his older years fighting the laws that would take their new rights away. Illustrated with colorful drawings.

Frederick Douglass: the black lion. Patricia and Fredrick McKissack. Children's, 1987. LC 86-32695, 136 p. (ISBN 0-516-03221-6; pbk 0-516-43221-4) Grades 4-6.

Part of the *People of Distinction* series. Details Douglass' evolution from his enslavement in Baltimore to his involvement in the abolitionist movement. Quotes from his own writings are used to highlight his own experiences. Sparsely illustrated with drawings and portraits.

George Washington Carver. Gene Adair. Chelsea House, 1989. LC 89-770, 112 p. (ISBN 1-55546-577-3; pbk 0-7910-0234-9) Grades 5 up.

Part of the *Black Americans of Achievement* series. George Washington Carver became a national folk hero when he testified before a Congressional agricultural committee and revealed his findings of 25 years of agricultural research with wit and quiet dignity. His real talent lay in teaching, and he helped many find independence because of his agricultural methods. His work lead to real economic solutions for the South by finding new uses for the peanut, sweet potato and other crops. Detailed background comes from historical and eyewitness sources, illustrated with drawings and photographs.

George Washington Carver. Suzanne M. Coil. Watts, 1990. LC 90-12283, 64 p. (ISBN 0-531-10864-3) Grades 5-8.

A *First book.* George Carver burned with the desire to learn. He wanted to be an artist, but turned to his love of plants and soon made a name for himself as an agriculturist. Booker T. Washington invited him to Tuskeegee to teach his skills to other blacks. Carver did just that, experimenting, teaching and developing products which helped those around him. An easier to read format is illustrated with drawings and photographs.

Hammer: Two legit two quit. Linda Saylor-Marchant. Macmillan, 1992. LC 92-4412, 64 p. (ISBN 0-87518-522-3) Grades 3 up.

Part of the *Taking Part* series. M.C. Hammer always loved to dance. At eleven, he made up a dancing act and performed it in the parking lot before the Oakland A's games. Focusing on spreading a Christian message through his music, Hammer went on to become a successful rap recording artist, scoring the first Billboard Top 100 hit in the genre. This slick, well-photographed biography portrays Hammer's unique style.

Harold Washington: mayor with a vision. Naurice Roberts. Children's Press, 1988. LC 88-7247, 32 p. (ISBN 0-516-03657-2; pbk 0-516-43657-0) Grades 2-4.

A *Picture story biography.* This book traces the career of Chicago's first black mayor in an easy-to-read format. Illustrated with photographs.

Harriet Tubman. Judith Bentley. Watts, 1990. LC 90-12319, 144 p. (ISBN 0-531-10948-8) Grades 9-12.

Part of the *Impact biography* series. Harriet spent her early, enslaved years at hard labor in the fields. Once she escaped to freedom, she helped many others escape and was known as "Moses." During the Civil War, she worked as a spy and a nurse using skills she learned helping with the Underground Railroad. Rich in historical detail, well illustrated with drawings and photographs, and includes a well-done bibliography.

Harriet Tubman and the Underground Railroad. Dan Elish. Millbrook, 1993. LC 92-9562, 32 p. (ISBN plb 1-56294-273-5) Grades 2-4.

Part of the *Gateway civil rights* series. Harriet Tubman's work to free slaves and her contribution to equal rights is the focus of this slick, brief biography. Her force of character made her underground railroad route a successful one, and she led more people out than anyone else after her own frightening escape. After the Civil War, she continued crusading for civil and women's rights. Well illustrated with photographs and drawings.

Harriet Tubman: conductor on the underground railroad. Ann Petry. HarperCollins, 1955. LC 55-9215, 247 p. (ISBN 0-690-37236-1); Cavendish, 1991. (ISBN plb 1-55905-097-7) Grades 6-10.

This classic has been reissued. In a flowing style, Harriet Tubman's story is woven into the context of the events and social conditions of the time. Parallel to her life were the lives of other famous people whose paths crossed hers. The action will hold older reader's attention. No illustrations.

Harriet Tubman: slavery and the Underground Railroad. Megan McClard. Silver Burdett, 1990. LC 90-32369, 160 p. (ISBN plb 0-382-09938-9; pbk 0-382-24047-2) Grades 5 up.

Part of the *History of the Civil War* series. This biography focuses on Harriet's role during the Civil War and her contributions to the fight. Time lines included.

Harriet Tubman: they called me Moses. Linda D. Meyer; J. Kerstelter, illus. Parenting Press, 1988. LC 87-43308, 32 p. (ISBN plb 0-943990-33-5; pbk 0-943990-32-7) Grades ps-4.

Part of the *Biographies for young Children* series. Using Tubman as a narrator, she describes her accomplishments in the Underground Railroad, nursing soldiers during the Civil War, and working with the Freedmen's Aid Society. Colorfully illustrated picturebook.

I am somebody: a biography of Jesse Jackson. James Haskins. Enslow, 1992. LC 91-34079, 112 p. (ISBN 0-89490-240-7) Grades 6 up.

Jesse Jackson dreams of a better world and society. This dream dictates his life. He has been criticized for being impulsive, but his drive is contagious. Jesse inspires people by saying, "I may be poor, but I am somebody." The focus of this biography is on Jesse's inner strength and how his ability to continue to fight against injustice has benefitted many. Illustrated with photographs.

Ida B. Wells-Barnett: a voice against violence. Patricia and Frederick McKissack; Ned Ostendorf, illus. Enslow, 1991. LC 90-49848, 32 p. (ISBN 0-89490-301-2) Grades 1-4.

Part of the *Great African-Americans* series. This very easy-to-read biography details Ida B. Wells-Barnett's struggle to stop violence against African-Americans. Born during the Civil War, Ida's parents wanted their children to have a good education. After they died, Ida worked as a teacher to keep her family together. She fought injustice by writing, organizing meetings, and taking legal action. Illustrated with colorful drawings.

Illustrated Black American profiles. Gene Machamer. Carlisle, 1991. LC 90-82937, 191 p. (ISBN 0-9627369-0-2) Grades 5 up.

This collection of very brief biographical sketches includes well-known and lesser known African-Americans who are successful as artists, writers, athletes, business people, entertainers, leaders, pioneers, and military figures. Illustrated with drawings.

Jackie Joyner-Kersee. Neil Cohen. Little, Brown, 1992. LC 91-43796, 144 p. (ISBN 0-316-15047-9) Grades 3-7.

Once Jackie Joyner decided to be a track and field athlete, she let nothing stand in her way. The focus of this biography is her determination to train. She overcame injuries and asthma to win the Olympic gold medal in the long jump and the heptathlon. The format and writing style is similar to the magazine, *Sports Illustrated for Kids;* includes statistics and action photographs.

Jackie Robinson. Carl R. Green; William R. Sanford. Macmillan, 1992. LC 91-23921, 48 p. (ISBN 0-89686-743-9) Grades 5-6.

Part of the *Sports Immortals* series. A fairly brief biography of the great baseball player who was the first African American to play in the major leagues. The focus of the book is Jackie's fight for acceptance from team members and fans as well as using his achievements on the playing field to prove his worth. Includes a trivia quiz, a glossary, and a bibliography.

Jackie Robinson and the breaking of the color barrier. Russell Shorto. Millbrook, 1991. LC 91-29907, 32 p. (ISBN 1-878841-15-7) Grades 4-6.

Part of the *Gateway Civil Rights* series. This book focuses on the contribution that Jackie made to the fight for civil rights, his birth on a Georgia farm, and his family's early hardships that shaped his early life. Even though he won a scholarship to college and served in the military, his only athletic opportunity was to play in the Negro baseball leagues. Branch Rickey, the owner of the Dodgers, discovered him and offered him a chance at the major leagues. His career made him a national figure which helped him become an effective spokesperson for the Civil Rights movement. Illustrated with photographs, includes a timeline, and bibliography including films.

Jackie Robinson: baseball pioneer. Howard Reiser. Watts, 1992. LC 91-28617, 64 p. (ISBN 0-531-20095-7) Grades 3-5.

Part of the *First book* series. Lavishly illustrated with photographs, this biography highlights the main events in Jackie Robinson's life. Includes glossary, bibliography, and index.

Jackie Robinson: baseball's first Black major-leaguer. Carol Greene; Steven Dobson, illus. Children's Press, 1990. LC 89-28816, 48 p. (ISBN 0-516-04211-4; pbk 0-516-44211-2) Grades 2-4.

Part of the *Rookie biography* series. This easy-to-read book focuses on the difficulties African Americans faced trying to find good jobs or play in professional sports. Jackie was able to break into professional baseball, but many threats were aimed at him. He fought back by playing his best, by demanding respect and by working for equal rights. Illustrated with photographs, including one of the hate letters he received.

Jackie Robinson: he was the first. David Adler. Holiday House, 1990. LC 88-23294, 48 p. (ISBN pbk 0-8234-0799-3) Grades 2-5.

This short biography, appropriate for read alouds, shows how Jackie used sports as a way to improve his life. Being the first African American in the major leagues was never easy, but Jackie preserved. Illustrated with paintings.

James Weldon Johnson: "Lift every voice and sing." Patricia and Fredrick McKissack. Children's Press, 1990. LC 89-77273, 32 p. (ISBN 0-516-04174-6; pbk 0-516-44174-4) Grades 2-5.

Part of the *Picture story biography* series. This is an easy-to-read biography about the man who wrote the song which symbolized to many in the African American community the heart of the struggle for civil rights and became known as the African American National anthem. Johnson saw hopes dying at the turn of the century as the law institutionalized racial separation. He contributed to equal rights through his songs, poems, speeches, and writing. This fairly easy to read biography is illustrated with photographs.

Janet Jackson. D. L. Mabery. Lerner, 1988. LC 88-2704, 48 p. (ISBN pbk 0-8225-1618-7) Grades 4-9.

Part of the *Entertainment World* series. Janet Jackson wanted to establish her own career and identity apart from her famous brother, Michael. She succeeded by establishing an acting and singing style of her own. This fairly easy to read biography features family pictures and glamorous photographs.

Jesse Jackson: a biography. Patricia McKissack. Scholastic, 1990. LC 89-10133, 112 p. (ISBN pbk 0-590-42395-9) Grades 3-7.

This dramatic success story tells of Jesse Jackson's beginnings in a small South Carolina town and his efforts to be the best at everything he did. It discusses his work with Martin Luther King, Jr., his accomplishments in civil rights, and his stirring public speeches. Jesse and his family are quoted to present his personal philosophy. Illustrated with photographs.

Jesse Owens. Rick Rennert. Chelsea House, 1991. LC 90-21161, 72 p. (ISBN 0-7910-1570-X) Grades 3-5.

Part of the *Junior world biography* series. Owens was a dedicated athlete who performed under tremendous pressure. The world wanted him to show Adolf Hitler the error in the Aryan superman ideal. Jesse wanted to win. He focused all of his energy on preparing for and winning gold medals in the 1936 Olympics. After he returned to the U.S., opportunities vanished. The book discusses his athletic career and how he persevered after the cheering stopped. Illustrated with photographs and includes a chronology and bibliography.

Jesse Owens. Carl Green; William Sanford. Macmillan, 1992. LC 91-27185, 48 p. (ISBN 0-89686-742-0) Grade 5.

Part of the *Sports immortals* series. Owens always had to fight: illness when he was young, shyness in school, lack of an academic background in college, financial hardship as an adult. But when he ran, he forgot adversity and felt free. He set records that amazed the world. This biography focuses on his accomplishments and includes a trivia quiz, a glossary, and a bibliography.

Jim Beckwourth: Black trapper and Indian chief. Wyatt Blassingame. Reprint of 1973 ed. Chelsea House, 1991. 80 p. (ISBN 0-7910-1404-5) Grades 2-6.

Part of the *Discovery biography* series. To escape cruel conditions in Missouri, Jim Beckwourth set out for the wild parts of the west. As a teenager, Jim worked with a mountain man, trapping and trading furs. The Indians of the region welcomed them and made them part of the tribe. When civilization caught up with them, Jim passed on his knowledge, yet he was never fully accepted by the settlers. Illustrated with drawings and photographs.

Jump at de sun: the story of Zora Neale Hurston. A.P. Porter. Carolrhoda, 1992. LC 91-37241, 88 p. (ISBN plb 0-87614-667-1; pbk 0-87614-546-2) Grades 2-6.

Part of the *Trailblazers* series. Zora struggled all her life with the dilemma of supporting herself by writing and being true to her artistic vision. She wrote fiction and plays when she could, but her work with preserving folklore earned her recognition. Her work reflected a part of society that had no voice. There are interesting personal notes of Zora's habits taken from interviews of family members. Illustrated with photographs.

Kareem Abdul-Jabbar: basketball great. Jacob Margolies. Watts, 1992. LC 91-31662, 64 p. (ISBN 0-531-20076-0) Grades 3-6.

Part of the *First book* series. Kareem Abdul-Jabbar had one of the longest careers ever in professional basketball, leading the Los Angeles Lakers to five world championships. The highlights of his life are described here. He perfected his graceful moves in spite of his tremendous height. While playing for the Milwaukee Bucks, he made public his Muslim faith changing his name from Lew Alcindor to Kareem Abdul-Jabbar. Includes a section on basketball history.

Katherine Dunham: Black dancer. Carol Greene; Steven Dobson, illus. Children's Press, 1992. LC 92-8769, 48 p. (ISBN 0-516-04252-1; pbk 0-516-44252-X) Grades K-3.

Part of the *Rookie biography* series. Katherine Dunham developed a unique style, using elements of black dance from Africa and the Caribbean. Dance always helped her through troubled times. Plagued with arthritis, Dunham established the Dunham Dance Company and School, ready to help anyone she could. This easy to read biography is illustrated with photographs and includes a timeline.

Ken Griffey, Jr. James R. Rothaus. Child's World, 1991. LC 91-24878, 32 p. (ISBN 0-89565-783-X; s.p. 0-485-55137-7) Grades 3 up.

Part of the *Sports superstars* series. In the 1990 All-Star game, Ken Griffey Jr. and Sr. played in the same game, representing their team: the Seattle Mariners. That season marked the first time in baseball history a father and son played for the same professional team. Exciting plays shown in color action photographs in a high interest, low reading format.

Kirby Puckett. Robert Italia. Abdo, 1992. LC 92-19752, 32 p. (ISBN plb 1-56239-125-9) Grades 2-5.

Part of the *MVP, most valuable player* series. Kirby was never in the right place at the right time. No recruiters came to his Chicago ghetto school and he had to attend a community college. He worked hard, learned from every coach he had, and finally got a break that landed him with the Minnesota Twins. Written with a sports style, this biography details Kirby's accomplishments in baseball and is illustrated with photographs.

Kirby Puckett. Jim Rothaus. Child's World, 1992. LC 92-6587, 32 p. (ISBN 0-89565-960-3; s.p. 0-685-60964-2) Grades 1-8.

Part of the *Sports biographies* series. Kirby Puckett plays baseball for the Minnesota Twins and is one of the best hitters in the game. He loves defense and robbing players of hits. His career with the Twins is described in a very low reading level and shown in color action photographs.

Langston Hughes: great American poet. Patricia and Frederick McKissack; Michael David Biegel, illus. Enslow, 1992. LC 92-2583, 32 p. (ISBN 0-89490-315-2) Grades 1-4.

Part of the *Great African-Americans* series. This easy to read biography describes Langston's early hardships, yet went on to gain fame as a writer and poet. Though he traveled a great deal, many of his poems and stories found inspiration in the stimulating atmosphere of Harlem in the 1920s. Includes a glossary and is illustrated with drawings and photographs.

Leontyne Price: opera superstar. Sylvia B. Williams. Revised ed. Children's Press, 1990. LC 84-7617, 32 p. (ISBN 0-516-03531-2; pbk 0-516-43531-0) Grades 2-5.

Part of the *Picture story biography* series. This easy to read book focuses on Leontyne Price's impressive operatic career and the honors bestowed on her. Illustrated with glamorous photographs from some of her stage roles.

Lewis Howard Latimer. Glennette Tilley Turner. Silver Burdett, 1990. LC 90-36264, 144 p. (ISBN plb 0-382-09524-3; pbk 0-382-24162-2) Grades 5-9.

Part of the *Pioneers in change* series. The son of escaped slaves, Lewis Latimer worked his way up from office boy in a patent office to an inventor in his own right. He built a career by refining the filament in light bulbs, eventually working for Thomas Edison. He introduced improvements to several everyday items outside of the electric industry. Sources include Latimer's writings, interviews with family, and historical documents. There are photographs, drawings and reprints of patents, and other historical documents.

Life and death of Martin Luther King, Jr. James Haskins. Morrow, 1992. LC 77-3157, 176 p. (ISBN pbk 0-688-11690-6) Grades 6 up.

This well-known biography of Martin Luther King, Jr. is reissued with a new afterword. Half the story is Martin's remarkable life and accomplishments; the other half concerns the events of the assassination in an hour by hour format, and results of the investigation. Martin knew his days were numbered, but he persevered with the work he had to do. For advanced readers, no illustrations.

Life in the ghetto. Anika D. Thomas. Landmark, 1991. LC 91-13944, 26 p. (ISBN plb 0-933849-34-6) Grades 5 up.

Part of the *Books for students by students* series. Thirteen-year-old Anika Thomas writes about her experiences in her Pittsburgh neighborhood, where prostitution, crime, drugs, and violence are everyday events. With the help of a strong and loving family, Anika is determined to obtain an education and find her way out of the ghetto. A unique story from this series, Anika's illustrations are drawings.

Li'l Sis and Uncle Willie: a story based on the life and painting of William H. Johnson. Gwen Everett. Hyperion, 1994. LC 91-14800, 32 p. (ISBN pbk 1-56282-593-3) Grades K-4.

The life and artistry of William Johnson is depicted through the eyes of his six year old niece, Li'l Sis. She relates the stories that he shared with her. The tales are often the background for the paintings which are reproduced to illustrate the book.

Louis Armstrong: a musician. Sam Tanenhaus. Chelsea House, 1989. LC 88-20208, 112 p. (ISBN 1-55546-571-4; pbk. 0-7910-0221-7) Grades 5 up.

Part of the *Black Americans of achievement* series. Louis Armstrong's talent for playing the coronet allowed him to escape the seamy slums of New Orleans. His long career gained him world-wide acclaim and affection from his fans. This biography contains historical detail and jazz background, illustrated with photographs and includes a chronology and a bibliography.

Louis Armstrong: jazz musician. Patricia and Fredrick McKissack; Ned Ostendorf, illus. Enslow, 1991. LC 91-12420, 32 p. (ISBN 0-89490-307-1) Grades 1-4.

Part of the *Great African Americans* series. This fairly easy-to-read biography describes the life of the great jazz musician called "Satchmo." Music got Louis out of a lot of trouble early in his career, but he eventually was able to develop his own style that earned him internatioanl renown. Illustrated with photographs and drawings.

Madame C.J. Walker. A'Lelia Perry Bundles. Chelsea House, 1991. LC 89-77285, 112 p. (ISBN 1-55546-615-X; pbk 0-7910-0251-9) Grades 5 up.

Part of the *Black Americans of achievement* series. Born Sarah Breedlove, Madam Walker's life was typical of an African American woman during Reconstruction. She worked as a sharecropper and later as a laundress in order to send her daughter to school. At thirty-seven she began developing hair care products and selling them door to door, in turn launching a business that would make her wealthy. She crusaded to improve life for African Americans. Written by her great,great granddaughter, this rags to riches biography is illustrated by photographs and includes a chronology and a bibliography.

Magic Johnson. Bob Italia. Abdo, 1992. LC 92-19754, 32 p.
(ISBN plb 1-56239-120-8) Grades 3-5.

Part of the *MVP, most valuable player* series. This easy-to-read story of Magic Johnson
includes the revelation that he was HIV positive. The book focuses on his basketball
career with the Lakers. Contains his address for fans who want to write to him.

Magic Johnson: basketball's smiling superstar. Rick L. Johnson.
Macmillan, 1992. LC 92-3175, 64 p. (ISBN 0-87518-553-3) Grades 3 up.

Part of the *Taking part* series. This easy to read biography features color pictures
and the admirable personality of "Magic" Johnson, one of the most loved celebrities
in sports today. His upbeat, winning attitude helped him succeed in the tough
world of basketball and still helps him face his battle against HIV.

Magic Johnson: champion with a cause. Keith Elliot Greenberg. Lerner,
1992. LC 91-31981, 64 p. (ISBN plb 0-8225-0546-0; pbk 0-8225-9612-1) Grades
4-9.

Part of the *Achievers* series. This updated biography deals with Magic's HIV virus,
and how the infection has altered his life. His career in basketball led to Magic's
inner strength, a quality which has helped him cope. Magic's plans for his future
illustrate his courage. Illustrated with photographs, some action, and includes a
chart of career statistics.

Malcolm X. Arnold Adoff; John Wilson, illus. HarperCollins, 1970. LC 70-
94787, 48 p. (ISBN plb 0-690-51414-X; pbk 0-06-446015-0) Grades 2-5.

Despite its publication date, this biography is a good introduction to the life and
achievements of Malcolm Little, aka Malcolm X. Malcolm's main message was that
Afro-Americans should find their own strength and identity through self respect
and self reliance. His life exemplified his views. He turned from a life of street
crime to become an internationally recognized crusader. Illustrated with drawings
and paintings.

Malcolm X and Black pride. Robert Cwiklik. Millbrook, 1991. LC 92-23687,
32 p. (ISBN 1-56294-042-2; pbk 1-878841-73-4) Grades 2-4.

Part of the *Gateway Civil Rights* series. Malcolm X was a leader of the Black Muslim movement, which advocates personal and racial pride. By developing that
pride, Malcolm X changed from a street criminal into a leader in the Nation of
Islam. He used his intelligence and charisma to urge people to change their lives as
well. This brief biography is illustrated with photographs and includes a chronology
and a bibliography.

Malcolm X: center of the storm. David Collins. Macmillan, 1992. LC 91-39951, 104 p. (ISBN 0-87518-498-7) Grades 5 up.

Part of the *People in focus* series. Malcolm X described himself as "the angriest man in America," and this anger motivated him throughout his life. He urged African Americans not to wait for freedom, but to seize it. Malcolm's life was filled with violence beginning with Ku Klux Klan visits to his childhood home to his death by assassination. Sparsely illustrated with photographs.

Marian Anderson. Charles Patterson. Watts, 1988. LC 88-10695, 160 p. (ISBN 0-531-10568-7) Grades 7 up.

An *Impact* biography. Anderson began singing in school and church choirs. Her performances were so good that famous musicians of the day offered to help her. She was the first African American to sing with the prestigious Metropolitan opera, but she constantly faced difficulty because of her race. In her later years, she was a United Nations representative. Uses quotes from published interviews and includes an insert with photographs.

Marian Anderson: a great singer. Patricia and Fredrick McKissack; Ned Ostendorf, illus. Enslow, 1991. LC 90-19163, 32 p. (ISBN 0-89490-303-9) Grades 1-4.

Part of the *Great African-Americans* series. Marian Anderson's artistry and singing ability overcame the persistent prejudice she faced. Presented in an easy to read format. Illustrated with photographs and drawings.

Marian Wright Edelman: defender of children's rights. Steven Otfinoski. Blackbirch, 1991. LC 91-598, 64 p. (ISBN 1-56711-029-0) Grades 3-7.

Part of the *Library of famous women* series. Marian has worked to ease people's suffering. While in law school, she helped register African Americans to vote in Mississippi. Later, she represented those who were arrested. She became concerned with children's rights, helping to form the Children's Defense Fund, and is now a powerful lobbyist for those who cannot help themselves. Well illustrated with photographs and includes a glossary and bibliography.

Martin Luther King. Rae Bains; Hal Frenck, illus. Troll, 1985. LC 84-2666, 32 p. (ISBN plb 0-8167-0160-1; pbk 0-8167-0161-X) Grades 3-6.

Tracing the idea of passive resistance through the philosophies of Thoreau and Gandhi, this biography focuses on the importance of non-violent protest to Dr. King's life and work. Illustrated with drawings.

Martin Luther King, Jr. Diane Patrick. Watts, 1990. LC 89-24800, 64 p. (ISBN 0-531-10892-9) Grades 3-6.

A *First book*. This short biography portrays King's life from his early year's to his leadership of the civil rights movement, and focuses on the impact of his work. Well illustrated with photographs and includes quotes from some of King's speeches.

Martin Luther King, Jr. Jean Darby. Lerner, 1990. LC 89-36797, 112 p. (ISBN 0-8225-4902-6; pbk 0-8225-9611-3) Grades 4-7.

In spite of hatred and violence, Martin remained steadfast in spreading his message of love and peace. His courage against incredible odds inspired others to take up the struggle. This biography has detailed historical background which acts to emphasize Martin's courage in the face of tremendous change. For older readers, the book is illustrated with photographs and includes a glossary and bibliography.

Martin Luther King, Jr.: a man to remember. Patricia McKissack. Children's Press, 1984. LC 83-23933, 128 p. (ISBN 0-516-03206-2; 0-516-43206-0) Grades 4 up.

Part of the *People of distinction* series. Even as a child, Martin questioned why African Americans and Anglo Americans could not work together, pray together, shop together, eat together, ride buses and trains together, play together, and live together in peace and brotherly love. By posing those questions all of his life, he challenged the way this country lived. Illustrated with drawings.

Martin Luther King, Jr.: a man who changed things. Carol Greene. Children's Press, 1989. LC 88-37714, 48 p. (ISBN 0-516-04205-X; pbk 0-516-44205-8) Grades 2-5.

A *Rookie* biography. This easy to read book shows the conditions that motivated Martin Luther King to lead the way for equal rights with his non-violent methods. Well illustrated with photographs and includes a chronology.

Martin Luther King, Jr. and the march toward freedom. Rita Hakim. Millbrook, 1991. LC 91-29906, 32 p. (ISBN 1-878841-13-0) Grades 2-4.

Part of the *Gateway Civil Rights* series. This slick, brief book chronicles Martin's fight for equal rights. Includes photographs, a glossary, and quotations from his speeches.

Martin Luther King, Jr.: free at last. David Adler; Robert Casilla, illus. Holiday House, 1986. LC 86-4670, 48 p. (ISBN 0-8234-0618-0; pbk 0-8234-0619-9) Grades 2-5.

This short picture book biography describes key events in Martin's life and his fight for a better world. Appropriate as a read aloud. Illustrated with paintings.

Martin Luther King, Jr.: leader in the struggle for civil rights. Valerie Schloredt; Beverley Birch, adapter. Gareth Stevens, 1990. LC 89-77587, 64 p. (ISBN 0-8368-0392-2) Grades 3-4.

Part of the *People who made a difference* series. Filled with photographs and quotations, this short biography describes Martin's commitment to civil rights, the results of his work, and the philosophy of nonviolent protest. Includes addresses for civil rights organizations, glossary, bibliography, and chronology.

Martin Luther King, Jr.: man of peace. Patricia and Fredrick McKissack; Ned Ostendorf, illus. Enslow, 1991. LC 90-19156, 32 p. (ISBN 0-89490-302-0) Grades 1-4.

Part of the *Great African Americans* series. This easy-to-read biography shows how Martin Luther King, Jr. used nonviolent protest as a way to get across his message of equal rights for all people. Highlights his "I have a dream" speech and his Nobel Peace Prize.

Mary Church Terrell: leader for equality. Patricia and Frederick McKissack; Ned Ostendorf, illus. Enslow, 1991. LC 91-3083, 32 p. (ISBN 0-89490-305-5) Grades 1-4.

In this easy to read biography, Mary's parents had to send her away to get an education because laws were passed to repress African Americans. She began a fight for equal right for men, women and African Americans that lasted her entire life. She established the National Association of Colored Women at the same time that her husband was appointed as the first black judge. Illustrated with photos, drawings, and glossary.

Mary McLeod Bethune. Rinna Evelyn Wolfe. Watts, 1992. LC 91-31660, 64 p. (ISBN 0-531-20103-1) Grades 3-5.

The biography emphasizes Mary McLeod Bethune's belief that education is the way to improvement for African Americans. Mary's scholarship led her to a church-run school where she decided that her mission was to serve African Americans. She worked tirelessly throughout her life to achieve great changes in education.

Mary McLeod Bethune: a great American educator. Patricia McKissack. Children's Press, 1985. LC 85-12843, 111 p. (ISBN 0-516-03218-6; pbk 0-516-43218-4) Grades 4 up.

Part of the *People of distinction* series. Mary was her parents' first free-born child. They believed she was destined to achieve great things. Education became the tool she used to leave the South Carolina cotton fields. Eventually, she became a teacher, crusader, and presidential advisor. Sparsely illustrated with drawings.

Mary McLeod Bethune: a great teacher. Patricia and Frederick McKissack; Ned Ostendorf, illus. Enslow, 1991. LC 91-8818, 32 p. (ISBN 0-89490-304-7) Grades 1-4.

Part of the *Great African-Americans* series. The life and accomplishments of the great educator Mary McLeod Bethune are presented in an easy to read format and illustrated with photographs and drawings. Includes a glossary.

Matthew Henson. Sean Dolan. Chelsea House, 1991. LC 90-20458, 72 p. (ISBN 0-7910-1568-8) Grades 3-5.

Part of the *Junior world biographies* series. In 1909, Matthew Henson and Robert Peary were on the first expedition to reach the North Pole. The details of each expedition show how difficult the struggle and how important Matthew's role was to the success of the mission. In the U.S., Peary was hailed as a hero, while Matthew was the hero to the Eskimos of Greenland. Ultimately, his achievements were recognized in the U.S. Illustrated with photographs and includes a chronology and glossary.

Meet Martin Luther King, Jr. James T. De Kay; Ted Burwell, illus. Random House, 1989. LC 88-26383, 72 p. (ISBN plb 0-394-91962-9; pbk 0-394-81962-4); Random House, 1993. (ISBN plb 0-679-95411-2; pbk 0-679-85411-8) Grades 2-5.

Part of the *Step-up* series and the *Bull's Eye* series. This fairly easy to read biography emphasizes how one man helped change the course of history. Includes photographs.

Michael Jordan. Dan McCune. Macmillan, 1988. LC 87-29021, 48 p. (ISBN 0-89686-364-6) Grades 5-6.

Part of the *Sports close-ups* series. People love to watch Michael Jordan play because of his great athletic ability and intensity. He joined the Chicago Bulls at the end of his third year in college. Written in a clipped sport style that emphasizes accomplishments in the sport. Many action photographs.

Michael Jordan. James R. Rothaus. Child's World, 1991. LC 92-18585, 32 p. (ISBN 0-89565-733-3; s.p. 0-685-55133-4) Grades 1-8.

Part of the *Sports Superstars* series. This high interest biography of Jordan focuses on his sports career with the Chicago Bulls and his unique style. Statistics are included. Jordan's retirement is not covered. Includes color action photographs.

Michael Jordan: basketball skywalker. Thomas Raber. Lerner, 1992. LC 92-8277, 54 p. (ISBN plb 0-8225-0549-5; pbk 0-8225-9625-3) Grades 4-7.

Part of the **Achievers** series. Jordan is recognized by coaches, fans, and other basketball greats as an outstanding player. He has a history of bolstering his team members and working for charity. Does not include his retirement. Illustrated with photographs, many action shots, and includes a chart of career statistics.

Michael Jordan: the Bull's air power. Mike Herbert. Revised ed. Childrens, 1987. LC 87-20868, 48 p. (ISBN 0-516-04362-5; pbk 0-516-44362-3) Grades 2 up.

Part of the *Sports Stars* series. Michael's own words describe his experiences along the road to his exceptional basketball career. His colleagues' remarks describe his talent and dedication. Michael's work with charities is mentioned as part of his character. Illustrated with photographs.

Nelson Mandela. Brian Feinberg. Chelsea House, 1991. LC 90-20974, 72 p. (ISBN 0-7910-1569-6) Grades 3-5.

Part of the *Junior world biographies* series. This book focuses on Nelson and Winnie Mandela's accomplishments in the face of imprisonment, police harassment, and physical danger. Using some quotes, the book includes a chronology, a glossary, and photographs.

Nelson Mandela. Richard Tames. Watts, 1991. LC 90-43956, 32 p. (ISBN 0-531-14124-1) Grades 5 up.

Part of the *Lifetimes* series. This is a short book detailing the life and accomplishments of Mandela. History, time lines, and a glossary are separate. Includes his release from prison.

Nelson Mandela: "no easy walk to freedom." Barry Denenberg. Scholastic, 1991. 160 p. (ISBN 0-590-44163-9; pbk 0-590-44154-X) Grades 3-9.

Nelson Mandela's life story is told against the detailed background of South African politics. Direct quotes from his writings offer insight into his beliefs. Sparsely illustrated with photographs. Includes a chronology and bibliography.

Nelson Mandela: voice of freedom. Libby Hughes. Macmillan, 1992. LC 91-31543, 144 p. (ISBN 0-87518-484-7) Grades 5-6.

Part of the *People in Focus* series. Mandela's African name translates as "stirred up trouble." His quiet dedication helped to force the world to focus on the injustices Black South Africans suffer. This book traces major influences on his life and work, as well as the suffering he has endured. Illustrated with photographs.

Nine African American inventors. Robert C. Hayden. Reprint of 1972 ed. Twenty-first century, 1992. LC 91-44193, 171 p. (ISBN 0-8050-2133-7) Grades 5-8.

Part of the *Achievers: African-Americans in science and technology* series. Many everyday items were invented by the special people included in this book: Garrett Morgan, Lewis Temple, Frederick McKinley Jones, Jan Matzeliger, Lewis Latimer, Elijah McCoy, Norbert Rillieux, Granville Woods, and Valerie Thomas. Other women inventors are included in the Thomas section. Each article discusses the importance of the inventor's work and a brief account of each's life, including portraits and drawings of various inventions.

One more river to cross: twelve black Americans. Jim Haskins. Scholastic, 1992. LC 91-8817, 160 p. (ISBN 0-590-42896-9) Grades 4-6.

Includes brief biographies of African Americans who were able to achieve despite many obstacles: Crispus Attucks, Madam C.J. Walker, Matthew Henson, Marian Anderson, Ralph Bunche, Charles Drew, Romare Bearden, Fannie Lou Hamer, Eddie Robinson, Shirley Chisholm, Malcolm X, and Ronald McNair. Each article is illustrated with a single photograph and includes a bibliography.

Oprah Winfrey: media success story. Anne Saidman. Lerner, 1990. LC 90-38059, 56 p. (ISBN 0-8225-0538-X; pbk 0-8225-9646-6) Grades 4-7.

Part of *The Achievers* series, this brief biography focuses on Oprah Winfrey's life and public image. It covers her relationships, her film production company, her restaurant, and her other entrepreneurial ventures. Illustrated with photographs and includes a chart of career accomplishments.

Oprah Winfrey. Geraldine Woods. Macmillan, 1991. LC 91-7818, 80 p. (ISBN 0-87518-463-4) Grades 3 up.

Part of the *Taking part* series. This biography is in a high interest/low reading level format. The focus is on Oprah's heritage, her belief in education, and her empathy, which makes her a successful talk-show host, actress, and business person. Her sexual abuse is mentioned and handled sensitively. Illustrated with photographs.

Oprah Winfrey: talk show host and actress. Lillie Patterson and Cornelia H. Wright. Enslow, 1990. LC 89-17002, 128 p. (ISBN 0-89490-289-X) Grades 6 up.

A *Contemporary women* series book. Oprah says the key to her success as a talk show host is being herself. This philosophy carried her from humble beginnings in Mississippi to film and broadcasting success. Illustrated with photographs. Includes chronology.

Outward dreams: Black inventors and their inventions. Jim Haskins. Walker, 1991. LC 90-12973, 128 p. (ISBN 0-8027-6993-4; plb 0-8027-6994-2) Grades 7 up.

These brief biographies of African American inventors include background information on the conditions that they had to work under, what they invented, and how these discoveries improved people's lives. Inventors include: Benjamin Banneker, Jan Matzeliger, Elijah McCoy, Granville Woods, Lewis Latimer, Madam C.J. Walker, and George Washington Carver.

Paul Robeson. Scott Ehrlich. Holloway, 1989. LC 87-23842, 112 p. (ISBN pbk 0-87067-552-4) Grades 5 up.

Part of the *Black Americans of achievement* series. Paul Robeson was an actor, singer and social activist who won worldwide acclaim. He brought great dignity to the African American art form of spirituals. Despite his world renown, the U.S. government blacklisted Robeson for his radical sympathies and halted his performances in this country. A pioneer civil rights leader, he stood firm in his advocacy for the improvement of conditions for poor and oppressed peoples everywhere. Illustrated with photographs and includes a chronology and bibliography.

Paul Robeson: hero before his time. Rebecca Larsen. Watts, 1989. LC 89-8880, 158 p. (ISBN 0-531-15117-4; plb. 0-531-10779-5) Grades 6-9.

Even though Paul Robeson aspired to be a lawyer, he became famous as an actor and singer. He won acclaim for roles such as Othello, Joe in *Show Boat,* yet he enjoyed more success in Europe than in America. When he praised Russia and other European countries for their acceptance of blacks, he was persecuted, and became a target for violence. Quotes published works and interviews, includes an insert with photographs and a bibliography.

Picture book of Harriet Tubman. David Adler; Samuel Byrd, illus. Holiday House, 1992. LC 91-19628, 32 p. (ISBN 0-8234-0926-0) Grades ps-3.

Part of the *Picture Book Biography* series. This book is suitable for reading aloud, and provides an early introduction to African-American history. It portrays the courage and strength of Harriet Tubman. Her life is traced from her birth on a Southern plantation, through her escape and abolitionist work, to her later years caring for the poor, sick, and homeless. Illustrated with paintings.

Picture book of Jesse Owens. David Adler; Robert Casilla, illus. Holiday House, 1992. LC 91-44735, 32 p. (ISBN 0-8234-0966-X) Grades ps-3.

Part of the *Picture book biography* series. Beginning with a vivid portrayal of his early life in a sharecropper's family, this story features Jesse's amazing accomplishments in track, his victory at the 1936 Olympics, and his life afterward. He had to contend with many difficulties arising from racism and lack of opportunity. A read aloud illustrated with paintings.

Picture book of Martin Luther King, Jr. David A. Adler; Robert Casilla, illus. Holiday House, 1989. LC 89-1930, 32 p. (ISBN 0-8234-0770-5; pbk 0-8234-0847-7) Grades ps-3.

This picture book biography highlights the major events of Martin's life, and emphasizes his philosophy of non-violent protest in the fight for equal rights. A read aloud with the characteristic paintings.

Pocketful of goobers: a story about George Washington Carver. Barbara Mitchell; Peter E. Hanson, illus. Reprint of 1986 ed. Lerner, 1987. LC 86-2690, 64 p. (ISBN pbk 0-87614-474-1) Grades 3-6.

Part of the *Creative Minds* series. An easy chapter book on Carver and his love of learning. At Tuskeegee, he began his agricultural experiments with the help of enthusiastic students. Carver convinced many people to plant peanuts after the boll weevil wiped out the cotton, but his credibility was threatened when the price of peanuts fell. He then searched for products from peanuts and sold them to the rest of the world in order to help his neighbors. Illustrated with drawings.

Prince. D. L. Mabery. Lerner, 1985. LC 84-26165, 48 p. (ISBN plb. 0-8225-1603-9) Grades 4-9.

He was born Prince Roger Nelson to parents who were jazz musicians. He started a rock and roll band in high school after his parent's divorced, finding an identity in the music he wrote. A recording studio owner liked what he heard, and Prince gradually built a career that included performing, songwriting, and movie acting. Illustrated with photographs.

Raggin': a story of Scott Joplin. Barbara Mitchell; Hetty Mitchell, illus. Carolrhoda, 1987. LC 87-9310, 64 p. (ISBN 0-87614-310-9; pbk 0-87614-589-6) Grades 3-6.

Part of the *Creative Minds* series. Scott Joplin came from poor beginnings in Texarkana. His mother had great faith in Scott's musical abilities. He began performing the music he liked best—rags—in a local club. Once established as a performer, Scott attempted to sell his music to the established musical world in New York. An easy chapter book illustrated with drawings.

Ralph J. Bunche: peacemaker. Patricia and Fredrick McKissack; Ned Ostendorf, illus. Enslow, 1991. LC 90-49849, 32 p. (ISBN 0-89490-300-4) Grades 1-4.

Part of the *Great African Americans* series. Ralph Bunche was fascinated by political science, especially the governments of Africa. Because of his work in Africa, he became part of the U.N. peace talks between the Arab countries and Israel. He was awarded the Nobel Peace Prize for this contribution. Illustrated with drawings and photographs.

Real McCoy: the life of an African-American inventor. Wendy Towle; Wil Clay, illus. Scholastic, 1993. LC 91-38895, 32 p. (ISBN 0-590-43596-5) Grades K-4.

The expression "the real McCoy" comes from the accomplishments of Elijah McCoy, an African American inventor of the late 1800s. His parents were escaped slaves who believed education was vital. As a result of his work with the railroad, his first invention was an automatic oil cup which lubricated heavy parts without having to stop the machinery. He went on to invent some fifty other patented items. An attractive read aloud illustrated with paintings.

Reflections of a black cowboy. Robert Miller; Richard Leonard, illus. Silver Burdett, 1991, 1992. LC 91-8661. (Series ISBN 0-382-24078-2; pbk 0-382-24083-9); V. 1, 90 p. (ISBN 0-382-24079-0; pbk 0-382-24084-7); V. 2, 90 p. (ISBN 0-382-24080-4; pbk 0-382-24085-5); V. 3, 102 p. (ISBN plb 0-382-24081-2; pbk 0-382-24086-3); V. 4, 81 p. (ISBN plb 0-382-24082-0; pbk 0-382-24087-1) Grades 4-6.

Using the voice of an old black cowboy, the biographies of African Americans who helped build the old West are told with the charm of a storyteller's narration. Each volume is illustrated with woodcuts. Vol. 1 is dedicated to such western figures as Nat Love, "Stagecoach" Mary Fields, Cherokee Bill, Willie Kennard, and Bill Pickett. Vol. 2 discusses buffalo soldiers such as Emanuel Stance, George Jordan, Henry O. Flippen, and the Tenth Calvary. Vol. 3 is about pioneers such as York, a guide and interpreter for the Lewis and clark expedition; Ed "Cut Nose" Rose, a hunter and fur trapper; Alvin Coffey, who paid for his freedom with earnings from gold mining; Biddy Mason, who won a suit for her freedom after walking from Missouri to California with a wagon train; and George Monroe, a Pony Express rider. Vol. 4 focuses on mountain men such as Esteban, a Spanish slave who searched for the Seven Cities of Gold; Jean Baptiste du Sable, founder of Chicago; Jim Beckwourth, a mountain man who found a way through the Rocky Mountains; and George McJunkin, discoverer of the Folsom archeological site in New Mexico.

Rosa Parks and the Montgomery bus boycott. Teresa Celsi. Millbrook, 1991. LC 91-29905, 32 p. (ISBN 1-878841-14-9; pbk 1-878841-34-3) Grades 2-4.

Part of the *Gateway Civil Rights* series. This short biography describes the fear and suffering Rosa Parks lived with as she grew up in the South. Rosa's refusal to give up her seat on a bus was not only a turning point in her life but one for the whole country as a major movement for civil rights began. Illustrated with photographs and paintings and includes a chronology and a bibliography.

Rosa Parks: mother to a movement. Rosa Parks and Jim Haskins. Dial, 1992. LC 89-1124, 200 p. (ISBN 08037-0673-1) Grades 5 up.

Rosa Parks' autobiography tells of her act of defiance in refusing to give up her seat on the bus. She explained her act by saying "The only tired I was, was tired of giving in." Illustrated with photographs.

Satchel Paige: the best arm in baseball. Patricia and Frederick McKissack; Michael David Biegel, illus. Enslow, 1992. LC 92-3583, 32 p. (ISBN 0-89490-317-9) Grades 1-4.

An easy to read biography of a great athlete, Satchel Paige, who was prevented from playing major league baseball for most of his career because of segregation. He had an outstanding record in the Negro leagues. After Jackie Robinson broke the color barrier, Satchel was signed by the Cleveland Indians. At 42, he was the first African American pitcher in the majors and later was admitted to the Baseball Hall of Fame. Illustrated with photographs and drawings and includes a glossary.

Seven African-American scientists. Robert C. Hayden. Reprint of 1970 ed. Twenty-first century, 1992. LC 91-44194, 173 p. (ISBN 0-8050-2134-5) Grades 5-8.

Part of the *Achievers: African Americans in science and technology* series. These brief biographies describe each scientist's life and work. They include: Benjamin Banneker, Charles Henry Turner, Ernest E. Just, Matthew Henson, George Washington Carver, Percy Julian, and Shirley Jackson. Illustrated with drawings.

Shaka, king of the Zulus. Diane Stanley and Peter Vennema; Diane Stanley, illus. Morrow, 1988. LC 87-27376, 40 p. (ISBN 0-688-07342-5; plb 0-688-07343-3); Reprint of 1988 ed. Morrow, 1994. LC 93-11730, 40 p. (ISBN pbk 0-688-13114-X) Grades K-4.

This read aloud picture book/biography depicts the powerful 19th century African Zulu chief and military genius. Illustrated with paintings.

Shirley Chisholm: teacher and congresswoman. Catherine Scheader. Enslow, 1990. LC 89-34451, 128 p. (ISBN 0-89490-285-7) Grades 6 up.

Part of the *Contemporary women* series. Shirley Chisholm, who believes that education is the key to success, began her career by teaching. As a politician, she tried to educate poor and African-American people about the importance of voting. She went from involvement in local politics to a Presidential nomination. She is quoted from her published work and interviews. Includes a chronology. Illustrated with photographs.

Sidney Poitier. Carol Bergman. Holloway, 1990. LC 87-24250, 112 p. (ISBN pbk 0-87067-566-4) Grades 5 up.

Part of the *Black Americans of achievement* series. Sidney Poitier is well-known for his dignified performances in major movies. His childhood in the Bahamas is a contrast to the elegant roles he won. In New York, he tried to use his prominence and film roles to change public perceptions of African Americans. Illustrated with photographs.

Sojourner Truth. Peter Krass. Chelsea House, 1988. LC 88-6107, 112 p. (ISBN 1-55546-611-7; pbk 0-7910-0215-2); Reprint. Holloway, 1990. (ISBN pbk 0-87067-559-1) Grades 5 up.

Part of the *Black Americans of achievement* series. Born Isabella, a slave, Sojourner endured the pain of separation from her family much of her life. She escaped slavery with the help of a Quaker family, became a traveling preacher, and later published her life story even though she could not read or write. She campaigned hard for the end of slavery and for rights of women. Her famous speeches helped to overcome male arguments against women's rights. Includes a great deal of historical detail, this biography uses quotes from Sojourner's works and is illustrated with photographs and drawings.

Sojourner Truth. Susan Taylor-Boyd. Reprint. Morehouse, 1990. LC 89-4345, 68 p. (ISBN pbk 0-8192-1541-4) Grades 5 up.

A *People who have helped the world* series book. The word that has been used most to describe Sojourner Truth is determined. Nothing stopped this former slave from fighting for equal rights for African Americans and women. Lavishly illustrated. Uses quotes from the period in side bars. Includes addresses from organizations, bibliography, glossary, and chronology.

Sojourner Truth and the voice of freedom. Jane Shumate. Millbrook, 1991. 32 p. (ISBN 1-56294-041-4) Grades 2-4.

Part of the *Gateway Civil Rights* series. This short biography portrays Sojourner Truth's life and struggles for equal rights. She tried to negotiate her freedom, but, in the end, her master refused. Only then did she run away. She changed her name to Sojourner and began preaching and selling her life story. Sojourner worked tirelessly, inspiring many to take up the cause of equal rights for African Americans and women. She won high praise from President Lincoln, eventually meeting him. Includes chronology, a bibliography, and photographs.

Space challenger: the story of Guion Bluford. James Haskins and Kathleen Benson. Carolrhoda, 1984. LC 84-4251, 64 p. (ISBN 0-87614-259-5) Grades 3-6.

Guion Bluford, the first African American to travel in space, served as a crew a member on the 1983 flight of the space shuttle Challenger. He has a Ph.D in aerospace engineering and laser physics. Yet in high school, a counselor told him to learn a trade because he wasn't "college material." Illustrated with mostly space flight photographs and includes a glossary.

Spike Lee: filmmaker. Bob Bernotas. Enslow, 1993. LC 92-41234, 112 p. (ISBN 0-89490-416-7) Grades 6 up.

Part of the *People to know* series. Spike Lee has become a spokesman for young African Americans, explaining black dissatisfaction through his expressive and controversial films. Spike has always maintained his individuality by keeping control over each aspect of his films. Quotes from Spike explain what he meant with each movie. They are then compared with critics' remarks. Spike has helped to change modern moviemaking. Sparsely illustrated with photographs and movie scenes.

Sports great Charles Barkley. Glen Macnow. Enslow, 1992. LC 91-45827, 64 p. (ISBN 0-89490-386-1) Grades 4-10.

Part of the *Sports Great* series. Written in a clipped sports style with game details, Charles Barkley was told that he could not play professional basketball. He was "too short and fat." But his desire to play overcame all obstacles. Includes action photographs and a chart of career statistics.

Sports Great Darryl Strawberry. John Albert Torres and Michael John Sullivan. Enslow, 1990. LC 89-28918, 64 p. (ISBN 0-89490-291-1) Grades 4-10.

This is a *Sports Great* biography with the characteristic sports style. Darryl practiced a lot to achieve his impressive statistics. He had an unbelievable start into professional baseball, but this book does not delve into his more recent problems. Includes action photographs and a chart of career statistics.

Sports Great Hakeem Olajuwon. Ron Knapp. Enslow, 1992. LC 91-41526, 64 p. (ISBN 0-89490-372-1) Grades 4-10.

Part of the *Sports Great* series. Hakeem Olajuwon quit basketball many times as he was growing up in Nigeria. He was frustrated because he could not "dunk" and do other lay-ups effectively. When he moved to the United States, basketball was his opportunity to improve. When he played at the University of Houston on a scholarship, he learned self-discipline. Hakeem has been a major force in bringing the Houston Rockets from the bottom of the NBA to near the top. Action photographs and a chart of career statistics are included.

Sports Great Herschel Walker. Jim Benagh. Enslow, 1990. LC 89-28385, 64 p. (ISBN 0-89490-207-5) Grades 4-10.

Part of the *Sports Great* series. Herschel Walker was a polite, quiet boy who decided he did not want to lose any more races to his sister. He began to exercise so that he could run faster. Herschel had clear goals, always working hard to achieve greatness. Concludes with him playing for the Minnesota Vikings. Includes action photographs and a chart of career statistics.

Sports great Kevin Mitchell. Glenn Dickey. Enslow, 1993. LC 92-24159, 64 p. (ISBN 0-89490-388-8) Grades 4-10.

Part of the *Sports Great* series. As a teenager, Kevin was part of a gang and in danger from guns and drugs. His grandmother convinced him to play baseball to keep off the streets. Even though he worked hard, he got into a lot of fights and was labeled a trouble-maker while in the minors. Eventually he found ways to control his temper. After being traded to the San Francisco Giants, he was named MVP for the National League. Includes action photographs and a chart of career statistics.

Sports great Patrick Ewing. Jack Kavanagh. Enslow, 1992. LC 91-41531, 64 p. (ISBN 0-89490-369-1) Grades 4-10.

Part of the *Sports Great* series. Patrick Ewing was raised in Jamaica. Until he came to the United States when he was twelve, he had never even touched a basketball. After working hard on his own and at Georgetown University, he became a valuable basketball player for the New York Knicks. Despite their losing season in 1985, Patrick was chosen NBA Rookie of the Year. The play action in this book shows his intensity and pride.

Stephen Biko. Diane Sanserver-Dreher. Bantam, 1991. 102 p. (ISBN 0-553-15931-3) Grades 4-7.

Part of the *Changing our world* series. Against the background of South African/British politics, Stephen Biko's accomplishments had great significance. Stephen committed his life to freeing Black Africans after hundreds of years of repression by convincing them that they must free themselves. He founded the Black Consciousness movement to challenge apartheid, and was killed for his beliefs. Sparsely illustrated with photographs.

Stokely Carmichael and Black power. Robert Cwiklik. Millbrook, 1993. LC 92-11560, 32 p. (ISBN plb 1-56294-276-X) Grades 2-4.

Part of the *Gateway Civil Rights* series. Stokely was the first to use the phrase "Black power" as a rallying cry, and to urge African Americans to claim equal rights with more aggressiveness. Stokely had always been motivated to make a difference. His opposition to Martin Luther King's non-violent methods seemed to explode after the death of Malcolm X. Stokely was blamed by some for the rioting following King's death. Illustrated with photographs and includes a bibliography.

Story of Booker T. Washington. Patricia and Frederick McKissack. Children's Press, 1991. LC 91-15895, 32 p. (ISBN 0-516-04758-2; pbk 0-516-44758-0) Grades 3-6.

Part of the *Cornerstones of freedom* series. Booker T. Washington drew a lot of criticism from African American activists, especially W. E. B. DuBois, for his attitude of subservience to Anglos who were responsible for killing their people. Washington believed that African Americans could earn respect and achieve security by learning a trade and providing services. His Tuskeegee Institute was a trade school that also gave excellent instruction in basic disciplines. An easy to read biography with historical detail that is illustrated with photographs.

Sundiata: lion king of Mali. David Wisniewski. Houghton Mifflin, 1992. LC 91-27951, 32 p. (ISBN 0-395-61302-7) Grades K-4.

As a handicapped child, Sundiata was destined to be a great king. Ridiculed and driven away from home, Sundiata gained strength, determination, and knowledge during his wanderings and returned to rule his country. Appropriate for reading aloud, this picture book is illustrated by intricate cut-paper illustrations.

Take a walk in their shoes. Glennette Tilley Turner; Elton C. Fax, illus. Dutton, 1989. LC 89-9700, 176 p. (ISBN 0-525-65006-7) Grades 4-8.

This collection of short skits portray the lives of many well-known African Americans. These can be performed as part of a classroom activity or a Black History Month presentation. Each short skit contains an event in the lives of important African Americans in order to encouraged empathy with these famous people. Participants imagine being Martin Luther King, Jr., Rosa Parks, Arthur Schomburg, Leontyne Price, Charles White, Garrett Morgan, Daniel "Chappie" James, Charles Drew, Frederick Douglass, Ida Wells, Oscar Micheaux, Mary McLeod Bethune, Leroy "Satchel" Paige, or Maggie Walker.

Teammates. Peter Golenbock; Paul Bacon, illus. Harcourt, 1990. LC 89-3816, 32 p. (ISBN 0-15-200603-6; pbk 0-15-284286-1) Grades ps-4.

In a picture book format, Jackie Robinson's struggles after he joined the Dodgers are shown. He suffered cruel and hateful rejection, feeling alone in his battle. But PeeWee Reese, the Dodgers' shortstop, accepted and supported Jackie, advancing the cause of integration in a personal way.

This is Michael Jackson. D. L. Mabery. Lerner, 1984. LC 84-10043, 48 p. (ISBN plb 0-8225-1600-4) Grades 4-9.

Part of the *Entertainment World* series. Michael Jackson has been performing since he was five years old. He creates a mysterious persona, but is really very shy. His life is full of peculiarities, but his singing and dancing remain fascinating to his fans. Illustrated with photographs.

Thurgood Marshall and equal rights. Seamus Cavan. Millbrook, 1993. LC 92-12995, 32 p. (ISBN 1-56294-277-8) Grades 2-4.

Part of the *Gateway Civil Rights* series. Thurgood Marshall had a life-long quest to see that African Americans had the guarantees offered in the constitution. As a lawyer, he worked with the NAACP. His most famous case was *Brown v. Board of Education of Topeka, Kansas,* which legally eliminated the "separate but equal" school policy. He was named the first African-American Supreme Court justice in 1965. Illustrated with photographs. Includes a bibliography.

Two tickets to freedom: the true story of Ellen and William Craft, fugitive slaves. Florence Freedman; Ezra Jack Keats, illus. Bedrick Books, 1989. LC 89-34109, 96 p. (ISBN 0-87226-330-4; pbk 0-87226-221-9) Grades 4 up.

Told in the style of a suspenseful adventure story, Ellen and William Craft were young slaves with a daring escape scheme. Ellen posed as a wealthy young gentleman traveling with a manservant. They were challenged and had many close calls, but the young couple finally made their home in England where they were sure they could be safe.

Walking the road to freedom: a story about Sojourner Truth. Jeri Ferris; Peter E. Hanson, illus. Lerner, 1989. 64 p. (ISBN pbk 0-87614-505-5); Carolrhoda, 1988. (ISBN 0-87614-318-4) Grades 3-6.

This **easy chapter** book describes Sojourner Truth as a fiery and inspirational orator, fighting for the rights of African Americans and women, despite many hardships and personal tragedies. Illustrated with drawings.

W. E. B. DuBois. Patricia and Fredrick McKissack. Watts, 1990. LC 90-37823, 128 p. (ISBN 0-531-10939-9) Grade 7-12.

An *Impact* biography. W.E.B. DuBois was a scholar who believed that an education was essential for African Americans to achieve. DuBois edited *The Crisis* magazine, and was one of the founders of the National Association for the Advancement of Colored People (NAACP). He was known for his strong dispute with Booker T. Washington's "collaborationist policies." This biography uses quotes from his published works to explain his philosophy and beliefs. Illustrated with photographs, includes bibliography.

A weed is a flower: the life of George Washington Carver. Aliki. Simon & Schuster, 1988. LC 87-22864, 32 p. (ISBN 0-671-66118-3; pbk 0-671-66490-5) Grades ps-3.

This picture book recounts the life of George Washington Carver. He was born of slave parents, and became a scientist who developed agricultural improvements. He was quoted as saying: " . . . a weed is a flower growing in the wrong place." Appropriate as a read aloud, this biography is illustrated with paintings.

Whitney Houston. Keith Elliot Greenberg. Lerner, 1988. LC 87-36062, 32 p. (ISBN 0-8225-1619-5) Grades 4-9.

Part of the *Entertainment World* series. Whitney Houston loves to sing, a commitment that kept her on a career path to stardom. Her modesty endears her to her fans. Illustrated with photographs.

Whoopi Goldberg: from street to stardom. Mary Agnes Adams. Macmillan, 1993. LC 92-23766, 64 p. (ISBN 0-87518-562-2) Grades 3 up.

Part of the *Taking part* series. Whoopie Goldberg won an Academy award for her performance in "Ghost" when she did not think she had a chance. She battled tremendous odds all her life: poverty, drug addiction, single motherhood, and dyslexia. Whoopie's comedy routines featured well-developed characters and her transition to movies was natural. Her struggles have shaped her philosophy and efforts to help others. Illustrated with photographs.

Willie Mays. John Grabowski. Chelsea House, 1990. LC 89-48947, 64 p. (ISBN 0-7910-1183-6; pbk 0-7910-1217-4) Grades 3 up.

Part of the *Baseball legends* series. This book describes the career of Willie Mays in a clipped sports style. He played in every All-Star game between 1954-1973, achieved impressive statistics, and was an inspiring athlete. Includes a chronology, bibliography and a chart of career statistics. Illustrated with photographs.

Young Martin Luther King, Jr.: I have a dream. Joanne Mattern; Allan Eitzen, illus. Troll, 1992. LC 91-26478, 32 p. (ISBN 0-8167-2544-6; pbk 0-8167-2545-4) Grades K-2.

Part of the *First start biographies* series. This simple biography is a read aloud book that emphasizes Martin's passion for equal treatment under the law. He worked constantly to change people's attitudes.

Zora Neale Hurston: a storyteller's life. Janelle Yates; David Adams, illus. Ward Hill, 1991. LC 91-065559, 104 p. (ISBN pbk 0-9623380-7-9); Enlarged ed. Ward Hill, 1993. (ISBN plb 0-9623380-3-6; pbk 0-9623380-1-X) Grades 4 up.

Part of the *Unsung Americans* series. Zora was a lively child who saw magic everywhere. Her imagination helped her endure the hardships of her life, later making her feel right at home as part of Harlem's artistic life. Zora gathered folk stories from her home in the South, and new adventures kept her from becoming discouraged. Her work preserved African American tales and traditions that were fading into extinction, some of which are included. Illustrated with woodcuts, this biography quotes from her published works.

Folklore

Adventures of High John the conqueror. Steve Sanfield; John Ward, illus. Orchard, 1989. LC 88-17946, 128 p. (ISBN 0-531-05807-7; plb 0-531-08407-8); Dell, 1992. (ISBN pbk 0-440-40556-4) Grades 4-7.

Everyone knows the African American stories of Brer Rabbit. Another folk-hero, High John, is not as well-known outside African American culture. He is a trickster who always manages to outsmart the Old Master, standing up for the slaves, and even drawing unwanted attention away from them.

Anansi and the moss-covered rock. Eric A. Kimmel; Janet Stevens, illus. Holiday House, 1988. LC 87-31766, 32 p. (ISBN plb 0-8234-0689-X; pbk 0-8234-0798-5) Grades ps-3.

Anansi the spider is a folk hero from West Africa. He finds powerful magic in a strange, moss-covered rock. He uses it to play a trick on all the animals in the forest. But Bush Deer sees what is happening and turns the trick around on Anansi. This story is a familiar one in the Caribbean, but comes originally from West Africa.

Anansi finds a fool. Verna Aardema; Bryna Waldman, illus. Dial, 1992. LC 91-21127, 32 p. (ISBN 0-8037-1164-6; plb 0-8037-1165-4) Grades ps-3.

Lazy Anansi wants to find a fool to go into the fishing business with him. Then the fool can be tricked into doing the work. When Bonsu hears about this, he tells Anansi that if he will do the work, Bonsu will get tired and do the suffering. After many misadventures, Anansi realizes he is the fool. In this version, Anansi is a man. Illustrations capture part of the rich West African culture.

Anansi goes fishing. Eric Kimmell; Janet Stevens, illus. Holiday House, 1992. LC 91-17813, 32 p. (ISBN 0-8234-0918-X; pbk 0-8234-1022-6) Grades ps-3.

Anansi the spider sees Turtle with a big fish, and decides to trick him into catching a fish for him. But Turtle tricks Anansi into weaving and setting the net, then catching and cooking the fish. However, Turtle eats it. Anansi is furious, but some good comes out of it: Anansi learns to weave a net, and teaches others. The net is his spider web.

Anansi the spider: a tale from the Ashanti. Gerald McDermott. Henry Holt, 1987. LC 76-150028, 48 p. (ISBN 0-8050-0310-X; pbk 0-8050-0311-0) Grades ps-2.

In this tale, Anansi encounters danger on a journey and his sons come to the rescue. He has a bright globe for the son who helps him the most. Because his sons are still arguing, the globe is still in the sky for everyone to see. Winner of the Caldecott award.

And in the beginning . . . Sheron Williams; Robert Roth, illus. Macmillan, 1992. LC 90-43094, 40 p. (ISBN 0-689-31650-X) Grades 1-5.

Beautiful watercolor illustrations evoke a special mood in this African American creation tale. Mahtmi, the Blessed One, makes a man from the darkest soil around Kilimanjaro and names him Kwanza, the first one. Kwanza wants to explore, but he returns to find that Mahtmi has created more people. Kwanza is jealous, but Mahtmi gives him a special mark as a blessing.

Baboon's umbrella. Ching; Mary Ching Walters, illus. Children's Press, 1991. LC 91-7952, 24 p. (ISBN 0-516-05131-8) Grades ps-3.

Part of the *Adventures in storytelling* series. In this African fable, Baboon always keeps his umbrella with him. One day it will not close, and he cannot feel the warm sun. A helpful chimpanzee suggests that he cut holes in the umbrella. All is well until the next time it rains. Text of story is printed in the back for storytelling. Other activities are included.

Beat the story drum, pum pum. Ashley Bryan. Macmillan, 1987. LC 80-12045, 80 p. (ISBN 0-689-31356-X; pbk 0-689-71107-7) Grades 3-6.

This collection of African stories is about getting along with others. Stories include: *Hen and frog; Why Bush Cow and Elephant are bad friends; The husband who counted the spoonfuls; Why frog and snake never play together;* and *How animals got their tails.*

Black folktales. Julius Lester; Tom Feelings, illus. Grove/Atlantic, 1991. LC 72-139259, 159 p. (ISBN 0-8021-3242-1) Grades 3-6.

Julius Lester says he picked African and African American stories that have meaning. He tells them in a way that is pertinent to today, in the best storytelling tradition. Lester groups them into: origins, love, heroes, and people.

Bringing the rain to Kapiti Plain. Verna Aardema; Beatriz Vidal, illus. Dial, 1981. LC 80-25886, 32 p. (ISBN 0-8037-0809-2; plb 0-8037-0807-6; pbk 0-8037-0904-8); Puffin, 1992. (ISBN pbk 0-14-054616-2; pbk + cassette 0-14-095052-4) Grades ps-3.

The end of a drought on an African plain is vividly told, using a cumulative rhyme to simulate the sound of rain. Older students will enjoy the poetry of the text.

Bury my bones but keep my words: African tales for retelling. Tony Fairman; Meshack Asare, illus. Holt, 1992. LC 92-25014, 192 p. (ISBN 0-8050-2333-X) Grades 5 up.

This collection of and guide to African stories goes beyond straight recitation of the plots. Background of the story-tellers is provided, together with music and description of movement. Stories include *The man with a tree on his head, There's one day the victim,* and *The two swindlers.*

Cow-tail switch and other West African stories. Harold Courlander and George Herzog; Madye Lee Chastain, illus. LC 47-30108, 160 p. Holt, 1987. (ISBN 0-8050-0288-X; pbk 0-8050-0298-7) Grades 2-4.

This collection of West African folktales is told with humor and dignity befitting the values of the people. Includes notes on each story and a pronunciation guide.

Dark-thirty: southern tales of the supernatural. Patricia McKissack; Brian Pinkney, illus. Knopf, 1992. LC 92-3021, 128 p. (ISBN 0-679-81863-4; plb 0-679-91863-9) Grades 3-7.

Dark-thirty is the time between day and darkness that the author's family engaged in some storytelling. These ghostly tales have African American roots. Stories include *Legend of Pin Oak; We organized; Justice; The 11:59; The sight; Woman in the snow; Conjure brother; Too mama; The gingi;* and *The chicken coop monster.* Illustrations are distinctive scratchboard.

Dark way: stories from the spirit world. Virginia Hamilton; Lambert Davis, illustrator. Harcourt, 1990. LC 90-36251, 154 p. (ISBN 0-15-222340-1; lmt.ed. 0-15-222341-X) Grades 3 up.

This collection of scary stories uses strange and supernatural phenomenon, and represents cultures from around the world. Stories with an African or African American background include: *Rolling Rio; The gray man, and death; The free spirits, Bouki and Malice; The girl who was swallowed by the earth;* and *The witch's skinny.*

Elephant's wrestling match. Judy Sierra; Brian Pinkney, illus. Dutton, 1992. LC 91-8107, 32 p. (ISBN 0-525-67366-0) Grades K-3.

The mighty elephant issues a challenge: who can beat him in a wrestling match? The leopard, crocodile, and rhinoceros all fail. But a bat buzzes in an elephant's ear until he rubs his ears on the ground, and is defeated. Pinkney's scratchboard illustrations give texture to this story from Cameroon.

Feathers and tails: animal fables from around the world. David Kherdian; Nonny Hogrogian, illus. Putnam, 1992. LC 91-31270, 96 p. (ISBN 0-399-21876-9) Grades 1 up.

Folk traditions everywhere contain stories about animals. The tales are from Native American, African, and European cultures, including *Anansi rides tiger* (African), *Coyote and the acorns* (Yurok Indians), *Lemming and the owl* (Eskimo), *Monkey*

(Chinese), *Heron and the hummingbird* (Muskogee Indians), and others. Some animals are friends to each other, some are enemies, but they all teach us something.

Fire children: a West African creation tale. Eric Maddern; Frane Lessac, illus. Dial, 1993. LC 92-34685, 32 p. (ISBN 0-8037-1477-7) Grades ps-3.

Nyame the Sky god made the Earth by filling a basket with soil, trees, flowers, and birds, leaving trap doors in the sky so he could look down. Two spirit people who lived inside Nyame were very curious and came out to live on the earth. They made clay figures, but always hid their "children" from Nyame. After firing, they came alive. Some stayed in the fire longer and became very dark; some did not and were much lighter. But the spirit people loved all their children.

Further tales of Uncle Remus: the misadventures of Brer Rabbit, Brer Fox, Brer Wolf, the Doodang, and other creatures. Julius Lester; Jerry Pinkney, illus. Dial, 1990. LC 88-20223, 160 p. (ISBN 0-8037-0610-3; plb. 0-8037-0611-1) Grades ps-3.

Yet another volume of Julius Lester's unique and humorous retelling of thirty-three Uncle Remus tales.

Honey hunters. Francesca Martin. Candlewick, 1992. LC 91-58736, 32 p. (ISBN 1-56402-086-X; pbk 1-56402-276-5) Grades ps-3.

In this traditional African folktale, man and the animals lived harmoniously together. They followed the honey guide—a little bird who showed them where the honey is. Once they found the honey, however, they argued and fought among themselves, rather than share. So the animals and man are now enemies.

How giraffe got such a long neck . . . and why rhino is so grumpy: a tale from East Africa. Michael Rosen; John Clementson, illus. Dial, 1993. LC 92-46662, 32 p. (ISBN 0-8037-1621-4) Grades ps-3.

At the beginning of time when grass was plentiful, Giraffe looked like a deer with a short neck. But a drought dried up the grass. The only leaves were high in a tree. Giraffe and Rhino went to Man for help and he promised magic if they returned the next day. Rhino was late, so Giraffe got both portions of the magic. Giraffe grew a long neck to reach the tender, juicy leaves—and Rhino did not.

How many spots does a leopard have?: and other tales. Julius Lester; David Shannon, illus. Scholastic, 1989. LC 88-33647, 72 p. (ISBN pbk 0-590-41973-0; 0-590-41972-2) Grades 2-7.

A collection of African and Jewish folktales come to life in this book: *Why the sun and moon live in the sky; The bird that made milk; The monster that swallowed every-thing; Tug of war; Why dogs chase cats; The town where snoring was not allowed; The town where sleeping was not allowed; The woman and the tree children; Why monkeys live in trees; What is the most important part of the body?; How many spots does a leopard have?;* and *The wonderful healing leaves.*

How stories came into the world: a folktale from West Africa. Joanna Troughton. Bedrick, 1990. LC 88-32159, 32 p. (ISBN 0-87226-411-4) Grades ps-3.

Part of the *Folk tales of the world* series. Here are four creation stories from Nigeria that Mouse discovered in her wanderings, and wove into a story tapestry. She explains how Sun and Moon got up in the sky; how the animals arrived on earth; how Hippo came to live in water; and the story of lightning and thunder.

How the animals got their colors: animal myths from around the world. Marcia Rosen; John Clementson, illus. Harcourt, 1992. LC 91-30113, 48 p. (ISBN 0-15-236783-7) Grades 2-5.

This collection of myths explains how a variety of animals got their colors—according to the people who live near them. The tale from the Africans tells about the leopard.

How the guinea fowl got her spots: a Swahili tale of friendship. Barbara Knutson. Carolrhoda, 1990. LC 89-25191, 24 p. (ISBN 0-87614-416-4; pbk 0-87614-537-3) Grades ps-4.

Nganga, the Guinea fowl, and her friend Cow know they should keep an eye out for Lion. Twice Nganga catches Lion sneaking up on Cow, and she startles Lion enough so that they can escape. Cow is so grateful that she sprinkles Nganga with milk. The next time Nganga sees Lion, he does not notice her because she blends in with her surroundings.

"I am not afraid!": Based on a Masai Tale. Kenny Mann; Richard Leonard, illus. Bantam, 1993. LC 92-13811, 32 p. (ISBN 0-553-09119-0; pbk 0-553-37108-8) Grades 1-3.

Part of the *Bank Street ready-to-read* series. This story is based on a Masai folktale. Leyo is afraid of everything. His older brother Tipilit has to help him do even the simplest tasks. After they face a demon, Leyo is determined to be more mature. Tipilit shows him how to approach the world with confidence.

John Henry: an American legend. Ezra Jack Keats. Knopf, 1987. LC 65-11444, 32 p. (ISBN plb 0-394-99052-8; pbk 0-394-89052-3) Grades ps-3.

Keats uses his unique style of illustration to present the legend of John Henry. This hero sacrificed himself to save the jobs of the men who worked with him.

Jump! The adventures of Brer Rabbit. Joel Chandler Harris; Vandyke Parks and Malcolm Jones, adapters; Barry Moser, illus. Harcourt, 1986. LC 86-7654, 40 p. (ISBN 0-15-241350-2) Grades ps-3.

Van Dyke Parks set many Brer Rabbit stories to music and recorded them on an album called "Jump!" That project led to picture story books with beautiful illustrations. Contents: *The comeuppance of Brer Wolf; Brer Fox goes hunting but Brer Rabbit bags the game; Brer Rabbit finds his match; Brer Rabbit grossly deceives Brer Fox;* and *The moon in the millpond.* Includes music and lyrics for *Hominy Grove.*

Jump again! More adventures of Brer Rabbit. Joel Chandler Harris; Van Dyke Parks, adapter; Barry Moser, illus. Harcourt, 1987. LC 86-33622, 40 p. (ISBN 0-15-241352-9) Grades ps-3.

Here is a retelling of Brer Rabbit tales with beautiful watercolor illustrations, but without the original African American dialect. Included is a song composed for the musical production. Stories: *Brer Rabbit, he's a good fisherman; Wonderful tar-baby story; How Brer Weasel was caught; Brer Rabbit and the mosquitoes;* and *Brer Rabbit's courtship.*

Jump on over! The adventures of Brer Rabbit and his family. Joel Chandler Harris; Van Dyke Parks, adapter; Barry Moser, illus. Harcourt, 1989. LC 89-7417, 40 p. (ISBN 0-15-241354-5) Grades ps-3.

Here are five more Brer Rabbit tales, illustrated with beautiful watercolor paintings. Includes the song "Home." Stories are: *Brer Rabbit and his family; Brer Rabbit and Brer Bear; Why Brer Wolf didn't eat the little Rabs; Another story about the little Rabs;* and *Brer Fox gets out-foxed.*

King and the tortoise. Tololwa Mollel; Kathy Blankley, illus. Houghton Mifflin, 1993. LC 92-12485, 32 p. (ISBN 0-395-64480-1) Grades K-3.

"There once was a king who considered himself the cleverest person in the world," and he devised a way to prove it to everyone else. He said if anyone could make him a robe of smoke, then they would be as clever as he was. Several tried, but only the tortoise came close. When the king promises to give him anything he needs to make the robe, he demands a thread of smoke. The king knew he had been tricked.

Knee-High man and other tales. Julius Lester; Ralph Pinto, illus. Dial, 1985. LC 72-181785, 32 p. (ISBN 0-8037-4593-1; pbk 0-8037-4607-5); Puffin, 1985. (ISBN pbk 0-8037-0234-5) Grades ps-3.

These six animal tales are part of the African American folk tradition. Contents:

Why the waves have whitecaps; Mr. Rabbit and Mr. Bear; Why dogs hate cats; The farmer and the snake; What is trouble; and *The knee-high man.*

Monkey-Monkey's trick. Patricia McKissack; Paul Meisel, illus. Random House, 1988. LC 88-3072, 48 p. (ISBN plb 0-394-99173-7; pbk 0-394-89173-7) Grades 1-3.

This easy to read book is based on an African folktale about a hyena who tricks a monkey out of his stew every day. But the monkey gets the last laugh.

More tales of Uncle Remus: further adventures of Brer Rabbit, his friends, enemies and others. Julius Lester; Jerry Pinkney, illus. Dial, 1988. LC 86-32890, 160 p. (ISBN 0-8037-0419-4; plb 0-8037-0420-8) Grades ps up.

More classic folktales featuring the lovable trickster Brer Rabbit. Great for reading aloud, as well as storytelling with any age group.

Mufaro's beautiful daughters: an African folktale. John Steptoe. Lothrop, 1987. LC 84-7158, 32 p. (ISBN 0-688-04045-4; plb 0-688-04046-2) Grades K-3.

A beautifully illustrated South African fairy tale shows the kind-spirited daughter, rather than the mean-tempered one, winning the heart of a prince.

Name of the tree: a Bantu Folktale. Celia Barker Lottridge; Ian Wallace, illus. Macmillan, 1990. LC 89-2430, 36 p. (ISBN 0-689-50490-X) Grades 1-5.

A famine comes to the land; all the animals are searching for food. They find a magic tree whose fruit is too high for them to reach. In order to obtain the food, the animals must call out the tree's name. The problem is, only a far-off king knows the name of the tree. The journey is long; the gazelle and the elephant forget the name of the tree by the time they return from the king. But a young turtle is able to remember despite all the difficulties of the journey. The animals are saved from starvation.

Orphan Boy: a Masai story. Tololwa M. Mollel; Paul Morin, illus. Houghton Mifflin, 1991. LC 90-2358, 32 p. (ISBN 0-685-53587-8; 0-89919-985-2) Grades K-3.

An old man who lived alone took comfort from seeing a sky full of stars. One night he noticed one of the stars was missing, but was distracted by a mysterious boy who said he wanted to live with him. The boy did amazing things, such as feeding the cattle in the midst of a drought. Soon the man's curiosity caused him to follow the boy. Once trust was broken, the boy shot up to the sky. The magic spell was broken.

People could fly: American Black folktales. Virginia Hamilton; Leo and Diane Dillon, illus. Knopf, 1985. LC 84-25020, 192 p. (ISBN 0-394-86925-7; plb 0-394-96925-1; pbk 0-679-84336-1; book + cassette 0-394-89183-X; pbk + cassette 0-679-85465-7) Grades ps-12.

These folktales are a creative product of oppression, sometimes called slave tales. They are retold here by Virginia Hamilton. She includes animal tales, stories resembling fairy tales, supernatural tales, and slave tales of freedom. With each one, she explains the origins and variations.

Piece of the wind and other stories to tell. Ruthilde Kronberg and Patricia McKissack. HarperCollins, 1990. LC 89-46249, 176 p. (ISBN pbk 0-06-064773-6) Grades 3-9.

These stories are to be shared. They are short enough to learn quickly. Their origins are varied: Europe, Africa, and contemporary America. There are suggestions in some of them for body movement and group participation, as well as guidelines in the introduction.

Princess who lost her hair: an Akamba legend. Tololwa M. Mollel; Charles Reasoner, illus. Troll, 1992. LC 92-13273, 32 p. (ISBN plb 0-8167-2815-1; pbk 0-8167-2816-X) Grades 2-5.

Part of the *Legends of the World* series. When a princess refuses to share her long hair, a drought comes to her country. A beggar boy, Muoma, has dreams which give him answers to the country's dilemma, but the king turns him away. Muoma goes on the quest anyway. He brings back a seed, the princess helps him grow it, and she finds a way to make restitution.

Promise to the sun: an African story. Tololwa M. Mollel; Beatriz Vidal, illus. Little, Brown, 1992. LC 90-13326, 32 p. (ISBN plb 0-316-57813-4) Grades ps-3.

During a great drought, a bat is chosen as the animals' spokesperson. He talks to everyone—the moon, the stars, the clouds, and the wind—to ask for rain. They are waiting for the sun to make steam. In return for his warmth, the sun wants a nest to rest in, instead of travelling around the earth. The bat promised, but later could not keep his word. Now the bat hides in shame, coming out only at night.

Rabbit makes a monkey of Lion. Verna Aardema; Jerry Pinkney, illus. Dial, 1989. LC 86-11523, 32 p. (ISBN 0-8037-0297-3; plb 0-8037-0298-1); Puffin, 1993. (ISBN pbk 0-14-054593-X) Grades ps-3.

Rabbit loves honey. When the honey guide shows her a supply of it, she worries because it belongs to Lion. Rabbit tricks Lion two times, barely escaping his ferocity. Lion hides in her house to pounce on her, but she is able to trick him again. At last, Rabbit learns to leave Lion's honey alone.

Raw head, bloody bones: African-American tales of the supernatural. Mary E. Lyons. Macmillan, 1991. LC 91-10690, 96 p. (ISBN 0-684-19333-7) Grades 5 up.

These fifteen scary stories share African and African American origins. Each is told with its own unique dialect. They can be read aloud, told, and acted out. Every story provides some background. Includes a bibliography.

Rhinos for lunch and elephants for supper!: a Masai tale. Tololwa M. Mollel; Barbara Sprull, illus. Houghton Mifflin, 1992. LC 91-19365, 32 p. (ISBN 0-395-60734-5) Grades ps-3.

A rabbit returns home, only to hear a horrible monster in her house. At least it sounds horrible. Everyone who tries to help is frightened away until a frog goes in. He discovers a caterpillar trying to take a nap.

Sebgugugu the glutton: a Bantu tale from Rwanda. Verna Aardema; Nancy Clouse, illus. Eerdmans, 1993. LC 92-44215, 40 p. (ISBN 0-8028-5073-1); Africa World Press, 1993. (ISBN 0-86543-377-1) Grades K-4.

Sebgugugu allows his greed for food to overcome his common sense, despite the warnings of Imana, the Lord of Rwanda. Every time Imana gives Sebgugugu and his family food, he squanders it and wants more. Finally Imana loses patience, the entire family is destroyed.

Singing snake. Stefan Czernecki; Timothy Rhodes. Hyperion, 1993. LC 92-85515, 40 p. (ISBN 1-56282-399-X; plb 1-56282-400-7) Grades ps-2.

This Australian folktale tells of a singing contest. Old Man is tired of the noise that surrounds him day and night. He feels that if the animals' sounds are organized into music, perhaps he can sleep. Snake wants to win the contest, but knows that Lark has the best voice. He puts her in his throat, so that it appears he is doing the singing. At the contest, Lark scratches his throat and makes Snake hiss in his real voice.

South and north, east and west: the Oxfam book of children's stories. Michael Rosen, editor. Candlewick, 1994. LC 91-58749, 96 p. (ISBN 1-56402-396-6) Grades ps-3.

Oxfam is a British organization that sends aid and education to poverty ridden areas. Some of these tales were heard by Oxfam staff working in the countries represented. African stories include: *Mansoon and the donkey* (North Africa); *Hare, hippo and elephant* (Central, Southern and East Africa); *Lion and the hare* (Botswana); *Snake, horse and toad* (West Africa); *Why do dogs chase cats?* (Northern Ghana); and *Greedy father* (Zimbabwe).

Spider and the sky god: an Akan legend. Deborah M. Newton Chocolate; Dave Albers, illus. Troll, 1992. LC 92-13277, 32 p. (ISBN plb 0-8167-2811-9; pbk 0-8167-2812-7) Grades 2-5.

Part of the *Legends of the world* series. Ananse the Spider faces a tough challenge from the Sky god. As payment for the god's stories, Ananse must capture the python, the hornets, the leopard, and the fairy. Kings have tried and failed, but Ananse uses trickery to ensnare all of them. Then he travels from town to town, telling his stories.

Story, a story. Gail Haley. Macmillan, 1970. LC 69-18961, 36 p. (ISBN 0-689-20511-2; pbk 0-689-71201-4) Grades ps-3.

This African tale relates how Ananse, the "spider man" bought his stories from the Sky God by capturing the leopard-of-the-terrible teeth, the-hornet-that-stings-like-fire, and the-fairy-whom-men-never-see. Winner of the 1971 Caldecott award.

Sukey and the mermaid. Robert D. San Souci; Brian Pinkney, illus. Macmillan, 1992. LC 90-24559, 32 p. (ISBN 0-02-778141-0) Grades K-3.

A folktale from the Sea Islands of Georgia and South Carolina. Sukey works hard, but gets only scoldings from her stepfather. With hurt feelings, she goes down to the beach where Mama Jo, a beautiful mermaid, hears her. Mama Jo soothes Sukey with gentle play and a gold coin for her parents. The coin makes the parents greedy for more.

Tales of Uncle Remus: the adventures of Brer Rabbit. Julius Lester; Jerry Pinkney, illus. Dial, 1987. LC 85-20449, 160 p. (ISBN 0-8037-0271-X; plb 0-8037-0272-8) Grades ps up.

The hilarious adventures of Brer Rabbit find a fresh, new voice in this retelling. The storytelling possibilities are abundant here.

Talking eggs. Robert D. San Souci; Jerry Pinkney, illus. Dial, 1989. LC 88-33469, 32 p. (ISBN 0-8037-0619-7; plb 0-8037-0620-0) Grades ps-3.

This Southern folktale shows that kindness will be rewarded. Blanche, the sweet sister, is given gifts of wealth by a mysterious old woman. Rose, the cruel sister, receives only toads and wasps.

Tower to heaven. Ruby Dee; Jennifer Bent, illus. Holt, 1991. LC 90-34131, 32 p. (ISBN 0-8050-1460-8) Grades ps-2.

Long ago, the great god of the sky lived near the earth; the people could talk to him every day. They got so busy that they forgot to talk to him unless they needed something. But every day Yaa, an old woman, came to talk. Yaa loved to talk and work, yet sometimes her pestal slipped and would hit the sky god. In frustration, he left. Yaa then built a tower enabling her to talk to him daily.

Traveling to Tondo: a tale of the Nkundo of Zaire. Verna Aardema; Will Hillenbrand, illus. Knopf, 1991. LC 90-39419, 40 p. (ISBN plb 0-679-90081-0) Grades K-4.

Bowane, the Nkundo, is too patient with his friends who are travelling with him to his wedding. They take so long getting to his bride's house that she has married someone else.

Village of round and square houses. Ann Grifalconi. Little, Brown, 1986. LC 85-24150, 32 p. (ISBN plb 0-316-32862-6) Grades 3-7.

In the village of Tos, the men live in square houses and the women live in round ones. Why is this? Gran'ma Tika explains that it all began when Naka the volcano, then at the village's end, awoke from a long sleep.

Wave in her pocket: stories from Trinidad. Lynn Joseph; Brian Pinkney, illus. Houghton Mifflin, 1991. LC 90-39359, 64 p. (ISBN 0-395-54432-7) Grades 3-7.

Amber tells us Tantie's stories, recreating the setting for each. The background that the reader gets from Amber puts folklore in a perspective of teaching rather than simply entertainment. The bond established between the teller and the listener make the tales more meaningful.

What's so funny, Ketu? Verna Aardema; Marc Brown, illus. Dial, 1983. LC 82-70195, 32 p. (ISBN 0-8037-9364-2; plb 0-8037-9370-7; pbk 0-8037-0646-4); Puffin, 1992. (ISBN pbk 0-14-054722-3) Grades ps-3.

Ketu's laugh gets him into trouble, but he can't help himself. When he saves a snake's life, Ketu receives the gift of hearing what animals think. And they have some very funny thoughts.

Who's in Rabbit's house? a Masai tale. Verna Aardema; Leo and Diane Dillon. Dial, 1977. LC 77-71514, 32 p. (ISBN 0-8037-9550-5; plb. 0-8037-9551-3; pbk 0-8037-9549-1) Grades K-3.

Rabbit cannot get into her house. The Long One has taken over her house and will not let her in. The help offered by the animals would destroy the house, but they finally scare the Long One out—and it's a caterpillar. Delightfully illustrated as a tribe putting on a play; masks represent the animals.

Why mosquitoes buzz in people's ears. Verna Aardema; Leo and Diane Dillon, illus. Dial, 1975. LC 74-2886, 32 p. (ISBN 0-8037-6089-2; plb 0-8037-6087-6); Puffin, 1978. (ISBN 0-8037-6088-4; 0-14-054905-6); Puffin, 1993. (ISBN big bk 0-14-054589-1; big bk + 6 pbks 0-14-778979-6) Grades ps-3.

Mosquito is held responsible for a crime; he is hiding from his fellow creatures. He buzzes in people's ears, whining "why is everyone still angry at me?" The response? A huge hand slaps the mosquito. Winner of the 1976 Caldecott award.

Why the sky is far away. Mary-Joan Gerson; Carla Golembe, illus. Little, Brown, 1992. LC 91-24949, 32 p. (ISBN 0-316-30852-8) Grades ps-3.

Once the sky was so close to the earth that people only had to cut off chunks for food. But it became angry when people took more than they could possibly use, then threw away the rest. The sky warned the people not to be wasteful. They were careful for a while, but one greedy woman forgot, causing the sky to go very far away. After that, people had to grow their own food. A traditional tale with a timely environmental message.

Fiction for younger readers
(Picture books and readers)

Abiyoyo: South African lullaby and folk story. Pete Seeger; Michael Hays, illus. Macmillan, 1985. LC 85-15341, 48 p. (ISBN 0-02-781490-4) Grades ps-4.

A little boy drove people crazy by playing his ukelele incessantly. His father annoyed them because his magic tricks made things disappear. The townspeople insisted that they leave, until a giant named Abiyoyo attacked. The same tricks that annoyed the townspeople saved them from the giant.

Africa brothers and sisters. Virginia Kroll; Vanessa French, illus. Macmillan, 1993. LC 91-20346, 32 p. (ISBN 0-02-751166-9) Grades ps-2.

Daddy and Jesse have played a game many times: it consists of questions and answers about the people of Africa. By exploring African people's past and present, Daddy and Jesse share a knowledge of their own uniqueness.

Afro-bets one two three book. Cheryl Willis Hudson. Just Us, 1988.
LC 87-82952, 24 p. (ISBN pbk 0-940975-01-7) Grades ps-3.

This is a number concept book which uses African American characters to introduce each number.

Amazing Aunt Agatha. Sheila Samton; Yvette Bandk, illus. Raintree Steck
Vaughn, 1990. LC 90-8016, 24 p. (ISBN plb 0-685-33572-0; 3
pbks 0-8114-2932-6) Grades ps-2.

An alphabet book featuring a fun-loving woman who enriches the life of her
nephew.

Amazing Grace. Mary Hoffman; Caroline Bunch, illus. Dial, 1991.
LC 90-25108, 32 p. (ISBN 0-8037-1040-2) Grades ps-3.

Grace acts out all the stories she hears. Yet, when she has a chance to play Peter Pan
in a school play, Grace receives an earful of reasons why she can't do it. Thanks to
her grandmother, Grace sees a beautiful dancer who inspires her to do what she
desires.

At the crossroads. Rachel Isadora. Greenwillow, 1991. LC 90-30751, 32 p.
(ISBN 0-688-05270-3; plb. 0-688-05271-1) Grades ps up.

These South African children are excited about their father's return after working
many months away from home. Their waiting seems endless and they become
tired. The youngest falls asleep. Finally, the bus comes and the celebration begins.

Aunt Flossie's hats, (and crab cakes later). Elizabeth Fitzgerald Howard;
James Ransome, illus. Houghton Mifflin, 1991. LC 90-33332, 32 p. (ISBN 0-395-
54682-6) Grades ps-1.

Sarah and Susan love to visit Aunt Flossie's house. They always share tea and cook-
ies, and later have crab cakes. But first they look through Flossie's hats; each one is
a fascinating story. One hat involves a very familiar tale that Sarah and Susan help
tell.

Aunt Harriet's Underground Railroad in the sky. Faith Ringgold. Crown,
1993. LC 92-20072, 32 p. (ISBN 0-517-58767-X; plb 0-517-58768-8) Grades ps-4.

Cassie and BeBe return from **Tar Beach** to join Harriet Tubman's freedom train.
They are separated as they relive the difficulties of escaping slavery on the Underground Railroad. Harriet takes Cassie along the route from the South to the North,
looking for signs of safety. Using Cassie's unique ability to fly, they go over Niagara
Falls and know they are free. Historical background included.

Aunt Martha and the golden coin. Anita Rodriquez. Crown, 1993.
LC 92-7316, 32 p. (ISBN 0-517-59337-8; plb 0-517-59338-6) Grades ps-2.

Aunt Martha is said to have magical powers because her apartment is never robbed
even though she lives on the ground floor. One day she tells neighborhood children
about finding a magic coin when she was a child in the South. It has protected her
many times. When a burglar breaks in, she uses the magic coin to protect herself.

Baby says. John Steptoe. Lothrop, 1988. LC 87-17296, 32 p. (ISBN 0-688-
07423-5; plb 0-688-07424-3); Morrow, 1992. (ISBN 0-688-11855-0) Grades ps up.

An older brother must learn to accept his baby brother's desire for attention. An
easy-to-read book.

Back home. Gloria Jean Pinkney; Jerry Pinkney, illus. Dial, 1992. LC 91-22610,
40 p. (ISBN 0-8037-1168-9; plb 0-8037-1169-7) Grades K-4.

Ernestine goes on a thrilling trip to visit her aunt, uncle, and cousin Jack. They
show her around the farm, the house where she was born, and her grandmother's
grave. She wears overalls that were her mother's. She tries very hard to make friends
with Jack. Ernestine wants him to see there is more to her than her city manners
and style.

Ben's trumpet. Rachel Isadora. Greenwillow, 1979. LC 78-12885; 32 p.
(ISBN 0-688-80194-3); Morrow, 1991. (ISBN 0-688-10988-8) Grades ps up.

Ben wants to play the trumpet. Watching the trumpet player at a nearby jazz club,
he pretends to play an imaginary trumpet until the club's trumpet player gives him
a chance to play a real one.

Best bug to be. Dolores Johnson. Macmillan, 1992. LC 90-22231, 32 p.
(ISBN 0-02-747842-4) Grades K-3.

Kelly had high hopes of getting the lead in the school play but they were dashed
when she was cast as a bumblebee. She could not get excited about being a bee, but
decided to do her best. When Kelly got up on stage, her smiles were the brightest, her
buzzes the most enthusiastic. She received the most applause for being the best bug.

Big friend, little friend. Eloise Greenfield; Jan Spivey Gilchrist, illus. Writers
and Readers, 1991. LC 91-072044, 12 p. (ISBN 0-86316-204-5) Grades ps-1.

This board book for preschoolers shows a lively toddler with two good friends—
one older, the other younger. The big friend is old enough to show him things he
does not know. The little friend can be taught new things.

Bigmama's. Donald Crews. Greenwillow, 1991. LC 90-33142, 32 p.
(ISBN 0-688-09950-5; plb 0-688-09951-3); Reading Adventures, 1993. (ISBN 0-685-64817-6; cassette 1-882869-75-3) Grades ps up.

Every year, this family visits their grandmother's farm. Bigmama is not big, but she is mother's mother. Once there, they find farm life exciting and unchanging from year to year: the chores, the well, the fishing, and the family fun.

Billy the great. Rosa Guy; Caroline Binch, illus. Delacorte, 1992. LC 92-34704, 32 p. (ISBN 0-385-30666-0; pbk 0-440-40920-9) Grades K-3.

Billy's parents would like to plan his future. They feel he would make a good teacher, doctor, or soccer player. They even try to pick his friends. But Billy has his own ideas.

Bimwili and the Zimwi. Verna Aardema; Susan Meddaugh, illus. Dial, 1985. LC 85-4449, 32 p. (ISBN 0-8037-0212-4; plb 0-8037-0213-2; pbk 0-8037-0553-0) Grades ps-3.

A young Swahili girl is allowed to go to the beach for the first time with her older sisters. She is captured by a Zimwi who wants her to sing for him. The love of her family allows her to be rescued.

Birthday. John Steptoe. Henry Holt, 1991. LC 72-182782, 32 p. (ISBN 0-8050-1849-2) Grades ps-2.

Today is Javaka's eighth birthday. He is the firstborn in a new African town created by blacks immigrants from all over the world. Everyone comes to his celebration. The party is a lot of fun: singing, dancing, steel drums, bongos, horns, and delicious food and drinks. Javaka makes his birthday wish: that "we can all live together like this forever."

Black is brown is tan. Arnold Adoff; Emily Arnold McCully, illus. Harper-Collins, 1973. LC 73-9855, 32 p. (ISBN 0-06-020083-9; plb 0-06-020084-7; pbk 0-06-443269-6) Grades ps-3.

An interracial family celebrates the things they love: cooking, singing, and playing.

Black like Kyra, white like me. Judith Vigna. Whitman, 1992. LC 92-1203, 32 p. (ISBN 0-8075-0778-4) Grades 2-6.

Christy's best friend at the youth center is Kyra. She is thrilled when Kyra and her family move in next door, but infuriated when her neighbors act rudely toward the African American family. Christy's friends are not allowed to play with her. Kyra's family is determined to stay in order to have a better life.

Black snowman. Phil Mendez; Carole Byard, illus. Scholastic, 1989.
LC 87-4774, 48 p. (ISBN 0-590-40552-7; pbk 0-590-44873-0) Grades 2-5.

In this modern fairy tale, a magical African kente cloth has the power to make a
black snowman come to life. By citing examples of noble African people, the snowman encourages Jacob to perform brave acts befitting his heritage.

Bright eyes, brown skin. Cheryl Willis Hudson; Bernette George Ford, illus.
Just Us Books, 1990. LC 90-81648, 24 p. (ISBN 0-940975-10-6; pbk 0-940975-
23-8) Grades ps-2.

Beautiful African American children romp through a day at a daycare center. They
color, play games, have lunch, dance, read, and finally pause for a nap.

Brother to the wind. Mildren Pitts Walter; Leo and Diane Dillon, illus.
Lothrop, 1985. LC 83-26800, 32 p. (ISBN plb 0-688-03812-3) Grades ps-2.

A young African boy is determined to fly. He decides to meet the Good Snake, who
tells him what he must do: make a kite and listen for the right wind.

Calypso alphabet. John Agard; Jennifer Bent, illus. Holt, 1989. LC 89-945617,
32 p. (ISBN 0-8050-1177-3) Grades ps-2.

This work captures the flavor of the Caribbean and its customs from Anancy to Zom-
bie. It is an easy read aloud book, with notes to explain the custom behind each word.

Can't sit still. Karen E. Lotz; Colleen Browning, illus. Dutton, 1993.
LC 92-28853, 48 p. (ISBN 0-525-45066-1) Grades ps-3.

A young girl who lives in the city celebrates the seasons. She hops, skips, and
dances through autumn leaves, winter snow, spring showers, and summer spray
from the hydrant. Her energy is evident on every page.

Carry go bring come. Vyanne Samuels; Jennifer Northway, illus. Macmillan,
1989. LC 89-1528, 32 p. (ISBN 0-02-778121-6) Grades ps-2.

Saturday is a big day! Leon's sister Marcia is getting married. Though Leon would
rather sleep, he gets up and is immediately asked to take things to people all over
the house. He is so loaded down that he cannot go another step. Leon is ready to
go back to bed.

Chalk doll. Charlotte Pomerantz; Frane Lessac, illus. HarperCollins, 1989.
LC 88-872, 32 p. (ISBN 0-397-32318-2; plb 0-397-32319-0) Grades K-3.

When Rose has to stay in bed because of a cold, she asks Mother for stories about her childhood in Jamaica. Mother tells her about making a rag doll, which she loved because she made it herself. She calls store-bought dolls "chalk dolls." Rose decides to make her own rag doll, just as Mother did.

Charlie Parker played be bop. Chris Raschka. Orchard, 1992. LC 91-38420, 32 p. (ISBN 0-531-05999-5; plb 0-531-08599-6) Grades ps-1.

Charlie Parker played a mean saxophone, and his style evolved into a genre called bebop. This book uses silly images and nonsense words to communicate a rhythm. When read aloud, one gets the sense of being dropped into a jazz song.

Charlie's house. Reviva Scheimbrucker; Niki Daly, illus. Viking, 1989. LC 90-50985, 32 p. (ISBN 0-670-84024-6) Grades ps-3.

Charlie lives in South Africa. He watches men build his house out of cement and iron sheets. He knows that his mother does not like the shelter. The next time it rains, Charlie builds a play house out of mud, and puts in everything his mother wants. He even makes a car, imagining himself living a grand life and making his mother happy.

Cherries and cherry pits. Vera B. Williams. Greenwillow, 1986. LC 85-17156, 40 p. (ISBN 0-688-05145-6; plb 0-688-05146-4); Morrow, 1991 (ISBN 0-688-10478-9) Grades ps up.

Bidemmi is a girl who loves to draw. All of her pictures and stories center around people "eating the cherries and spitting out the pits."

Chicken Sunday. Patricia Polacco. Putnam, 1992. LC 91-16030, 32 p. (ISBN 0-399-22133-6) Grades ps-3.

Because Stewart and Winston take a Ukrainian girl in as family, their grandma is her's too. They all wish to get grandma the Easter bonnet she wants very badly. They decide to sell decorated Easter eggs to earn enough money to buy the hat.

Chita's Christmas tree. Elizabeth Fitzgerald Howard; Floyd Cooper, illus. Macmillan, 1989. LC 88-26250, 32 p. (ISBN 0-02-744621-2; pbk 0-689-71739-3) Grades ps-2.

A family plans a special Christmas celebration in turn of the century Baltimore. Chita and her father take their buggy into the woods and put her name on the tree they choose. On Christmas, Chita finds her tree decorated and surrounded with presents.

Clean your room, Harvey Moon. Pat Cummings. Macmillan, 1991. LC 89-23863, 32 p. (ISBN 0-02-725511-5) Grades ps-2.

Mom is determined that Harvey clean his room before watching anymore TV. And what a mess he has there! If he hurries, maybe he will not have to miss too much TV. Put a few things under the rug, and he will be done. Mom is not fooled.

Corduroy. Don Freeman. Viking, 1968. LC 68-16068, 32 p. (ISBN 0-670-24133-4); Live Oak, 1982. (ISBN book + cassette 0-941078-08-6; pbk + cassette 0-941078-06-X; 4 pbks + cassette 0-941078-07-8); Puffin, 1993. (ISBN pbk 0-14-050173-8; Story Tape 0-14-095114-8; 0-14-095063-X) Grades ps-3.

Corduroy is a bear in a department store waiting for someone to buy him. He sees the perfect girl and she sees him. Her mother says that he doesn't look new because he is missing a button from his shoulder strap. So Corduroy decides to look for a button.

Cornrows. Camille Yarbrough; Carole Byard, illus. Putnam, 1992. LC 78-24010, 32 p. (ISBN pbk 0-698-20709-2) Grades 2-6.

Sister and little brother, Me Too, receive a treat at hairbraiding time. Mama and Great-Grammaw cuddle them as their fingers weave the hair into a design. Sister wants to know about the design, so the story is told of woven hair's history, and the African tradition it signifies.

Dancing with the Indians. Angela Shelf Medearis; Samuel Byrd, illus. Holiday House, 1991. LC 90-28666, 32 p. (ISBN 0-8234-0893-0; pbk 0-8234-1023-4) Grades ps-3.

This story deals with the relationship between an escaped slave and the Seminole Indians who took him in. The slave's family has continued to visit the Indians, and his granddaughter describes one of these annual events. The African American family arrives and watches shyly at first. But they are encouraged to join the dance, until they are whirling and twirling in the Ribbon and Rattlesnake dances, and finally the Indian Stomp dance.

Daniel's dog. Jo Ellen Bogart. Scholastic, 1992. LC 89-35258, 32 p. (ISBN pbk 0-590-43401-2) Grades ps-2.

Daniel has a new baby sister. He now has to play by himself. But he does not have to be by himself when he imagines he has a dog named Lucy. When Daniel's friend Norman is sad about his father going away on a business trip, Daniel offers him an imaginary dog for company.

Darkness and the butterfly. Ann Grifalconi. Little, Brown, 1987.
LC 86-27561, 32 p. (ISBN 0-316-32863-4) Grades ps-3.

Osa, an African girl, is afraid of the dark even though she is fearless during the day.
The village wise woman tells her about a little yellow butterfly that flies in the dark.
Osa dreams that she flies like the butterfly, seeing beautiful things. Then she is not
afraid to go home by herself in the dark.

Dinner at Aunt Connie's house. Faith Ringgold. Hyperion, 1993.
LC 92-54871, 32 p. (ISBN 1-56282-425-2; plb 1-56282-426-0) Grades 1-4.

When Melody visits her Aunt Connie's house, she is fascinated by her aunt's paintings, especially when the paintings talk. Each one is an African American woman of
distinction, telling her own story. Imagine the dinner guests' surprise when the
paintings are moved to the dining room.

Do like Kyla. Angela Johnson; James E. Ransome, illus. Orchard, 1990.
LC 89-16229, 32 p. (ISBN 0-531-05852-2; plb. 0-531-08452-3) Grades ps-2.

Kyla's little sister does everything like her. She's begins with calling the birds early in
the morning. At bedtime that night, Kyla taps at the window—just like little sister.

Double Dutch and the voodoo shoes: an urban folktale. Melodye Rosales; original story by Warren Colman. Children's Press, 1991. LC 91-13153, 32 p.
(ISBN 0-516-05133-4; pbk 0-516-45133-2) Grades ps-3.

Part of the *Adventures in storytelling* series. Two girls compete in a Double Dutch
jumping rope contest. Shalesea always jumps in the same worn-out shoes which she
considers her good luck charm. A condition of the contest is to jump without the
shoes. Shalesea still jumps well, and the shoes help in their own magical way. Illustrations and text are printed separately, to encourage storytelling activities.

Dove. Dianne Stewart; Jude Daly, illus. Greenwillow, 1993. LC 91-45798, 32 p.
(ISBN 0-688-11264-1; plb 0-688-11265-X) Grades ps up.

Grandmother Maloka and Lindi worry after the flood hits their part of South
Africa. They cannot plant crops, and will have no food. They make beautiful key
rings and necklaces, but cannot sell them. Then they remember a dove who visited
them after the flood, and the hope it gave them. Inspired, they make a beaded
dove. It sells, and they make many more until they can plant again.

Easter. Miriam Nerlove. Whitman, 1989. LC 89-35394, 24 p. (ISBN 0-8075-
1871-9; pbk 0-8075-1872-7) Grades ps-1.

A family celebrates Easter in a loving, supportive home. The Easter traditions include coloring eggs, a special basket, going to church in new clothes, hearing the Easter story, and sharing dinner. Of course, everyone hunts eggs.

Eat up, Gemma. Sarah Hayes; Jan Ormerod, illus. Lothrop, 1988. LC 87-36205, 32 p. (ISBN 0-688-08149-5) Grades ps-1.

Baby Gemma does not eat any of the wonderful food she is offered. She *does* try to eat the fruit off a lady's hat in church. So big brother makes her food look like the hat—and she eats every bite.

Elijah's angel: a story for Chanukah and Christmas. Michael Rosen; Aminah Brenda Lynn Robinson, illus. Harcourt, 1992. LC 91-37552, 32 p. (ISBN 0-15-225394-7) Grades K-3.

Michael, a nine-year-old Jewish boy, loves to visit Elijah, an eighty-year-old barber who makes beautiful wood carvings. Most of the carvings express his Christian beliefs, so Michael is concerned when Elijah gives him a carved angel. Once Michael realizes that it's merely a gift of friendship, he makes a gift in return: a menorah. Elijah adds a candle each night of Chanukah to show his friendship.

Enchanted hair tale. Alexis DeVeaux; Cheryl Hanna, illus. HarperCollins, 1987. LC 85-45824, 40 p. (ISBN 0-06-021623-9; plb 0-06-021624-7); Puffin, 1993. (ISBN pbk 0-14-054406-2) Grades K-3.

Sudan has wonderful hair: it giggles and roars, and even sprouts wings. Everyone teases him about it until he gets very angry and runs away. He discovers some circus performers who can do marvelous tricks. They all have hair like his. He tries some of their tricks, and keeps the memory of the exciting afternoon when he returns home.

Evan's corner. Elizabeth Starr Hill; Sandra Speidel, illus. Viking, 1991. LC 92-25334, 32 p. (ISBN 0-670-82830-0); Puffin, 1993. (ISBN pbk 0-14-054406-2) Grades ps-3.

Evan needs his own place, one that is just his. Eight people live in his apartment, so he chooses a corner to decorate and spend time in. Something is missing. When he shares the corner with his younger brother, he finds what is missing.

Everett Anderson's Christmas coming. Lucille Clifton; Jan S. Gilchrist, illus. Holt, 1991. LC 91-2041, 32 p. (ISBN 0-8050-1549-3; pbk 0-8050-2949-4) Grades ps-4.

Despite things that can make people sad, such as Daddy's absence, Christmas is a very special time for Everett and his mother. It is one of anticipation, parties, snow, a tree in the living room, and love.

Everett Anderson's goodbye. Lucille Clifton; Ann Grifalconi, illus. Henry Holt, 1983. LC 82-23426, 32 p. (ISBN 0-8050-0235-9; pbk 0-8050-0800-4) Grades ps-2.

Everett has to deal with his father's death. He struggles through the stages of grief: denial, anger, bargaining, depression, and acceptance.

Everett Anderson's nine month long. Lucille Clifton; Ann Grifalconi, illus. Henry Holt, 1978. LC 78-4202, 32 p. (ISBN 0-8050-0287-1; pbk 0-8050-0295-2) Grades ps-2.

Now that Everett's mother is Mrs. Perry, something is different about her. She is going to have a baby and Everett feels left out. He wants to play with the baby, but has to wait. Then even his mother doesn't seem to pay attention to him any more. But the Perrys are a family and Everett finds his place there.

Father and son. Denize Lauture; Jonathan Green, illus. Putnam, 1993. LC 91-29413, 32 p. (ISBN 0-399-21867-X) Grades ps-3.

This simple poem, with vivid illustrations, celebrates the relationship between a father and his son. They spend a relaxing day together: walking, flying a kite, going to church, fishing, reading, and sharing.

First pink light. Eloise Greenfield; Jan Spivey Gilchrist, illus. Writers and Readers Pub., 1991. LC 91-07248, 32 p. (ISBN 0-86316-207-X; pbk 0-86316-212-6) Grades ps-3.

Daddy has been away for a long time, and Tyree misses him. So Tyree wants to hide and surprise his father when he comes home. Mommy says Daddy will not be home until early morning, that he can wait up, but somehow he cannot keep his eyes open.

Finding the green stone. Alice Walker; Catherine Deeter, illus. Harcourt, 1991. LC 90-33038, 32 p. (ISBN 0-15-227538-X) Grades ps up.

Everyone has a beautiful glowing green stone, but Johnny loses his. In his anxiety, he lashes out at his peers. When he admits his bad feelings, everyone understands and helps him look for it. He realizes the only way he can find his stone—by being kind and loving.

Flyaway girl. Ann Grifalconi. Little, Brown, 1992. LC 90-39799, 32 p. (ISBN 0-316-32866-9) Grades ps-3.

Nsia is a busy African girl. Her mother wants her to enjoy childhood as long as possible, but she needs Nsia's help. Mother sends her to gather rushes to weave for the

New Year Ceremony of Beginning. In spite of many distractions, Nsia completes this important task and demonstrates her growing maturity.

Follow the drinking gourd. Jeanette Winter. Knopf, 1988. LC 88-9661, 48 p. (ISBN 0-394-89694-7; plb 0-394-99694-1) Grades 1-4.

This picture book portrays an old sailor teaching slaves a folk song containing directions to the Underground Railroad. "Follow the drinking gourd" advises looking to the constellation of the Big Dipper for directions and follows one family who escaped. Music included.

Fortune tellers. Lloyd Alexander; Trina Schart Hyman, illus. Dutton, 1992. LC 91-30684, 32 p. (ISBN 0-525-44849-7) Grades K-3.

A dissatisfied carpenter goes to a fortune teller. Hearing only what he wants to, he surmises that he will be rich. When he returns to ask another question, a woman mistakes *him* for the fortune teller. The carpenter finds a new career telling others what they want to hear.

Golden bear. Ruth Young; Rachel Isadora, illus. Viking, 1992. LC 89-24843, 32 p. (ISBN 0-670-82577-8; pbk 0-14-050959-3) Grades ps-1.

Golden Bear does so many things with his son. Together they dance, play the violin, watch a bug, ice skate, build a snowman, watch tulips grow, work in the garden, talk on the telephone, take a bath, and make a bedtime wish.

Grandpa's face. Eloise Greenfield; Floyd Cooper, illus. Putnam, 1988. LC 87-16729, 32 p. (ISBN 0-399-21525-5; pbk 0-399-22106-9) Grades ps-2.

After seeing her grandfather make an angry face when he was rehearsing for a play, Tamika worries about him losing his temper with her.

Green lion of Zion Street. Julia Fields; Jerry Pinkney, illus. Macmillan, 1988. LC 87-15519, 32 p. (ISBN 0-689-50414-4; pbk 0-689-71693-1) Grades K-3.

At first, children waiting at a bus stop are frightened by a stone lion. When they find out it is a statue, they entertain themselves by making up stories about the majestic lion.

Habari gani? What's the news?: a Kwanzaa story. Sundaira Morninghouse; Jody Kim, illus. Open Hand, 1992. LC 92-12272, 32 p. (ISBN 0-940880-39-3) Grades K-4.

This storybook shows an African American family incorporating the concepts of

Kwanzaa into their everyday lives. Each day's principle becomes an activity: the family works for unity and harmony, the children express their individuality and creativity, and they work together to help their community. Through these goals and activities, the family solidifies their beliefs.

Half a moon and one whole star. Crescent Dragonwagon; Jerry Pinkney, illus. Macmillan, 1986. LC 85-13818, 32 p. (ISBN 0-02-733120-2; pbk 0-689-71415-7) Grades K-3.

After Susan goes to bed, a whole world continues just outside of her awareness. There are stars and the moon, forest animals, flowers, people talking, and others working; all while Susan sleeps and dreams.

Hard to be six. Arnold Adoff; Cheryl Hanna, illus. Lothrop, Lee & Shepard, 1990. LC 89-45903, 32 p. (ISBN 0-688-09013-3; plb 0-688-09579-8) Grades K-3.

A little boy is anxious to grow up, especially when his sister has a birthday. He jumps on her new bicycle, but it is too big for him and he crashes. His family is understanding and helpful. He learns that to be himself is a good thing—at any age.

Home field. David Spohn. Lothrop, 1993. LC 92-5459, 32 p. (ISBN 0-688-11172-6; plb 0-688-11173-4) Grades ps-2.

Dad and Matt share a special time on a summer morning. They play a game of baseball, with just the two of them as an imaginary crowd. This is just one way that they show their love for each other. A warm, bi-racial family story.

How many stars in the sky? Lenny Hort; James E. Ransome, illus. Morrow, 1991. LC 90-36044, 32 p. (ISBN 0-688-10103-8; plb 0-688-10104-6) Grades ps-3.

Mama is away from home for a night: her son cannot sleep. He decides to count stars until he feels tired. Daddy discovers him outside and they go for a drive to look for a place to count stars.

Hue boy. Rita Phillips Mitchell; Caroline Binch, illus. Dial, 1993. LC 92-18560, 32 p. (ISBN 0-8037-1448-3) Grades ps-3.

Hue Boy is the smallest boy in his Caribbean village and he begins to worry. His mama is anxious to see him grow and he gets teased at school. Everyone tries to tell him how to grow, and Hue Boy works at it very hard. Then his father returns from his job working on a ship. As Hue Boy walks with him, he is sure that he must be tall now.

I can do it by myself. Lessie Jones Little and Eloise Greenfield; Carole Byard, illus. HarperCollins, 1978. LC 77-11554, 32 p. (ISBN 0-690-01369-8; plb 0-690-03851-8) Grades K-2.

Donnie has a plan to get his mother a birthday present. He picked out a plant, and is going to get it all by himself. His brother says he is too little, but he has everything worked out—as long as he can get by the dog.

I love my family. Wade Hudson; Cal Massey, illus. Scholastic, 1993. LC 92-9773, 32 p. (ISBN 0-590-45763-2) Grades ps-2.

A young boy describes the fun of his annual family reunion. He loves seeing his cousins and talks about each relatives' uniqueness. The family plays games, sings, dances, listens to Grandpa's scary stories, eats lots of food, and takes pictures.

I make music. Eloise Greenfield; Jan Spivey Gilchrist, illus. Writers and Readers, 1991. LC 91-072046, 12 p. (ISBN 0-86316-205-3) Grades ps-1.

This board book for preschoolers features a lively music maker. She delights her parents by playing a variety of instruments, always confident that whatever she plays will be special because she made the music.

I need a lunch box. Jeannette Caines; Pat Cummings, illus. HarperCollins, 1993. LC 85-45829, 32 p. (ISBN 0-06-020984-4; plb 0-06-020985-2; pbk 0-06-443341-2) Grades ps-1.

Even though he is not starting school like his sister, a little boy wants his very own lunch box.

I remember "121." Francine Haskins. Children's Book Press, 1991. LC 91-16647, 32 p. (ISBN 0-89239-100-6) Grades K-5.

This autobiographical account of an African American family in 1950's Washington, D.C. celebrates the life they shared. The daily activities are treasured memories: the birth of a younger brother, family gatherings, playing dress-up, street games, and finally moving day.

Irene and the big, fine nickel. Irene Smalls-Hector; Tyrone Geter, illus. Little, Brown, 1991. LC 89-32816, 32 p. (ISBN 0-316-79871-1) Grades ps-3.

Of all the adventures Irene has on a 1950's Harlem Saturday morning, the most exciting is finding a nickel and sharing the raisin bun she buys with it.

Island baby. Holly Keller. Greenwillow, 1992. LC 91-32491, 32 p. (ISBN 0-688-10579-3; plb 0-688-10580-7) Grades ps-2.

Simon loves to help Pops run the animal hospital where they nurse injured birds. Simon finds a flamingo with a broken leg. He nurses it all summer, and is sad to let it go. When he sees a flock of flamingos, Simon is proud that he was able to help the bird on its way.

Jafta—the town. Hugh Lewin; Lisa Kopper, illus. Carolrhoda, 1984. LC 84-4950, 24 p. (ISBN plb 0-87614-266-8) Grades ps-3.

Jafta and his mother travel to the city to visit his father. There is so much to do and see—and it is very easy for a boy to get separated from his parents.

Jafta's father. Hugh Lewin; Lisa Kopper, illus. Lerner, 1989. LC 82-12837, 24 p. (ISBN pbk 0-87614-496-2); Carolrhoda, 1983. (ISBN plb 0-87614-209-9) Grades ps-3.

Jafta, an African boy, remembers special times with his father and the things he helped him build. When his father has to work in town, Jafta yearns to see him again.

Jafta's mother. Hugh Lewin; Lisa Kopper, illus. Carolrhoda, 1988. LC 82-12863, 24 p. (ISBN pbk 0-87614-208-0); Lerner, 1989. (ISBN pbk 0-87614-495-4) Grades ps-3.

Jafta recounts stories about his mother and the times they share together.

Jamaica tag-along. Juanita Havill; Anne Sibley O'Brien, illus. Houghton Mifflin, 1989. LC 88-13478, 32 p. (ISBN 0-395-49602-0; pbk 0-395-54949-3) Grades ps-3.

When Jamaica's brother, Ossie, tells her not to tag along, she follows anyway. Her feelings are hurt when he yells at her, so she begins building a sandcastle. When a younger child wants to help her, she realizes she can include him, just as she wishes she were part of Ossie's plans.

Jamaica's find. Juanita Havill; Anne Sibley O'Brien, illus. Houghton Mifflin, 1986. LC 85-14542, 32 p. (ISBN 0-395-39376-0; pbk 0-395-45357-7) Grades ps-3.

Jamaica finds a hat and a stuffed dog at the park. She takes the hat to the lost and found, but decides to keep the stuffed dog. She feels bad about keeping the little dog, and when she takes it to the lost and found, she meets the girl who lost the dog.

Jamal and the angel. Anita Rodriquez. Crown, 1992. LC 92-11636, 32 p. (ISBN 0-517-58601-0; plb 0-517-59115-4) Grades ps-2.

Jamal has a guardian angel. He did not know this for a long time, because angels are invisible. Jamal works hard and saves his money to fulfill his dream of getting a guitar. When he unselfishly uses his money to buy Christmas presents, the guardian angel reveals himself. He shows Jamal where to find a part-time job, and soon he has his guitar.

Jamal's busy day. Wade Hudson; George Ford, illus. Just Us, 1991. LC 90-81646, 24 p. (ISBN 0-940975-21-1; pbk 0-940975-24-6) Grades 1-3.

Part of the *Feeling Good* series. Jamal describes his day. School is his work, just as his father is an architect and his mother is an accountant. Jamal works hard at his "job," occasionally helping his "supervisor" and "co-workers." When his parents talk about their busy day, Jamal can say: "I know just what you mean."

Jambo means hello: Swahili alphabet book. Muriel Feelings; Tom Feelings, illus. Dial, 1985. LC 73-15441, 56 p. (ISBN 0-8037-4346-7; plb 0-8037-4350-5); Puffin, 1985. (ISBN pbk 0-8037-4428-5) Grades K-3.

This alphabet book introduces young readers to Swahili language and culture. Each letter of the alphabet has a Swahili word, a phonetic pronunciation, and a brief explanation. The muted illustrations show an aspect of village life connected with the word.

Jenny. Beth P. Wilson; Dolores Johnson, illus. Macmillan, 1990. LC 89-8135, 32 p. (ISBN 0-02-793120-X) Grades K-3.

In a series of prose poems, Jenny portrays her life: school, home, church, and Grandma's house. Jenny does not like the fact that her father lives in Ohio, and that she and her mother are alone. She also describes things she likes such as a wedding and Grandpa's snoring.

Jenny's journey. Sheila White Samtom. Viking, 1991. LC 90-25745, 32 p. (ISBN 0-670-83490-4; pbk 0-14-054308-2) Grades ps-3.

Jenny is lonely after her best friend, Maria, moves to an island far away. So Jenny writes her a letter, and draws pictures to describe how she will travel in her boat to see Maria.

Jonathan and his mommy. Irene Smalls-Hector; Michael Hays, illus. Little, Brown, 1992. LC 91-31797, 32 p. (ISBN 0-316-79870-3) Grades ps-3.

When Jonathan and his mommy go for a walk, it is exciting. They walk in so many different ways: zigzag steps, reggae steps, giant steps, and crisscross ones. Against a city backdrop, they explore their neighborhood and enjoy the time together.

Joshua's Masai mask. Dakari Hru; Anna Rich, illus. Lee and Low, 1993. LC 92-73219, 32 p. (ISBN 1-880000-02-4) Grades K-3.

Joshua loves playing the kalimba, an African instrument taught to him by his Uncle Zambezi. But playing it in the school talent show is quite another matter. His parents are thrilled, but Joshua is afraid everyone will laugh at him for not being cool. Then Uncle Zambezi gives him a magical Masai mask. Joshua finds out what life is like for the "cool" people he admires. He then decides to play his kalimba with pride.

Julius. Angela Johnson; Dav Pilkey, illus. Orchard, 1993. LC 92-24175, 32 p. (ISBN 0-531-05465-9; plb 0-531-08615-1) Grades ps-1.

Maya's grandfather has given her a special surprise: Julius the pig. Maya loves Julius because he does such unexpected things. Her parents do not love him, because of the messes he makes. But Julius and Maya have a lot of fun.

Just us women. Jeannette Caines; Pat Cummings, illus. HarperCollins, 1982. LC 81-48655, 32 p. (ISBN plb 0-06-020942-9; pbk 0-06-443056-1) Grades K-3.

A young girl savors the preparations for a car trip that she and her favorite aunt will make by themselves.

Kelly in the mirror. Martha M. Vertreace; Sandra Speidel, illus. Whitman, 1993. LC 92-22655, 32 p. (ISBN 0-8075-4152-4) Grades ps-2.

Her brother has her father's eyes. Her sister's eyebrows curve just like Mama's. But Kelly does not look like any of them and that makes her sad. She likes to go to the attic when that happens. While exploring, Kelly finds an old photo album and sees that she looks just like her mother when she was a girl.

Kinda blue. Ann Grifalconi. Little, Brown, 1993. LC 92-1399, 32 p. (ISBN 0-316-32869-3) Grades ps-3.

Sissy is feeling grumpy, moping around, missing her father who died some years earlier. She wonders if anyone notices her. Then her Uncle Dan comes and takes her for a ride on his shoulders.

King of another country. Fiona French. Scholastic, 1993. LC 92-12661, 32 p. (ISBN 0-590-46369-1) Grades ps-3.

Ojo played his drums early in the morning, and always said "no" when someone asked him to do something. The king of the forest offered Ojo his own kingdom if he said "yes" as well as "no." The only forbidden thing was to open the carved door. Ojo now said "yes" to everything and was very successful as a result. When his new wife wants to open the carved door, Ojo learns one must sometimes say "no."

Laney's lost Momma. Diane Johnston Hamm; Sally G. Ward, illus. Whitman, 1991. LC 90-26824, 32 p. (ISBN 0-8075-4340-3) Grades ps-2.

Laney suddenly realizes that the woman she thought was her momma is not. She looks all over the store, and cannot find her momma anywhere. Her mother had told her to never leave the store and, if she ever got in trouble, to ask for help. Laney follows those instructions and mother and daughter are reunited.

Leaving morning. Angela Johnson; David Soman, illus. Orchard, 1992. LC 91-21123, 32 p. (ISBN 0-531-05992-8; plb 0-531-08592-9) Grades ps-2.

A family is moving. They had to say good-bye to friends and familiar things and pack. When moving day finally arrives, they find that their final good-bye is the hardest.

Little Eight John. Jan Wahl; Wil Clay, illus. Dutton, 1992. LC 91-2707, 32 p. (ISBN 0-525-67367-9) Grades K-3.

Little Eight John looked fine, but he was mean. He did exactly the opposite of what his mother said, just to cause problems. Little Eight John disobeyed his mother once too often, and he was pursued by the fearsome "Old Raw Head Bloody Bones." Now he always minds his mother!

Mac and Marie and the train toss surprise. Elizabeth Fitzgerald Howard; Gail Gordon Carter, illus. Macmillan, 1993. LC 92-17918, 32 p. (ISBN 0-02-744640) Grades ps-2.

Mac and Marie are waiting at the railroad track. They know exactly when the train comes. Their uncle Clem works on it, and promised to toss them a surprise package. As darkness settles, Mac and Marie see the package thrown from the train. It is a wonderful present—a conch shell from Florida with the sound of the ocean.

Mary Guy. Kilty Binger. Lothrop, 1993. LC 92-10261, 32 p. (ISBN 0-688-10783-4; plb 0-688-10784-2) Grades K-3.

Mary Guy's favorite song is a nonsense song that she sings all the time on her Caribbean island. The governor does not allow any fun, and is determined to outsmart Mary Guy. She outsmarts him.

Mary had a little lamb. Sarah Josepha Hale. Scholastic, 1990. LC 89-24391, 32 p. (ISBN 0-590-43773-9; pbk 0-590-43774-7) Grades ps-1.

This old nursery rhyme has an exciting new look, including a thoroughly modern, African American Mary. Color photographs.

Masai and I. Virginia Kroll; Nancy Carpenter, illus. Macmillan, 1992. LC 91-24561, 32 p. (ISBN 0-02-751165-0) Grades K-2.

When Linda learns about East Africa, she imagines how her life would change if she were Masai. Customs involving food, family life, home, and work would be very different. Still, she loves her family and will always be herself.

Matthew and Tilly. Rebecca Jones; Beth Peck, illus. Dutton, 1991. LC 90-3730, 32 p. (ISBN 0-525-44684-2) Grades ps-3.

Matthew and Tilly did everything together: they played, ate ice cream, and rescued a cat. One day, they get sick of each other. It was just a little thing, but they shouted, stomped, then each played alone. Soon they could not stand being apart and made up.

Million fish . . . more or less. Patricia C. McKissack; Dena Schutzer, illus. Knopf, 1992. LC 90-34322, 40 p. (ISBN 0-679-80692-X; plb 0-679-90692-4) Grades ps-3.

Strange things can happen on the Bayou Clapateaux. Hugh Thomas catches a million fish, but only gets home with three because alligators, raccoons, and cats take most of them.

Mirandy and Brother Wind. Patricia McKissack; Jerry Pinkney, illus. Knopf, 1988. LC 87-349, 32 p. (ISBN 0-394-88765-4; plb 0-394-98765-9; book + cassette 0-679-82668-8) Grades ps-3.

Hoping to win first prize at her first cakewalk, Mirandy wants Brother Wind to be her dance partner. She ends winning more than the contest.

"More, more, more," said the baby. Vera B. Williams. Greenwillow, 1990. LC 89-2023, 32 p. (ISBN 0-688-09173-3; plb 0-688-09174-1) Grades ps up.

The love between babies and grownups is shown in triplicate in this energetic, sweet story.

Mother Crocodile : Maman-Caiman. Birago Diop; Rosa Guy; John Steptoe, illus. Doubleday, 1993. LC 80-393, 32 p. (ISBN 0-385-30803-5) Grades ps-3.

Mother Crocodile tells stories about the past and about humans. The impatient little crocodiles want stories about adventure and faraway places. They believe the monkey who says that Mother Crocodile is crazy. Then a war between humans comes to their quiet river. The little crocodiles refuse to leave with Mother until the humans try to take them. Then they remember the escape their mother told them about in her stories.

Mrs. Katz and Tush. Patricia Polacco. Bantam, 1992. LC 91-18710, 32 p. (ISBN 0-553-08122-5; pbk 0-440-40936-5) Grades ps-3.

Mrs. Katz and Larnel become friends as they care for a kitten named Tush. It was abandoned because it was ugly and had no tail. The lonely Jewish widow and the young African American boy talk about the suffering and triumphs of their ancestors. They celebrate Passover together, and panic when Tush disappears.

My best friend. Pat Hutchins. Greenwillow, 1993. LC 91-48354, 32 p. (ISBN 0-688-11485-7; plb 0-688-11486-5) Grades ps up.

This is a story of two friends with different talents. One friend runs faster, climbs higher, eats spaghetti, and fingerpaints neater. The other friend is brave in the dark, knowing there is no monster lurking there.

My Daddy and I. Eloise Greenfield; Jan Spivey Gilchrist, illus. Writers and Readers, 1991. LC 91-072045, 12 p. (ISBN 0-86316-206-1) Grades ps-1.

In this toddler board book, Daddy knows how to make a kid feel special—by doing things together.

My doll, Keshia. Eloise Greenfield; Jan Spivey Gilchrist, illus. Writers and Readers, 1991. LC 91-072047, 12 p. (ISBN 0-86316-203-7) Grades ps-1.

This toddler board book shows the unusual things that dolls can do when loving friends help them.

My little island. Frane Lessac. HarperCollins, 1985. LC 84-48355, 48 p. (ISBN 0-397-32114-7; plb 0-397-32215-5; pbk 0-06-443146-0) Grades ps-3.

A young boy and his best friend travel to the Caribbean island where he was born. They enjoy many things there: visiting family, marketing, eating special food, hearing calypso and reggae music, and a celebration.

Nettie Jo's friends. Patricia C. McKissack; Scott Cook, illus. Knopf, 1989. LC 87-14080, 40 p. (ISBN 0-394-89158-9; plb 0-394-99158-3; pbk 0-679-86573-X) Grades ps-4.

Nettie Jo must have a new dress for her favorite doll, but all the needles are being used. So she visits her friends, the animals. She finds that they have problems of their own. After Nettie Jo helps them, they seem to forget her. When she most needs their help, the animals do come through for her.

Not yet, Yvette. Helen Ketteman; Irene Trivas, illus. Whitman, 1992. LC 91-19608, 24 p. (ISBN 0-8075-5771-4) Grades ps-2.

There are many things for Yvette and her father to do in preparing a surprise birthday party for her mother: house cleaning; baking the cake; shopping for presents; wrapping them. The effort pays off when they jump out and say, "Happy Birthday."

Now let me fly: the story of a slave family. Dolores Johnson. Macmillan, 1993. LC 92-33683, 32 p. (ISBN 0-02-747699-5) Grades K-5.

Minna's story begins in Africa. She is kidnapped and sold into slavery, betrayed by a banished tribesman. On the slave ship, Amadi befriends her. They are sold to the same master, marry, and have children. Later they are separated and each one yearns to reunite the family.

Not so fast, Songolo. Niki Daley. Macmillan, 1986. LC 85-71034, 32 p. (ISBN 0-689-50367-9; pbk 0-14-050715-9) Grades K-3.

Malusi likes doing things slowly. When his grandmother takes him shopping, he dawdles to look at things, plays games, and sings. But after grandmother buys him a pair of red tennis shoes, she has to tell him not to walk so fast.

Oh, that cat! Norma Simon; Dora Leder, illus. Whitman, 1986. LC 85-15546, 32 p. (ISBN 0-8075-5919-9) Grades ps-4.

Max the cat does whatever he wants to do. At one time or another, everyone in the family has been mad at him. There are also times when he is the sweetest, funniest, most lovable cat in the world.

On the riverbank. Charles Temple; Melanie Hall, illus. Houghton Mifflin, 1992. LC 91-43942, 32 p. (ISBN 0-395-61591-7) Grades ps-3.

This rhyming text evokes the feeling of a jaunty family fishing outing after a long winter. They enjoy the sounds of spring, and the anticipation of catching fish. When there's a tug on the line, the excitement begins.

One of three. Angela Johnson; David Soman, illus. Orchard, 1991. LC 90-29316, 32 p. (ISBN 0-531-05955-3; plb 0-531-08555-4) Grades ps-1.

The youngest of three girls loves her role with the others. Sometimes the older sisters do things without her, and she feels lonely. Then Mama and Daddy are there, and she is one of three again, although in a different way.

One smiling grandma: a Caribbean counting book. Ann Marie Linden; Lynne Russell, illus. Dial, 1992. LC 91-30826, 32 p. (ISBN 0-8037-1132-8) Grades ps-3.

This bright, colorful counting book draws on Caribbean wildlife and culture to demonstrate number concepts. The rhyming text and the actions of a young girl are lively.

Osa's pride. Ann Grifalconi. Little, Brown, 1990. LC 88-28828, 32 p. (ISBN 0-316-32865-0) Grades ps-3.

Osa's grandmother uses storytelling to help her realize that selfish pride only alienates her friends.

Over the green hills. Rachel Isadora. Greenwillow, 1992. LC 91-12761, 32 p. (ISBN 0-688-10509-2; plb 0-688-10510-6) Grades ps up.

Zolani lives in rural, Black South Africa. He and his mother are going to visit grandmother. Along the way, they have interesting experiences, and meet friendly people. Once at grandmother's house, she is not there and Zolani must wait. Soon she arrives, they rejoice and play their pennywhistles.

Papa Lucky's shadow. Niki Daly. Macmillan, 1992. LC 91-24283, 32 p. (ISBN 0-689-50541-8) Grades K-3.

Papa Lucky loved to dance, but he gave up dancing once he got a steady job and married grandma. Then he comes to live with his granddaughter and he starts dancing again. He puts an "act" together and they do street performances to earn money. They put bottle caps on the girl's shoes so she can dance with him in "Me and my shadow."

Patchwork Quilt. Valerie Flournoy; Jerry Pinkney, illus. Dial, 1985. LC 84-1711, 32 p. (ISBN 0-8037-0097-0; plb 0-8037-0098-9) Grades 4-8.

Making a patchwork quilt binds a grandmother, a mother, and a young girl together through different seasons and adversity. A *Reading rainbow* book.

Pretend you're a cat. Jean Marzollo; Jerry Pinkney, illus. Dial, 1990. LC 89-34546, 32 p. (ISBN plb 0-8037-0774-6) Grades ps-3.

Each verse in this book asks the reader to do things that the animal in the poem does. Cats climb, leap stretch, sleep, hiss, scat, and purr—can you? Can you pretend you are a dog, a fish, a bee, a chick, a bird, a squirrel, a pig, a cow, a horse, a seal, a snake, or a bear.

Princess Gorilla and a new kind of water. Verna Aardema; Victoria Chase, illus. Dial, 1988. LC 86-32888, 32 p. (ISBN 0-8037-0412-7; plb 0-8037-0413-5; pbk 0-8037-0914-5) Grades ps-3.

King Gorilla finds a barrel of strong "water" (which had vinegar printed on the side) and decides that whoever drank the whole barrel will marry his beautiful daughter. The princess and the handsome gorilla she admires have to think of something quick.

Rachel Parker, kindergarten show off. Ann M. Martin; Nancy Poydar, illus. Holiday House, 1992. LC 91-25793, 40 p. (ISBN 0-8234-0935-X; pbk 0-8234-1067-6) Grades ps-3.

Olivia is five years old. She loves kindergarten and lives with her mother, father, and Rosie the cat. Then Rachel moves in next door. Olivia does not like Rachel because she is a show off. When Olivia and Rachel have to work together, they discover they can be friends.

Ragtime Tumpie. Alan Schroeder; Bernie Fuchs, illus. Little, Brown, 1989. LC 87-37221, 32 p. (ISBN 0-316-77497-9; pbk 0-316-77504-5) Grades ps-3.

Paintings capture the energy of this fictionalized account of an event in Josephine Baker's childhood: she wins a dancing contest.

Rain talk. Mary Serfozo; Keiko Narahashi, illus. Macmillan, 1990. LC 89-12178, 32 p. (ISBN 0-689-50496-9; pbk 0-689-71699-0) Grades K-3.

A young girl takes in every enjoyable moment of a rainy day from the sound of the rain drops on her umbrella to the drops glistening on a spider web.

Rains are coming. Sanna Stanley. Greenwillow, 1993. LC 92-1347, 24 p. (ISBN 0-688-10948-9; plb 0-688-10949-7) Grades ps up.

Aimee and her family recently moved to Zaire, where her father is a missionary. For Aimee's birthday, she and her mother have planned a party, but the skies look threatening. Aimee hurries around the village trying to get her party together, while everyone is preparing for the coming storm. They get to her house just as the rains come.

Red dancing shoes. Denise Lewis Patrick; James E. Ransome, illus. Tambourine, 1993. LC 91-32666, 32 p. (ISBN 0-688-10392-8; plb 0-688-10393-6) Grades ps up.

Grandmama brings presents for everyone, but the youngest girl gets the best one—a pair of shiny, red shoes. She loves those shoes, and dances in them. When she goes to her aunt's house, disaster strikes. She falls, and scuffs her new shoes in the dust. Fortunately her aunt knows how to shine them up.

Robby visits the doctor. Martine Davison; Nancy Stevenson, illus. Random House, 1992. LC 91-30193, 32 p. (ISBN plb 0-679-91819-1; pbk 0-679-81819-7) Grades ps-2.

Part of the *AMA kids book* series. Robby is worried when he wakes up with a bad earache and learns that he must go to the doctor. He worries the entire time he waits, but the doctor helps him. After he takes his medicine for a while, Robby feels better.

A Rose for Abby. Donna Guthrie; Dennis Hockerman, illus. Abingdon, 1988. LC 88-10577, 32 p. (ISBN pbk 0-687-36586-4) Grades 2 up.

Abby sees a homeless old woman searching in trash cans and sleeping in a cardboard box near her father's church. She worries about her not having food and shelter. She decides to ask neighbors to pitch in, and they find a way to aid many street people, including the woman that Abby first helped.

Shape space. Cathryn Falwell. Houghton Mifflin, 1992. LC 91-32274, 32 p. (ISBN 0-395-61305-1) Grades ps-2.

This concept book features a lively young gymnast who finds a box of wonderful play things: shapes. She dances with the shapes, builds with them, wears them, and makes friends with them.

Shortcut. Donald Crews. Greenwillow, 1992. LC 91-36312, 32 p. (ISBN 0-688-06436-1; plb 0-688-06437-X) Grades ps-6.

While visiting Bigmama's, the children are out late. They decide to take the shortcut on the railroad tracks, even though they are not supposed to. After a close run-in with a freight train, the children acknowledge that shortcuts are not worth it.

Sofie's role. Amy Heath; Sheila Hamanaka, illus. Macmillan, 1992. LC 91-33488, 40 p. (ISBN 0-02-743505-9) Grades K-2.

On the day before Christmas, things get very busy at Broadway Pastries. So this year Mama says Sofie can help. Everyone has their own job, but Sophie finds a way to help that is very important.

Somewhere in Africa. Ingrid Mennen and Niki Daly; Nicolaas Maritz, illus. Dutton, 1992. LC 91-19379, 32 p. (ISBN 0-525-44848-9) Grades ps-3.

Ashraf lives in Africa. Not the wild Africa with elephants and tigers, but a city with streets, traffic lights, and cars. Ashraf has seen wild Africa only in a library book.

Storm in the night. Mary Stolz; Pat Cummings, illus. HarperCollins, 1988. LC 85-45838, 32 p. (ISBN 0-06-025912-4; plb 0-06-025913-2; pbk 0-06-443256-4) Grades K-3.

When the lights are knocked out by a storm, Thomas and his grandfather share a story.

Sweet Clara and the freedom quilt. Deborah Hopkinson; James Ransome, illus. Knopf, 1993. LC 91-11601, 40 p. (ISBN 0-679-82311-5; plb 0-679-92311-X) Grades K-5.

As a young slave who works as a seamstress, Clara hears people talk about running away and gathers clues from them. She creates a map sewn into the pattern of her quilt. After she escapes, she leaves her quilt as a guide for others to follow.

Tailypo! Jan Wahl; Wil Clay, illus. Henry Holt, 1991. LC 90-39491, 32 p. (ISBN 0-8050-0687-7) Grades ps-2.

An old man lives by himself in the woods of Tennessee. One night, a strange creature with a great, long tail creeps into his cabin. When the man lops off the tail, cooks it and eats it, the creature haunts him, looking for his "tailypo." Wonderfully detailed paintings illustrate this dark tale.

Tar beach. Faith Ringgold. Crown, 1991. LC 90-40410, 32 p. (ISBN 0-517-58030-6; plb 0-517-58031-4; book + doll 0-517-59961-9) Grades ps-3.

It's easy to fly in Cassie's dreams. She can do anything then—fly over her Harlem home, claim buildings for her family, and see to it that they will be secure. A child-like faith that everything can be right on a summer night is expressed in the author's fascinating artistic style.

Tell me a story, Mama. Angela Johnson; David Soman, illus. Orchard, 1989. LC 88-17917, 32 p. (ISBN 0-531-05794-1; plb 0-531-08394-2; pbk 0-531-07032-8) Grades ps-1.

A young girl knows her family's stories so well that after she asks her mother to tell one, she tells it herself.

Three wishes. Lucille Clifton; Stephanie Douglas, illus. Dell, 1994. LC 75-5579, 32 p. (ISBN 0-385-30497-8; pbk 0-440-40921-7) Grades ps-3.

Be careful of your wishes, as Nobie finds out. She almost loses her friend Victor over some silly wishes she has after finding a penny on New Years Day, with her birth year on it. Before it is too late, she wishes to have her friend back—the really important thing in life.

Train to Lulu's. Elizabeth Fitzgerald Howard; Robert Casilla, illus. Macmillan, 1988. LC 86-33429, 32 p. (ISBN 0-02-744620-4; pbk 0-689-71797-0) Grades ps-2.

Set in the late thirties, Beppy and Babs, travel by train to visit their aunt in Baltimore. Despite being scared, the two sisters enjoy the adventure.

Turtle knows your name. Ashley Bryan. Macmillan, 1989. LC 89-2, 32 p. (ISBN 0-689-31578-3); Macmillan, 1993. LC 92-33553, 32 p. (ISBN pbk 0-689-71728-8) Grades ps-3.

Once upon a time, there was a boy with a very long name. His granny helps him learn to remember it.

Two and too much. Mildred Pitts Walter; Pat Cummings, illus. Macmillan, 1990. LC 88-14888, 32 p. (ISBN 0-02-792290-1) Grades ps-2.

When Brandon offers to help his mother get ready for a party, she asks him to watch two-year-old Gina. His sister makes one mess after another. Yet, he panics when the house is too quiet.

We keep a store. Anne Shelby; John Ward, illus. Orchard, 1990. LC 89-35105, 32 p. (ISBN 0-531-05856-5; plb 0-531-08456-6) Grades ps-2.

There are so many delights in a family-run country store. The best things happen when the neighbors gather to tell stories, put up fruit, or play down by the creek.

What kind of babysitter is this? Dolores Johnson. Macmillan, 1991. LC 90-42860, 32 p. (ISBN 0-02-747846-7) Grades ps-2.

Kevin is mad that he has another babysitter. All they do is paint their toenails and read "kissy-kissy" books. When Aunt Lovey arrives, she watches the baseball game, waves a pennant, and begins to read a baseball book. Kevin begins to change his mind about this babysitter.

What will Mommy do when I'm at school? Dolores Johnson. Macmillan, 1990. LC 90-5559, 32 p. (ISBN 0-02-747845-9) Grades ps-1.

When a little girl thinks about starting school, she worries about her mother being lonely at home by herself.

Wheels: a tale of Trotter Street. Shirley Hughes. Lothrop, 1991. LC 90-40473, 32 p. (ISBN 0-688-09880-0; plb 0-688-09881-9) Grades ps-3.

Carlos wants a new bicycle. When Carlos asks, his mother says there is no money. However, his brother gives him something even better.

When Africa was home. Karen Lynn Williams; Floyd Cooper, illus. Orchard, 1991. LC 90-7684, 32 p. (ISBN 0-531-05925-1; plb 0-531-08525-2; pbk 0-531-07043-3) Grades ps-2.

Peter loves his home in Africa. When his parents say it is time to go "home" to America, nothing there feels right.

When I am old with you. Angela Johnson; David Soman, illus. Orchard, 1990. LC 89-70928, 32 p. (ISBN 0-531-05884-0; plb 0-531-08484-1; pbk 0-531-07035-2) Grades ps-3.

A young boy wonders what he and his Grandaddy could do together when they both grow older. They could go fishing, play cards, and keep each other company—just like they do now.

When I was little. Toyomi Igus; Higgins Bond, illus. Just Us, 1992. LC 92-72006, 32 p. (ISBN 0-940975-32-7; pbk 0-940975-33-5) Grades 1-up.

While on a fishing trip, Noel asks grandfather what things were like when he was a boy. Noel cannot believe it: no television, no jets, horse drawn wagons instead of cars, an ice box instead of a refrigerator. When Noel catches a fish, Grandpa recalls his first catch.

When I'm Alone. Carol Partridge Ochs; Vicki Jo Redenbaugh, illus. Carolrhoda, 1993. LC 93-6348, 32 p. (ISBN 0-87614-752-X; pbk 0-87614-620-5) Grades ps-3.

When this little girl is alone, the strangest things happen. An assortment of animals visit her, make a mess, and leave her with the blame. Counting down in rhyme from ten aardvarks to one sleeping kitten, she has quite a problem: she cannot convince her mother that the animals did it.

Where does the trail lead? Burton Albert; Brian Pinkney, illus. Simon & Schuster, 1991. LC 90-21450, 40 p. (ISBN 0-671-73409-1; pbk 0-671-79617-8) Grades ps-3.

A boy explores the world of seashore delights on a summer afternoon. He runs, climbs, jumps on rocks, cavorts in tide pools and fields of flowers, and feels the sea spray.

Wild wild sunflower child Anna. Nancy White Carlstrom; Jerry Pinkney, illus. Macmillan, 1987. LC 86-18226, 32 p. (ISBN 0-02-717360-7; pbk 0-689-71445-9) Grades ps-1.

Anna romps outdoors—enjoying the sun, sky, grass, flowers, berries, frogs, ants, and beetles. The text is a verse that bounces as much as Anna does.

Will there be a lap for me? Dorothy Corey; Nancy Poydar, illus. Whitman, 1992. LC 91-20324, 24 p. (ISBN 0-8075-9109-2) Grades ps-1.

Kyle had a special place—his mother's lap. But as she progresses through pregnancy, his special place becomes smaller and smaller. Finally his baby brother is born, and Mother is busy with the baby. Kyle is grumpy—until Mother makes some quiet time just for him and he sits on her lap again.

William and the good old days. Eloise Greenfield; Jan Spivey Gilchrist, illus. HarperCollins, 1993. LC 91-47030, 32 p. (ISBN 0-06-021093-1; plb 0-06-021094-X) Grades K-3.

William likes the good old days better than the present. Now Grandma is sick. William imagines how she was—and how she will be after she gets well.

Willie's not the hugging kind. Joyce Durham Barrett; Pat Cummings, illus. HarperCollins, 1989. LC 89-1868, 32 p. (ISBN 0-06-020416-8; plb 0-06-020417-6; pbk 0-06-443264-5) Grades K-3.

Jo-Jo convinces Willie that hugging is silly. Willie's family stops hugging him until he cannot stand it any longer.

Wood-Hoopoe Willie. Virginia Kroll; Katherine Roundtree, illus. Charlesbridge, 1993. LC 92-74501, 32 p. (ISBN 0-88106-409-2; plb 0-88106-410-6) Grades ps-4.

Willie is constantly tapping a rhythm with whatever is in his hands. Grandma said he must have a wood-hoopoe in him. A wood-hoopoe is an African bird that is always tapping on trees. Then the family goes to a Kwanzaa festival. The drummer cannot come—but Willie is able to let the wood hoopoe out and play.

Working cotton. Sherley Anne Williams; Carole Byard, illus. Harcourt, 1992. LC 91-21586, 32 p. (ISBN 0-15-299624-9) Grades K-4.

Shelan describes one of her days in the cotton fields. They begin before the sun is up, and does not end until the sun goes down. Their life is very hard, but they are grateful that their family is together. Shelan admires her father's speed, her baby sister's cuteness, and her mother's lunch. At the end of an exhausting day, they see a late season cotton blossom, which they think will bring them good luck.

You can't catch me. Annabel Collis. Little, Brown, 1993. LC 92-54486, 32 p. (ISBN 0-316-15237-4) Grades ps-1.

A little brother invents a wonderful game when his older sister and brother take him to the playground. He imagines running away with a monkey. Their romp takes them to an imaginary island inhabited by all sorts of animals.

Your dad was just like you. Dolores Johnson. Macmillan, 1993. LC 92-6347, 32 p. (ISBN 0-02-747838-6) Grades K-3.

Peter knows that his father is very angry at him for breaking some big purple thing. He goes to his grandfather's to see if he can run away from home. Grandfather tells Peter a revealing story about Peter's dad when he was young.

You're my Nikki. Phyllis Rose Eisenberg; Jill Kastner, illus. Dial, 1992. LC 91-2670, 32 p. (ISBN 0-8037-1127-1; plb 0-8037-1129-8) Grades ps-3.

Nikki's mother is starting a new job. Nikki is worried that her mother will forget her. At first, Nikki's mother is so tired that she does forget to do their routine, but she does not forget to tuck Nikki into bed.

Zebra-riding cowboy: a folk song of the old West. Angela Shelf Medearis; Maria Cristina Brusca, illus. Holt, 1992. LC 91-27941, 32 p. (ISBN 0-8050-1712-7) Grades ps-2.

A Western folk song tells the story of a man who looked more like "a greenhorn just escaped from town" than a cowboy. He proved that he was one when he was given the wildest horse available. An afterword describes the heritage of African American cowboys.

Fiction for Middle Readers

All Jahdu storybook. Virginia Hamilton; Barry Moser, illus. Harcourt, 1991. LC 90-47847, 108 p. (ISBN 0-15-239498-2) Grades 3 up.

Jahdu is a trickster, always playing, always running. Some of these stories have been previously published. In this collection, they are reworked and organized so that Jahdu goes from one adventure to another.

Ballad of Belle Dorcas. William H. Hooks; Brian Pinkney, illus. Knopf, 1990. LC 89-2715, 48 p. (ISBN 0-394-84645-1; plb 0-394-94645-6) Grades 2-7.

Belle Dorcas would do anything to keep her true love, Joshua, with her. When Joshua is to be sold, Belle uses the magic of a conjure woman with surprising results.

Bells of Christmas. Virginia Hamilton; Lambert Davis, illus. Harcourt, 1989. LC 89-7468, 59 p. (ISBN 0-15-206450-8) Grades ps up.

A nostalgic look at Christmas in 1890. Jason celebrates the holiday in the best way: with a loving family.

Case of the elevator duck. Polly Berrien Berends; Diane Allison, illus. Random House, 1989. LC 88-23971, 64 p. (ISBN pbk 0-394-82646-9; plb 0-394-92646-3) Grades 2-4.

A *Stepping stone* book. Gilbert wants to be a detective, and gets an early start by solving cases in his housing project. He finds a duck and takes it in until he can find its owner. Tenants are not allowed to have pets and Gilbert almost gets caught. When he has to let the duck go, the owners come forward: a Hispanic family who had to get rid of their pet to stay in the project.

Cay. Theodore Taylor. Doubleday, 1987. LC 69-15161, 160 p. (ISBN pbk 0-385-07906-0); Avon, 1977. (ISBN 0-390-00142-X; pbk 0-380-01003-8); Bantam, 1990. (ISBN large print 1-55736-163-0) Grades 5-6.

Phillip and his mother attempt to leave the Caribbean after Nazi submarines attack their island's oil refinery, but their ship is torpedoed. Blinded, Phillip and a black man named Timothy escape to a little island (or cay). At first Phillip worries about Timothy being black. After they survive together, Phillip loses his prejudiced thoughts. When Timothy dies protecting him in a hurricane, Phillip realizes he lost a good friend.

Charlie Pippin. Candy Dawson Boyd. Macmillan, 1987. LC 86-23780, 192 p. (ISBN 0-02-726350-9; pbk 0-14-032587-5) Grades 3-7.

Charlie becomes obsessed with understanding the Vietnam war—at first because of a school assignment, then in an attempt to understand her strict father. Knowing she will have to deal with his anger, she uncovers the facts about her father's Vietnam experiences.

Chevrolet Saturdays. Candy Dawson Boyd. Macmillan, 1993. LC 92-32119, 176 p. (ISBN 0-02-711765-0) Grades 3-7.

Joey is really unhappy. His parents divorced and his mother remarried. Joey resents his stepfather and his dog Josie. At school, he is always in trouble. Then Joey leaves the gate open, and Josie gets out. In order to face his angry stepfather, Joey tracks Josie down and finds a job to help pay the vet bills.

Cousins. Virginia Hamilton. Putnam, 1990. LC 90-31451, 128 p. (ISBN 0-399-22164-6); Scholastic, 1993. (ISBN pbk 0-590-45436-6) Grades 3-6.

Cammie loves her family. She worries about her grandmother in a nursing home. She does not like to get in trouble, but she cannot seem to help it around her cousins—especially Patty Ann, her "too perfect" cousin. When Patty Ann is killed in an accident, Cammie feels guilty about her anger.

Do you know me? Nancy Farmer; Shelley Jackson, illus. Orchard, 1993. LC 92-34068, 112 p. (ISBN 0-531-05474-8; plb 0-531-08624-0; pbk 0-14-036946-5) Grades 3-7.

Uncle Zeka arrives at Tapiwa's home after bandits burned his village in Mozambique. Zeka knows a lot about surviving in the bush, but city life is quite different. Even though he means well, he constantly gets into trouble, often involving Tapiwa in the hijinks. Finally, Tapiwa's father finds Uncle Zeka the perfect job: working at a wildlife preserve.

Down in the piney woods. Ethel Footman Smothers. Knopf, 1992. LC 91-328, 144 p. (ISBN 0-679-80360-2; plb 0-679-90360-7); Random House, 1994. (ISBN pbk 0-679-84714-6) Grades 4-8.

Life isn't easy for ten-year-old Annie Rye and her family. They are sharecroppers in Georgia. It gets harder when they take in her three half-sisters with their uppity ways. When a confrontation with an Anglo family leads to threats, fear binds Annie Rye's family together.

Drinking gourd. F.N. Mongo; Fred Brenner, illus. HarperCollins, 1970.
LC 92-10823, 64 p. (ISBN 0-06-024329-5; plb 0-06-024330-9; pbk 0-06-444042-7) Grades K-3.

Part of the *I can read* series. Tommy Fuller is surprised to find runaway slaves in his barn, and even more surprised to discover that his deacon father is part of the Underground Railroad. Tommy is troubled by the slave family's plight, and his father's breaking the law by helping them. When he is confronted by the slave catchers, Tommy realizes that he, too, must help.

Drylongso. Virginia Hamilton; Jerry Pinkney, illus. Harcourt, 1992.
LC 91-25575, 56 p. (ISBN 0-15-224241-4) Grades 3-6.

A family is struggling to maintain their farm during a severe drought. Just as a dust storm hits, a strange boy stumbles out of the clouds. He says his name is Drylongso: wherever he goes, life gets better. He helps the family find an underground spring and advises them where to plant their crops. Then he disappears.

Duey's tale. Pearl Bailey. Harcourt, 1975. LC 74-22278, 59 p. (ISBN 0-15-126576-3) Grades 3-12.

On one level, an exciting adventure; on the other, a lesson about life. This simple allegory has a message about finding one's place in the world. A seedling, separated from his mother tree, wanders around. It makes friends with a log and a bottle as the river carries them to their destiny. The seedling becomes a strong maple tree that gives shade to those around him.

Dustland. Virginia Hamilton. Greenwillow, 1980. LC 79-19003, 192 p. (ISBN 0-688-80228-1; plb 0-688-84228-3); Harcourt, 1989. (ISBN pbk 0-15-224315) Grades 6 up.

The second part of the *Justice Cycle* series. Justice, her brothers Thomas and Levi, and their friend Dorian use extrasensory powers to travel in the future. Dustland, the barren wasteland that they find, is inhabited by strange creatures who also have powers that the four possess. Their destiny lies in Dustland, but they are confused and frustrated about why they are called to this land.

Escape from slavery: five journeys to freedom. Doreen Rappaport; Charles Lilly, illus. HarperCollins, 1991. LC 90-38170, 128 p. (ISBN 0-06-021631-X; plb 0-06-021632-8) Grades 4-7.

Five short stories recount the experiences of slaves who escaped to find freedom in the North. Excellent storytelling materials.

Everywhere. Bruce Brooks. HarperCollins, 1990. LC 90-4073, 80 p.
(ISBN 0-06-020728-0; plb 0-06-020729-9; pbk 0-06-440443-1) Grades 4 up.

A boy is worried about his grandfather who has just had a heart attack. Dooley, the
nephew of a local nurse, suggests they perform the ritual of soul switching. This
involves sacrificing an animal in order to allow a person to keep on living. Dooley
wants to try the bizarre plan so the boy can prove how much he loves his grandfather.

Fast Sam, Cool Clyde and Stuff. Walter Dean Myers. Puffin, 1988.
LC 74-32383, 190 p. (ISBN pbk 0-14-032613-8) Grades 5-9.

When Francis moves to 116th Street, he does not know anyone. He is soon given
the nickname "Stuff" by kids in his building. Through a series of mishaps, they all
become great friends.

Finding Buck McHenry. Alfred Slote. HarperCollins, 1991. LC 90-39190, 256
p. (ISBN 0-06-021652; plb 0-06-021653-0; pbk 0-06-440469-2) Grades 4-6.

Jason Ross thinks that he has found the great baseball player, Buck McHenry, a
pitcher from the old Negro Leagues whose players were not allowed in the majors.
Their school janitor, Mack Henry, fits Buck's description just when the Little
League's "rejects" team needs a coach.

Fish and Bones. Ray Prather. HarperCollins, 1992. LC 91-44227, 272 p.
(ISBN 0-06-025121-2; plb 0-06-025122-0) Grades 5-9.

Thirteen-year-old Bones is only worried about how to beat the heat in a small Florida
town until the bank is robbed. He and his father's helper try to find the money and
collect the reward before anyone else can solve the mystery. Then the money starts
showing up everywhere, and Bones gets so close that his life is in danger.

Friendship. Mildred D. Taylor, Max Ginsberg, illus. Dial, 1987. LC 86-29309,
56 p. (ISBN 0-8037-0417-8; plb 0-8037-0418-6) Grades 2-6.

Sent on an errand to get medicine for a sick aunt, four African American children
decide to visit an Anglo-owned country store they usually avoid. It is an unfriendly
and dangerous place. They are eventually served, but not before being insulted and
frightened. Tom Bee, an old black man, reveals he saved the life of the owner, but the
owner's sons cannot tolerate the familiarity between the two men. A tragedy ensues.

Gathering. Virginia Hamilton. Harcourt, 1989. LC 80-12512, 214 p. (ISBN pbk
0-15-230592-0) Grades 7 up.

The third book of the Justice Cycle trilogy. The four youngsters return to Dustland because of the threats of Mal: a strange, horrifying creature who attacks without warning. They are able to trace the beginnings of Dustland to their own earth and time, and all the inhabitants of earth have been reduced to a primitive state.

Get on out of here, Philip Hall. Bette Greene. Dial, 1981. LC 79-50151, 160 p. (ISBN 0-8037-2871-9; plb 0-8037-2872-7); Dell, 1984. (ISBN 0-440-43038-0) Grades 4-7.

Sequel to *Philip Hall likes me, I reckon maybe.* Beth Lambert is humiliated in front of the entire church congregation when she gets up to receive a leadership award, and Philip Hall's name is called instead. It seems that everything else she does after that goes wrong. Beth learns that winning can be as simple as cooperating with others.

Gift-giver. Joyce Hansen. Houghton Mifflin, 1980. LC 79-13812, 128 p. (ISBN 0-395-29433-9); Ticknor, 1989. (ISBN pbk 0-89919-852-X) Grades 3-6.

Doris hates anything that does not conform to her friends' lives. Her parents do not care what her friends think and she is constantly embarrassed by their strict ways. Then Amir joins her class. He is a loner, but has a lot of insight. He helps Doris gain self-confidence, especially when her father is laid off. Amir supports Doris in ways that her other friends do not.

Go fish. Mary Stolz; Pat Cummings, illus. HarperCollins, 1991. LC 90-4860, 80 p. (ISBN 0-06-025820-9; plb 0-06-025822-5; pbk 0-06-440466-8) Grades 2-6.

The day is long and lazy, but Thomas cannot sit still. He is not satisfied watching Grandfather read. So they go fishing in their favorite spot. They do a lot of talking while waiting for a fish to bite, and this leads Thomas to ask for a story—a tale of Africa and Grandfather's grandfather's grandfather.

Gold Cadillac. Mildred D. Taylor; Michael Hays, illus. Dial, 1987. LC 86-11526, 48 p. (ISBN 0-8037-0342-2; plb 0-8037-0343-0) Grades 2-6.

The acquisition of a gold Cadillac brings strife to a Northern African-American family, especially when they take the car to Mississippi for a visit and encounter racism.

Have a happy . . . Mildred Pitts Walter; Carole Byard, illus. Lothrop, 1989. LC 88-8962, 144 p. (ISBN 0-688-06923-1); Avon, 1990. (ISBN 0-380-71314-4) Grades 3-6.

Chris is confused about all the holidays that occur at the same time: his birthday, Christmas and Kwanzaa. But these holidays bind his family together and help them through the unhappy fact of his father's unemployment.

House of Dies Drear. Virginia Hamilton; Eros Keith, illus. Macmillan, 1984. LC 68-23059, 256 p. (ISBN 0-02-742500-2; pbk 0-02-043520-7) Grades 6-9.

Thomas and his family move into a historic house that was owned by a man who helped slaves escape through the Underground Railroad. Thomas thinks the house is haunted by ghosts who want his family to leave.

How to survive third grade. Laurie Lawlor. Whitman, 1988. LC 87-25430, 72 p. (ISBN plb 0-8075-3433-1); Pocket, 1991. (ISBN 0-671-67713-6) Grades 2-5.

Ernest is always picked on. He has no friends in his class; he is alone after school. Then Jomo arrives from Kenya. Ernest would really like to be his friend, but is afraid that no one will like Jomo if the two of them are friendly. Jomo appreciates Ernest's timid overtures and they become friends.

I be somebody. Hadley Irwin. Dutton, 1988. LC 84-490, 160 p. (ISBN pbk 0-451-15303-0) Grades 4-6.

Everyone in Creekview, Oklahoma is talking about a place called Athabasca as if it were paradise. Rap learns that it is in far-off Canada. The African Americans in his town want to go there to escape Jim Crow laws. After much debate, Rap and his Aunt Spicy make the long trip. Along the way, Rap witnesses hate and violence toward African Americans. He also sees the love that binds them together, and he decides to stay in Athabasca. Based on a true incident.

Journey to Jo'burg: a South African story. Beverly Naidoo; Eric Velasquez, illus. HarperCollins, 1985. LC 85-45508, 96 p. (ISBN 0-397-32168-6; plb 0-397-32169-4; pbk 0-06-440237-1) Grades 4-7.

Naledi is very worried. Her baby sister is extremely ill, and her mother is working in Johannesburg. Naledi knows her mother can help, so Naledi and her brother Tiro take a perilous journey to find her. Away from home, Naledi realizes how oppressed blacks are in their country, and she vows to make a difference someday.

Julian, dream doctor. Ann Cameron; Ann Strugnell, illus. Random House, 1993. LC 89-37562, 64 p. (ISBN 0-679-90524-3; pbk. 0-679-80524-9) Grades 2-4.

A *Stepping Stone* book. Julian wants to get his father a special birthday present: something dad has always dreamed about. But how does a kid find out a grown-up's secret wish? Julian tries mental telepathy, but it doesn't work. So he tries to get him to talk in his sleep.

Julian, secret agent. Ann Cameron; Diane Allison, illus. Random House, 1988. LC 88-4228, 64 p. (ISBN plb 0-394-91949-1; pbk 0-394-81949-7) Grades 2-4.

This easy to read book finds Julian, his brother Huey, and his friend Gloria going into the crimebusting business. While looking for criminals, they do good deeds. When they actually find a possible criminal, they may have gotten more than they bargained for.

Jump ship to freedom. James L. Collier and Christopher Collier. Delacorte, 1981. LC 81-65492, 192 p. (ISBN pbk 0-385-28484-5); Dell, 1987. (ISBN 0-440-44323-7) Grades 4-6.

Daniel Arabus, a resourceful fourteen year old slave, has a lot of trouble hanging on to the money that his dad earned as a soldier in the Revolutionary war. First his mistress says she will "hold it," then his master puts him on a slave ship bound for the West Indies. Dan jumps ship in New York. He tries to find his Congressman to learn if the money is any good, but learns that he is in Philadelphia at the Constitutional Convention.

Just like Martin. Ossie Davis. Simon & Schuster, 1992. LC 91-4672, 215 p. (ISBN 0-671-73202-1) Grades 6 up.

Young Isaac Stone is proud to be Junior Assistant Pastor and help organize events in his church—such as the 1964 march on Washington. He believes in Dr. Martin Luther King, Jr.'s nonviolent tactics. But his father, Isaac Sr., returned from Korea an angry and bitter man; he cannot accept the nonviolent way. After he is beaten during a protest and a bomb kills two of his friends, Stone worries that his father will break down.

Justice and her brothers. Virginia Hamilton. Peter Smith, 1989. LC 78-54684, 217 p. (ISBN 0-8446-6577-0); Harcourt, 1989. (ISBN pbk 0-15-241640-4) Grades 5 up.

Part one of the *Justice cycle* series. What begins as a hot and lonely summer for Justice and her twin brothers turns into a frightening battle of wills. Justice finds herself testing her extrasensory powers against those of a domineering brother, and this struggle takes them to a strange barren world.

Justin and the best biscuits in the world. Mildred Pitts Walter; Catherine Stock, illus. Lothrop, 1986. LC 86-7148, 128 p. (ISBN 0-688-06645-3) Grades 3-7.

Justin learns a lesson in independence when his Grandpa lets him visit his ranch. With the patient tutelage of his grandfather, Justin learns, among other things, how to make prize-winning biscuits. This impresses his bossy sisters. Winner of the 1987 Coretta Scott King Award for fiction.

Koya Delaney and the good girl blues. Eloise Greenfield. Scholastic, 1992. LC 91-10530, 176 p. (ISBN 0-590-43300-8) Grades 3-6.

Koya's cousin Del, a famous rock musician, is coming to visit her family. Events occur that could ruin the visit and cause her to be angry, but she tries to hold it all in. Their friend Dawn snubs her sister, then Del is mobbed by fans during their quiet family time. Koya learns that if she does not find a way to express her anger, she is miserable and makes everyone else miserable, too.

Last summer with Maizon. Jacqueline Woodson. Doubleday, 1990. LC 89-23403, 105 p. (ISBN 0-385-30045-X; pbk 0-440-40555-6) Grades 5 up.

Maizon and Margaret are best friends in Brooklyn. The summer they turn eleven, Margaret's life is disrupted by her father's death. Then, Maizon is accepted at a boarding school, and Margaret realizes she will have to go on alone. Slowly and painfully, Margaret makes the adjustment by writing poetry to express her feelings, and one of her poems wins a contest. When Maizon calls to say she is coming back, Margaret wonders if things will change again.

Maizon at Blue Hill. Jacqueline Woodson. Delacorte, 1992. LC 91-44295, 144 p. (ISBN 0-385-30796-9; pbk 0-440-40899-7) Grades 4-7.

Maizon is accepted into a boarding school where her Grandma feels she will be academically challenged. Maizon is afraid to be away from home and her best friend Margaret. She's worried about being one of five African American students. Maizon feels that she does not fit in at school, and she wonders if she will ever fit in anywhere.

Mariah keeps cool. Mildred Pitts Walter. Macmillan, 1990. LC 89-23981, 144 p. (ISBN 0-02-792295-2) Grades 3-7.

Sequel to **Mariah loves rock**. Mariah must learn to get along with her half-sister, Denise, while trying to form a swimming team with her friends.

Mariah loves rock. Mildred Pitts Walter; Pat Cummings, illus. Troll, 1989. LC 88-2595, 128 p. (ISBN 0-8167-1838-5) Grades 3-9.

Eleven-year-old Mariah idolizes a rock star. The only thing that distracts her from thoughts of Sheik Bashara is the turmoil her family faces when a half sister plans to live in their home.

M.C. Higgins, the great. Virginia Hamilton. Macmillan, 1974. LC 72-92439, 288 p. (ISBN 0-02-742480-4; pbk 0-02-043490); Dell, 1976. (ISBN 0-440-95598-

X); Bantam, 1988. (ISBN large print 1-55736-075-8); Second edition. Macmillan, 1993. (ISBN 0-689-71694-1) Grades 5 up.

All M.C. can think about is leaving his home in the isolated Ohio mountains. A company has strip mined the area above his home and a spoil heap is oozing toward it. Two strangers arrive and change his life, enabling M.C. to begin planning for the future.

Me, Mop and the Moondance Kid. Walter Dean Myers; Rodney Pate, illus. Delacorte, 1988. LC 88-6503, 128 p. (ISBN 0-440-50065-6); Doubleday, 1988. (ISBN 0-385-30147-2); Dell, 1991. (ISBN pbk 0-440-40396-0) Grades 3-7.

A Little League baseball team trying to win over an obnoxious rival helps three orphans remain close friends. T.J. and the Moondance Kid are getting used to being part of a new family. Mop tries desperately to become adopted.

Meet Addy: an American girl. Connie Porter; Melodye Rosales, illus. Pleasant Co., 1993. LC 92-38680, 69 p. (ISBN 1-56247-076-0; pbk 1-56247-075-2) Grades 2-5.

Part of the *American girls collection* series. Addy's family lives on a North Carolina plantation during the Civil War. She overhears her parents plotting to run away, but before they can put their plan into action, her father and brother are sold. It is up to her and her mother to escape on their own.

Mississippi bridge. Mildred Taylor; Max Ginsburg, illus. Dial, 1990. LC 89-27898, 64 p. (ISBN 0-8037-0426-7; plb 0-8037-0427-5); Bantam, 1992. (ISBN 0-553-15992-5) Grades 3-6.

Jeremy Simms is embarrassed by the way his father and friends treat African-Americans. He wants to make amends any way he can. Jeremy is upset when a bus driver forces the African-Americans off to make room for whites. The climactic scene comes when, in the driving rain, he sees the bus go off the bridge.

Mop, Moondance and the Nagasaki knights. Walter Dean Myers. Delacorte, 1992. LC 91-36824, 160 p. (ISBN 0-385-30687-3; pbk 0-440-40914-4) Grades 3-7.

Now that T.J., his brother Moondance, and their friend Mop are adopted, they are adjusting to their new homes. Their baseball team has a chance to go to Japan if they win the league championship. In preparation for the trip, they are getting acquainted with teams from all over the world. T.J.'s team gets a new player, Greg. When they realize that he is homeless, they want to help, but do not know how to do that without telling adults.

More stories Julian tell. Ann Cameron; Ann Strugnell, illus. Knopf, 1986. LC 84-10095, 96 p. (ISBN 0-394-86969-9; plb 0-394-96969-3; pbk 0-394-82454-7) Grades 2-6.

These are five more stories featuring Julian, his brother Huey, and his best friend Gloria. They all learn new lessons about getting along.

Muddy Banks. Ruby C. Tolliver; Walle Conoly, illus. TCU Press, 1987. LC 85-20851, 154 p. (ISBN 0-87565-062-7; 0-87565-049-X) Grades 4 up.

Boy, a runaway slave, is rescued by a widow named Bethel Banks. Still, he yearns for his own freedom. The longer he stays with Miz Banks, the more he cares for her. She teaches and nurtures him. Suddenly the Battle of Sabine Pass provides an opportunity for escape—or destroy the new life he can have with Miz Banks.

My name is not Angelica. Scott O'Dell. Houghton Mifflin, 1989. LC 89-1864, 130 p. (ISBN 0-395-51061-9); Dell, 1990. (ISBN 0-440-40379-0) Grades 5-9.

Konje and Raisha are part of a prestigious African clan that negotiates with a powerful lord who deals in the slave trade. They are captured and sold into slavery. Life in a Danish household in Jamaica is humiliating and they look for ways to escape. Konje runs away and forms a rebel band to fight the whites. As the final confrontation comes closer, Konje and Raisha see the hopelessness of their struggle. They each find a way to be true to themselves.

Oh, brother. Johnniece Marshall Wilson. Scholastic, 1989. LC 87-4478, 128 p. (ISBN pbk 0-590-41001-6) Grades 3-7.

Alex is mad at his big brother Andrew. He borrows Alex's bike without asking, throws his stuff all over the room, and leaves him to babysit so he can play ball with his friends. Alex's anger pushes him to work harder to earn the money for a new bicycle. His anger also goads him into a fight with Andrew's bully friend. Andrew finally admits he is jealous of how much little brother Alex does.

Oren Bell. Barbara Hood Burgess. Delacorte, 1991. LC 90-41810, 182 p. (ISBN 0-385-30325-4; pbk 0-440-40747-8) Grades 5 up.

Because Oren does not carry out a superstitious ceremony, he believes he is responsible for the tragedies that he and his family must endure.

Out from this place. Joyce Hansen. Walker, 1988. LC 88-5594, 144 p. (ISBN 0-8027-6816-4) Avon, 1992. (ISBN 0-380-71409-4) Grades 3-6.

Sequel to **Which way freedom?** Obi and Easter separate to search for a new place.

She decides to go back for Jason, her little brother, and they join a hard-working community. Easter must decide what to do with her life: settle down as a farmer's wife, or go North for an education.

Paris, Pee Wee and Big Dog. Rosa Guy; Caroline Binch, illus. Delacorte, 1985. LC 85-1654, 112 p. (ISBN 0-385-29407-7; pbk 0-440-40072-4) Grades 4-6.

Paris was home alone on a Saturday morning. His mother had to work and insisted that he clean the house. Then Pee Wee came by and they went out "for a while." One thing led to another and, suddenly, the day was over, the house was still dirty, and his mother was going to be mad.

Philip Hall likes me. I reckon maybe. Bette Greene; Charles Lilly, illus. Dial, 1974. LC 74-2887, 160 p. (ISBN 0-8037-6098-1; plb. 0-8037-6096-5; pbk 0-440-45755-6; large print 1-55736-106-1) Grades 3-6.

A lively competition between Philip Hall and Beth Lambert is complicated by her crush on him. A Newbery Honor Book for 1975.

Planet of Junior Brown. Virginia Hamilton. Macmillan, 1971. LC 71-155264, 240 p. (ISBN 0-02-742510-X; pbk 0-02-043540-1); Hall, 1988. (ISBN large print 0-8161-4642-X); Reprint, 2nd edition. Macmillan, 1993. LC 92-40350, 224 p. (ISBN pbk 0-689-71721-0) Grades 5-9.

Junior Brown and Buddy Clark have found refuge in the basement of their school, thanks to the janitor, Mr. Pool. Buddy is homeless and lives alone in a deserted building. Junior is a 300 pound boy who wants to play the piano, but his stress causes him to retreat into a fantasy world. Together, they try to solve their problems.

Poor girl, rich girl. Johnniece Marshall Wilson. Scholastic, 1992. LC 91-19296, 176 p. (ISBN 0-590-44732-7; pbk 0-590-44733-5) Grades 4-7.

Miranda badly wants a pair of contact lenses, but her parents say they cannot afford them. So she decides to get a job. Between helping her mother by babysitting, she wonders if she'll have time or energy to get a real job. Miranda learns a few things about working and accomplishment.

Righteous revenge of Artemis Bonner. Walter Dean Myers. HarperCollins, 1992. LC 91-42401, 144 p. (ISBN 0-06-020844; plb 0-06-020846-5; pbk 0-06-440462-5) Grades 5-9.

This fast-paced, humorous historical novel tells of Artemis Bonner's search for the man who killed his uncle. Artemis also hopes to find his uncle's treasure. His travels take him to New Mexico, old Mexico, Seattle, Alaska, San Francisco, and Tombstone.

Robin on his own. Johnniece Marshall Wilson. Scholastic, 1992. LC 90-32927, 160 p. (ISBN pbk 0-590-41809-2) Grade 4 up.

Robin's grief over his mother's death changes to desperation when his aunt marries and moves away and his father also talks of moving.

Samuel's choice. Richard Berleth; James Watling, illus. Whitman, 1990. LC 89-77186, 40 p. (ISBN 0-8075-7218-7) Grades 3-6.

Samuel is a fourteen year old slave. Other slaves argue that the freedom revolutionaries advocate will not be theirs. They think that they should not aid the rebels in the war. But retreating rebel forces need Samuel's aid and he decides to help. Then his master has to give all his property to the Army and Samuel has a chance for freedom.

Scorpions. Walter Dean Myers. HarperCollins, 1988. LC 85-45815, 160 p. (ISBN 0-06-024364-3; plb 0-06-024365-1; pbk 0-06-447066-0) Grades 7 up.

Jamal is forced into leading his brother's Harlem gang, the Scorpions. He thinks that a gun will help him handle the job. The Scorpions and the gun nearly destroy him and the people he cares about most.

Secret of Gumbo Grove. Eleanora Tate. Bantam, 1988. LC 86-26742, 266 p. (ISBN 0-553-27226-8) Grades 7 up.

Raisin Stackhouse uses her love of history and insatiable curiosity to learn valuable lessons about her ancestors and some of the community's first settlers. Everyone is not happy about Raisin's discoveries.

Shimmershine Queens. Camille Yarbrough. Putnam, 1989. LC 88-11539, 128 p. (ISBN 0-399-21465-8) Grades 5-8.

Angie realizes that her dreams can be more than escape. They can uplift her in spite of her family's problems and her classmates' taunting.

Sister. Eloise Greenfield; Moneta Barnett, illus. HarperCollins, 1974. LC 73-22182, 96 p. (ISBN 0-690-00497-4; pbk 0-06-440199-5) Grades 3-6.

This journal of a young girl shows how her father's death has torn her family apart. Even as she reports the events, she questions them.

Slave dancer. Paula Fox; Eros Keith, illus. Macmillan, 1982. LC 73-80642, 192 p. (ISBN 0-02-735560-8; pbk 0-440-96132-7; pbk 0-440-40402-9; large print 1-55736-029-4) Grades 5-8.

Thirteen year old Jessie Bollier was kidnapped and put to work on a slave ship. He had played his fife to earn a few coins on the street; now the Captain needed someone to play for and pacify the slaves. As human cargo, Jessie wondered if he would live to see his home again. Newbery winner.

Song of the trees. Mildred D. Taylor; Jerry Pinkney, illus. Dial, 1975. LC 74-18598, 56 p. (ISBN 0-8037-5452-3; plb 0-8037-5453-1; pbk 0-553-27587-9) Grades 2-5.

This story involves the characters of **Roll of thunder, hear my cry** in which beloved trees on Cassie's family's property are cut down due to financial difficulty and racial tension. Winner in the Council on Interracial Books Award/African American category and the Jane Adams Children's Book award.

Sounder. William H. Armstrong. HarperCollins, 1969. LC 70-85030, 128 p. (ISBN 0-06-020143-6; plb 0-06-020144-4; pbk 0-06-440020-4; pbk 0-06-080379-7); Bantam, 1987. (ISBN large type 1-55736-003-0); Reprint Harper-Collins, 1989. (ISBN pbk 0-06-080975-2) Grades 5 up.

This moving story depicts the suffering of a sharecropper's family when the father is arrested for stealing food so his family can eat. Winner of the Newbery Award.

Steal away. Jennifer Armstrong. Orchard, 1992. LC 91-18504, 224 p. (ISBN 0-531-05983-9; plb 0-531-08583-X); Scholastic, 1993. (ISBN pbk 0-590-46921-5) Grades 6 up.

Two women, of different backgrounds narrate this story of growing up and getting along. In 1855, they were thirteen. One was a lonesome orphaned Anglo American girl; the other a frightened African American slave. They each felt compelled to go north. The journey was risky but worth the danger. By talking about their experiences with their granddaughters, they find a way to live with their differences.

Stealing home. Mary Stolz. HarperCollins, 1992. LC 92-5226, 160 p. (ISBN 0-06-021154-7; plb 0-06-021157-1; pbk 0-06-440528-1) Grades 3-6.

Thomas and Grandfather have comfortable patterns of baseball and fishing, and evenings of puzzles and games. Thomas is afraid that his Great Aunt Linzy will disrupt their lives—and she does. She moves Thomas out of his room and cleans everything in sight. Just when he gets used to this, things change again. This novel resumes Thomas' story from **Storm in the night** and **Go fish.**

Stories Julian tells. Ann Cameron; Ann Strugnell, illus. Pantheon, 1981. LC 80-18023, 96 p. (ISBN 0-394-84301-0; plb 0-394-94301-5); Reprint Knopf, 1989. (ISBN 0-394-82892-5) Grades K-5.

This early chapter book features Julian, a boy who tells stories. Sometimes his stories are meant to get himself out of trouble and other times he is misinformed. Julian's tales are warm slices of life.

Summer wheels. Eve Bunting; Thomas Allen, illus. Harcourt, 1992. LC 90-49758, 48 p. (ISBN 0-15-207000-1) Grades 2-4.

The Bicycle Man fixes up old bicycles and loans them to kids. If something happens to the bike while someone has signed it out, they have to fix it. Along comes a guy named "Abraham Lincoln," who knows the rules but does not follow them. The neighborhood kids set him straight.

Susannah and the purple mongoose. Patricia Elmore; Bob Marshall, illus. Dutton, 1992. LC 91-43643, 120 p. (ISBN 0-525-44907-8) Grades 3-7.

Lucy and Susannah's latest mystery involves arson. First, their neighbor Quiggy's porch burns, followed by the house next to it. They first suspect Theresa, their neighbor's new foster daughter, because she set a school storage shed on fire. Then they wonder about a real estate agent who wants Quiggy's house. After receiving vital clues from a neighborhood boy, Susannah realizes that the fires are part of a bigger crime.

Sweet whispers, Brother Rush. Virginia Hamilton. Putnam, 1982. LC 81-22745, 224 p. (ISBN 0-399-20894-1; pbk 0-380-65193-9) Grades 7 up.

Fourteen year old Teresa, called Tree, has to take care of her handicapped brother, Dabney, while her mother works. She meets Brother Rush, a handsome young man she can only see in a mirror. He takes her through events from her family's recent past. Just as she begins to understand them, Brother Rush disappears.

Tails of the Bronx: a Tale of the Bronx. Jill Pinkwater. Macmillan, 1991. LC 90-48914, 176 p. (ISBN 0-02-774652-6; pbk 0-689-71671-0) Grades 3-7.

Everyone knows everyone on Burnridge Avenue—they work together, play together, take care of things together. So when cats and garbage vanish, the kids decide to solve the mystery. They then meet some special homeless people.

Talk about a family. Eloise Greenfield; James Calvin, illus. HarperCollins, 1991. LC 77-164212, 64 p. (ISBN 0-397-32504-5; pbk 0-06-440444-7) Grades 2-5.

Genny's big brother Larry is coming home from the military. He is very good at mediating problems, such as a fuss between some of her brothers and sisters. She is sure that Larry can lessen the anger her parents always feel, but even he can't do that. Then Genny gets angry at everyone: her parents, her sisters, and even Larry.

Thank you, Dr. Martin Luther King, Jr. Eleanora E. Tate. Bantam, 1992. LC 89-70665, 237 p. (ISBN 0-553-15886-4) Grades 4-7.

Mary Eloise learns the importance of being herself after working on a play for Black history month. Sequel to **Secret of Gumbo Grove**, involving the younger characters of that town.

They're all named Wildfire. Nancy Springer. Macmillan, 1989. LC 88-27497, 112 p. (ISBN 0-689-31450-7) Grades 4 up.

Jenny dreaded having new neighbors, especially when her mom expected her to walk the new girl to school. It was not that the new family was African American, it was just that Jenny wanted to be with her friends. After she learns that Shanterey loves horses as much as she does, they become best friends. That friendship will be sorely tried, as hate crimes are aimed at Shanterey and her family. Jenny is right in the middle.

Thief in the village and other stories. James Berry. Orchard, 1988. LC 87-24695, 160 p. (ISBN 0-531-05745-3; plb 0-531-08345-4); Puffin, 1990. (ISBN pbk 0-14-034357-1) Grades 6 up.

A collection of short stories that show the special flavor of Jamaican life.

To hell with dying. Alice Walker; Catherine Dexter, illus. Harcourt, 1988. LC 86-27122, 32 p. (ISBN 0-15-289075-0; pbk 0-15-289074-2) Grades ps-6.

Mr. Sweet was a tragic figure in the life of the young girl who narrates. When they were children, she and her brother loved the old man so much that their attention brought him back from death. Even as a young woman, she hopes that her love can call him back.

Toning the sweep. Angela Johnson. Orchard, 1993. LC 92-34062, 112 p. (ISBN 0-531-05476-4; plb 0-531-08626-7) Grades 6 up.

Emily loves the annual visits to her unconventional grandmother, Ola. This year the visit is different. Ola has cancer and they must bring her back to live in their house. The visit is a frenzy of good-byes and memories. As they relive them, their exploration of the past becomes a desperate search for meaning.

Two hundred thirteen Valentines. Barbara Cohen; Will Clay, illus. Henry Holt, 1991. LC 91-7151, 64 p. (ISBN 0-8050-1536-1; pbk 0-8050-2627-4) Grades 2-4.

Wade Thompson is not thrilled to be in the gifted and talented program. He has to change schools, leave most of his friends, and learn to get along with new snobby classmates. Even worse, they have to exchange valentines. Wade is so sure no one will send him any that he decides to send himself 213 valentines, all signed by celebrities.

Ty's one-man band. Mildred Pitts Walter; Margot Tomes, illus. Macmillan, 1987. LC 80-11224, 32 p. (ISBN 0-02-792300-2; pbk 0-590-40178-5) Grades K-3.

One lazy summer day, Ty meets a wonderful man with a peg-leg. He asks Ty to gather the oddest things: a washboard, spoons, a comb, and a pail. He begins to make exciting music that fills everyone with energy. Then he slips away into the night.

Uncle Shamus. James Duffy. Macmillan, 1992. LC 92-19217, 144 p. (ISBN 0-684-19434-1) Grades 4-6.

Life is tough for Akers Johnson. He lives on the poor side of town and does not have any friends. Even Marleena Radford pretends she lives in another part of town. Then Uncle Shamus arrives. He is a blind ex-convict who has come back to get the money he stole thirty years earlier. And he wants Akers and Marleena to help him.

Underground man. Milton Meltzer. Harcourt, 1990. LC 72-80317, 220 p. (ISBN pbk 0-15-292846-4) Grades 3-7.

In 1835, tensions at home make Josh leave his family farm. He is not sure what he wants to do with his life. When Josh wanders into a logging camp and meets Sam, a runaway slave, he decides to dedicate his life to the abolition of slavery.

Ups and downs of Carl Davis III. Rosa Guy. Delacorte, 1989. LC 88-23693, 113 p. (ISBN 0-385-29724-6; pbk 0-440-40744-3) Grade 6 up.

Through letters, Carl Davis tells about what happened since he moved from New York City to his grandmother's house in South Carolina. But he is most puzzled by why was he sent away in the first place.

Wagon wheels. Barbara Brenner; Don Bolognese, illus. HarperCollins, 1978. LC 92-18780, 64 p. (ISBN 0-06-020668-3; plb. 0-06-020669-1) Grades K-3.

An *I can read* history book. An African American family goes to Kansas seeking free land. After they survive winter, the father leaves them to find a better place for a homestead.

Three brothers must take care of themselves and then travel 150 miles to join him.

Which way freedom? Joyce Hansen. Avon, 1992. LC 85-29547, 128 p. (ISBN 0-390-71408-6) Grades 6 up.

Part of the *Walker's American History Series for young people*. After escaping from his master's farm, Obi has to make a choice: work as a farm laborer or earn a living as a soldier for the Union. Based on original sources.

Whose side are you on? Emily Moore. Farrar, 1988. LC 87-46392, 128 p. (ISBN 0-374-38409-6; pbk 0-374-48373-6) Grades 3-7.

Barbra is having a lot of trouble in sixth grade—her grades are poor, her teacher does not like her, and T.J. is always pestering her. She is horrified when T.J. becomes her student tutor. Yet, she begins to like him a little and her grades start improving. When T.J. disappears, no one will help her find him. Barbra uses desperate but resourceful measures.

Yellow Bird and me. Joyce Hansen. Houghton Mifflin, 1986. LC 85-484, 155 p. (ISBN 0-89919-335-8; pbk 0-395-55388-1) Grades 3-7.

Sequel to **The Gift-Giver**. Doris' best friend, Amir, moves and leaves a void in her life. All she can think of is finding a way to visit him, until she begins helping Yellow Bird with his homework. She sees that he is smart, but he shows signs of dyslexia.

Young landlords. Walter Dean Myers. Peter Smith, 1992. LC 79-13264, 197 p. (ISBN 0-8446-6569-X); Puffin, 1989. (ISBN pbk 0-14-034244-3) Grades 5 up.

Paul Williams and his friends decide to protest to the landlord about conditions in his apartment building. In frustration, the man turns the building over to them. They simultaneously try to maintain the place, fight off a zealous reporter, and help a friend who is accused of stealing.

Reference and Scholarly Works

Before the Mayflower: a history of Black America. Lerone Bennett Jr. 6th edition revised. Viking, 1993. LC 82-082391, 720 p. (ISBN pbk 0-14-017822-8); William Thomas, 1992. (ISBN 1-56956-192-3); Viking, 1984. (ISBN pbk 0-14-007214-4); Johnson, 1982. (ISBN 0-87485-029-0).

This history begins with a look at "The African Past." In addition to extensive historical accounts, this volume contains a thorough chronology from 1619 through 1987, a list of African American "firsts," and a detailed index.

Biographical dictionary of Afro-American and African musicians.
Eileen Southern. Greenwood Press, 1982. LC 81-2586, 478 p.
(ISBN 0-313-21339-9).

Part of the *Encyclopedia of Black Music* series. A thoroughly researched and comprehensive volume, this work treats over 1,400 musicians of Afro-American or African descent born between 1640 and 1955. Many entries include comments, bibliographies, and discographies.

Black children and American institutions: an ecological review and resource guide.
Valora Washington, Velma LaPoint. Garland Publishing, 1988. LC 88-16490, 464 p. (ISBN 0-8240-8517-5).

Part of the *Garland Reference Library of Social Science*. This book deals with topics such as the status of African American child development in the educational system, family support, public assistance and welfare services, children and youth in the criminal justice system, and physical and mental health. Also included is a resource guide for child advocacy, and a list of community institutions and action groups. The book concludes with a lengthy reference and annotated bibliographic section.

Black dance in America: a history through its people.
James Haskins. HarperCollins, 1990. LC 89-35529, 240 p. (ISBN 0-690-04657-X; plb 0-690-04659-6; pbk 0-06-446121-1).

This work shows unique dance skills brought from Africa. Jazz and tap dancing are only two of the many forms that can be traced to Africa. There are biographies of extraordinary performers and choreographers like: Bill "Bojangles" Robinson, Katherine Dunham, Pearl Primus, Alvin Ailey, and Arthur Mitchell.

Black music in America.
James Haskins. HarperCollins, 1987. LC 85-47885, 224 p. (ISBN 0-690-04460-7; plb 0-690-04462-3; pbk 0-06-446136-X).

Covers the major eras of African American music as it evolved in the United States, from early slave music, to ragtime and blues, to jazz and soul, through the 70's and 80's. Includes concise biographies of African American musicians as well as historical background. A complete index and extensive illustrations are included.

Dictionary of American Negro biography.
Rayford W. Logan; Michael R. Winston. Norton, 1983. LC 81-9629, 680 p. (ISBN 0-393-01513-0).

This volume contains biographical information on African Americans who are no longer living. The cut-off date for inclusion is 1970. The purpose of the book is to assess the historical significance of these individuals. Many entries include suggested additional readings.

Directory of Blacks in the performing arts. Edward Mapp. 2nd ed. Scarecrow, 1990. LC 89-30477, 612 p. (ISBN 0-8108-2222-9); Scarecrow, 1978. LC 78-2436, 444 p. (ISBN 0-8108-1126-X).

Contains biographical and career information on 800 African Americans who have made significant contributions to the performing arts. Dance, film, music, radio, television, and theater are included.

Encyclopedia of Black America. W. Augusta Low; Virgil A. Clift, editors. De Cappo, 1984. LC 80-13247, 941 p. (ISBN pbk 0-306-80221-X); McGraw Hill, 1981. (ISBN hardcover text 0-07-038834-2).

Despite the uneven quality of its essays, this work is a capable ready-reference tool. Some 1,700 entries provide comprehensive coverage of African American history, life, and culture. Emphasis is on brief biographies (1,400). Also includes thematic essays on a broad spectrum of topics.

Extraordinary Black Americans from colonial to contemporary times. Susan Altman. Children's Press, 1989. LC 88-11977, 240 p. (ISBN 0-516-00581-2).

Consists of short biographies on African Americans. Each article is approximately two pages long. Includes pictures, birth and death dates, and achievements.

Famous first facts about Negroes. Romeo B. Garrett. Ayer Company, 1972. LC 75-172613, 224 p. (ISBN 0-405-01987-4).

This book records famous "firsts" for African Americans. The work is arranged in alphabetical categories. It is recommended for school libraries as fascinating reading.

From slavery to freedom: a history of Negro Americans. John Hope Franklin. 7th ed. McGraw Hill, 1994. LC 93-44726, 608 p. (ISBN pbk 0-07-021907-9); Knopf, 1994. (ISBN 0-679-43087-3); Knopf, 1987. 6th ed. LC 87-45341, 624 p. (ISBN 0-394-56362-X; pbk 0-394-37013-9); McGraw Hill, 1988. (ISBN pbk 0-07-554041-X).

This work traces the history of African Americans, from African origins through the Vietnamese War. It concentrates on African Americans as a people, rather than just a few outstanding individuals.

Negro Almanac: a reference work on the African-American. Harry A.
Ploski, James Williams, compilers. 6th ed. Gale, 1993. LC 86-72654.
(ISBN 0-8103-5409-8); 5th ed. Gale, 1989. (ISBN 0-8103-7706-3); Bellwether,
1989. (ISBN 0-913144-09-6); 4th ed. Bellwether, 1983. (ISBN 0-685-17467-0).

The current edition of this important reference source, (previous editions printed in
1967, 1971, and 1976) shows considerable updating. This profusely illustrated text
consists of a chronology of African American history since 1600, a section on social
and cultural life, numerous biographical sketches, statistical/historical tables and
charts, and more.

Quotations in Black. Anita King. Greenwood Press, 1981. LC 80-1794, 320 p.
(ISBN 0-313-22128-6).

Includes over 1,100 quotations from over 200 individuals and over 400 proverbs,
reflecting rich African American contributions to our culture. Emphasis is on quotations from historical figures. The volume is a worthy expansion of material
appearing in Bartlett's Familiar Quotations and other standard works.

**Research in Black child development: doctoral dissertation
abstracts, 1927-1979.** Hector F. Myers, Phyllis Gabriel-Rana, Ronee Harris-
Epps, and Rhonda J. Jones, compilers. Greenwood, 1982. LC 81-13425, 737 p.
(ISBN 0-313-22631-8).

Abstracts of studies identified in the Dissertation Abstracts International for the
years 1927-1979 that included African American children in their samples. It
addresses issues relevant to the development and functioning of African American
children and adolescents. Includes index.

Non-fiction

About Martin Luther King day. Mary Virginia Fox. Enslow, 1989. LC 88-
23230, 64 p. (ISBN 0-89490-200-8) Grades 4-7.

The African American struggle for civil rights provides background for Martin
Luther King Jr.'s accomplishments. In addition, a history of legislation to make
King's birthday a holiday and the continued work of King's family and his follow-
ers is given.

African-American holidays. James Anyike. Popular Truth, 1991. LC 91-067532, 85 p. (ISBN 0-9631547-0-2) All ages.

This guide furnishes historical background, and suggests activities for a variety of holidays, that highlight African American social contributions. By increasing cultural awareness among African American youth, the author sees holiday celebration as a way to build self-esteem. Holidays include Martin Luther King's Birthday, Black History Month, African Liberation Day, Juneteenth, Kwanzaa, and others.

African Journey. John Chiasson. Macmillan, 1987. LC 86-8233, 64 p. (ISBN 0-02-718530-3).

Describes the culture and habitat of the people in six distinctly different regions of Africa: the Sahel, the plains of Benin, the city of Dakar, the Atlantic coast, river ports along the banks of the Niger, and Ethiopia. The pictures make this book truly unique. These photo-essays comprise stark, compelling documentation of the continent. Art activities and recipes from Africa are presented with instructions. Traditional designs can be easily transferred to cloth or other materials. There are directions for the use of such items as beads, games, masks, dolls, and food.

Afro-Americans. Howard Smead. Chelsea House, 1989. LC 88-20300, 120 p. (ISBN plb 0-87754-854-4; pbk 0-7910-0256-X) Grades 5-6.

Part of the *Peoples of North America* series. This book provides an overview of the history of African Americans by discussing early slave culture and tracing major events in the fight for equal rights.

Afro-Bets first book about Africa: an introduction for young readers. Veronica Freeman Ellis; George Ford, illus. Just Us Books, 1990. LC 89-85157, 32 p. (ISBN plb 0 940975 12 2; pbk 0-940975-03-3) Grades 1-4.

A brief history of Africa, including some of its customs and folk tales, is presented in a read-aloud format. Illustrated with colorful drawings and photographs.

Aida. Leontyne Price; Leo and Diane Dillon, illus. Harcourt, 1990. LC 89-3643, 32 p. (ISBN 0-15-200405-X) Grades 1-6.

Aida is an Ethiopian princess who is captured and enslaved in Egypt. There she falls in love with the captain of the army, but this leads to tragedy. Based on G. Verdi's opera, "Aida."

All night, all day: a child's first book of African-American spirituals.
Ashley Bryan; David M. Thomas, musical arrangements. Atheneum, 1991.
LC 90-753145, 48 p. (ISBN 0-689-31662-3) Grades K-6.

Beautiful illustrations and easy musical arrangements highlight this book of 20
spirituals.

Ashanti to Zulu: African traditions. Margaret Musgrove; Leo and Diane
Dillon, illus. Pied Piper, 1976. LC 76-6610, 32 p. (ISBN pbk 0-8037-0308-2)
Grades K-4.

Each letter of the alphabet introduces an aspect of African culture and customs.
Twenty-six African tribes are represented. Winner of the 1977 Caldecott award.

Black heroes of the American revolution. Burke Davis. Harcourt, 1992.
LC 75-42218, 80 p. (ISBN pbk 0-15-208561-0) Grades 5-6.

History books have too often neglected the courageous contributions that African
American men and women made to this country's struggle for independence. One
of the first casualties was Crispus Attucks in the Boston Massacre. James Armistead
contributed to the surrender of General Cornwallis. Others served as sailors, scouts,
guides, and soldiers in the revolution.

Black heroes of the wild west. Ruth Pelz; illus. Leandro Della Piana. Open
Hand Publishing, 1989. LC 89-63500, 55 p. (ISBN 0-940880-25-3; pbk 0-940880-
26-1) Grades 4-12.

Short biographies describe the accomplishments of lesser-known, heroic men and
women who braved the unsettled frontiers of the West.

Caribbean carnival: songs of the West Indies. Irving Burgie; Frane
Lessac, illus.; Rosa Guy, afterword. Tambourine, 1992. LC 91-760838, 32 p.
(ISBN 0-688-10779-6; plb 0-688-10780-X) Grades 1-up.

Primitive paintings and easy musical arrangements express the celebration of life
found in Calypso music. Songs include: *Day-O; Michael row the boat; Yellow bird;
Panama tombe; Chi chi bird; Missy lost the gold ring; Que bonita bandera; Kingston
market; Little girl in the ring; I carry my ackee; Judy drowned-ed; Carolina Karo;* and
Jamaica farewell.

**Children of promise: African-American literature and art for young
people.** Charles Sullivan, editor. Abrams, 1991. LC 91-7566, 128 p.
(ISBN 0-8109-3170-2) Grades 4-6.

This book of poetry, prose, and speeches presents painting reproductions and drawings in loosely chronological order. Shows the history of a people through their artistic endeavors.

Childtimes: a three generation memoir. Eloise Greenfield; Lessie Jones Little. HarperCollins, 1993. LC 77-26581, 192 p. (ISBN pbk 0-06-446134-3) Grades 4-6.

Three generations of women write about their childhoods and living through social change.

The civil rights movement in America from 1865 to the present. Second edition. Patricia and Fredrick McKissack. Children's, 1991. LC 86-9636, 352 p. (ISBN 0-516-00579-0) Grades 4-up.

The struggle to achieve civil rights is chronicled from Reconstruction to the present. The historic background is expanded by discussions of the struggles of other ethnic groups in the same period. Includes time lines and historic illustrations.

Climbing Jacob's ladder; heroes of the Bible in African-American spirituals. John Langstaff; Ashley Bryan, illus; John Andrew Ross, musical arranger. Macmillan, 1991. LC 90-27297, 32 p. (ISBN 0-689-50494-2) Grades K-6.

Old Testament heroes' stories are described, illustrated by colorful paintings, and immortalized with spirituals. The Biblical characters include: Noah, Abraham, Jacob, Moses, Joshua, David, Ezekiel, Daniel, and Jonah. Musical arrangements are for piano and voice. A companion to **What a morning!: the Christmas story in Black spirituals.**

Count your way through Africa. Jim Haskins; Barbara Knutson, illus. Carolrhoda, 1989. LC 88-25896, 24 p. (ISBN plb 0-87614-347-8; pbk 0-87614-514-4) Grades 1-4.

Part of the *Count Your Way* series. Every number in Swahili, from one to ten, is used to introduce concepts about African customs, land, and culture.

Ethnic celebrations around the world. Nancy Everix. Good Apple, 1991. 160 p. (ISBN 0-86653-607-8) GA 1326. Grades 3-8.

Contains games, puzzles, maps, coloring pages, and craft instructions that projects teachers can use to highlight holidays of different countries. Each holiday is discussed with an accompanying bibliography. African countries include Kenya and Nigeria.

Get on board: the story of the Underground Railroad. Jim Haskins. Scholastic, 1993. LC 92-13247, 160 p. (ISBN 0-590-45418-8) Grades 4-7.

The only hope most slaves had of finding freedom was using the Underground Railroad. This device involved a loosely organized group of people determined to help. This book describes the people: the ones who hid the escaping slaves, those who helped transport them from hiding place to hiding place, and those who escaped. A picture emerges of a movement of people committed to righting a terrible injustice.

Great migration: an American story. Jacob Lawrence. HarperCollins, 1993. LC 93-16788, 48 p. (ISBN 0-06-023037-1; plb 0-06-023038-X) Grades 3-7.

After World War I, African Americans found life in the South difficult: no work, ruined crops, little food. They hoped to find a better life in the industrialized North. They courageously migrated, but found little improvement in the large northern cities. Illustrated by a series of vivid paintings.

How my family lives in America. Susan Kuklin. Macmillan, 1992. LC 91-22949, 40 p. (ISBN 0-02-751239-8) Grades ps-3.

Children from three families tell how they are adjusting to American traditions, while maintaining unique aspects of other cultures. Sanu's father is from Senegal, and a visit there taught her about what it means to be African. Includes a recipe for tiebou dienn.

I am a Jesse White tumbler. Diane Schmidt. Whitman, 1990. LC 89-16590, 40 p. (ISBN plb 0-8075-3444-7) Grades 2-8.

The Jesse White tumbling team is an organization for Chicago's inner city kids. Most of them are from the Cabrini-Green housing project. Kenyon tells the story of the team by relating his experiences, emphasizing that he has to keep up good grades and stay out of trouble to remain on the team.

In for winter, out for spring. Arnold Adoff; Jerry Pinkney, illus. Harcourt, 1991. LC 90-33185, 43 p. (ISBN 0-15-238637-8) Grades ps-3.

This poetry collection celebrates the way people's lives are tied to nature. Each season brings its own delight, and people enjoy special treats: snow flakes, butterflies, and harvesting the garden.

Inspirations: stories about women artists. Leslie Sills. Whitman, 1989. LC 88-80, 56 p. (ISBN 0-8075-3649-0) Grades 4-up.

The life experiences of four artists are reflected in their artistry. Faith Ringgold is the only African American represented in the book. Her students taught her to use everyday materials, such as beads and cloth, in her art. Faith's work reflects her communal pride in her African American heritage.

Kids explore America's African-American heritage. Westridge Writers Workshop. John Muir, 1993. LC 92-32275, 112 p. (ISBN pbk 1-56261-090-2) Grades 3-up.

Part of the *Kids explore* series. This book, written by students in grades 3-8 highlights African American history and contributions. In addition to short biographies of prominent citizens, the work includes: celebrations, recipes, art activities, folktales, and a phrase guide. Students also write about people who have influenced them.

Kwanzaa. Dorothy Rhodes Freeman; Dianne M. MacMillan. Enslow, 1992. LC 91-43100, 48 p. (ISBN 0-89490-381-0) Grades 1-4.

Part of the *Best Holiday Books* series. In an easy-to-read format, the history and observance of Kwanzaa is introduced. Kwanzaa is based on African harvest celebrations, and emphasizes reflection about family ancestors, African history, and American history. This leads one to look to the future with hope. Every one of the seven days deals with a principle related to strength of character and family bonding. Defines many Swahili words, and includes an index.

Kwanzaa. Deborah M. Newton Chocolate; Melodye Rosales, illus. Children's, 1990. LC 89-25418, 32 p. (ISBN plb 0-516-03991-1; pbk 0-516-43991-X) Grades ps-3.

Part of the *Holiday celebration* series. This book gives background on the holiday, and is a good read-aloud for young children. Two young brothers show how their family contributes to the celebration.

Kwanzaa. A. P. Porter, Bobby van Buren, illus. Carolrhoda, 1991. LC 90-28605, 48 p. (ISBN plb 0-87614-668-X; pbk 0-87614-545-4) Grades K-4.

An *On my own* book. Kwanzaa is a holiday especially for families to celebrate their African American heritage. The history and practices are explained. Each day of the week long celebration is devoted to Kwanzaa's goals. There are lists of terms and items to use in the celebration.

Learning to swim in Swaziland: a child's eye view of a southern African country. Nila K. Leigh. Scholastic, 1993. LC 92-13223, 48 p. (ISBN 0-590-45938-4) Grades K-3.

Nila was eight years old when she and her parents moved to Swaziland. This is a compilation of what she learned. She tells of the people and how they live, how things are different and the same, the games kids play, what school is like, what food they eat, even a (modern) folktale. Nila tells her story in her own words and writing, using drawings and photographs to make her point.

Let freedom ring: a ballad of Martin Luther King. Myra Cohn Livingston; Samuel Byrd, illus. Holiday House, 1992. LC 91-28245, 32 p. (ISBN 0-8234-0957-0) Grades 1-4.

This biography is a poem, using quotes from Martin's speeches to highlight his personal philosophy. The illustrations capture the energy expressed by his words.

Life doesn't frighten me. Maya Angelou; Jean-Michel Basquiat, illus. Stewart, Tabori, and Chang, 1993. LC 92-40409, 32 p. (ISBN 1-55670-288-4) Grades K-3.

Maya Angelou's poem about fear is illustrated by brightly colored, contemporary paintings. The narrator scares away the things that try to frighten: i.e., shadows, noises, barking dogs, clouds with ghosts, dragons.

Long Hard Journey: the story of the Pullman porter. Patricia and Fredrick McKissack. Walker, 1990. LC 89-9139, 144 p. (ISBN 0-8027-6884-9; plb 0-8027-6885-7) Grades 7-9.

This "David and Goliath" story portrays the struggle of the first African American union: the Pullman porters against a corporate giant—the Pullman company. Winner of the Coretta Scott King award.

Many thousand gone: African-Americans from slavery to freedom. Virginia Hamilton; Leo and Diane Dillon, illus. Knopf, 1992. LC 89-19988, 160 p. (ISBN 0-394-82873-9; plb 0-394-92873-3) Grades 4-9.

Short, individual biographies tell the story of the people who journeyed to freedom via the Underground Railroad. The style has a folk tale quality. Useful bibliography included.

March on Washington. James Haskins. HarperCollins, 1993. LC 92-13626, 128 p. (ISBN 0-06-021289-6; plb 0-06-021290-X) Gr. 5-up.

The 1963 March on Washington proved that people could peaceably demonstrate for equal rights on a grand scale. Despite disagreements on the purpose of the march, the African American leaders came together in a show of strength to lobby for jobs, education, and voting rights. They included A. Phillip Randolph, Martin Luther King, Jr., Roy Wilkins, Whitney Young, James Farmer, and John Lewis. After huge numbers of people gathered, the day had an emotional ending with King's "I have a dream" speech.

Martin Luther King Day. Linda Lowery; Hetty Mitchell, illus. Lerner, 1987. LC 86-20758, 56 p. (ISBN pbk 0-87614-468-7); Live Oak, 1987. (ISBN book + cassette 0-87499-071-8; pbk + cassette 0-87499-070-X; set of 4 pbks + cassette 0-87499-072-6) Grades K-4.

An *On My Own* book. Martin Luther King Jr.'s life and accomplishments are recounted in an easy-to-read format and the national holiday established in his honor is also discussed.

My black me: a beginning book of black poetry. Arnold Adoff, editor. Dutton, 1974. LC 73-16445, 96 p. (ISBN 0-525-35460-3); Dutton, 1994. (ISBN 0-525-45216-8) Grades 3 up.

This collection focuses on poems about being African American. Includes authors such as Langston Hughes, Lucille Clifton, Nikki Giovanni, Imamu Amiri Baraka, and Sonia Sanchez.

Nathaniel talking. Eloise Greenfield; Jan Spivey Gilchrist, illus. Writers and Readers Publishers, 1988. LC 88-51019, 32 p. (ISBN 0-86316-200-2) Grades K-5.

Nathaniel tells what he is thinking using his own "rap" technique. His thoughts cover his age, his friends, his mother who died, his teacher and grandmother, his daddy playing the blues, and even himself.

Night on neighborhood street. Eloise Greenfield; Jan Spivey Gilchrist, illus. Dial, 1991. LC 89-23480, 32 p. (ISBN 0-8037-0777-0; plb 0-8037-0778-9) Grades ps-3.

Each of the poems provide a slice-of-life about a family who cares for one another as only families can—in times of crisis or tenderness, danger or security.

Now is your time: the African-American struggle for freedom. Walter Dean Myers. HarperCollins, 1992. LC 91-314, 304 p. (ISBN 0-06-024370-8; plb 0-06-024371 6; pbk 0 06 446120-3) Grades 6-up.

This cultural history of African Americans considers the need for freedom as felt by those Africans who were captured and brought to America as slaves. For instance, some Africans were royalty in their natural societies. Here, they were degraded and subjugated. Africans fought for their freedom in many ways: fighting in the Revolutionary and Civil wars, fighting for education, fighting for the right to express themselves.

Pass it on: African-American poetry for children. Wade Hudson; Floyd Cooper, illus. Scholastic, 1993. LC 92-16034, 32 p. (ISBN 0-590-45770-5) Grades K-4.

Includes works by some of the best known African American poets: Langston

Hughes, Paul Laurence Dunbar, Eloise Greenfield, Nikki Giovanni, and Gwendolyn Brooks. Each poem evokes a tender in childhood. Illustrated.

Red dog/blue fly: poems for a football season. Sharon Mathis; Jan Spivey Gilchrist, illus. Viking, 1991. LC 91-50266, 32 p. (ISBN 0-670-83623-0) Grades ps-3.

Football for young players comes alive in these poems. The dreams of victory, the terror of injury, the anxiety of learning the plays, pleasing the coach, and winning the trophies.

Shadow. Blaise Cendrars; Marcia Brown, trans. and illus. Macmillan, 1982. LC 81-9424, 40 p. (ISBN 0-684-17226-7); Macmillan, 1986. (ISBN pbk 0-689-71084-4); Macmillan, 1994. (ISBN pbk 0-689-71875-6) Grades ps-up.

Marcia Brown's beautiful collage illustrations evoke the mood of Africa's mysticism. *Shadow* is always present, an Africa which once was, but is not the same now. It is a blend of shadow and substance, of reality and spirituality. Winner of the Caldecott award.

Shake it to the one that you love the best: play songs and lullabies from Black musical traditions. Cheryl Warren Mattox; Varnette Honeywood and Brenda Joysmith, illus. Warren-Mattox, 1990. 56 p. (ISBN pbk 0-9623381-0-9) Grades K-6.

This collection of songs is intended to make people aware of African American music and art. Each song has a music arrangement. Game instructions accompany the art works.

Sing to the sun. Ashley Bryan. HarperCollins, 1992. LC 91-38359, 32 p. (ISBN 0-06-020829-5; plb 0-06-020833-3) Grades 2-up.

These poems are alive with emotion, but different in tone and subject. Each poem is a slice of life, some good, some bad. All are honest and heart-felt. The illustrations are bright and beautiful. Ashley Bryan has a unique, primitive style.

Something on my mind. Nikki Grimes; Tom Feelings, illus. Dial, 1986. LC 77-86266, 32 p. (ISBN pbk 0-8037-0273-6) Grades 2-up.

Each poem contains a myriad of experiences like hope, fear, joy, sorrow, and growing up.

Spin a soft black song. Nikki Grimes; George Martins, illus. Revised ed. Hill and Wang, 1985. LC 84-19287, 64 p. (ISBN 0-8090-8796-0); Farrar, 1987. (ISBN 0-374-46469-3) Grades K-up.

This collection of poetry captures the essence of an African American child's life with energy and affection.

To be a slave. Julius Lester. Dial, 1968. LC 68-28738, 160 p. (ISBN 0-8037-8955-6); Scholastic, 1986. (ISBN pbk 0-590-42460-2) Grades 7-12.

Lester uses some of the most overlooked sources of information on the conditions of slavery: dialogues with actual slaves and narratives from men, women, and children who lived through this period. Many have not been published previously, and some are extracts from sources long out of print. Documentation is placed beneath quoted material. Lester ties passages together with sympathetic commentary in a work that is readable and compelling. This work begins with the arrival of the first Africans in 1619, and continues into the 1900s. Bibliography included.

Tommy Traveler in the world of Black history. Tom Feelings. Writers and Readers, 1991. LC 90-071223, 48 p. (ISBN 0-86316-202-9; pbk 0-86316-211-8) Grades 3-6.

Using a comic strip format, Tommy Traveler is fascinated by all the African American books in Dr. Gray's library. He dreams of meeting all the historical figures that he reads about. He meets Phoebe Fraunces, who saves George Washington's life; Emmet Till, a fourteen year old lynched for whistling at an Anglo girl; Aesop, famous fable teller; Frederick Douglass, and his fight for freedom; Crispus Attucks, revolutionary war hero; and Joe Louis, boxer.

Tree of life: the world of the African Baobab. Barbara Bash. Little, Brown, 1989. LC 89-6028, 32 p. (ISBN 0-316-08305-4; pbk 0-316-08322-4) Grades ps-5.

The life cycle of the African Baobab tree is more than a thousand years, though it looks dead most of its life. Many animals, birds, and insects depend on it. Birds and insects build their nests, baboons love the fruit, and people gather all its products. Eventually the tree collapses in on itself, and a new tree grows from it.

Under the Sunday tree. Eloise Greenfield; Amos Ferguson, illus. Harper-Collins, 1988. LC 87-29373, 48 p. (ISBN plb 0-06-022257-3; pbk 0-06-443257-2) Grades 1-up.

This collection of poems and paintings presents a unique view of life in the Bahamas.

Undying glory. Clinton Cox. Scholastic, 1991. LC 90-22303, 167 p. (ISBN 0-590-44170-1; pbk 0-590-44171-X) Grades 4-7.

A highly readable account of the Massachusetts 54th Regiment, an African American Civil War unit. They fought valiantly and proved their worth to win freedom from slavery.

Voices from America's past. Raintree Steck-Vaughn, 1990. LC 90-44955, 128 p. (ISBN 0-8114-2770-6) Grades 4-6.

Different eras of American history are described by the people who lived them. Historical documents such as letters, speeches, diaries, and reminiscences set the tone for the eyewitness accounts of events. African Americans are represented by a colonial soldier requesting a pension, a slave shipping himself north, George Washington Carver's discoveries, and Martin Luther King's "I have a dream" speech.

What a morning: the Christmas story in Black spirituals. John Langstaff; Ashley Bryan, illus.; John Andrew Ross, musical arranger. Macmillan, 1987. LC 87-750130, 32 p. (ISBN 0-689-50422-5) Grades ps-6.

Spirituals are used to tell the Christmas story. Includes musical arrangements and beautiful illustrations featuring African characters. There are suggestions to teachers, parents, and instrumentalists on performing the songs. A companion to *Climbing Jacob's Ladder: heroes of the Bible in African American spirituals.*

Year they walked: Rosa Parks and the Montgomery bus boycott. Beatrice Siegel. Macmillan, 1992. LC 91-14078, 128 p. (ISBN 0-02-782631-7) Grades 4-7.

The life of Rosa Parks and the African-American nonviolent protest movement became intertwined due to one courageous act: Parks' refusal to give up her seat. That action violated a city ordinance. The court case that resulted galvanized the African American community into action: a year long boycott of the bus company. The year changed the course of Rosa Parks' life, and that of the entire country.

✿ REFERENCES ✿

Dictionary of American immigration history. Francesco Cordasco, editor. Scarecrow Press, 1990. LC 89-37041, 810 p. (ISBN 0-8108-2241-5).

This is a unique dictionary of American immigration history that contains 2,500 cross-referenced, signed entries, including biographical sketches, ethnic groups, associations, unions, legislation, social movements, and major themes, (e.g., ethnicity, assimilation, and nativism). The emphasis of this book is on the period from the 1880s, when the U.S. Congress began to actively administer immigration laws, to the passage of the Immigration and Control Act in 1986. Most entries have a short bibliography, and a 130-item bibliography appears at the end of the volume.

Dictionary of race and ethnic relations. E. Ellis Cashmore, editor. 3rd edition. Routledge, 1989. 320 p. (ISBN 0-415-02511-7) A3547.

Largely the work of American and British sociologists, this is a basic handbook of selected terminology in the field of race and ethnic relations. Despite its British origins, it has useful definitions of key terms, such as ethnicity, prejudice, and racism.

Ethnic Almanac. Stephanie Bernardo. Doubleday, 1981. LC 78-14694, 560 p. (ISBN 0-385-14143-2; pbk 0-385-141440)

Although now out of print, this witty potpourri of useful information about numerous ethnic groups is valuable. This unusual volume covers inventions, comic strips, folk medicine, food, racial stereotypes, slang, superstitutions, etc.

Ethnic genealogy: a research guide. Jessie Carney Smith, editor. Greenwood, 1983. LC 82-12245, 440 p. (ISBN 0-313-22593-1).

The best general handbook on ethnic genealogy research, this work leads both novices and experts through basic source materials and archival collections. The last three chapters focus on Asian American, African American, and Hispanic American records and research.

Ethnic groups in American life. James P. Shenton, advisory editor; Gene Brown, editor. Ayer, 1978. LC 77-11053, 422 p. (ISBN 0-405-10310-7).

Part of the *Great Contemporary Issues* series. This work reprints *New York Times* articles from the 1860s to 1978, arranged under five headings: Native Americans, immigrants from Europe and Asia, migration patterns of those immigrants, race and poverty, and problems of a multi-ethnic society.

Ethnic information sources of the United States. Wasserman. 3rd edition. Gale, 1995. (ISBN 0-8103-5508-6).

An excellent comprehensive listing of organizations, agencies, institutions, media, libraries and museums, religious organizations and many other agencies. Well organized and easy to use.

Ethnic NewsWatch. Softline Information.

A new electronic publisher, based in Stamford, Conn., release its first product, *Ethnic NewsWatch (ENW)*, early in 1992. Both an online and a CD-ROM product, ENW features selected articles from approximately 100 ethnic newspapers and magazines published in the United States. *ENW* provides users with directory information on the publications, full indexing for the entire newspaper/magazine, and full text for the available articles. Publications are in English and Spanish. All subject headings in *ENW* are in English. Databases are updated monthly.

Ethnic periodicals in contemporary America: an annotated guide. Sandra L. Jones Ireland, compiler. Greenwood press, 1990. 256p. (ISBN 0-313-26817-7).

This book lists 290 U.S. periodicals aimed at ethnic interest groups. Arranged by groups, the periodical citations contain full publication information, including title, editor, address, telephone number, publisher, subscription terms, language used in text, and print process. Entries for publications that are still active also include annotations. An index and selected bibliography are provided. *Ethnic Periodicals in Contemporary America* is No. 3 in Greenwood Press's Bibliographies and Indexes in Ethnic Studies series.

Harvard encyclopedia of American ethnic groups. Stephan Thernstrom; Ann Orlov; Oscar Handlin. Harvard University Press, 1980. LC 80-17756, 1102 p. (ISBN 0-674-37512-2)

This scholarly tome, invaluable in all types of libraries, includes authoritative information on 108 American ethnic groups from Afro-Americans to Yankees. The essays, many of which are lengthy, treat the historical, cultural, religious, and socioeconomic aspects of each group. Other entries are thematic essays on topics such as intermarriage, labor, and politics. Maps and tables support the volume.

Minorities: a changing role in American society. Carl Foster, Diznak Church, Mark A. Siegal, editors. Revised ed. Information Plus, 1992. 132 p. (ISBN pbk 1-878623-40-0).

This reference source provides a compilation of statistics on minorities in the U.S. published by various federal agencies including the Bureau of Census, National Center for Health Statistics, Bureau of Labor Statistics, Department of Education, and the Department of Justice. The chapters are arranged by subject area, such as demography, labor force participation, and occupations. Within each chapter are bold headings for information on different minority groups. It includes a brief index, tables, graphs, and charts. Much of the information and statistics is for broad categories, such as Black, Hispanic, Asian, and American Indian, however there is also information on more specific minorities.

Multicultural projects index: things to make and do to celebrate festivals, cultures, and holidays around the world. Mary Anne Pilger. Libraries Unlimited, 1992. LC 92-13731, 300 p. (ISBN pbk 0-87287-867-8).

This index provides access to a multitude of how-to instructions for cultural activities which have appeared in books. Contains bibliographic information on sources cited. Appropriate for use with all primary grades.

Multicultural review. Greenwood Publishing Group.

A quarterly journal which debuted in January, 1992 helps librarians select multicultural books, periodicals, and AV products. This journal is devoted exclusively to the interdisciplinary and multimedia materials and issues associated with American ethnic, racial, and religious experiences. The journal has three objectives: 1) increased awareness of and sensitivity to pluralism; 2) celebration of diverse cultures and common bonds; 3) creation of a comprehensive, timely, authoritative, affordable, and efficient tool for reviewing material on and relating to multiculturalism. *Multicultural Review* provides reviews organized by broad subject categories; each review contains thorough citation information as well as an evaluative discussion of the material. Reviews are indexed by author and title. In addition, a shelflist by ethnic group is provided. The *Review* offers columns in each issue on serials, poetry, and regular articles, and reviews on audio/video products, electronic media, and juvenile materials, as well as numerous other topics.

Strangers to these shores: race and ethnic relations in the U.S. Vincent Parrillo. 4th ed. Macmillan, 1993. LC 93-12047. (ISBN 0-02-391752-0).

This book covers the broad subject of minorities, specifically, European Americans, both "old" and "new"; racial minorities; religious minorities; and women. It then returns to broad discussion of minorities and their place in the present and future of America. It is a wonderful work, containing illustrations and photos, as well as comments from interviews with immigrants.

World directory of minorities. Minority Rights Group Staff. St. James Press, 1990. 427 p. (ISBN 1-55862-016-8).

This is a directory of minorities in all areas of the world. It includes groups who have been considered a minority for at least 40 to 50 years and is divided into 11 world regions. The recognized minorities of those areas are then listed alphabetically, and an overall definition is given of that group. It includes a history of the group, recent developments, organizations of the group and its present economic and social status, and current issues. A fascinating collection of general information about minorities, due to racial and religious differences in all parts of the world.

❀ INDEX ❀

Author/Illustrator/Title

❀ INDEX ❀

Subject